# Ricardo Darín and the Construction of Latin American Film Stardom

**International Film Stars**
Series Editor: Homer B. Pettey and R. Barton Palmer

This series is devoted to the artistic and commercial influence of performers who shaped major genres and movements in international film history. Books in the series will:

- Reveal performative features that defined signature cinematic styles
- Demonstrate how the global market relied upon performers' generic contributions
- Analyse specific film productions as case studies that transformed cinema acting
- Construct models for redefining international star studies that emphasise materialist approaches
- Provide accounts of stars' influences in the international cinema marketplace

Titles available:

*Close-Up: Great Cinematic Performances Volume 1: America*
Edited by Murray Pomerance and Kyle Stevens

*Close-Up: Great Cinematic Performances Volume 2: International*
Edited by Murray Pomerance and Kyle Stevens

*Chinese Stardom in Participatory Cyberculture*
By Dorothy Wai Sim Lau

*Geraldine Chaplin: The Gift of Film Performance*
By Steven Rybin

*Tyrone Power: Gender, Genre and Image in Classical Hollywood Cinema*
By Gillian Kelly

*Film Stardom in Southeast Asia*
By Jonathan Driskell

*Diana Dors: Film Star and Actor*
By Martin Shingler

*Yul Brynner: Exoticism, Cosmopolitanism and Screen Masculinity*
By Susanna Paasonen

Ricardo Darín and the Construction of Latin American Film Stardom
By Clara Garavelli

www.euppublishing.com/series/ifs

# Ricardo Darín and the Construction of Latin American Film Stardom

Clara Garavelli

Edinburgh University Press is one of the leading university presses in the UK. We publish academic books and journals in our selected subject areas across the humanities and social sciences, combining cutting-edge scholarship with high editorial and production values to produce academic works of lasting importance. For more information visit our website: edinburghuniversitypress.com

© Clara Garavelli, 2023, 2025

Grateful acknowledgement is made to the sources listed in the List of Figures for permission to reproduce material previously published elsewhere. Every effort has been made to trace the copyright holders, but if any have been inadvertently overlooked, the publisher will be pleased to make the necessary arrangements at the first opportunity.

Edinburgh University Press Ltd
13 Infirmary Street
Edinburgh EH1 1LT

First published in hardback by Edinburgh University Press 2023

Typeset in 12/14 Arno and Myriad by
IDSUK (Dataconnection) Ltd

A CIP record for this book is available from the British Library

ISBN 978 1 4744 5895 5 (hardback)
ISBN 978 1 4744 5896 2 (paperback)
ISBN 978 1 4744 5897 9 (webready PDF)
ISBN 978 1 4744 5898 6 (epub)

The right of Clara Garavelli to be identified as the author of this work has been asserted in accordance with the Copyright, Designs and Patents Act 1988, and the Copyright and Related Rights Regulations 2003 (SI No. 2498).

# Contents

List of Figures vi
Acknowledgements vii

Introduction 1

## PART I: From Gardel to Darín: Film Stardom in Argentina
Chapter 1: Origin and establishment of the Argentine star system 21
Chapter 2: Stardom during the rise of television and the 1960s film wave 43
Chapter 3: The challenges of a (non-)star system in a post-dictatorship period 68

## PART II: From Child Theatre Performer and TV Celebrity to Film Star
Chapter 4: Childhood and first performances 99
Chapter 5: *Telenovelas* and music-based youth films 116
Chapter 6: Theatre performances 134
Chapter 7: Comedy roles and 1980s–1990s work in cinema 152
Chapter 8: Contemporary productions and the ageing star 172

## PART III: A 'Hispanic' Star
Chapter 9: Spanish *conquistador* 193
Chapter 10: Transnational mobility and cross-cultural exchanges 211
Chapter 11: Discourses of scandal, politics, activism and legacies 231

Appendices 257
Index 266

# Figures

| | | |
|---|---|---|
| Figure 2.1 | Pinky interviews Darín in 2001 (Channel 7 – Historical Archive of Argentine Radio and Television) | 57 |
| Figure 2.2 | Mirtha Legrand and Juana Viale with Ricardo Darín, Diego Torres, Darío Barassi and Jey Mammon (Channel 13, December 2021) | 60 |
| Figure 3.1 | Adrián Suar, Juan José Campanella, Ricardo Darín and Norma Aleandro at the Oscar's for *The Son of the Bride* in 2002 (*Revista Gente* Archive) | 87 |
| Figure 4.1 | Ricardo Darín in *He nacido en la ribera* (Catrani 1972) | 109 |
| Figure 5.1 | Ricardo Darín and Alicia Zanca in *Una escalera al cielo* (Channel 9, 1979, Grandes de la Escena Nacional Archive) | 122 |
| Figure 5.2 | Cover of the satirical magazine *Humor Registrado*, no. 65, September 1981, courtesy of *Revista Humor Registrado* | 125 |
| Figure 5.3 | Record cover *De a dos* (1979) | 128 |
| Figure 6.1 | Ricardo Darín and Carlos Calvo (*Clarín* Archive) | 139 |
| Figure 7.1 | Luis Brandoni and Ricardo Darín in *Mi cuñado* (1991, *Clarín* Archive) | 154 |
| Figure 7.2 | Darín in *Expreso a la emboscada* (Béhat 1986) | 159 |
| Figure 8.1 | Ricardo Darín in *Nieve negra* (Hodara 2017) | 181 |
| Figure 10.1 | Ricardo Darín and Andrea Del Boca in *Estrellita Mia* (1987) | 222 |
| Figure 11.1 | Darín enters the football pitch in one of the galancitos games for Almirante Brown, courtesy of Fernando Fuentes | 233 |
| Figure 11.2 | *Revista Gente*'s cover, January 1989 | 245 |

# Acknowledgements

I am indebted to the publishers, Edinburgh University Press, and to the team of Gillian Leslie, Richard Strachan and Sam Johnson, for believing in this project and supporting me all the way through it with great patience. Thanks also to the peer reviewers for their role in making this project possible, and to the series editors, Homer B. Pettey and R. Barton Palmer, for their kind words and for including this book in this stimulating series on international stars. Liverpool University Press generously granted permission to reproduce in Chapter 9 parts of: Garavelli, C. (2015) 'Conquering the Conquerors: Ricardo Darín's Rise to Stardom in Spanish Film Culture', *Bulletin of Hispanic Studies*, 92.4, pp. 411–428.

I am fortunate to have been able to work with Adrián Muoyo, director of the ENERC-INCAA library, and all of his highly knowledgeable team, who provided invaluable guidance on the contents of their archive of Darín. I could not have had better research assistants in Brenda Salama, Cecilia Garavelli, Karol Valderrama Burgos, Michela Baldo and Natalia Christofoletti Barrenha, who provided outstanding data and comments at different stages. I have also benefited from constant above-and-beyond support from my dear friend and colleague Emma Staniland, who read the whole manuscript and helped me, tactfully and patiently, with proofreading and much-needed moral support.

I would like to thank also the generous support of the University of Leicester (UoL), which granted me a sabbatical semester to write parts of this manuscript. I have been fortunate to have joined UoL at a particular moment when a caring and supportive community of colleagues was in place; one that has not just made stressful times bearable, but helped sustain enjoyment of our work together regardless. Carolina Rocha was the first person who invited me to write about Darín, in an edited collection that in the end never saw the light of day, but which took me away from the world of experimental video and granted me a new challenge. For that I will be always grateful. That project also gathered together different scholars who over the years have supported and encouraged my Darín adventure. Among them, I should mention Beatriz Urraca – who also invited me to write on Darín for different projects – Santiago Oyarzábal and María Valdéz, whose all-important notes I hope I have done justice. Back in 2012, when I started researching this topic, Alberto Elena provided insightful comments, and so did Marina Díaz López, María Luisa Ortega Gálvez and my *Secuencias. Revista de historia del cine* collaborators.

Other colleagues, friends and relatives who made this project possible thanks to their wonderful spirit, knowledge and camaraderie are Andrea Cuarterolo, Ana Laura Lusnich, Cecilia Sosa, Patricia Bossio, Tomás Crowder-Tarraborrelli, Deborah Shaw, Sarah Barrow, Kristi Wilson, Pablo Piedras, Javier Campo, Georgina Ricci, Beatriz Tadeo Fuica, Elizabeth Ramírez, Lichi Corsiglia, Carla Petroccelli, Catherine Morley, Nuria Escudero Pérez, Simona Storchi, Michelle Harrison, Maite Usoz de la Fuente and Marion Krauthaker. I am extremely grateful to my brother Marcos Garavelli, who supported me in times of desperation and always had something interesting to say about Darín. Carlos Garavelli and Ana María Talmón offered me a wonderful place to stay in Buenos Aires, as did María Ángela Delgado and Carlo Crivelli in Madrid. María Cristina Sacco and Gustavo Bellotti bought all the tacky magazines I asked them to buy with love – thanks a lot. My beautiful little family, Carlos and Greta Crivelli, with whom I share my passion for cinema, had to put up with my mood changes when the writing process was not going as expected. I love you both for understanding why I needed to borrow some of our time together to work on this. Thanks also to directors and producers Damián Szifrón and Javier and Héctor Olivera for their contacts and information, and to Tamara Cortés Crespo and Gonzalo Roldán – aka Walter Aniston – Darín's biggest fans.

My grandmother, Aracelis Gallardo – also known as 'Perla Garavelli', a real star played by Graciela Borges in the film *Las manos* (Doria 2006) – took my mother and me to the theatre to see Darín on stage when I was deciding whether or not to embark on this project. That night at the Maipo, with those two extraordinary women talking about Darín, lies at the heart of this book. Although they are not here anymore to see the end result, their spirit, contagious laughter and wisdom about life appear on every page and guided my research and writing process.

Last, but certainly not least, I would like to express my sincere gratitude to Ricardo Darín himself, a real gentleman who could not care less about stardom, but who still dedicated valuable time writing to and talking with me on several occasions during a globally devastating pandemic, with great patience and enthusiasm – there wouldn't be a book without him! Gracias Richard.

To my mother, the brilliant artist Graciela Sacco,
*por el regalo de la ilusión.*

# Introduction

Over the past two decades, Ricardo Darín has become the most famous actor in Argentina, and yet his star persona remains unexplored in both Hispanic and Anglophone academia. His name is synonymous with commercial success within the national film industry, so much so that he plays himself in *Delirium* (Kaimakamian 2014), a film which focuses – in a self-reflexive and parodical way – on two amateur filmmakers who are convinced that Darín's presence in their first feature film will guarantee its resounding triumph and make them rich. In that same comic vein, in 2015 a Brazilian film blog invented the news that the Argentine Minister of Culture was considering sponsoring a film without Darín as part of the cast (Cacofonias 2015). Even though these two examples exaggerate Darín's role in the dynamics of the local film industry, it cannot be denied that he has become a regular presence in most mainstream Argentine productions and a key economic factor in the definition and shaping of popular conceptions of national identity and film culture.

Although his success has been mainly circumscribed to Spanish-speaking countries, his name has been associated with the renewal of Argentine cinema in international film circuits. Darín gained worldwide recognition through Fabián Bielinsky's *Nueve reinas* [*Nine Queens*] (2000) and Juan José Campanella's *El hijo de la novia* [*The Son of the Bride*] (2001). In 2010, the film *El secreto de sus ojos* [*The Secret in their Eyes*] (Campanella 2009), starring Darín, won the Academy Award for Best Foreign Film of that year. Some Hollywood offers followed these successes – which he rejected, claiming that he does not have the intention of falling into stereotypical 'Latino' roles. Thanks to the release of the film *Relatos salvajes* [*Wild Tales*] (Szifrón 2014), he also gained significant attention in UK media. When reviewing this film for *The Guardian*, Peter Bradshaw (2015) recognised that: 'Ricardo Darín is the film's big star name', in spite of the cast being populated with some of the most internationally renowned Argentine film performers of the past decades, such as Leonardo Sbaraglia, Darío Grandinetti and Óscar Martínez. At the time of writing these words, the film *Argentina, 1985*, starring Darín and directed by Santiago Mitre, is about to be released, and is considered in international circuits to be one of the 'top 100 most anticipated films of 2022' (Lavallée 2022).

Now in his mid-sixties, and at the apex of his national and international career, the time is right to dedicate a monograph to the leading actor of the Argentine box office, who challenges the stereotypes and misconceptions of the 'Latin American star' as popularly defined or understood. Accordingly, this book fills a gap both in Hispanic and Anglophone academia in terms of understanding how Ricardo Darín's rise to stardom carried him from his beginnings in a family of theatre and radio performers, through to his roles as a soap opera heart-throb, to finally becoming a star of the big screen. As a corollary to this focus on his individual career and place in Argentine cinematic culture and history, this study interrogates whether or not Ricardo Darín can be understood to embody the epitome of the contemporary Latin American or Hispanic star, and whether the characteristics of the Hollywood star system, in fact, can be usefully applied in the context of Argentine cinema, where the distinction between so-called 'industrial' and 'independent' cinemas is very difficult to discern.

Interest in Darín and his career is visible in recent academic articles and book chapters, some of which have begun consideration of his star persona. Articles by Beatriz Urraca (2014), Constanza Burucúa (2014), Carolina Rocha (2016), Carolina Soria (2014), Dolores Tierney, Victoria Ruétalo and Roberto Carlos Ortiz (2017), Nahuel Ribke and Jerome Bourdon (2017), Eamon McCarthy (2022), and my own articles and book chapters (2013, 2015, 2016), have begun exploration of this cinematic figure but only provide short accounts of Darín's importance for the local and international film culture and industry. They examine his performance and star construction in connection to specific contemporary films – such as *Elefante blanco* [*White Elephant*] (Trapero 2012), *El secreto de sus ojos* or *La señal* [*The Signal*] (Darín and Hodara 2007) – or the topic of his raise to stardom in the Spanish peninsula (Garavelli 2013, 2015). None of these writings explores the process of constructing Darín as a 'star' or his cultural significance in relation to the dynamics of Argentine film industry, or in connection with the stereotypes circulating around the notion of the Latin American and Hispanic 'star'. Additionally, there are no academic studies that analyse Darín's works in theatre and TV, or his light-hearted, music-driven films from the 1980s. Thus, this study of the figure of Ricardo Darín will explore not only how he emerged as the must-see actor of contemporary Argentine cinema, but will also delve into new latitudes and examine issues still not fully examined, such as: How are Argentine, Latin American, and Hispanic stars constructed? Does the leading actor of contemporary Argentine cinema embody a wider social group and historical moment? Do his performances define the contemporary Argentine mainstream cinematographic canon?

Given the extent of Darín's prolific and diverse career, the book will focus on a retrospective analysis, and wil not consider productions due for release in 2022 or already in the pipeline for this year onwards. It will look back at his performances as a child actor and in other lesser-known productions not yet analysed in Hispanic or Anglophone Film Studies literature. While some films are discussed at length, others receive less attention, either because they have already been widely analysed – as is the case of *Nueve reinas*, *El Hijo de la novia*, *El aura* [*The Aura*] (Bielinsky 2005), *XXY* (Puenzo 2007), *El secreto de sus ojos*, *Relatos salvajes*, and *Elefante blanco* [*White Elephant*] (Trapero 2012) – or for reasons that will be made apparent. It will also look at his career progression in comparison to other Argentine male and female stars, from historical figures such as Carlos Gardel and Libertad Lamarque, to more contemporary ones like Leonardo Sbaraglia, Héctor Alterio, Norma Aleandro, Darío Grandinetti, Federico Luppi, Pablo Echarri, Cecilia Roth, Adrián Suar, Natalia Oreiro, Diego Peretti and Guillermo Francella.

In his critical guide to Star Studies, Martin Shingler states that books devoted to the examination of the work, image and appeal of an individual star still remain a rarity in Film Studies (2012: 13). Since those words were proffered ten years ago, the field has changed significantly. The British Film Institute's Film Star series, co-edited by Shingler himself, aimed to tackle this lacuna. Of its seventeen titles, seven were dedicated to non-US stars, demonstrating the importance of challenging the Hollywood-centric view that has long dominated Film Studies. It is just that kind of revisionist approach that informs the series of which this study is a part; through which the editors, Homer B. Pettey and R. Barton Palmer, have endeavoured to create a forum for explorations of the artistic and commercial influence in the international cinema market of actors who move outside Anglophone circuits (Pettey and Palmer, Edinburgh University Press, 2019–present).

This monograph contributes to the overall series, and thereby field, by moving away from such top-down analysis and seeking to look at the specific characteristics of the Latin American star system in connection to one of its major contemporary stars. Moreover, this study builds on previous theoretical works on stars in world cinema that have themselves drawn from Ella Shohat and Robert Stam's polycentric approach (Bandhauer and Royer 2015; Nagib, Perriam and Dudrah 2012), whereby 'the world has many dynamic cultural locations, many possible vantage points' and in which 'no single community or part of the world, whatever its economic or political power, should be epistemologically privileged' (Shohat and Stam 2014: 48). Thus, instead of reading Latin American and, more specifically, Argentine stardom as peripheral, it will be explored on its own terms, for all the unique cultural and power dynamics at play.

In their analysis of Catherine Deneuve, Lisa Downing and Sue Harris emphasised how a single star case study enables exploration of 'the developments, breaks and lines of continuity that constitute her image over the course of a career' (2007: 8). Darín's case also enables the examination of a wide range of works over various socio-political periods, of appeal to a range of audiences and which inform of the development of the field over the course of history. Additionally, considering that he comes from a family of actors and that his son is also on the verge of becoming a film star himself, Darín serves as a springboard for exploring how the film industry – or lack of one – functions at various historical moments in Argentine history.

In line with Andrea Bandhauer and Michelle Royer's analysis in *Stars in World Cinema* (2015), this book does not aim to be a survey of stars in Latin America nor in Argentina. Instead of sustaining the distant gaze that is inherent to such broad-reaching studies, my study of Darín's career and persona allows for a close encounter with various stars and forms of stardom that feed into the dynamics of a rich Hispanophone culture, and reveal the possibility of other, less untouchable and more immeasurable, forms of moving image figures.

## Latin American stardom

> The Head of Hollywood Cosmetics. I should talk very little, command a lot of authority, dress very stylish and not pay too much attention to the customers. 'Do like the American supervisor who came last year, she didn't get friendly with anybody,' and of course she didn't talk because she knew very little Spanish. So since I already look American, I took advantage of it not to pay attention to anybody [...] You know something? All of Mecha Ortiz's hairdos look good on me. There isn't an actress I like better in Argentine movies.
>
> Manuel Puig (1984: 40–41)

*Betrayed by Rita Hayworth* (1968) is the novel that initiated Manuel Puig's career, and his eventual positioning as one of the greatest writers of twentieth-century Latin American literature. The story, as with many that followed, is very much influenced by cinema, and its characters – as the above citation of protagonist Choli's words exemplifies – live their everyday life emulating the stars they see on the big screen. Among the many merits of Puig's novels, as John King explains when analysing stardom in Latin America, is the fact they 'address some of the dominant concerns of film studies, in particular the ways in which ordinary moviegoers express their pleasure' (2003: 146). The cited dialogue indeed shows how stars become that 'ideal other' (McDonald 1998: 191) the characters identify with, imitating their actions and copying their clothes and hairstyles. But whilst Hollywood's influence is evident in the attempt of Choli to behave like the American supervisor, significant local specificities prevail – embodied here by the fascination for Argentine actress Mecha Ortiz. Mexican essayist Carlos Monsiváis, considered a pioneer of Stardom Studies in Latin America (King 2003: 145), further explains that

> (…) for a long period, despite their admiration and amazement at the landscape of shadows sent by the US, Latin Americans did not entrust and could not entrust to Hollywood their own representation and sentimental formation. For that they relied on Mexican, Argentine and Brazilian cinema. 'This is how we speak, this is how we look, this is how we move, this is how we treat our fellows.' (1995: 57, cited in King 2003: 145)

Indeed, the era described here, known as the Golden Age or classical industrial period – covering, roughly, the advent of sound in the 1930s to the end of the 1950s – saw how the local audiences of the three biggest film producers of the region (Argentina, Brazil and Mexico) 'listened to and watched their own stars. Carlos Gardel, Pedro Armendáriz, Jorge Negrete, Cantinflas, Dolores del Río, María Felix, were all models to be emulated' (King 2003: 145). While the world of Puig's novel is located in the 1940s, at the peak of Argentina's cinematographic Golden Age, the fascination for cinema, and more specifically for film stars, is evident in all his works, regardless of their setting in different historical periods.[1] Significantly for my interests here, though, is that what transpires in stories located in later decades is that the emphasis has shifted, and Hollywood stars begin to dominate the narrative surrounding the characters. Monsiváis argues, as

King also explains, that Hollywood, 'and certain Latin American films, were key mediators and teachers in the transition to modernity in Latin America' (King 2003: 145).

At the time Puig's novel was published, however, there was a growing critical rejection of US cultural imperialism, which became more significant as dictatorships spread across the region. John King believes that the lack of Star Studies in Latin America was precisely an outcome of the New Latin American Cinema Wave that emerged in these years and their overt rejection of stardom as belonging to a neocolonialist consumerist tradition they were trying to move away from (2003: 143). The Argentine researcher Alina Mazzaferro (2018) in her book on the rise of Stardom in Argentina – *La cultura de la celebridad* – mentions that the lack of studies in this area is mostly due to the fact that they are misconceived as shallow, not worthy of academic attention. This idea comes from twentieth-century debates over culture, media and globalisation, whereby the cult of celebrity tended to be viewed as a destroyer of core positive values, particularly from a Marxist point of view (Hinerman 2000: 193–194).[2] In light of this, the fact that Puig's novel was highly praised indicates that popular culture was slowly starting to be conceived of in more positive terms, even though it took slightly longer to have that same impact in scholarly circles.

In recent years, with the growing literature exploring various aspects of industrial consolidation and dynamics, and particularly since the consolidation of Star Studies at the end of the 1990s (Shingler 2012: 11), there has been an upsurge of articles and chapters starting to explore the existence of stardom in Latin America, and what it implies in a world that has been arguably dominated by Hollywood. As Leah Kemp rightly states when reviewing the concept of stardom in Spanish America, 'it is commonplace in Latin American cinema studies to decry the continual focus on Hollywood' (2017: 37). Ana López, when analysing the case of Mexican star Dolores del Río, affirms the tendency to believe that stardom in general is synonymous with stardom in Hollywood (1998: 6). For Nahuel Ribke and Jerome Bourdon, the US film industry exerts such an overwhelming control over Latin American markets that they prefer to talk about Peripheral Stardom despite signs of vitality in the local industries, because stars coming out of these regions simply 'cannot have the global or international reach of Hollywood stardom' (2017: 713).

Yet, as Tytti Soila explains in relation to the case of European stardom, whilst no star system in Latin America is identical to that of Hollywood production, 'the notion of national stardom has been a lived and unquestioned praxis in many places, and singular stars – definitely peer to the American ones – have become objects of intense admiration in their respective countries' (2009: 2). Indeed, in their analysis of Brazilian stars and stardom, Lisa Shaw and Tim Bergfelder ratify that this new trend in national film histories has, since the late 1980s, been challenging the notion that stars were by and large a Hollywood phenomenon (2017: 2). At a moment when online, on-demand platforms are dominating the global industry, it has become both more crucial and more complex to think in terms of national, transnational and international stardom. And with the displacement of Hollywood's hegemony in favour of a global understanding of the phenomenon, there has been a shift as well 'from a focus on stardom that is exclusively associated with cinema towards an acknowledgement that stars regularly cross media boundaries between film and television, the music industry, sports and other entertainment fields' (Shaw and Bergfelder 2017: 2). Accordingly, the following pages propose, through the figure of one of Latin America's most famous contemporary stars, to assert the extraordinary qualities of a number of multimedia personalities and, using Soila's approach, to think about stars from Hollywood and Latin America as 'peers'.

When analysing the figure of Mexican actress María Félix, the great Mexican writer Octavio Paz concluded that a star should be defined as an actor that

> has gone beyond what her craft demands: she has invented herself, she has become her own persona. An invention that is also a transfiguration: the new persona is and is not the actor. It is a creature that whilst sharing the same face and body, emanates all the strange and magnetic attributes that belong to fable and myth. She has become a star as the popular expression has it. The expression is exact: stars are celestial bodies that we can see and even photograph, but which we cannot touch. (Paz 1992: 9–10; translated by King 2003: 140)

Considering that human beings have now walked on the moon on several occasions, have had the opportunity to extract scientific samples from remote planets of the universe, and now even engage in orbital space tourism, it seems highly pertinent to redefine the metaphor of the star, and to bring it further back down to earth. The case of Ricardo Darín serves, in this respect, as a wonderful prism through which to rethink film stars in Latin America; to read them less in terms of an unattainable ideal and more for the unique qualities that single out particular individuals in the audience's imaginary and who contribute to box-office success. When Diego Lerer interviewed Darín for *Clarín*'s cultural magazine back in 2001 – when his cinematographic career was just gaining momentum – he asked the actor if he had ever considered himself a star. Darín's reply was:

> No. Neither in the past, nor now, nor in the future. I know how this career goes. I know that it fluctuates, that today I'm the best of the best and tomorrow a nobody. Besides, I'm not cut out for it. I think stars become stars when they stop being in contact with other humans. And I will never stop having that contact. You know why? Because then you lose the best part. I believe there are stars, yes – those who live as stars and promote their lives as stars and, of course, to achieve that, they have to cut out other things. For example, the pleasure of walking down the street, talking to people, stopping, wasting some time. Stars don't have time to lose. But I still have some.
>
> [No. Ni antes, ni ahora, ni después. Sé cómo es esta profesión, sé que tiene vaivenes, que hoy sos un fenómeno y mañana el cuatro de copas. Y aparte no me da el cuero para eso. Yo creo que las estrellas se transforman en estrellas cuando dejan de tener contacto con los humanos. Y yo, la verdad, no voy a dejar de tener contacto nunca con la gente. ¿Sabés por qué? Porque te perdés la mejor parte. Creo, sí, que hay estrellas. Que viven de estrellas, fomentan su vida de estrellas y que, por supuesto, para poder conseguirlo tienen que … amputarse otras zonas. Por ejemplo, el placer de caminar por la calle, hablar con la gente, detenerse, perder un poco de tiempo. Las estrellas no tienen tiempo para perder. Yo todavía tengo un poco.] (Lerer 2001: 22)

In this sense, Darín would come to represent what Lorraine York (2018) has defined as a 'reluctant celebrity', someone who is torn between being and not being a celebrity. According to York, this characteristic is more prominent in 'white, straight males who inhabit their race, sexed and gendered privilege with widely varying degrees of self-awareness, for it is that privilege that allows them to fashion their reluctance and to place it so confidently on public display' (2018: 2). Following this line of thought, Darín's rejection of 'Latino' roles in Hollywood might, to some extent, be read as an unconscious process of whitening himself as a Latin American actor.[3] There is indeed a certain privilege that comes with the ability to express reluctance, but it is argued that in Darín's case that privilege comes from belonging to a lineage of stage actors:

> I am the son of actors, but not the son of stars. A lot of San Martín, a lot of Cervantes. I saw my mum crying for lack of work while others, with more or less talent but surely with more luck, got more opportunities. I spent more time in the kitchen than in the drawing room, so I cannot go along with this idea that I'm a star, no.
>
> [Yo soy hijo de actores, pero no hijo de estrellas. Mucho San Martín, mucho Cervantes. Yo la vi llorar a mi vieja por falta de laburo mientras por al lado pasaban tipos con más o menos talento, pero seguro con mucha más suerte. Yo conocí la cocina antes que el salón, entonces comerme la película de la Estrella, no.] (Darín quoted in *Radar* 1999: 14–15)

As the following pages will explore, the fact that he insists on the importance of being connected to others demonstrates that Darín is not simply a 'reluctant star', but rather a twenty-first-century Latin American star who – in spite of himself – makes necessary a redefinition of what it means to be a star in the global south.

In line with Gillian Kelly's statement when analysing Hollywood star Tyrone Power, 'as with any scholarly account of a star, this book is indebted to the pioneering work of Edgar Morin (1961) and Richard Dyer (1979)' (2021: 9–10). Other names which populate these pages and which have become regular references in any writings on stars are Christine Gledhill, Paul McDonald, Richard deCordova, Ginette Vincendeau, Martin Shingler, Jeanine Basinger, Sabrina Qiong Yu, Guy Austin, Jeremy Butler, Jackie Stacey, Sean Redmond and Su Holmes, to name but a few. In the specific case of Latin American stardom, a comprehensive bibliography would also be impossible here, but some of the most important names in the field include the aforementioned John King (2003), as well as Carlos Monsiváis (1993, 1995), Octavio Paz (1992), Ana López (1998), Julia Tuñón (2003), Jeffrey Pilcher (2002), Marina Díaz López (2017), Linda Hall (2013), Jethro Soutar (2008) and Joanne Hershfield (2000), who delve into the Mexican case, and Lisa Shaw (2013, 2017), Kathryn Bishop-Sanchez (2016), Heloísa Buarque de Hollanda (1991), Ismail Xavier (1978), João Carlos Rodrigues (1988/2001), and Fernão Ramos and Luiz Felipe (2000) for the Brazilian case. In terms of Argentina, the third biggest film industry in the region, the aforementioned Alina Mazzaferro (2018) should be singled out, for providing a book-length study on the history of Argentine stardom, alongside a myriad of articles and book chapters from various scholars, including Soledad Pardo, Carolina Rocha, Beatriz Urraca, Jorge Sala, Claudio España, Ricardo

Manetti and María Valdez, which will be brought into play in the course of these pages.

## About this book

The chapters that follow situate Ricardo Darín within the history of Argentine cinema with the aim of navigating the socio-historical, cultural and industrial dynamics that have shaped Argentine stardom over the years. They approach Darín both conceptually and historically, considering how specific tropes of Star Studies operate in the Latin American context. The main body of this work is comprised of three parts. Part I, entitled 'From Gardel to Darín: Film Stardom in Argentina', is composed of three chapters that contextualise the Argentine star system. In order to do so, this part will explore in chronological order the industrial and cultural uses and significance of film stars in Argentina, in order to provide the necessary background to understanding Darín's stardom construction. Accordingly, this section will establish points of comparison with other historical and internationally known Argentine stars, and it will also look at macro-structural synergies, including those with production companies, government policies and aesthetic cinematographic waves.

Bearing this in mind, Chapter 1, 'Origin and establishment of the Argentine star system', will examine the creation and consolidation of the Argentine star system from the silent to the classical-industrial period. It will consider the impact of the creation of production companies such as *Argentina Sono Film* and *Lumiton*. It will pay specific attention to the cases of Carlos Gardel, Hugo del Carril, Libertad Lamarque, Tita Merello and Luis Sandrini. By looking at both men's and women's first steps in the development of a national star system, it aims to move beyond the readings on masculinity associated with Darín (Rocha 2012; Ruétalo in Tierney et al. 2017; McCarthy 2022), instead placing focus on addressing his career development as part of a wider industrial process. Thus, the chapter explores how these performers gained public recognition within and outside the country; how they worked in an increasingly transnational way in different countries; their relationship with Hollywood and the studio system; and whether or not they represent wider social groups and historical moments.

Chapter 2, entitled 'Stardom during the rise of television and the 1960s film wave', will look at the emergence of television in the early 1950s and how the small screen impacted on the development of a star system shared with the film industry. In global terms, the appearance of television and the mass-mediatisation of culture generated growing conceptual differences between celebrities and film stars. Nevertheless, in Argentina, with the fall of the film studios, television acquired a renewed status, erasing the stark dichotomy that tended to separate film and television stardom in other latitudes. Therefore, this chapter will explore the complex intricacies between these terms and whether they are connected to wider market strategies and/or cultural and sociological strands both in popular media and the film industry. In this vein, the chapter will consider how Darín, at this gestational moment, constructed his star image on the platform provided by the emerging medium of television, drawing on its interdisciplinarity and fast pace. The chapter will also contemplate the new wave of auteur films by directors such as David José Kohon, Lautaro Murúa, Rodolfo Kuhn, Manuel Antín, Simón Feldman, Leopoldo Torre Nilsson and Leonardo Favio which appeared following this particular historical moment, and what impact this new wave had in the creation and consolidation of new film stars – such as Alfredo Alcón, Graciela Borges, Héctor Alterio, Norma Aleandro, Soledad Silveyra and Federico Luppi – many of whom have worked with Darín at different stages of their careers. Lastly, the chapter will consider to what extent 'stars became elided' (King 2003) under the militant anti-imperialist film productions of the New Latin American Cinema wave that also emerged during this period.

Chapter 3, 'The challenges of a (non-)star system in a post-dictatorship period', will consider how the dictatorship and the transitional period affected the national film industry and its stars. The increasing international recognition of Argentine cinema that started at the beginning of the 1980s, thanks to the Academy Award for Best Foreign Language Film being given to *La historia oficial* [*The Official Story*] (Puenzo 1985), will be explored in conjunction with the internal process of dismantling many of the most iconic production companies. This process reached its most critical moment during the Menemist era, in which Argentine cinema experienced a crisis that left the industry at the verge of extinction. Paradoxically, the industry's collapse produced the emergence, at the end of the 1990s, of a new wave of productions made on a shoestring by young directors working with non-professional actors. How this New Argentine Cinema affected the national star system will be explored in connection to the most important performers' career development in other media, including Adrián Suar, Gastón Pauls, Leonardo Sbaraglia, Valeria Bertuccelli, Mercedes Morán, Guillermo Francella and Cecilia Roth. The chapter will conclude with a brief analysis of the cultural shift carried out by the Kirchner administrations and its impact on the film industry, acknowledging Ricardo Darín's place within this (non-)industrial period and in the renewal of the contemporary Argentine star system.

Part II, 'From Child Theatre Performer and TV Celebrity to Film Star', comprises five chapters that explore the heretofore uncharted territory of Darín's performance in theatre and TV, as well as his more familiar works in cinema. The chapters run in chronological order, but each one of them focuses on a specific aspect of his career by looking at his work in different mediums – theatre, television, cinema and other media. Central to this section will be the analysis of the changes of Darín's power over audience and market expectations over time. The first chapter of this section, 'Childhood and first performances' (Chapter 4), will look at Darín's early days in a family-run theatre and his first steps as a child TV performer – at a time when TV was at its early stages of development in the country. Archive material and Darín's own words about the importance of his upbringing will be considered alongside the development of the star system in Argentina in the mid-1960s and early 1970s. The violence of those years, the proscription of Peronism, and the emergence of a new wave of film directors will all be taken into account in the analysis of TV shows like *La pandilla del tranvía* [*The Trolley Car Gang*] (Channel 9, 1968), *Alta comedia* [*High Comedy*] (Channel 9, 1974–1975), the soap opera *Estación Retiro* [*Retiro Station*] (Channel 9, 1971–1972) and his first film performance in *He nacido en la ribera* [*I Was Born on the Riverbank*] (Catrani 1972). The chapter will carefully weave a tapestry depicting the network of performers, directors, producers and representatives who started to become connected with Darín through these different works and personal relationships, and who came to be the backbone of the Argentine star system of the time.

The second chapter of Part II – '*Telenovelas* and music-based youth films' – will examine Darín's performances as soap opera heart-throb – including the subsequent coming-of-age of his celebrity status. It is precisely his *galán* features – a local term connoting a man of handsome features and gentlemanly manners – which gave root to his popularity in the 1980s, through his participation in booming, audience-pleasing melodramas such as *Estrellita mía* [*My Little Star*] (Channel 11, 1987, co-starring the soap-opera diva of the time, Andrea del Boca) and *Rebelde* [*Rebel*] (Channel 9, 1989, starring another famous TV actress, Grecia Colmenares). As mentioned in my short contribution to the *Directory of World Cinema: Argentina Vol. II* (2016), in those years he performed in myriad of small supporting roles in films with tendencies towards promoting family and good moral values, such as the remake of the historical family drama *Así es la vida* [*That's Life*] (Carreras 1977) and the moralistic youth rehabilitation story *Juventud sin barreras* [*Youth Without Limits*] (Montes 1979). This latter film was also part of a common film strategy of the time that consisted of including singing acts randomly inserted in the film plots to promote local singers, which was also the case of the 'love films' Darín worked on during this period, where the songs tended to be more important than the actual plot, and Darín's performance – generally as the lover – was only anecdotical, yet was persistently present in the social imaginary. In this regard, the chapter will explore Darín's cross-media performances and his growing popularity and 'celebrity' status, paying particular attention to the importance of *telenovelas* and television in general for the consolidation of Latin American stardom.

Chapter 6 will look at Darín's performances in the theatre, from musicals such as *Sugar* (1986) to comedies such as *Art* (1998–2008) and *Escenas de la vida conyugal* [*Scenes from a Marriage*] (2013–2022). The chapter will focus on different performance styles – how repeating the same show over and over during a period of time, with various acting partners, in front of a live audience, involves different bodily postures/gestures than those used in front of a TV camera or on a film set, where the emphasis in the last years has been to focus on close-ups of Darín's facial expressions and eyes (Ruétalo in Tierney et al. 2017). Accordingly, these pages will delve into the complex relationship between acting and stardom, paying particular attention to those plays that have meaningfully contributed to the construction of his stardom, thanks to his negotiation of this maze of different practices.

Chapter 7 explores Darín's work in 1980s–1990s cinema and his involvement in New Argentine Cinema. It will examine how he tried to move away from his impersonation of the charismatic swindler 'Chiqui' Fornari in the celebrated sitcom *Mi cuñado* [*My Brother-in-law*] (Channel Telefé, 1993–1998), which curated the lovable guy-next-door image that was Darín's trademark during the 1990s. Since comedy stardom can be quite idiosyncratic, his comedy career will be discussed in relation to the perceived ordinariness of comedy and television performance, demonstrating that both can coexist with, and inform, the alleged extraordinariness of film stardom.

Chapter 8 will examine 'Contemporary productions and the ageing star', looking at how film stars must continuously negotiate their stardom status as they grow older in a highly mediated world where youth is considered a prime value. It will look at Darín's performance in blockbuster and award-winning films like *El hijo de la novia*, *El secreto de sus ojos* and *Relatos salvajes*. It will also pay specific attention to those films that have scarcely been considered to date, especially because of their contemporary nature – as films made in the latter moments of his life and career – such as *Nieve negra* [*Black Snow*] (Hodara 2017), *La cordillera* [*The Summit*] (Mitre 2017), *Todos lo saben* [*Everybody Knows*] (Farhadi 2018), stars Penélope Cruz and Javier Bardem, and *El amor menos pensado* [*An Unexpected Love*] (Vera 2018). The fact that he managed to move away, in the process of the consolidation of his cinematographic career, from stereotypical roles that could have typecast him as an epitome of youthful masculinity seems to have granted Darín the opportunity to revalue age as wisdom.

The final section, Part III, will examine the concept of the 'Hispanic' Star. It consists of three chapters which analyse the rise of Ricardo Darín's stardom outside of Argentina. Thus, it will study his career development in Spain, and will also explore his non-relationship with Hollywood – i.e. his choice to remain outside the big North American star factory and thereby avoid the process of 'self-exoticisation' that Latin American stars often go through in order to conform to its audience expectations (Ribke and Bourdon 2017). And, finally, it will consider his reception and career paths in other Latin American countries and in the UK. In this vein, Part III will examine whether or not it is possible to conceive of such a notion as a stereotypical 'Hispanic' star, what such a stereotype would entail, and to what extent Hollywood creates this stereotype as its 'other'. This part of the book will also include a final chapter reflecting on the research findings about, and what can be understood as, the particularities of a star system in Argentina, where the film industry constantly pushes at the boundaries of definition.

The first chapter of this final part (Chapter 9) will develop the work begun in my article 'Conquering the Conquerors: Ricardo Darín's Rise to Stardom in Spanish Film Culture', published in *Bulletin of Hispanic Studies* (2015). Accordingly, it will delve into the reception of Darín in Spain, paying particular attention to his latest works; those not included in my first approaches to the topic, such as *Truman* (Gay 2015) and *Todos lo saben* (Farhadi 2018). The chapter will also consider the increased transnational flow of cast and crew members that speaks to a common, mixed and imaginary geopolitical community formed by Spain and Argentina.

In this regard, it will unpick the complex figure of 'Darín the Argentinian' by looking at his new role as a member of the patronage of the Instituto Cervantes (accepted in 2018) and the assumption of a double nationality when he became a Spanish citizen in 2006.[4]

Chapter 10 will investigate the challenges related to 'Transnational mobility and cross-cultural exchanges' of the 'Hispanic stars'. Hence, it will look at the reception of Darín's image in the USA and the UK. It will also explore Darín's perspective on Hollywood, and why he has been reluctant to be part of it. The chapter will challenge the concepts of transnational, global or regional stardom. In order to do so, it will look at the recent connection of Darín with Javier Bardem and Penélope Cruz, and it will consider whether or not these cases of contemporary Hispanic stars who made it in Hollywood keep a sense of cultural and historical identity beyond the Hollywood canon. The final chapter (Chapter 11) considers the impact on star consecration of the 'Discourses of scandal, politics, activism and legacies', as the title suggests. It will engage multiple questions regarding the wider culture of Darín's films, proclamations and image, and what those reveal about Argentine cinema, and, more broadly, questions about Latin American and Hispanic cinemas and their stars. It will also consider Darín's legacy and family endeavours – including his son's recognition in film and TV and his sister's work in the industry as the president of the Argentine Actor's Association. The final remarks will focus on the particularities of the contemporary Argentine star system, commenting on whether or not we can think of it as a system in a traditional sense, and on the growing hybrid characteristics it shares with television and new digital platforms.

## Notes

1. Works such as *Kiss of the Spider Woman* (1976) and *Pubis Angelical* (1979).
2. Horkheimer and Adorno, in their seminal work on the cultural industry, argued that modern entertainment and media corporations use stardom and celebrity to pacify the masses. These two representatives of the Marxist Frankfurt School wrote this text in 1944 while in exile in the US, tainting the concept of stardom with a pessimistic view of the impact of popular culture on the masses – a system that spread the illusion of progression to benefit the ruling classes (reprinted in 2002: 43–72).
3. My thanks to Niamh Thornton, from the University of Liverpool, for this insight.
4. And, at the time of writing these words, he also obtained Uruguyan nationality (*Página12* 2022).

## References

Bandhauer, A. and Royer, M. (2015) 'Introduction: Star Studies and World Cinema', in Bandhauer, A. and Royer, M. (eds), *Stars in World Cinema. Screen Icons and Star Systems Across Cultures*, London and New York: I. B. Tauris.

Bishop-Sanchez, K. (2016) *Creating Carmen Miranda. Race, Camp, and Transnational Stardom*, Nashville, TN: Vanderbilt University Press.

Bradshaw, P. (2015) 'Wild Tales (*Relatos salvajes*) Review: Gripping Argentinian Revenge Portmanteau', in *The Guardian*, Thursday 26 March, available online at: http://www.theguardian.com/film/2015/mar/26/wild-tales-relatos-salvajes-review (accessed 1 May 2015).

Buarque de Hollanda, H. (ed.) (1991) *Quase Catálogo 3: Estrelas do cinema mudo Brasil, 1908–1930*, Rio de Janeiro: CIEC-Escola de Comunicação/UFRJ and Museo de Imagem e do Som do Rio de Janeiro.

Burucúa, C. (2014). 'Identidad, crisis y reevaluación de la historia: Ricardo Darín en *El secreto de sus ojos* y *Un cuento chino*', in *Imagofagia*, 10.

Cacofonias (2015) 'Argentinos pensam em lançar primeiro filme sem Ricardo Darín', in *Sensacionalista*. http://sensacionalista.uol.com.br/2015/01/23/argentinos-pensam-em-lancar-primeiro-filme-sem-ricardo-darin/ (accessed 19 December 2017).

Díaz López, M. (2017) 'La estelarización de Cantinflas y su presencia en el imaginario ranchero/How Cantinflas Became a Star and his Presence in the Ranch Comedy Imaginary', in *Secuencias Revista de Historia del Cine*, no. 43–44.

Downing, L. and Harris, S. (eds) (2007) *From Perversion to Purity: The Stardom of Catherine Deneuve*, Manchester and New York: Manchester University Press.

Dyer, R. (1979) *Stars*, London: BFI.

Garavelli, C. (2013), 'A Shared Star Imagery: The Argentine Actor Ricardo Darín Through Spanish Film Posters', in *Ol3Media*, no. 13.

Garavelli, C. (2015), 'Conquering the Conquerors: Ricardo Darín's Rise to Stardom in Spanish Film Culture', in *Bulletin of Hispanic Studies*, 92.4, pp. 411–428.

Garavelli, C. (2016), 'Ricardo Darín', in Urraca, B. and Kramer, G. M. (eds), *Directory of World Cinema: Argentina, Vol. II*, Bristol: Intellect.

Hall, L. (2013) *Dolores del Río. Beauty in Light and Shade*, Stanford, CA: Stanford University Press.

Hershfield, J. (2000), *The Invention of Dolores del Río*, Minnesota: University of Minnesota Press.

Hinerman, S. (2000) 'Star Culture', in Lull, J. (ed.), *Culture in the Communication Age*, London: Routledge.

Horkheimer, M. and Adorno, T. W. (2002) 'The Culture Industry: Enlightenment as Mass Deception', in Schmid Noerr, G. (ed.), *Dialectic of Enlightenment: Philosophical Fragments*, Stanford, CA: Stanford University Press.

Kelly, G. (2021) *Tyrone Power. Gender, Genre and Image in Classical Hollywood Cinema*, Edinburgh: Edinburgh University Press.

Kemp, L. (2017) 'Stardom in Spanish America', in Delgado, M., Hart, S. and Johnson, R. (eds), *A Companion to Latin American Cinema*, UK: John Wiley and Sons.

King, J. (2003) 'Stars: Mapping the Firmament', in Hart, S. and Young, R. (eds), *Contemporary Latin American Cultural Studies*, London: Arnold.

Lavallée, E. (2022) 'Annual Top Films Lists', in *ioncinema.com*. https://www.ioncinema.com/news/annual-top-films-lists/santiago-mitre-argentina-1985 (accessed 24 April 2022).

Lerer, D. (2001) Interview with Ricardo Darín, in *Revista Ñ/Clarín*, pp. 17–23.

López, A. (1998) 'From Hollywood and Back: Dolores del Rio, a Trans(National) Star', in *Studies in Latin American Popular Culture*, 17, pp. 5–33.

McCarthy, E. (2022), 'Starring Ricardo Darín: National Identity and Masculinity in Films by Juan José Campanella and Pablo Trapero', in *Modern Languages Open*, 1, pp. 1–15.

McDonald, P. (1998) 'Reconceptualising Stardom', in Dyer, R. (ed.), *Stars*, London: British Film Institute, pp. 174–200.

Mazzaferro, L. (2018) *La cultura de la celebridad*, Buenos Aires: Eudeba.

Monsiváis, C. (1995) 'All the People Came and Did Not Fit onto the Screen: Notes on the Cinema Audience in Mexico', in Paranaguá, P. A. (ed.), *Mexican Cinema*, translated by A. M. López, London: BFI, pp. 145–151.

Monsiváis, C. (1993) *Rostros del cine mexicano*, Mexico City: IMCINE.

Morin, E. (1961) *The Stars: An Account of the Star System in Motion Pictures*, New York: Grove Press.

Nagib, L., Perriam, C. and Dudrah, R. (eds) (2012) *Theorizing World Cinema*, London and New York: I. B. Tauris.

*Página12* (2022) 'Ricardo Darín respondió a las críticas recibidas por tramitar la ciudadanía uruguaya: "No me fui a vivir a ningún lado"', *Página12*, available at: https://www.pagina12.com.ar/438219-ricardo-darin-respondio-a-las-criticas-recibidas-por-tramita (accessed 1 September 2022).

Paz, O. (1992) *Razón y elogio de María Félix*, Mexico: Secretaría de Gobernación, Dirección General de Radio, Televisión, y Cinematografía, Cineteca Nacional.

Pilcher, J. (2002) *Cantinflas and the Chaos of Mexican Modernity*, Wilmington, DE: Scholarly Resources.

Puig, M. (1984) *Betrayed by Rita Hayworth*, London: Arena Book, Arrow Books Limited.

*Radar* (1999) 'Ricardo Darín se confiesa', in *Página/12*, *Radar* supplement, 3 October, pp. 14–15.

Ramos, F. and Luiz Felipe (2000) *Enciclopédia do cinema brasileiro*, San Pablo: Editora SENAC.

Ribke, N. and Bourdon, J. (2017) 'Peripheral Stardom, Ethnicity, and Nationality: The Rise of the Argentinian Ricardo Darin From Local Celebrity to Transnational Recognition', in *Communication, Culture & Critique*, 10, pp. 712–728.

Rocha, C. (2012) *Masculinities in Contemporary Argentine Popular Cinema*, New York: Palgrave Macmillan.

Rocha, C. (2016) 'A Hero's Challenged Masculinity: Darín in *La señal*', in *Journal of Iberian and Latin American Studies*, 22:2, pp. 139–150.

Rodrigues, J. C. (1988/2001) *O negro brasileiro e o cinema*, Rio de Janeiro: Editora Globo.

Shaw, L. (2013) *Carmen Miranda*, London: BFI.

Shaw, L. and Bergfelder, T. (2017) 'Introduction', in Bergfelder, T., Shaw, L. and Vieira, J. L. (eds), *Stars and Stardom in Brazilian Cinema*, New York and Oxford: Berghahn.

Shingler, M. (2012) *Star Studies: A Critical Guide*, London: Palgrave Macmillan/BFI.

Shohat, E. and Stam, R. (2014) *Unthinking Eurocentrism: Multiculturalism and the Media*, 2nd edition, New York and Oxon: Routledge.

Soila, T. (2009) 'Introduction', in Soila, T. (ed.), *Stellar Encounters. Stardom in Popular European Cinema*, UK: John Libbey Publishing Ltd.

Soria, C. (2014) 'The Star as Antihero: Ricardo Darín in *Carancho*', in *Argus-a Artes y Humanidades*, vol. III, no. 13, July, available at: https://www.argus-a.com/archivos-dinamicas/the-star-as-antihero.pdf (accessed 20 August 2022).

Soutar, J. (2008) *Gael García Bernal and the Latin American New Wave*, London: Anova Book Company Ltd.

Tierney, D., Ruétalo, V. and Ortiz, R. C. (2017) 'New Latin American Stardom', in D'Lugo, M. et al. (eds), *The Routledge Companion to Latin American Cinema*, London and New York: Routledge.

Tuñón, J. (2003) *Los rostros de un mito. Personajes femeninos en las películas de Emilio Indio Fernández*, Mexico: Arte e Imagen.

Urraca, B. (2014), 'Rituals of Performance: Ricardo Darín as Father Julián in *El Elefante blanco*', in *Revista de Estudios Hispánicos*, 48, pp. 356–372.

Xavier, I. (1978) *Sétima arte, um culto moderno: o idealismo estético e o cinema*, San Pablo: Perspectiva.

York, L. (2018) *Reluctant Celebrity. Affect and Privilege in Contemporary Stardom*, Switzerland: Palgrave Macmillan.

PART I

# From Gardel to Darín: Film Stardom in Argentina

# Chapter 1

# Origin and establishment of the Argentine star system

Cinema is a product of the emergence of modern life (Benet 2004: 17–34). The mass migration of people from rural to urban areas at the turn of the century brought with it the need to regulate time, space and labour, which promoted new forms of entertainment and leisure (Charney and Schwartz 1995: 3). The development of a mass culture came alongside the fascination for new technologies and modes of representation. What started as a medium to capture time and movement was soon transformed into an art form that had to negotiate its place among – and in connection to – other popular cultural practices, such as theatre, music and fine art. Longer film strips enabled the creation of more complex stories and the configuration of an institutional mode of representation (Bürch 1991). The turn to fiction as a leading film product (Thompson and Bordwell 2019: 20), and the need to increase the respectability of film, generated a discourse on acting in film that heightened its status to that of the already highly regarded stage acting (Shail 2019: 3). The development of a general cinematic language included the exploration of continuity effects and the regular use of close-up shots where facial expression started to prevail over physical gesticulation to enhance argument development (Gubern 1994). As has been demonstrated by various scholars (deCordova 1991; Shail 2019; Lusnich 1996), all these formal changes, in serving to give film performers more visibility, are part of the foundations of a 'star system'.

The star phenomenon was not only an outcome of new representational regulations, aesthetic improvements and cutting-edge discourses on acting and art quality, but also of the professionalisation of the production and consumption processes of motion pictures. In the first decade of the twentieth century, different film industries started to flourish across the globe. The United States became dominant, as it had the largest market, with more theatres per capita than any other country (Thompson and Bordwell 2019: 17). It was there where film production companies realised that the star image was an important source of economic value (McDonald 2000: 118). The shifted status of film as commodity meant that the filmed body was 'established as a site of textual productivity' (deCordova 1991: 50), not 'just a source of labour but also a form of capital' (McDonald 2000: 10). Thus, the identities of performers allowed the achievement of greater degrees of product differentiation in a competitive market (Shail 2019: 4; deCordova 1991: 46).

In their quest to expand their profit margins, the big American film companies soon started to look south of the border. Argentina was an ideal destination. It experienced an upsurge of immigration at the end of the nineteenth century that brought to its shores the new motion picture technologies, becoming one of the first countries in the world to discover its wonders (Finkielman 2004: 5; García Oliveri 2011). During the so-called silent period, Hollywood's productions gained control over the territory – a domain that remains up until this day.[1] Even though Argentina's cinematographic production was one of the most important of Latin America at the time (Mafud 2016: 13; García Oliveri 2011), local productions tended to be isolated efforts that did not manage to establish a regular work force (Di Núbila 1998: 51). As Alina Mazzaferro explains in her history of the star system in Argentina:

> in spite of the efforts and enthusiasm of particular individuals, local silent cinema was not able to consolidate a star system of its own that could compete against Hollywood. It was also unable to consolidate a regular audience, see the production companies flourish, or films bring profits, and there were no more than a handful of successes in the first twenty years of [its] national cinema.
>
> [A pesar de los esfuerzos y el entusiasmo, el cine mudo local no pudo consolidar un star system propio que compitiera con el de Hollywood, así como tampoco logró conformar un público, ni prosperaron las productoras, ni los films brindaron importantes ganancias, ni existieron más de un puñado de éxitos en los primeros veinte años de vida del cine nacional.] (2018: 38)

The country was going through an identity crisis at the time, caused by the fact that one third of the population was of foreign origin (Cuarterolo 2019: 234). Therefore, state efforts were channelled into the promotion of nationalist ideals that would consolidate the nation. Most artistic manifestations were in tune with this aim to educate the masses, and cinema, due to its capacity to reach wider illiterate audiences, proved to be an ideal medium by which to configure a collective imaginary. To this end, pioneer films included the commemoration of special events of significant relevance for the country, such as the wars of independence.[2] It is quite paradoxical, considering the symbolic dimension of these first films, that this task of promoting a national identity was in the hands of newly-arrived Europeans, including Belgian Henri Lepage, French Eugenio Py, Austrian Max Glücksmann, and Italians Federico Valle, Emilio Peruzzi, Mario Gallo and Atilio Lipizzi (Cuarterolo 2019: 234; Di Núbila 1998: 11–22). As Argentine cinema specialist Andrea Cuarterolo has pointed out, these realities evidence that cinema in Argentina at that moment was an import product (2019: 235). As such, it is not surprising that it took its time to find its roots and build a corpus of professionals that would consolidate a national industry strong enough to compete with the productions and performers coming from the north.

Even though we cannot talk about an Argentine star system in these first two decades, there were nonetheless a few films that had significant impact and whose performers paved the way for a notion of local stardom to flourish later on in the classical-industrial period. *Nobleza guacha* [*Gaucho Nobility*] (Cairo, Martínez de la Pera, Gunche), released in 1915, was the first major success of the silent era that should be mentioned in this respect (Di Núbila 1998: 17). It cost 20,000 pesos to make and grossed over one million (Barsky and Barsky 2017: 30). Jorge Finkielman, in his cultural history of the film industry in Argentina, states that the film was exhibited 'simultaneously in twenty-five Buenos Aires theatres, and also shown in Brazil, Spain and other Latin American countries', a success which motivated the desire to consolidate a local industry (2004: 16).[3] This desire was fuelled by the fall in import of foreign films caused by the First World War, and the fact that American supremacy was not yet completely manifest (Finkielman 2004: 16). Cast members in this production included Orfilia Rico, Margot Segré, Julio Scarcella, María Padín, Ángel Boyano, Celestino Petray, Arauco Radal and Arturo Mario – many of whom became regular faces of the silent period and made a fairly prosperous transition into the sound era.

*Nobleza gaucha*'s cinematographers, Martínez de la Pera and Gunche, separated from Cairo and invested in their own production, *Hasta después de muerta* [*Till After Her Death*] (1916). The film was written by no other than theatre sensation Florencio Parravicini, who also performed in it – his first adventure in cinema before his stellar career as a true film star skyrocketed in the 1930s. Orfilia Rico was cast again, alongside other important performers of the time, such as Silvia Parodi, María Fernanda Ladrón de Guevara, Argentino Gómez, Pedro Quartucci and

Enrique Serrano. Both Parodi and Gómez went on to perform in *Flor de Durazno* [*Peach Blossom*] (Defilippis Novoa 1917), the debut film of a young Carlos Gardel, who was quite hesitant to participate in a silent production considering he was already a respected Tango singer at the time, performing folk music in a duo formed with José Razzano (Barsky and Barsky 2017: 41).

The fact that Gardel was not able to demonstrate his singing ability and that he was overweight prompted many criticisms on his choice for the cast. Nonetheless, he had long been singled out in the media for his natural acting capacity while singing, and he had close relationships with artists that would become the leading film performers of this period, including the Podestá family, Alippi and Cassaux (Barsky and Barsky 2017). Thus, Federico Valle, from Patria Film, and Defilippis Novoa, the director, believed in his power of attraction and natural flair for the performative, seeing the exchange value of performers whose popularity off-screen could be capitalised in cinema.

*Flor de Durazno* included a mixture of experienced and new actors, like Ilde Pirovano, Celestino Petray and Diego Figueroa. Even though it did not have the success of *Nobleza gaucha*, it became another milestone of Argentine cinema, screened 'more than 500 times at the cinema where it was released' (Finkielman 2004: 21). Most importantly, it showed how the use of a popular face from the music industry, placed alongside a well-known theatre performer like Celestino Petray,[4] was a good marketing strategy with which to attract a massive audience. It was first announced as the new film written by doctor Martínez Zuviría – also known as Hugo Wast, an ascending writer and politician – but soon the newspapers showed images of Gardel to refer to the film, demonstrating the importance of his image in the promotion process (Barsky and Barsky 2017: 56). It should be noted that Gardel's physique fit very well with the character, who was not meant to be a gentleman from the city, but rather a rustic strongman from the countryside (Barsky and Barsky 2017: 43). Whilst the local canon of masculine beauty was starting to change with the growing impact of Hollywood films in the region, larger men were still considered in the press to be the preferred choice of 'the female audience' and, therefore, a benchmark of identification and aspiration for male spectators in a highly heteronormative society.[5]

When reviewing the most popular screen actors of the 1920s, Mazzaferro called attention to the names of Parravicini and Rico, together with that of Angelina Pagano, Blanca Podestá, Enrique Muiño, Elías

Alippi, Roberto Casaux and César Ratti (2018: 24).⁶ It was a particular moment when variety shows and the so-called '*género chico*' (little genre) plays – short, light plays with musical elements, such as one-act lyrical farces – were a mass phenomenon (Mazzaferro 2018: 25). It was also at that time when the actor's métier was professionalised and the performing companies were mainly formed by members of the same family – or used to operate as if they were one. As Mazzaferro rightly explains:

> either the actor inherited the metier, born in a family of performers that would facilitate his/her practical training (the most paradigmatic example is that of the Podestá family); or s/he was an outsider that had a gift for the craft and could start a career with the support of an artistic godfather
>
> [o el actor había heredado el *metier*; nacido en el seno de una familia de actores que facilitaba su formación práctica (el ejemplo paradigmático es la familia Podestá); o era un outsider que poseía un don para la disciplina y emprendía su carrera de la mano de un padrino artístico.] (2018: 26)

Ricardo Darín, to a certain extent, belongs to this tradition. As will be further explored in Chapter 4, he was born into a family of performers, a generational legacy which now continues with his own son, Ricardo 'Chino' Darín, and his nephew, Fausto Bengoechea – son of Darín's sister, Alejandra Darín, also an actress and president of the Argentine Actors Association. He has always talked about how he was born into the business and that he learnt the trade on a stage, by watching not only his parents perform, but also family friends who were respected theatre performers and who became big film stars as well, such as Norma Aleandro, Héctor Alterio, Alfredo Alarcón and Lautaro Murúa (cited in Parejas 2008). His grandfather, Andrés Antonio Darín, was an Italian immigrant who, in the 1940s and 1950s, co-owned the theatre Teatro Marconi (Darín, personal communication), where many of the well-known performers from this period acted, including the aforementioned Blanca Podestá.

## Talking pictures and the Golden Age of the star system (1933–1957)

At the beginning of the 1920s, Argentine cinema entered a period of depression that was only ended thanks to the arrival of sound. With more than 100 premieres a year, theatre, together with music, radio and various sports events – notably football and boxing, provided the popular forms of entertainment that local silent films appeared to be unable to match (Di Núbila 1998: 37). The working classes were formed mainly by immigrants that found the reading of intertitles in Spanish quite challenging. The upsurge in immigration was still experiencing its heyday at the beginning of the 1930s, which prolonged those issues. Cinema, therefore, was for the consumption of Spanish-literate audiences that preferred American or European productions (España 2000: 24).

Moreover, from 1915 on, Hollywood studios started making some films that located their plots in Argentina, an element that had previously been the main attraction of local productions. And, as Finkielman states, 'many great stars took part in those productions' (2004: 81) – such as Douglas Fairbanks in *The Gaucho* (Jones 1927). While, in general, these works where not well received in Argentina, for their questionable views on the country and its customs, their use of movie stars to attract an audience inspired many local producers. A paradigmatic example is that of Julián De Ajuria. Upon unsuccessfully trying to convince various American companies to produce films that would be in tune with the Argentine spirit of the time, he decided to finance the United States-based production of the film *Una nueva y gloriosa nación* [*The Charge of the Gauchos*] (Kelley 1928) himself. The film focused on a typically nationalist topic: the events surrounding the 1810 May Revolution.[7] De Arjuria understood that, in order to obtain distribution opportunities for the film against major Hollywood productions, he needed to use recognisable faces that would guarantee media coverage.

Francis X. Bushman was cast in the leading role as Manuel Belgrano. In those years, Bushman was popularly known as 'the king of Photoplay' – the popular American magazine that dedicated a special section to unveiling film performers' lives off the screen. He had made more than 170 films and was one of the biggest Hollywood stars of the silent era, still enjoying the success of his role in *Ben-Hur* (Niblo 1925). The heroine of the romance was played by Jaqueline Logan, who was also coming out of performing one of the most important roles of her career as Mary Magdalene in the box-office sensation *The King of Kings* (De Mille 1927). Other cast members included Italian Guido Trento, Argentine Paul Ellis and Canadian Charles Hill Mailes, all regular performers at the time, well known by audiences both in the USA and their home countries.[8] According to Finkielman, *Una nueva y gloriosa nación* was 'the most successful silent film of all', screened for two full years in Argentina, only finally removed from circulation when the sound film revolution began (2004: 84).

There were other cases in this pre-sound period that showed a growing use of the strategies implemented by Hollywood's star system to drive an audience and keep a national film production afloat. Nelo Cosimi, for instance, began his career as film director in the early 1920s, directing all kinds of movies and using imaginative and clever promotion techniques during the production of his films. This included, for example, filtering information to the press that was not related to the actual process of making the film – such as the announcement of his own marriage to actress Chita Foras while filming *Corazón ante la ley* in 1929 (Finkielman 2004: 80).[9] José Agustín Ferreyra, a prolific director of this era, also had some close relationships with the protagonists of his films – notably Lidia Liss and then María Turgenova – and fed the media titbits about an extravagant off-screen lifestyle that garnered attention for his on-screen personalities and productions (Couselo 1969).[10] In spite of these isolated cases, though, the reality is that stardom in Argentina only really originated in tandem with the sound revolution, when the star systems in the United States and in Europe were already experiencing a second phase in their evolution. While many of those systems' strategies were emulated, in the local system the star became more linked to a particular role or genre, rather than to a studio (Casale 2018: 248).

The expansion of the film and radio industries in the 1930s eventually allowed for the establishment and consolidation of a true local star system (Mazzaferro 2018: 23). Broadcasting in Argentina originated in 1920, almost simultaneously to in other parts of the world. At first, it was only live transmission of events, but by 1924 the existing technical difficulties in transmission and reception were surpassed, and the alliance between the broadcasting and recording industries came into effect (Finkielman 2004: 112). In that same year, Jaime Yankelevich bought Radio Belgrano, a company that initiated pioneer contracts of exclusivity with various artists whose constant presence and popularity in other media guaranteed high audience levels (Di Núbila 1998: 52). The 1930s would see the widespread entrance of the radio into houses all over the country, transforming the way prestigious artists understood the new media (Mazzaferro 2018: 43). The incipient film industry did not take long in maximising on radio's potential for promotion of its productions.

In 1927, for example, Radio La Nación 'presented a weekly program called Radio Club Metro-Goldwyn-Mayer, with information about the lives of the movie stars, Hollywood news and prizes consisting of autographed photographs or tickets to see a movie' (Finkielman 2004: 116).

In terms of the film industry's national expansion, as previously mentioned this developed in the 1930s thanks to the advent of sound technology. The first sound film arrived in Argentina on 12 June 1929, amidst the struggles of a global economic crisis, in the form of the American film *The Divine Lady* (Lloyd 1926). This was a silent film which had a synchronised musical score and sound effects, and it laid one of the first stepping stones in the advent of the new sound systems (España 2000: 25). There were previous local efforts in synchronising films with a recorded soundtrack, including Eugenio Py and Max Glücksmann's attempts in the early 1910s, and José Ferreyra's unsuccessful trial at showing *La muchacha del arrabal* with simultaneous playing of records in 1923 at the Esmeralda Cinema (Finkielmann 2004: 119). But there were no technical or financial means to make sound films in Argentina, which delayed the internal production process (Finkielmann 2004: 139).

The first Argentine film to have a soundtrack was *Adiós Argentina* [*Goodbye Argentina*] (Parpagnoli 1930).[11] It was the debut film of Libertad Lamarque, who would eventually become one of the icons of Argentine and Mexican Golden Age cinema.[12] At first the film was a resounding failure, with no real plot or proper character development. Federico Valle, its producer, requested the film to be taken out of circulation and re-edited, resulting in a modest improvement (Finkielmann 2004: 140). Other works came after this one, but the first true success of Argentine sound cinema took place in 1933, with Luis José Moglia Barth's film *¡Tango!* (Di Núbila 1998: 71). The film counted on multiple stars from various backgrounds, including famous singers, orchestras and dancers. It also presented realistic dialogues plagued with local expressions and charismatic *porteño* personalities, which led many to suggest that Buenos Aires itself was another star in the film (Kairuz 2001; España 2000). But, most significantly, it marked the beginning of Argentina Sono Film, one of the leading production companies in the consolidation of a national industry, relying heavily on the power of attraction of film stars and, as the name suggests, on the importance of sound for local cinema (Casale 2018: 249; Manetti 2000: 163).[13]

Although the argument was quite simple and similar to previous silent films – the clash between the values and lifestyle of the countryside against those of the big city – the way of producing the film was more ambitious and aligned with an intention to invest in an incipient star system. Film historian Claudio España has explained that Ángel Mentasti, who used to distribute European films in the region, was dreaming of making his own sound film with Tango music, similar to those Gardel was doing in Paris and New York, and which were so popular in Latin America (2000: 25).[14] Therefore, together with Moglia Barth, they thought the way forward was to include the most popular faces of the local theatre, radio and recording companies, including Maipo theatre regular Pepe Arias, Libertad Lamarque, who was the leading voice of RCA Victor company, Tita Merello, who was enjoying the success of the play *El conventillo de la Paloma*, and a young Luis Sandrini, who was starting to garner considerable attention as a comedian in Enrique Muiño and Elías Alippi's theatre company, with the play *Los tres berretines* [*The Three Whims*] (2000: 27).[15] Meneca Tailhade and Alicia Vignoli, also from the Maipo; Azucena Maizani, Mercedes Simone and Alberto Gómez's popular voices; Juan de Dios Filiberto, Osvaldo Fresedo, Edgardo Donato and Ernesto Ponzio and Bazán's tango orchestras, in conjunction with the king of tango dancing, José Ovidio Bianquet, completed a super-stellar cast that was never gathered together again (España 2000: 27).

¡*Tango!* not only initiated the so-called Golden Age of Argentine cinema – also known as the classical-industrial period – but also consolidated the star image of many of the performers who would come to form its star system.[16] The scene in which Libertad Lamarque's character cries melodramatically on the floor, for instance, shows an action that would become a regular feature of her future beloved characters (Kairuz 2001). After a failed start in *Adiós Argentina*, and being called 'too fat to be a movie star' (Lamarque 1986: 152), Lamarque decided to exploit her talent as a tango singer, working her way up through a small production company (the Murúa brothers' SIDE), and in roles portraying naïve, poor girls, who suffer all sorts of misfortunes, which connected her to the masses. Mentasti invited her to work in ¡*Tango!* and, towards the end of the 1930s, Argentina Sono Film started actively using her name to gain distribution and exhibition deals for its upcoming films, becoming one of the first Argentine studios to give special treatment to one of its performers (Paladino 1999: 63–64). In short, Lamarque became the heroine of popular melodrama and, according to some critics, the biggest star not only of Argentina but of all Latin America (Mazzaferro 2018: 58).

Pepe Arias, in turn, plays for the first time in ¡Tango! the role of the picaresque wheeler-dealer that he would exploit throughout his career.[17] Tita Merello plays a woman who appears lost and confused, a recurrent state of many characters in her filmography (Kairuz 2001).[18] Luis Sandrini presents all the typical elements that he will sustain throughout his life: the poor but honest, funny, lovable and trustworthy guy (Mazzaferro 2018: 59). Even forty years later, in the film that will see him join Darín in 1977 – *Así es la vida* (Carreras) – we will see remnants of this good-natured funny-guy type that originated in this moment.[19] It is in fact his performance that same year of 1933, in the film adaptation of the play he was working on at the time, that would consolidate his comic archetype and star image. *Los tres berretines*, directed by Enrique Telémaco Susini, was released only a few days after ¡Tango!, becoming the second Argentine sound film, and launching the second largest studio of the time: Lumiton (Fabbro 2000: 223).[20]

The founders of Lumiton were pioneers not only in their sound experiments and facilities, but also in their focus on the production process of signing up both, star performers as well as star directors (Fabbro 2000: 224).[21] Their first two productions, *Los tres berretines* and *Ayer y hoy*, were made by a technical team lead by Susini that ranked the name of the actors in order of popularity in the opening credits, and simply did not mention a director (Di Núbila 1998: 77). Upon their second film's failure, they hired Francisco 'Pepe' Oyarzábal, who changed the company's fate with *Noches de Buenos Aires* [*Buenos Aires Nights*] (Romero 1935), starring Tita Merello and Fernando Ochoa, and consolidated the stardom of actresses like Niní Marshall.[22] He was, in fact, in the process of developing a project with Carlos Gardel – with whom he coincided in the production of *Luces de Buenos Aires* in Paris – but their collaboration never materialised due to the singer's tragic death in a plane crash in Colombia (Fabbro 2000: 225).

Some of the stellar directors of this period included Mario Soffici, Daniel Tinayre, Manuel Romero, Luis Saslavsky and Alberto de Zavalía.[23] Their films tried to move away from formulaic proposals generated by producers who were trying to sell more projects from their companies by using the name of specific stars – which caused a number of low-quality productions that not even a famous name could rescue (Martínez Suárez 1990: 98).[24] Di Núbila noted in these films, particularly in those of Romero and Soffici, an improvement in the quality of the performances. In addition to the above-mentioned stars, the names of José Gola, Arturo García Buhr – who worked with Darín in 1978 in *La rabona* (David) and in 1984 in *La Rosales* (Lipszyc) – Elsa O'Connor, Enrique Serrano, Francisco Petrone, Santiago Arrieta, Olinda Bozán and Irma Córdoba (Di Núbila 1998: 114) were also mentioned by Di Núbila as the actors who made the cinema of this period more attractive (1998: 114).[25]

In summary, sound films allowed the language barrier to disappear and, thus, the rise in popularity of a cinema spoken in Spanish (España 2000: 23). The Argentine and Mexican industries became so successful that Hollywood itself decided to start making films in Spanish (Heinink and Dickson 1990).[26] Studio production then consolidated an industry in Argentina between 1933 and 1956 (Fabbro 2000: 160).[27] It was a similar case in Mexico, which experienced its Golden Age between 1936 and 1956.[28] Many scholars have pointed out the key role played by domestic film stars in the expansion and consolidation of these local industries (Paladino 1999; España 2000). Most of the performers who reached star recognition in this period were able to do so thanks to their migration from different media – mainly radio, theatre and cinema – and their ability to adapt to different acting styles and media demands (Mazzaferro 2018: 50). Moreover, the success of a sound cinema with a local flavour promoted the development of national publications specialised in cinema and its stars. This growth took place at the same time that the *género chico* plays began to decline (Mazzaferro 2018: 39–41).

In Argentina, publications such as *Radiolandia*, *Sintonía*, *Antena* and *Set* dedicated many pages to exploring the intricacies of stardom, demonstrating an acute understanding of how film stars were constructed. In their pages you could read discussions on the stars' clothes and make-up, as well as their links to production companies, their extensive network of friends and enemies, and even an acknowledgement of their status as commodities (Pardo 2018: 6). In this sense, these publications anticipated the origin of Film Stardom Studies and envisaged how 'to use a star system is therefore to adopt a degree of exclusivity in using employees' identities as production values' (McLean 2001: 423; Shail 2019: 7). While these first publications began with a focus on radio and theatre performers and, to lesser degree, film stars, this focus soon shifted. By 1940, three new magazines dedicated exclusively to cinema emerged: *Nuestra revista*, *Cámara: Noticias del cine argentino* and *Nuestro cine*. At that stage, the amount of letters these publications were receiving from readers showed the existence of popular fan clubs, like the one dedicated to the Legrand sisters, which evinced the final consolidation of a local star system (Casale 2018: 249).

## The star system under turbulent political times

In September 1930, a military *coup d'état* ended Hipólito Yrigoyen's government and decades of constitutional order (Di Núbila 1998: 65). This initiated a period of de facto presidents known as 'The Infamous Decade', which culminated with the election of Juan Domingo Perón in 1946.[29] While film cameras were, as César Maranghello explains, unconsciously looking at this military intervention with optimism, several cinematographic companies were not able to survive the rising economic crisis that it generated (2005: 63). Unemployment soared and, with the lack of capital circulation, many local film theatres had to close (Maranghello 2005: 64). Nevertheless, as previously discussed, with the advent of sound in 1933, and of a cinema spoken in the Argentine dialect, the distribution of foreign productions was reduced, and the general public started to choose local films as a form of entertainment. In this political climate, a conservative and populist cinema prevailed, whereby the lowly were portrayed as noble and the rich as despotic, in stories plagued with moral innuendos (Maranghello 2005: 72).

One of the stars to suffer from the political upheavals of this period was Niní Marshall. At first, she benefited from this focus on the working class. She knew well how to alter her speech and body gestures to capture the essence of the immigrants, which resonated across the country, thus becoming one of the most sought-after figures outside Buenos Aires (Mazzaferro 2018: 64–66). In this respect, the characters of Cándida and Catita, based on various popular archetypes, were her most famous (Mazzaferro 2018: 65; Posadas 1993), to the extent that they saved Lumiton and EFA's finances in 1940 (Di Núbila 1998: 302). Argentina Sono Film, banned from using those characters due to their exclusivity contract with other studios, also managed to benefit from Marshall's stardom by appealing, precisely, to her star image: *Hay que educar a Niní* [*Educating Niní*] (1940), directed by Luis César Amadori, fused character and performer in such a self-referential way that Niní played a version of herself, demonstrating a new height in her status (Di Núbila 1998: 303).[30]

But in 1943 the military government prohibited Marshall's characters in an attempt to purge Argentine Spanish of what they considered a promotion of corrosive linguistic misuses (Mazzaferro 2018: 67). Accordingly, she had to rescind many of her broadcasting contracts and put aside her successful cinema roles, instead privileging new characters. Her multiple prohibitions – the second one came during Perón's government in 1950, when she was put on a blacklist and was forbidden to work in the country (Posadas 1993: 95) – did not diminish her value and importance in show business (Mazzaferro 2018: 67).³¹ On the contrary, the local audience supported her, she kept winning important awards, and her exile sparked a fruitful international career in Mexico and Spain – as was also the case for other stars who had to work in exile in the 1940s and 1950s, like Amanda Ledesma and Libertad Lamarque (Mazzaferro 2018: 68).

Mirtha Legrand's filmography serves as a perfect example of the type of cinema promoted in the country during this period. In *Los martes orquídeas* [*On Tuesdays, Orchids*] (Mugica 1941) an almost imperceptible kiss takes place between the leading characters towards the end.³² Legrand plays a middle-class, naïve and virginal girl; a character whose beauty and fragility would be a constant trait in roles throughout her stellar career. Subsequent films would be even more conservative in their approach. As Mazzaferro explains, in *Claro de Luna* [*Moonlight*] (Amadori 1942) or *La pequeña señora de Pérez* [*Pérez's wife*] (Christensen 1944), the audience had to imagine that a kiss takes place between the lovers (2018: 144). For the local imaginary, stardom still represented a threat against the idea that women could only be fulfilled in the role of wives or mothers (Mazzaferro 2018: 149). While in North America the rules of the star system implied that an actress could reach star status through a scandal, in Argentina female performers could not risk stepping off the path of what was morally accepted as ladylike behaviour (Mazzaferro 2018: 159).

In the early 1940s, Argentina started to experience the impact of the Second World War. Its products were not exported as much as they used to be, and there was a growing lack of film stock with which to produce films (Di Núbila 1998: 314). The Second World War's exigencies and alliances then also prompted the USA to look south of the border in an attempt to consolidate its power. Thus, the Roosevelt administration (1933–1945) implemented the Good Neighbour Policy, with the aim of improving reciprocal trade agreements with Latin America and reasserting US impact in the region. Yet, as José Piedra noted, 'the unadvertised reason for the U.S. interest had much to do with the commercial exploitation of Latin lands and peoples of the Americas in the wake of a war-torn Europe' (1994: n.p.). The policy was highly promoted through cinema, following a common agreement between Roosevelt's government and Hollywood's studios. A variety of films were produced, including classic genre films shot on both sides of the border and Disney's South American projects.³³

The most successful were musical comedies set either in Latin America or in the USA and featuring well-known stars (López 1993: 70).

As Ana M. López has explained, 'after decades of portraying Latin Americans lackadaisically and sporadically as lazy peasants [...] Hollywood films [...] featuring Latin American stars, music, locations and stories flooded US and international markets' between 1939 and 1947 (1993: 69). This implied that during this period an array of Latin American stars moved to Hollywood to perform in various productions filled with Latin rhythms and promises to the audience of an adventure that would take them *Flying Down to Rio* (Freeland 1933),[34] *Down Argentine Way* (Zanuck 1940)[35] or to spend a *Weekend in Havana* (Lang 1941) (Burton 1992: 23).[36] Many studies have been produced on key figures of this era, such as Dolores del Río (López 1998; Herschfield 2000; Tuñón 2000; Hall 2013), Lupe Velez (Vogel 2012) and Carmen Miranda (Shaw 2013, 2015; Vieira 1999; Bergfelder, Shaw and Vieira 2017).

By the end of the war, Argentina was struggling in the wake of its political neutrality during the conflict – it only declared war on the Axis powers in March 1945. Not only did the lack of film stock affect production, but also the market was starting to favour Mexican films instead of those coming from Argentina due to the boycott put in place by the USA as a consequence for the nation's sustained neutrality (Kriger 2009: 34). The country went from producing fifty-six films in 1942 to twenty-three in 1945 (Kriger 2009: 39). The state then began to intervene and decreed the compulsory showing of national products in local cinemas. When Perón became president in June 1946, the film industry was declared 'of national interest' and benefited from financial state support (Kriger 2009: 43).

As a cultural, aesthetic, historical, economic and social phenomenon, cinema became the ideal medium and industry for channelling national desires and exerting popular narratives of self-identification. Since the emergence of Peronism was an outcome of a process of appropriation and resignification of working-class rituals and symbols, cinema became an important political capital (Mazzaferro 2018: 102–103). As Mazzaferro (2018: 103) rightly explains, the interplay between ordinary and extraordinary that was at the core of Peronism, with Perón presenting himself as one more *descamizado* and his wife Evita as a plebeian princess (Sarlo 2003: 84), is the same paradoxical oxymoron that lies at the base of film stardom. The star is close and familiar, yet remote and singular at the same time. Hence, during Perón's administrations the star system was transformed through its dialogue with political alliances: to be ascribed to

Peronism was more important than talent or artistic training (Mazzaferro 2018: 119).

The unprecedented spectacularisation of politics and the politicisation of the cinematographic star system is undoubtedly connected to Peronism's reliance on the construction of a symbolic capital that would give political identity to Argentine society (Kriger 2009: 133). The fact that, before becoming the First Lady, Eva Duarte was trying to be a film star herself is also significant. At the time she started her relationship with Perón, she was an actress of little renown (Mazzaferro 2018: 88). But soon her association with the General allowed her to obtain more and better roles and contracts; something which caused tensions with her peers.[37] While shooting *La Cabalgata del circo* [*Circus Cavalcade*] (Soffici and Boneo 1945), starring Libertad Lamarque, for the first time a production schedule suffered several alterations due to a supporting actress's agenda – even at the expense of the leading performers' commitments (Mazzaferro 2018: 93).[38] Tensions with the industry mounted again during the shooting of *La pródiga* [*The Prodigal Woman*] (Soffici 1945) – her first and only leading role – when the union denounced an abuse of power in connection to her treatment of staff members.[39] After these incidents, and her ascension as First Lady, she would instead find her desired stardom in politics, implementing her own aesthetic – one very much inspired by the film industry's stardom strategies.

In terms of the importance of political alliances in the industry at this time, Hugo del Carril is a paradigmatic example. As Mazzaferro outlines, he embodied two of the most iconic values of popular culture in the 1940s and 1950s: Tango and Peronism (2018: 68). He reached star status in 1939, when he played the great Carlos Gardel in Alberto de Zavalía's *La vida de Carlos Gardel* [*Carlos Gardel's Life*]. His fusion with the character in the public imaginary granted him a mythical aura.[40] By 1949, he recorded the Peronist anthem and became the public face of the party (Kriger 2009: 187). Zully Moreno, another great diva from the Golden Age, also did not shy away from publicly stating that her elegance and feminine reference – which arguably granted her stardom – did not come from Hollywood, but from the First Lady Eva Perón (Mazzaferro 2018: 81). Tita Merello, who used to be placed as the antipodes of Zully Moreno's prevailing beauty canon in the media, was also a fervent Peronist whose characters referenced the First Lady: excluded women who manage to surpass themselves through work (Kriger 2009: 242). Crucially, as a consequence of the 1955 *coup d'état* that ousted Perón, and the following proscription of Peronism, many of the big stars linked to the party had to leave the country, and the star system had to be redefined (Mazzaferro 2018: 16).

## Notes

1. The silent period in Argentina comprises the years since the first films were made on Argentine soil, so from 1896 to 1932 (Di Núbila 1998). Although some scholars prefer to limit this period to the years when feature-length fiction films started to be made, before the advent of sound – 1914 to 1932 (Mafud 2016).
2. The first films created in the country serve as examples of this, including *La bandera argentina* [*The Argentine Flag*] (Py 1897), *La revolución de mayo* [*The May Revolution*] (Gallo 1909) and *El fusilamiento de Dorrego* [*Dorrego's Murder By Firing Squad*] (Gallo 1908). The latter included famous theatre performers of the time, such as Salvador Rosich, Eliseo Gutiérrez and Roberto Casaux, showing producers' increasing interest in incorporating well-known faces in their films as a way of attracting audiences.
3. Between 1915 and 1921 around 100 Argentine films were released (Di Núbila 1998: 20).
4. Celestino Petray was a theatre actor who belonged to Pepe Podestá's theatre company. He also acted in *Nobleza guacha*, in the role of Cocoliche (Barsky and Barsky 2017).
5. Reviewing the success of *Nobleza gaucha* in 1915, Elina Tranchini states that many famous performers from the theatre and the 'circo criollo' [folkloric circle] participated in its achievements, including the 'handsome Julio Scarcella, who was the preferred option of the feminine audience at the time for his chubbiness' (cited in Barsky and Barsky 2017: 44).
6. Parravicini's case is quite paradigmatic of an emerging star system. Podestá discovered him in a small suburban theatre and invited him to join his theatre company in 1906. His powerful personality tended to blur the boundaries of his characters and his own persona. He loved bragging about his adventurous past and insisted he was a descendent of Napoleon and Casanova, which increased his mythical construction and power of attraction (Castillo 1943).
7. De Ajuria produced some of the first feature-length Argentine films, including *La Revolución de Mayo* (1909) and *Nobleza gaucha* (1915). He made his fortune distributing American films in Argentina (Cuarterolo 2013: 4).
8. Guido Trento had a successful career in Italy as a theatre and silent film actor, performing in more than seventy films. During the Second World War he emigrated to the USA. His work in front of the camera stopped with the emergence of sound cinema, although he continued working on dubbing for some time. Charles Hill Mailes was an active performer during the silent era, appearing in more than 290 films, including those of famous directors such as D. W. Griffith. He had retired by the time of the advent of sound and passed away in 1937. Paul Ellis was the artistic name of Benjamin Ítalo José Ingenito Paralupi O'Higgins, an Argentine actor,

scriptwriter and producer who had a long career in the USA. He started working in the 1920s in the pre-sound era and had a successful career in sound cinema as a handsome Latino, playing alongside stars such as Greta Garbo and Bela Lugosi.
9. Nelo Cosimi was born in Italy in 1894 and moved to Argentina when he was four years old. At a very young age he started working in theatre, and in 1916, while working for Elías Alippi's company, he started acting in Ferreyra's *Venganza gaucha*. Then came his first leading role in *El tango de la muerte* (Ferreyra 1917) (Di Núbila 1998: 44; Couselo 1969). His wife, actress Chita Foras, was also born in Italy and became an iconic figure of Argentina's performing arts scene for over three decades. She was part of Leonor Rinaldi's theatre company, worked in LRA National Radio, participated in Cordero-Sandrini's theatre company, and in cinema acted in more than a dozen films, spanning the silent and sound periods.
10. In his book on Argentine cinema history, film historian César Maranghello mentions that the film *Palomas rubias* [*Blond Doves*] (Ferreyra 1920), which initiated the work of the Torres Ríos brothers, included in its leading roles the 'beautiful' Lidia Liss and Mary Clay, paving the way for a local star system to emerge (2005: 37). María Turgenova was born in Spain but became one of the leading actresses of Argentine silent cinema. She spent a period as Tango singer, as well as working regularly in theatre. She was married to José Agustín Ferreyra from 1924 until 1931.
11. This is still considered a silent film by some scholars (Mazzaferro 2018: 57). Maranghello states that the first Argentine sound film was *Mosaico criollo* (Yribarren 1930) (2005: 61; Martínez Suárez 1990: 95). He also mentions that in that year, 1930, Valle's company produced a series of short films directed by Eduardo Morera starring Carlos Gardel, in what could be considered the origin of local music videoclips.
12. Other cast members included the director himself, Pierina Dealessi, Ada Cornaro, Ana Fábregas and Silvio Romano.
13. It is also in this year that the National Film Institute was created, and a new government regulation was put in place to start supporting the development of a national industry (Kriger 2009: 27).
14. Gardel embarked on a music tour in France in 1931, which led him to sign a contract with the American company Paramount to shoot a film in their studio located in Joinville-le-Pont. The musical *Las Luces de Buenos Aires* [*Buenos Aires's Lights*] (Millar 1931) launched Gardel's career as an international film star. Mazzaferro states that Gardel's local stardom is actually owed to his European tours and his work with Paramount (2018: 63). The great actress Imperio Argentina also worked for Paramount at their Joinville studio during this period.
15. After this film, Moglia Barth directed *Dancing* (1933), which also promoted some of the biggest stars of this period, such as tango singer Amanda Ledesma. Ledesma went on to work with Luis Sandrini, Osvaldo Miranda and Hugo del Carril, and in radio was the main rival of Libertad Lamarque. She moved to Mexico in 1942, working there with iconic figures of the music and film industries, such as Jorge Negrete.
16. Saying this, as Diana Paladino has rightly pointed out, the notion of the star and the narrative strategies implemented for their exploitation were not yet properly defined at local level when ¡*Tango!* took place (1999: 62).

17. Pepe Arias had starred in twenty-four films by the mid-1960s, including two comedies that explored, in a reflexive way, the role of stars in Argentine society: *El fabricante de estrellas* [Stars Maker] (Romero 1943) and *Estrellas de Buenos Aires* [Buenos Aires' Stars] (Land 1956). This last one was directed by Kurt Land, who went on to direct Darín's father in the film *La culpa* [The Guilt] in 1969 – a film normally wrongly attributed to Darín himself.
18. These features correspond to the reading that Merello tended always to play the same role: that of the self-abnegating mother (Mazzaferro 2018: 70; Manetti 2000: 228)
19. Sandrini himself declared that he used to play 'either of Cachuso or of Sandrini' ['Yo hacía de Cachuso o de Sandrini] (quoted in Pellettieri 2001: 181), suggesting that his characters were intrinsically linked to his off-screen personality, and consolidating the mythical construction at the core of his stardom.
20. Cast members included Luis Arata, Héctor Quintanilla, Florindo Ferrario, Miguel A. Lauri, Luis Díaz, Mario Danesi, Luisa Vehil – who received the Konex de Brillante Award in 1981 with Alfredo Alcón – and Benita Puértolas.
21. Lumiton was originally founded by César José Guerrico, Enrique T. Susini, Luis Romero Carranza and Miguel Mugica (Di Núbila 1998: 76).
22. The film was directed by Manuel Romero, who shot thirteen films in forty-two months for Lumiton. They also hired Mugica to direct nine films within the same period, and Christensen to direct their films for five years (Martínez Suárez 1990: 97).
23. Throughout this study, other great directors of this Golden Age have been mentioned, including Luis César Amadori, Luis Moglia Barth, Leopoldo Torres Ríos, Carlos Christiansen, Hugo Del Carril, Lucas Demare, Francisco Múgica, Carlos Borcosque, Carlos Schlieper and Luis Bayón de Herrera.
24. In his analysis of stardom, Richard Dyer also noted that 'even in Hollywood's heyday, stars did not absolutely guarantee the success of a film' (1998: 11).
25. Olinda Bozán also worked with Darín in 1977, in the film *La nueva cigarra* [The New Cicada] (Siro), to be discussed in more depth in Chapter 7.
26. There was greater mobility of stars between Latin America and Hollywood during this period. A good local example is that of Fernando Lamas, who reached stardom in Argentina in the 1940s and who at the beginning of the 1950s signed a contract of exclusivity with Metro-Goldwyn-Mayer. According to Mario Gallina, in the 1950s Lamas and the Mexican Ricardo Montalbán became the Latino actors with more influence in Hollywood (1999: 252). Carlos Cores is another example who shows the fluidity between the Mexican and Argentine industries in this period. Upon reaching stardom in Argentina in the 1940s, he moved to Mexico at the beginning of the 1950s to participate in a series of films in that country.
27. It was not only Argentina Sono Film and Lumiton that emerged during this period, but also a myriad of production companies such as Pampa Film, Baires, Compañía Argentina de Films Río de la Plata, Estudios San Miguel, Emelco, Estudios Mapol, Artistas Argentinos Asociados, Productora General Belgrano, Cinematográfica Cinco SIDE (Sociedad Impresora de Discos Electrofónicos) and EFA (Establecimientos Filmadores Argentinos), which focused on particular film stars.
28. With film stars of the calibre of Dolores del Río, Pedro Armendáriz, María Félix, Arturo de Córdova, Pedro Infante, Cantinflas, and directors like Emilio Fernández and Fernando Fuentes.

29. It is generally stated that *La década infame* actually ended in 1943 with the *coup d'état* that put an end to the conservative government of Ramón Castillo.
30. The sisters Mirtha and Silvia Legrand played secondary roles in the film as students. Other cast members included Francisco Álvarez, Pablo Palitos and Héctor Calcagno.
31. The Peronist blacklist restricted many important personalities of Argentine culture from actively participating in their areas of expertise in the country. Film stars affected by it included Libertad Lamarque, Niní Marshall, Arturo García Buhr, Delia Garcés, Pepe Arias and María Duval.
32. The film included important stars of the period, such as Enrique Serrano, Felisa Mary, Juan Carlos Thorry, Nury Montsé, Silvana Roth and Zully Moreno (Di Núbila 1998: 328).
33. Such as *South of the Border with Disney* (1941), *Saludos Amigos* (1943) and *The Three Caballeros* (1945).
34. Casting Dolores del Río with Fred Astaire and Ginger Rogers.
35. Including Ricardo Quintana, Betty Grable and a special performance by Carmen Miranda.
36. Including Alice Faye, Carmen Miranda, John Payne, César Romero and Sheldon Leonard.
37. Right before getting married to Perón she became one of the best-paid radio actresses in Radio Belgrano, which was one of the leading broadcasting companies of the time (Mazzaferro 2018: 90).
38. It has been stated that the tensions between Lamarque and Duarte in the shooting of this film led to the former's exile during Perón's administrations (Mazzaferro 2018: 93). The film included stars like Hugo del Carril, Armando Bo, Orestes Caviglia, Elvira Quiroga and Pepe Arias.
39. The film was not released in the end until 1984 because Eva married Perón, who was running for president, and it was considered inappropriate for her new position. Cast members included Juan José Míguez, Angelina Pagano, Ernesto Raquén, Alberto Closas and Manuel Alcón.
40. For further information on Del Carril's star configuration and participation in the Peronist movement please refer to Kriger (2009), Calzon Flores (2016) and the recent volume edited by Calzon Flores and Kozak (2021).

# References

Barsky, J. and Barsky, O. (2017) *El cine de Gardel. Vol. 1 De Patria Films a Joinville (1917–1932)*, Buenos Aires: Teseo & UAI Editorial.

Benet, V. (2004) *La cultura del cine. Introducción a la historia y la estética del cine*, Barcelona: Ediciones Paidós Ibérica, S.A.

Bergfelder, T., Shaw, L. and Vieira, J. L. (eds) (2017) *Stars and Stardom in Brazilian Cinema*, New York/Oxford: Berghahn.

Bürch, N. (1991) *El tragaluz del infinito*, Madrid: Cátedra.

Burton, J. (1992) 'Don (Juanito) Duck and the Imperial-Patriarchal Unconscious: Disney Studios, the Good Neighbor Policy, and the Packaging of Latin America', in Parker, A. (ed.), *Nationalism and Sexualities*, New York: Routledge.

Calzon Flores, M. F. (2016) 'Hugo del Carril y su trayectoria como ídolo popular: astro del tango, galán-cantor y director de cine, 1935–1955', in *Cuadernos de Ideas*, 10.10, December. https://perio.unlp.edu.ar/ojs/index.php/cps/article/view/3476/2977 (accessed 8 March 2022).

Calzon Flores, F. and Kozak, D. (eds) (2021) *Más allá de la Estrella. Nuevas miradas sobre Hugo Del Carril*, Ciudad Autónoma de Buenos Aires: Autoría.

Casale, M. (2018) 'El actor en el star system argentino ¿Trabajador privilegiado o mero producto?', in *telóndefondo/27*, January–June, pp. 245–254.

Castillo, A. (1943) *La vida de Florencio Parravicini*, Buenos Aires: Not Known.

Charney, L. and Schwartz, V. (1995) *Cinema and the Invention of Modern Life*, Berkeley: University of California Press.

Couselo, J. M. (1969) *El negro Ferreyra, un cine por instinto*, Buenos Aires: Editorial Freeland.

Cuarterolo, A. (2013) '*Una nueva y gloriosa nación* (Albert Kelley, 1928): entre la "ficción orientadora" y la "fantasia histórica"', in *Imagofagia*, 8. http://www.asaeca.org/imagofagia/index.php/imagofagia/article/view/592/572 (accessed 13 January 2022).

Cuarterolo, A. (2019) 'El cine histórico argentine durante el período silente: Dos modelos estéticos e ideológicos en pugna', in *Vivomatografías*, 5. http://www.vivomatografias.com/index.php/vmfs/article/view/258 (accessed 13 January 2022).

deCordova, R. (1991) 'The Emergence of the Star System in America', in Gledhill, C. (ed.), *Stardom: Industry of Desire*, London: Routledge.

Di Núbila, D. (1998) *La época de oro. Historia del cine argentine I*, Buenos Aires: Ediciones del Jilguero.

Dyer, R. (1998) *Stars*, London: BFI.

España, C. (2000) 'El modelo institucional. Formas de representación en la edad de oro', in España, C. (ed.), *Cine Argentino. Industria y clasicismo 1933/1956 Vol. 1*, Buenos Aires: Fondo Nacional de las Artes.

Fabbro, G. (2000) 'Lumiton: El berretín del cine', in España, C. (ed.), *Cine Argentino. Industria y clasicismo 1933/1956 Vol. 1*, Buenos Aires: Fondo Nacional de las Artes.

Finkielman, J. (2004) *The Film Industry in Argentina: An Illustrated Cultural History*, North Carolina: McFarland & Company, Inc. Publishers.

Gallina, M. (1999) *De Gardel a Norma Aleandro: Diccionario sobre figuras del cine argentino en el exterior*, Buenos Aires: Ediciones Corregidor.

García Oliveri, R. (2011) *Diccionario del Cine Iberoamericano*, España/Portugal: SGAE, vol. 1, pp. 420–442.

Gubern, R. (1994) 'La herencia del star system', in 'Las estrellas: vejez de un mito en la era técnica', *Archivos de la filmoteca*, 18, October, Valencia: Filmoteca de la Generalitat Valenciana.

Hall, L. (2013) *Dolores del Río: Beauty in Light and Shade*, Stanford, CA: Stanford University Press.

Heinink, J. and Dickson, R. G. (1990) *Cita en Hollywood. Antología de las películas norteamericanas habladas en español*, Bilbao: Edic. Mensajero.

Hershfield, J. (2000), *The Invention of Dolores del Río*, Minneapolis: University of Minnesota Press.

Kairuz, M. (2001) 'Made in Argentina', in *Suplemento Radar: Página 12*. https://www.pagina12.com.ar/2001/suple/Radar/01-11/01-11-18/NOTA4.HTM (accessed 22 January 2022).

Kriger, C. (2009) *Cine y Peronismo: El Estado en escena*, Buenos Aires: Siglo Veintiuno Editores.

Lamarque, L. (1986) *Libertad Lamarque. Autobiografía*, Buenos Aires: Javier Vergara Editor.

López, A. M. (1993) 'Are All Latins From Manhattan? Hollywood, Ethnography and Cultural Colonialism', in King, J., López, A. M. and Alvarado, M. (eds), *Mediating Two Worlds: Cinematic Encounters in the Americas*, London: BFI Publishing.

López, A. M. (1998) 'From Hollywood and Back: Dolores del Río, A Trans(National) Star', in *Studies in Latin American Popular Culture*, 17.5, pp. 5–32.

Lusnich, A. L. (1996) 'El *star-system*. Transformación y permanencia de un fenómeno con historia', in *Imagen de la cultura y el arte latinoamericano. Boletín del Instituto de Historia del Arte Argentino y Latinoamericano*, year 1, 1, pp. 113–117. Buenos Aires: Secretaría de Publicaciones de la Facultad de Filosofía y Letras, Universidad de Buenos Aires.

McDonald, P. (2000) *The Star System: Hollywood's Production of Popular Identities*, London: Wallflower Press.

McLean, A. (2001) 'Star System', in Pearson, R. and Simpson, P. (eds), *Critical Dictionary of Film and Television Theory*, London: Routledge, pp. 423–424.

Mafud, L. (2016) *La imagen ausente. El cine mudo argentino en publicaciones gráficas. Catálogo. El cine de ficción (1914–1923)*, Buenos Aires: Editorial Teseo.

Manetti, R. (2000) 'Argentina Sono Film. Más estrellas que en el cielo', in España, C. (ed.), *Cine Argentino. Industria y clasicismo 1933/1956 Vol. 1*, Buenos Aires: Fondo Nacional de las Artes.

Maranghello, C. (2005) *Breve historia del cine argentino*, Barcelona: Laertes S.A.

Martínez Suárez, J. (1990) 'Los estudios cinematográficos argentinos y el star-system' in Oroz, S. et al. (eds), *Cine Latinoamericano años 30-40-50*, Mexico: Universidad Nacional Autónoma de Mexico.

Mazzaferro, A. (2018) *La cultura de la celebridad: Una historia del star system en Argentina*, Buenos Aires: Eudeba.

Paladino, D. (1999) 'Libertad Lamarque: La reina de la lágrima', in *Archivos de la Filmoteca*, 31, February, pp. 60–75.

Pardo, S. (2018) *La construcción de una estrella cinematográfica. El caso de Zuly Moreno en el marco del star-system argentine del período clásico-industrial*, unpublished PhD thesis.

Parejas, S. (2008) '"Me he dado a conocer como soy": Ricardo Darín', in *Revista 7 días*. https://susanaparejas.com/2012/11/20/me-he-dado-a-conocer-como-soy-susana-parejas_-ricardo-darin/ (accessed 5 January 2022).

Pellettieri, O. (Dir.) (2001) *De Toto a Sandrini. Del cómico italiano al "actor nacional" argentino*, Buenos Aires: Galerna S.R.L.

Piedra, J. (1994) 'The Three Caballeros: Pato Donald's gender ducking', in *Jump Cut: A Review of Contemporary Media*, 39, June, available at: http://www.ejumpcut.org/archive/onlinessays/JC39folder/3caballeros.html (viewed 9 March 2020).

Posadas, A. (1993) *Niní Marshall. Desde un ayer lejano*, Buenos Aires: Ediciones Colihue.

Sarlo, B. (2003) *La pasión y la excepción*, Buenos Aires: Siglo XXI.

Shail, A. (2019) *The Origins of the Film Star System: Persona, Publicity, and Economics in Early Cinema*, London and New York: Bloomsbury Publishing Plc.

Shaw, L. (2013) *Carmen Miranda*, London: BFI, Palgrave Macmillan.

Shaw, L. (2015) 'Carmen Miranda: From Brazilian Film Star to International "Tropical Other"', in Bandhauer, A. and Royer, M. (eds), *Stars in World Cinema: Screen Icons and Star Systems Across Cultures*, London and New York: I. B. Tauris.

Thompson, K. and Bordwell, D. (2019) *Film History: An Introduction*, University of Wisconsin-Madison: MacGraw Hill Education.

Tuñón, J. (2000) *Los rostros de un mito. Personajes femeninos en las películas de Emilio Indio Fernández*, Mexico: CONACULTA-IMCINE.

Vieira, J. L. (1999) 'Brasil-Hollywood: Carmen Miranda The Brazilian Bombshell', in *Archivos de la Filmoteca*, 31, February, pp. 36–47.

Vogel, M. (2012) *Lupe Vélez: The Life and Career of Hollywood's "Mexican Spitfire"*, Jefferson, NC: McFarland & Co Inc.

# Chapter 2

# Stardom during the rise of television and the 1960s film wave

The *Revolución Libertadora* [*Liberating Revolution*]'s 1955 *coup d'état* put an end to Perón's government and its Peronist star system. Many of the iconic artists from the period, such as Hugo del Carril, Tita Merello and Zully Moreno, were persecuted and had to live in exile (Mazzaferro 2018: 120). After years of lack of investment in new equipment, new talents and foreign distribution, the industry suffered another crisis (Maranghello 2005: 114). The production of low-cost films for general entertainment which moved away from a rich cinematographic local tradition resulted in Argentine cinema losing its influence in Latin American markets and, therefore, many studios had to close their doors (Maranghello 2005: 114).[1] This closure was also the outcome of the annulment of the Peronist Film Law, which up until this point had supported the industry by granting a screen quota to national productions and by offering various forms of subsidies to the sector (Kriger 2009: 91).[2]

Even once the witch-hunt of Peronist supporters in the industry diminished, there were some artists who never recovered – such as Fanny Navarro (Posadas 1994: 236).[3] With the disarticulation of the domestic show business came a renewed focus on foreign stars and their systems – mainly from Hollywood and Europe (Mazzaferro 2018: 120). By 1958, when elections were called once more, most of the covers of *Antena* magazine were dedicated to foreign performers.[4] Local figures such as Mirtha Legrand, Mecha Ortiz, Laura Hidalgo and Lolita Torres had to share their spotlight with Marilyn Monroe, Debbie Reynolds, Paul Newman, Elizabeth Taylor, Audrey Hepburn, James Dean, Anita Ekberg and Gina Lollobrigida (Mazzaferro 2018: 138).[5] As these names suggest, at an international level the 1950s saw the transformation of film stars into glamorised objects charged with sex appeal. The crisis in Hollywood studios brought with it an exacerbation of the stars' features more than the restructuring of the stellar model (Mazzaferro 2018: 152). This was particularly the case for female stars, whose bodies became the centre of attention of the industry.

Whilst the focus on performers' sex appeal and physical attributes was inspired by foreign star systems, its implementation in Argentina followed a different path. As Mazzaferro has rightly explained, under the dictatorship Argentine sex appeal 'had to be more discreet and lose a great deal of its sexual references' ['debió ser más discreto y perder gran parte de su referencialidad sexual'] (2018: 127). A double moral standard prevailed. For local audiences, international stars generated both attraction and rejection. They offered the possibility to imagine new ways of articulating star images, but they also marked the limits of a conservative audience that was not ready to accept from its native stars any transgressions of what was socially – and thus commercially – acceptable (Mazzaferro 2018: 127). Women were still under the influence of long-standing discourses whereby modesty and chastity were considered prime feminine values. Accordingly, under the moral and cultural conservatism imposed by the regime, a female star system based on sexual nuances had to be toned down whilst still trying to align with the female liberation happening on-screen in other latitudes. Their male counterparts, on the contrary, tended to present a more homogenous image (with minor variations and exemptions), akin to a classic, Clark Gable-esque gallantry and heteronormative masculinity that presented no threat to the status quo (Mazzaferro 2018: 135).

Mazzaferro states that the year 1958 marked a crucial change for the star system worldwide. At an international level, this change was mainly due to the impact of Brigitte Bardot. And locally, it was thanks to the irruption of Isabel Sarli, who broke all the norms of the field (Mazzaferro 2018: 17). When analysing the emergence of the 'new sexy girls' ['las nuevas sexies'] in the 1960s in Argentina, María Valdez further explains that Brigitte Bardot's body exposure in *Et Dieu... créa la femme* [*And God Created Women*] (Vadim 1956) came to demonstrate the constrained female universe within Western moral values (2005: 30). Following Marilyn Monroe's legacy as the eroticised woman who breaks away from dominant discourses of acceptable feminine behaviour (Vincendeau 2016: 100), Bardot embodied both the old values of French cinema and the new ones of the 'emerging youth culture that rejected bourgeois hypocrisy' (Leahy 2003: 71; Vincendeau 1992).

By appearing *au naturel*, Bardot constructed her own myth based on 'the materiality of a star sign located firmly in her body' (Leahy 2003: 73).

This was also the case for Sarli, despite her multiple physical and cultural differences with the French goddess. The partial democratic opening of 1958 brought the opportunity for local stars to align with the trends dominating the international arena. In Sarli's case, she dared to undress in front of the camera in the film *El trueno entre las hojas* [*Thunder Among the Leaves*] (Bó 1958), inaugurating an erotic national cinema and her stellar career (Mazzaferro 2018: 173; Ruétalo 2004: 79).[6] The fact that nudity offered new routes into stardom made the comparison between Sarli and Bardot more prominent in the local media. This comparison intensified when, in 1960, Armando Bó released . . . *Y el demonio creó a los hombres* [*. . . And the Demon Created Men*], starring Sarli, which was, as the title suggests, in close dialogue with the Roger Vadim film that launched Bardot's career into new heights.[7]

In spite of media efforts to compare the two stars, as previously mentioned, they were fundamentally different. Bardot was lean, blonde, child-like and from a bourgeois background. Sarli, on the contrary, was curvy, brunette, she looked her age and had a working-class upbringing. Her voluptuous figure, humble origins and sudden social mobility made her the quintessential popular star in Argentina, even more so for the resemblance to Evita's own career (Mazzaferro 2018: 175). Although that connection could not be formulated at a time of Peronist proscription, her star image was increasingly grounded in lower-class attributes that tended to exalt suppressed Peronists values (Ruétalo 2004: 83). In relation to this, Ruétalo explains that Sarli was a contentious figure, 'simultaneously ostracised and adored (. . .) much like her idol Eva Perón, locked within the lumpen-proletariat who were to succeed in breaking through many gender-specific taboos while within the confines of gendered roles' (2004: 82). Her career indeed started under Perón's administration, when she was crowned Miss Argentina in 1955.[8] Yet her association with the party was not considered of concern by the new regime. With time, however, the tone of the film censors harshened as they argued that Sarli's body was 'too provocative and ostentatious' to uphold the morals of Argentina (Fernández and Nagy 1999: 144; Ruétalo 2004: 83). And, ironically, by 1974, in spite of these Peronist links, both her and Bó started to receive threats from the Triple A, the extreme right-wing faction of Peronism, for the 'immoral and obscene' content of their films (Ruétalo 2004: 83; Romano 1995: 131).

Sarli's stardom, as Ruétalo rightly states, became the 'controversially provocative and most glaringly distinctive commodity of the Sarli-Bo films' (2004: 81), which consisted of a series of twenty-seven productions that spanned from 1958 until 1980. Egle Martin, Thelma Tixou, Libertad Leblanc and Élida Marletta would follow Sarli's steps and base their cinematographic careers on their scantily clad bodies. The *Vedettes* coming from Buenos Aires's music halls and vaudevilles would provide, from then on, many important names in the erotic comedy films that started to emerge as an outcome of Sarli's influence in the commercial sphere. María Valdez includes within this group the artists Nora Núñez, Rosángela Balbo, Marcela López Rey, Lolo Prat and Zulma Faiad (2005: 31–32). This trend also incited the creation of a subgenre: the hotel films, with works like *La cigarra no es un bicho* [*The Cicada is Not an Insect*] (Tinayre 1963).[9] A few years later, as will be explored in more depth in Chapter 7, we will find our own Ricardo Darín venturing into this subgenre and having an off-screen romantic relationship with one of the most famous vedettes of the 1970s and 1980s: Susana Giménez.

The mixed and passionate reactions to these sorts of films evinced the deep fracture that would divide Argentine cinema from the 1960s onwards. On the one hand, there existed an industrial cinema that would continue implementing old narrative techniques and well-known faces, and which would depend on a corrupt system of subsidies to survive (España 2005: 20); on the other hand, a New Argentine Cinema that promoted an exploration of contemporary issues, using their own specialist technicians and performers (Maranghello 2005: 163). While the latter – also known as the '1960s Generation' –was coming to an end by the time of Onganía's military dictatorship in 1966, this division between industrial/commercial and independent cinema has managed to endure until the present day, with various degrees of impact on the local star system (España 2005: 21).

## Stardom in the first wave of New Argentine cinema

Many scholars have defined the period of 1961 to 1966 in Argentine cinema as a period characterised by a process of modernisation and censorship (España 2005: 20; Maranghello 2005: 164; Castagna 1994). The fall of Perón and of the studios allowed the emergence of a new generation of filmmakers who were highly influenced by European productions and who aimed to create independent, auteur-driven productions that provided a window into contemporary local issues. Known as the

'1960s Film Generation', this group of young filmmakers offered a fresh perspective detached from the industrial model. In this regard, they were informed both by the appearance of an anti-Peronist middle class in the cultural sphere, and by the struggles of fighting against corruption and content restriction at the centre of the National Film Institute during a very unstable moment for the country's democracy.[10]

Director Leopoldo Torre Nilsson became a key, though liminal, figure in navigating both the old studio system and leading this new wave – a role played as well by Fernando Ayala and, to lesser degree, by José Martínez Suárez. Most of the members of this generation had a background in short film, like Rodolfo Kuhn, David José Kohon, Simón Feldman and Manuel Antín. An exception to note for the present analysis of film stars is Lautaro Murúa. He was a Chilean-born actor who had, instead, a background in theatre and he became not only an important director of this new wave – with films such as *Shunko* (1960), *Alias Gardelito* [*Alias Big Shot*] (1962), *Un guapo del 900* [*A Bully in 900*] (1971) and *La Raulito* [*Little Ralph*] (1975) – but also one of the leading male performers of the 1970s and 1980s in Argentina, having participated in iconic films such as *Invasión* [*Invasion*] (Muchnik 1969), *No habrá más penas ni olvido* [*Funny Dirty Little War*] (Olivera 1983) and *El exilio de Gardel (Tangos)* [*Tangos, The Exile of Gardel*] (Solanas 1985). It has been suggested that his commercial failure as a director during this new wave forced him to give priority to his acting career in the end (Maranghello 2005: 167), though he has won as many accolades as a director as he did as a performer. Another interesting case is that of Leonardo Favio, who had a background both in short film and as an actor. In 2000, his directorial debut, *Crónica de un niño solo* [*Chronicle of a Boy Alone*] (1964), was ranked as the best Argentine film of all time in a survey run by Buenos Aires's Cinema Museum (De Vita 2011: 7).[11] Before this project, he had become a well-known performer for his work in important films of the period, such as *El jefe* [*The Boss*] (Ayala 1958), *Fin de fiesta* [*The Party is Over*] (Torre Nilsson 1960) and *La mano en la trampa* [*The Hand in the Trap*] (Torre Nilsson 1961). Maranghello (2005: 171) also considers the veteran René Múgica as part of this wave; someone who, like Murúa, had a background as theatre actor.[12]

Whilst there was stylistic and thematic disparity in the films associated with this group of filmmakers, there were some common elements that distinguished them as belonging to this label. First, there was a generational rejection of their predecessors' cinema, which was particularly evident in multiple young characters expressing disenchantment with or rejection of the father figure (Castagna 1994: 249; Sala 2015: 11–12). Second, there was a need to explore urban realism, dissecting in the dialogues feelings of loneliness, marginalisation, boredom and discontent, through a complex rhetoric of the ordinary. Third, following local literature's tendencies, they initiated a process of challenging old myths and contending enshrined values (Castagna 1994: 249). Through these foci, these directors started to denounce the harshness of everyday life, breaking down taboos that were hidden in studio cinema – such as a freer exposure of bodies and sexuality (Sala 2015: 13). Lastly, and most importantly for our subject in these pages, they favoured the use of a limited number of characters – and, thus, of actors – privileging new faces not worn out in studio productions. Hence, modern cinema paid particular attention to a young stellar system whereby the generational change implied a collective response, the creation of 'a troupe', rather than a focus on the individual (Sala 2015: 11).

According to Castagna, during this period the star system in Argentina tended to follow the US model, which based most of its on-and-off-screen personas on a number of limited stereotypes. Therefore, 'naïve girls, divas, gentlemen, local thugs, secondary archetype roles and gender politics marked, [according to him], more than twenty years of national cinema' [... ingenuas, divas, galanes, malevos vernáculos, arquetipos secundarios y política de género señalaron más de veinte años de cine nacional] (1994: 249). Or at least this was the case for more commercial products. When it came to the new wave, they looked rather to Europe than Hollywood. In relation to this, Jorge Sala (2017) goes a step further and identifies in this modern Argentine cinema the emergence of a new prototype: 'the white-collar worker' ['el trabajador de cuello blanco']. This stereotype would mark the careers of a series of actors that went on to become film stars in the 1970s and 1980s, including Héctor Alterio, Walter Vidarte, Luis Brandoni and Federico Luppi – all of whom, with the exception of the Uruguayan Vidarte, worked with Darín in cinema at a later stage, when they were already consecrated actors.

The advent of these new archetypical roles showed the desire to create a more realistic portrayal of the everyday man. Thus, in its attempt to break away from studio tradition, this wave of directors offered down-to-earth stars instead of cultivating the image of distant figures of the classical stardom model (Sala 2017: 4). In some cases, inspired by Italian Neorealism, they recurred to what Sala described as 'temporary actors' ['actores eventuales']. This term describes actors not known to the general public but it moves away from the more popular concept of 'non-professional actors' associated with the European wave, which did not fully acknowledge the rejection of the idea of professionalisation that many independent theatre actors of the 1960s in Argentina had – including in that group, for instance, Héctor Alterio (Sala 2017: 15). In the end, these 'temporary' actors tended to be mixed with some recognisable faces, as José Martínez Suárez highlights, due to the fact that 'it was not the time to have a whole team made up of unknown people because the distributors would reject the film' ['todavía no era el momento de armar un equipo de gente desconocida porque el distribuidor rechazaba la película] (cited in Valles 2014: 137).

This technique of blending performers of various levels of expertise was in fact a common strategy of Italian Neorealism as well. André Bazin identifies in the Italian school an 'amalgam of players' and further explains that 'the technical inexperience of the amateur is helped out by the experience of the professionals, while the professionals themselves benefit from the general atmosphere of authenticity' (2011: 36). As mentioned, it was precisely that aim to capture the authentic that drove this 1960s generation to implement non-professionals – or 'temporary' actors – responding to their suitability for the part because, paraphrasing Bazin, 'they fit it physically or [...] there is some parallel between the role and their lives' (2011: 36). In his analysis, Sala brings to the fore a good example of this latter point. He states that Héctor Alterio's star configuration is highly connected to his humble origins. The image of working-class *porteño* coming from the outskirts of the city is at the heart of Martín Santomé – the leading character of *La tregua* [*The Truce*] (Renán 1974) – which recuperates Alterio's own personal experiences, launching in this process what would become a stellar career, thanks in large part to the success of the film (Sala 2017: 7).[13]

Ana María Picchio, Alterio's co-protagonist in *La tregua* and one of the leading actresses of this generation, who has worked with Darín in subsequent years, further exemplified Bazin's statement when she declared that: 'I think that one of the reasons why *The Truce* is a success is because Alterio and I are both common people. Similar to the majority of the population' ['Pienso que uno de los motivos por los que "La tregua" es un gran éxito es porque Alterio y yo somos dos seres communes. Iguales a la mayoría de la gente'] (cited in Salas 2017: 6; Barreiro 1974). These words put a particular emphasis on the physical attributes that made the group of performers of this new wave so unique. In this sense, it should be noted that in their attempt to promote more earthly stars, this 1960s generation broke away from classical canons of beauty. Instead of the cold and distant image that carried a mythical aura characteristic of the film stars of the classical-industrial period, these new performers exposed an inner beauty and more humane features, which were built on their physical imperfections. Sala identifies, for example, 'Alberto Argibay's myopia, Norma Aleandro's aquiline nose, and Jorge Rivera López's prominent baldness, as attributing a sense of familiarity to these stars [for the viewer]' ['La miopía de Alberto Argibay, la nariz aguileña de Norma Aleandro o la calvicie prominente de Jorge Rivera López aportaron una carnadura de inmediatez a las estrellas'] (2017: 5–6).

Breaking away from glamour and flawless beauty models implied a paradigm shift in the local star system, even more so due to the fact that these directors were working outside an industry that had come to sustain such a system. The configuration of the star image during this new wave, therefore, relied heavily on quirkiness and proximity. That is the reason why, as Sala explains (2017: 6), an actor like Raúl Parini, defined in one interview as 'the man with a weird face' ['el hombre de la cara rara'] (*Platea* 1961; Sala 2017: 6) was able to forge a successful career in cinema and actively contribute to a generational phenomenon. Nonetheless, some directors felt they were moving away from any possible star-related narratives in their casting choices. Upon reflection on his first experiences as director, Lautaro Murúa declared, for instance, that 'with *Shunko* and *Alias Gardelito* I managed to destroy part of the myth of the film star' ['con *Shunko* y *Alias Gardelito* he logrado destruir parte del mito de las estrellas'] (cited in De Marco 1961). It should be contended, however, that the aura and untouchability of the studio stars might have been broken, but only to be reconfigured in more terrestrial terms. These actors still performed, in all their peculiarity, the vital role of positioning the film in the market place, thanks to the attractiveness of the unique star persona that they constructed/was constructed for them, on and off the screen.

It bears mentioning that there were still stars who appeared in the films of these directors who comply with classical beauty principles, as the faces of Graciela Borges, María Vaner, Elsa Daniel and Bárbara Múgica well demonstrate. In the case of Borges, she was only a teenager when she appeared in Hugo Del Carril's *Una cita con la vida* [*A Date with Life*] (1958). From that moment, as has been repeatedly stated in the press, 'everybody fell in love with her eyes, with features that seemed to be handmade, with her perfect face and mouth' ['todo el mundo enamorado de los ojos, de los rasgos terminados a mano, perfectos, la carita, la boca']

(*La Nación* 2003). Likewise, the public was enamoured with her multiple friendships and affairs with celebrities such as Enzo Ferrari, Paul Newman and Juan Manuel Fangio (De Vita 2021).[14] Vaner, who belonged to a family of actors, became known as 'the muse of Favio and the 1960s' ['fue musa de Favio y de los 60'] (Sendrós 2008). It was said that she had one of the most expressive faces; one that bewitched directors like Kohon in *Tres veces Ana* [*Three Times Ana*] (1961), Kuhn in *Los jóvenes viejos* [*The Old Young People*] (1962) and Múgica in *El octavo infierno* [*The Eighth Hell*] (1964) (*MinutoUno* 2008).[15]

Daniel, on her part, started her career in 1953 after winning Radio El Mundo's Miss *Sonrisa* [Smile] contest. By all accounts, she had one of the most beautiful faces of her generation, inspiring multiple directors, such as Torre Nilsson in *La casa del ángel* [*The House of the Angel*] (1957), and she was regularly compared with Ingrid Bergman by the media (De Vita 2017; Avigliano 2017). Múgica, on the other hand, used to be described as a 'peculiar beauty' (Podestá 2020). She was, like Vaner, from an artistic background: her mother was the actress Alba Múgica and her uncle was the director René Múgica. She started acting as a teenager, appearing in two films by Torres Ríos – father of Torre Nilsson. Víctor Laplace, who worked with Múgica on several occasions, declared upon her sudden death in 1990 that 'she had a very particular beauty. She never dyed her hair, nor had any surgery done, and yet she was so pretty, so beautiful as a person that it was a pleasure to be with her' ['Era de una belleza muy particular. Nunca se tiñó el pelo, ni se hizo cirugías y era tan bella, tan bonita persona que daba placer estar con ella'] (Podestá 2020). These words suggest that Múgica was one of those personalities located in-between the traditional star system, with its beauty standards, and the more ordinary features of the new group of unconventional stars of the new wave.[16]

In terms of male performers of this 1960s generation who portrayed a classical masculine beauty, we should mention Alfredo Alcón, and Héctor Pellegrini.[17] Alcón initiated his drama courses at the Buenos Aires Drama Conservatory when he was a teenager, thanks to the fact that one of the tutors thought he was 'good-looking' ['lindo'] (cited in *La Nación* 2005). From 1954, he played several roles as the *galán* [handsome fellow type] for Radio El Mundo. His debut in cinema took place in *El amor nunca muere* [*Love Never Dies*] (Amadori 1955), alongside big film stars of the period such as Zully Moreno, Tita Merello and Mirtha Legrand. He fluctuated between studio productions and iconic films of the new wave and also succeeded in theatre, winning multiple awards as actor and director.[18] Pellegrini had a more unusual look, in line with the new generation's intention to show realistic stars. His first work in cinema was in Murúa's *Alias Gardelito* and, shortly after, 'that face and his handsome physique, with tender smile, dreamy eyes, rough or gentle gestures, would captivate director Rodolfo Kuhn, who cast him to star in *Pajarito Gómez* alongside María Cristina Laurenz' ['ese rostro y su figura de nuevo galán con sonrisa tierna, ojos soñadores, gestos rudos o lánguidos, hicieron que el director Rodolfo Kuhn lo eligiera para protagonizar *Pajarito Gómez*, junto a María Cristina Laurenz'] (*Cadena Nueve* 2014). This role, where he played a parody of Palito Ortega, the big 1960s star of commercial cinema, would lead to the fusion of actor and character in the public imaginary (Manrupe and Portela 2001: 340).[19] Moreover, it would reveal another feature of this new wave of directors: their rejection of the youth portrayed in contemporary commercial films, devoid of passion and conflict (Sala 2015: 13–14).

While there were many actors who played roles of sexually attractive men during this decade, their attractiveness tended to fall on personality traits rather than physical attributes. This was the case of actors who were both part of the new wave or working in studio productions. Unlike their female counterparts, these men were able to base their sex appeal either on their witty sense of humour, their intelligent remarks or their heroic acts and depth of character, instead of on their appearance, as is well exemplified by Humberto Ortiz, Alberto Olmedo, Óscar Orlegui, José Slavin, Pepe Soriano, Óscar Viale and Rodolfo Ranni. As we will explore in more depth in the next section, most of them had a very successful career in television that fed into their cinematographic ventures, and their characters tended to rely on their distinctive imperfections, like Olmedo's baldness and Ranni's hairy chubbiness.

## 'Stars eclipsed': the New Latin American Cinema movement

It has been widely documented that the New Latin American Cinema movement, which aimed at an ideal of political revolution, emerged in this period of the new wave, inspired by the outcome of the Cuban Revolution and the European student revolts (Del Valle Dávila 2021; Shohat and Stam 2000). Thus, when analysing Argentine cinema in the 1960s, it should be noted that there were in fact two different 1960s generations of filmmakers that existed in parallel of the studio production directors. The first wave appeared at the beginning of the decade and took the form of the above-mentioned *auteur* trend of directors like Manuel Antín, Lautaro Murúa, Fernando Ayala, Leonardo Favio and Leopoldo Torre Nilsson. As discussed, their star system operated a paradigm shift and focused on terrestrial and mundane stars, whilst positioning the directors themselves as stars on account of the commodity value they acquired.[20] This wave came to an end with the onset of Onganía's military dictatorship in 1966, due to several factors, including the group's disparity, lack of economic profits – owing to box-office failure and poor connection with a wider popular audience – and constant struggles with various established sectors of the film industry (Castagna 1994: 261; Maranghello 2005: 163).

The second wave took place in the second half of the decade and was connected to the upsurge of a New Latin American Cinema movement and the revolutionary discourses epitomised in Argentina by Fernando Pino Solanas and Octavio Getino's manifesto, 'Towards a Third Cinema' (1969).[21] In that publication they openly declared their rejection to 'first cinema', which referred to the imperialist domain of Hollywood and the USA. They also stated that they wanted to move away from an *auteur* cinema – referred to as 'second cinema' – such as that coming from Europe and which was foundational for the new wave directors. Instead they proposed a 'Third Cinema', one of destruction and construction: 'destruction of the image that neocolonialism has created of itself and of us, and construction of a throbbing, living reality which recaptures truth in any of its expressions' (Solanas and Getino 1969: 123). Accordingly, in Ella Shohat and Robert Stam's words, 'the manifestoes of the 1960s and 1970s valorized an alternative, independent, anti-imperialist cinema more concerned with provocation and militancy than with auteurist expression or consumer satisfaction' (2000: 248). This rejection of commercial traditions included one of its most common elements, the film star.

In respect of this, John King rightly states in his study on stardom in Latin America, that during this militant wave 'stars were eclipsed' (2003: 142). He explains that this is because these directors 'were opposed to the triumphant individualism of studio film stars and developed what Vincendeau has called "collective" stardom (2000: ix)' (King 2003: 143). Their way of crediting their works was in line with this, attributing their productions to a group, instead of an individual, as the names *Grupo Cine Liberación* and *Grupo Cine de la Base* demonstrate.[22] With the aim of killing off the bourgeois artist that all filmmakers have inside (Getino and

Velleggia 2002: 133), they broke away from an *auteur* approach and from the personality cult that forms the basis of stardom.[23] According to King, this is evident in the case of *Grupo Ukamau* in Bolivia, which replaced the close-up '– the preferred framing of the star – with the sequence shot [which] offered a more "collective" framing, in keeping (...) with the belief structures and social organisation of the Quechua-Aymara peoples' that were the focus of most of their films (King 2003: 143). The end result, in King's words, is that

> Stars thus became elided in theory and practice for two reasons. First, because the 'new' cinema movements the world over from the 1950s proposed modes of film-making that were 'atheistic' with regard to the screen gods and goddesses of previous times. Second, because criticism, especially Anglo-American criticism, tended to share the critical assumptions of the 'third cinema' thesis, albeit in less strident terms. (2003: 143)

The impact of Third Cinema was so significant at an international level that it had a lasting effect on all productions that have come afterwards, and on ways of thinking about and producing films throughout Latin America. This was mainly due to the fact that, by the time this wave was coming to an end in the local arena in the early 1980s, its key films started to gain momentum via their inclusion in the texts written by an array of Anglo-American writers, who created a revolutionary canon 'that became a touchstone for other work in the region' (King 2003: 144). A main outcome was the tendency to believe that all films coming out of Latin America have to be socio-politically committed and militant in nature. Moreover, the use of non-professional actors, the tendency to shoot on location and focus on giving visibility to those working and living at the margins of society became a trademark, being at the core of the New Argentine Cinema that emerged at the end of the 1990s that we will explore in the following chapter. King (2003) believes that the lack of Star Studies in Latin America was precisely an outcome of the New Latin American Cinema Wave of the 1960s and 1970s, due to their overt rejection of stardom as belonging to a consumerist neocolonialist tradition from which they were trying to move away.

## Stars and celebrities: the impact of television

The first public television broadcast took place in Argentina on the Peronist 'Loyalty Day' on 17 October 1951. During its first decade, television imported actors and actresses from other areas of show business, such as cinema, radio and theatre. However, its various technical difficulties, lack of good quality projects, low audiences due to the high price of TV sets, and low pay for artists, meant that many of the stars from film and radio rejected work in that medium (Mazzaferro 2018: 197). It was not until 1958 that television became a product of mass consumption, when a public tendering led to a change from the solely state-funded channel model to a private and competitive commercial scheme. This prompted the emergence of several channels – including Channel 9 and Channel 13 in 1960, and Channel 11 in 1961 (Mazzaferro 2018: 189). In her analysis of the origin of television in Argentina, Mirta Varela calls the period of 1960 to 1969 'the second decade', because it was the time when what was once simply the 'TV set' became what is now known as 'television' – in other words, the creation of a mass communication medium, a spectacle, an audience, a language, took place (Varela 2005: 14–16). The advent of this new urban way of spending free time was worshipped by those who saw it as a modern way of life, in harmony with the most progressive societies. However, at the same time, it was heavily criticised for its power to commodify the everyday and subjugate the masses (Garavelli 2019: 219).

With the crisis of film studios and the radio being replaced by TV as the principal entertainment medium in people's homes, rising television stars also began to gain more recognition than the old film stars of the Golden Age (Mazzaferro 2018: 186). Thus, soon, all artists wanted to work in television. In contrast to what happened in the USA, where film actors and actresses continued to uphold a dominant position in the entertainment world in spite of television's popularity, in Argentina the star system began to grow mostly from television (Mazzaferro 2018: 186). In this sense, as Mazzaferro has explained, the local star system did not follow John Ellis's (1982) hypothesis that television was a medium that produces personalities but never stars, and that those personalities were simply ordinary (Mazzaferro 2018: 186; Bennett 2008: 32–33). Instead, the star system that television promoted in Argentina sparked new desires in the audience and generated new forms of subsidiary circulation of the stars' images.

It is true, however, that television imposed a more varied star system that did not necessarily rely on acting abilities. Beauty became one of the main capitals for those in search of artistic stardom in the medium. This was the case, for instance, of Lidia Elsa Satragno – aka Pinky – the first famous person to emerge from the Argentine small screen (Mazzaferro 2018: 202). Her work at the beginning was mainly as a TV presenter, embodying some of the distinctive features of the new figures launched by television: sudden fame accompanied by a large salary, the capacity to connect more directly with the audience without the mediation of a character, and a charismatic personality. Moreover, her clothes and body gestures evinced the conservative tone acquired by the medium, which became a beacon of family values (Mazzaferro 2018: 201, 216). In this sense, she can be read in Ellis's terms as a 'television personality', or in the words used by Argentine magazines in the early 1970s, a 'famous' person – i.e. a celebrity. Nevertheless, instead of reaffirming stark binary terms which attempt to define what a true star is all about, in which film and television stardom remain separate, we have to consider the Argentine star system from this period as coming primarily from the small screen, due to the combined situation of Argentine cinema at the time and the social and cultural impact of television. Following Deborah Jermyn's work (2006), and Andy Medhurst's before it (1991), it can be asserted that artists like Pinky demonstrate that 'the television personality is capable of achieving the kind of intertextual coverage assumed to be the preserve of [movie] stars' (Bennett 2008: 33).

Pinky was also the first famous personality constructed in television who was exported to cinema (Mazzaferro 2018: 203). Her debut film was as a supporting actress in Torre Nilsson's *La caída* [*The fall*] (1959), starring Elsa Daniel and Lautaro Murúa. She then worked in René Múgica's *El demonio en la sangre* [*Demon in the Blood*] (1964), leaving her small mark on 1960s New Argentine Cinema. Yet her cinematographic career was short-lived, with her last experience being the film *Ritmo, amor y juventud* [*Rhythm, Love, and Youth*] (De Rosas 1966) just two years later, which was the typical commercial studio production which served as pretext to promote in cinema the music stars resonating on TV.[24] This last work complies with Mazzaferro's analysis, whereby many of the television stars made it in cinema, but only in 'light' or 'commercial' films that tended to continue their work in television (2018: 215). Pinky's success as broadcaster was, nonetheless, unparalleled and respected. In 1980, she was selected to inaugurate *Argentina Televisora Color* (ATC), announcing the end of black and white television and the arrival of colour. She conducted many important programmes, including an extensive interview with Ricardo Darín in 2001, in connection to the release of the film *La fuga* (Mignogna 2001), in which she made clear how successful and talented the actor was.[25]

Thus, the emergence of the first small screen stars caused a shift in the local star system. It was not only presenters with charismatic personalities

**Figure 2.1** Pinky Interviews Darín in 2001 (Channel 7 – Historical Archive of Argentine Radio and Television)

and big smiles who started to draw an audience and be the centre of attention of various tabloids and publicity campaigns, but also other artists from various disciplines, including theatre performers, comedians, writers, directors and musicians, whose image was re-signified in their transition through the studio channels. In this regard, performers of '*teleteatro*' [the television play] flourished, including Atilio Marinelli, Nora Cárpena, Guillermo Bredeston, María Aurelia Bisutti, Bárbara Múgica, Delfy de Ortega, Soledad Silveyra, and Claudio García Satur – many of whom, as we will explore in the following chapters, have worked with Darín on various projects.[26] The great comedians who would lead the commercial comedy genre on the big screen – in its multiple forms, such as family-oriented films or the new soft-porn trend that implemented *vedettes* – all came from television, as the names of Alberto Olmedo, Jorge Porcel, Tato Bores, Carlitos Balá, Juan Carlos Altavista ('Minguito'), Javier Portales, José Marrone, Pepe Biondi and Juan Verdaguer exemplify.[27]

There was an array of singers created by and for television who became new youth idols: Palito Ortega, Violeta Rivas, Johnny Tedesco, Leo Dan and Sandro. They used to participate in a programme called 'El Club del Clan' (Channel 13, Mejía and Andrés, 1962–1964) which launched the stellar careers of many young musicians. Of those performers, Ramón Bautista Ortega – aka Palito Ortega – and Roberto Sánchez Ocampo (known as 'Sandro') had the most successful cinematographic careers. The former was even considered to be 'the most radiant star of the 1960s' (Anchou 2005: 248).[28] Argentina Sono Film knew well how to capitalise on this popular television phenomenon by producing, in 1963, the film also bearing the title *El Club del Clan* (Carreras), and by using Palito's musical number in the opening scene. From that moment on, the TV programme gained unprecedented ratings and the record label RCA Victor, which produced the album 'Palito Ortega', sold copies like hot cakes. Palito was a sociological marvel: a mixture of Elvis Presley with the common physiognomy of a rural working-class labourer who became the symbol of an aspirational rapid social and class mobility (Anchou 2005: 248).

According to Argentine film scholar Ricardo Manetti, Sandro was 'the other side of the same coin' (2005: 429). While Palito embodied the dreams of popular triumph and economic wealth of provincial *muchachitos* [teenagers], Sandro was an 'enigmatic *gitano* [gipsy]' whose mysterious life drove women crazy. Palito's films promoted family values and the most stringent moral conduct imposed by Onganía's dictatorship. Sandro's, on the contrary, exploited the melodramatic tone of *telenovelas*, locating his star image on his eroticised body and pelvic movements.

David Stivel was one of the directors who, in a short period of time, became a famous television personality (Mazzaferro 2018: 212).[29] He gathered together a group of actors and actresses with a background in theatre to participate in a series of TV programmes. Under the name of *Gente de teatro* [Theatre People] – also popularly known as 'Clan Stivel' [Stivel's Group] – stars such as Norma Aleandro, Carlos Carella, Federico Luppi, Emilio Alfaro, Juan Carlos Gené, Marilina Ross and Bárbara Múgica managed to find a privileged position in television that allowed them to avoid the judgement of the anti-television intellectuals and sustain their respectable careers in cinema and theatre. Their most cherished work was the single-episode series *Cosa juzgada* (Channel 11, Gené and Stivel, 1969–1971). Every episode was based on real-life police cases that were drawn from the Argentine judicial archive, bringing to the small screen original stories that crossed the boundaries between fiction and reality in an unusual way for the time. With regards to this programme, Darín himself has stated that

> I was lucky enough, when I was ten years old, to work with Alterio in two or three television series shown on what used to be Channel 7

that were outstanding. One of them was based on universal theatre and the other on Argentine theatre. Then came *Cosa juzgada*, from the Stivel group, which was also marvellous – rife with extraordinary actors of diverse acting ability, working on a show that was socio-politically committed. In that moment, they marked a before and after for Argentine television.

[He tenido la suerte, cuando tenía 10 años, de trabajar con Alterio en dos o tres ciclos, emitidos en el viejo Canal 7, que eran gloriosos. Uno era de teatro universal y otro, de teatro argentino. Luego estuvo *Cosa juzgada*, del clan Stivel, que también fue glorioso, plagado de extraordinarios actores con una gama de posibilidades muy amplia, muy comprometida y que en su momento marcaron la televisión e hicieron escuela]. (Quoted in González Acevedo 2005: 47)

As mentioned in the cases of Sandro and Palito, the very few film studios in operation at the time – mostly Argentina Sono Film – drew quite significantly from television and its new star system. In 1958, Héctor Olivera and Fernando Ayala founded the production company Aries Cinematográfica S.A., knowing very well how to take advantage of such a star system – particularly with names like Alberto de Mendoza, Olga Zubarry and Alfredo Alcón (Posadas 1994: 237). At first, they focused on major issues, such as juvenile delinquency in *El jefe* [*The Boss*] (Ayala 1958), and political corruption in *El candidato* [*The Candidate*] (Ayala 1959).[30] But soon they started to explore blockbuster themes, exploiting the figure of Luis Sandrini or the success of the hotel films – as in *Hotel alojamiento* (Ayala 1965), starring Olinda Bozán, Atilio Marinelli, Pepe Soriano, Emilio Alfaro, Gilda Lousek, Marilina Ross and Rodolfo Bebán.

Many of the old Golden Age stars managed to reinvent themselves in the new medium as well, finding in the small screen a new opening for their diminishing cinematographic careers.[31] Claudio España has surveyed the most iconic personalities who weathered these storms of media and system changes in his chapter on the 'Dawn and Persistence of the Stars' ['Ocaso y perduración de las estrellas'] (2005). The most significant case to mention is that of Mirtha Legrand. Her last work in cinema was in Ayala's *Con gusto a rabia* (1965), where she shared the leading role with Alfredo Alcón and Marcela López Rey. In 1968, after a short period away from the spotlight, she became the TV host of *Almorzando con las estrellas* [*Having Lunch with the Stars*] (Channel 9), which soon after changed its name to *Almorzando con Mirtha Legrand* [*Having Lunch with Mirtha Legrand*] (Channel 9 and then Channel 13). The programme became the main space of consecration for an expanded star system: anyone who

**Figure 2.2** Mirtha Legrand and Juana Viale with Ricardo Darín, Diego Torres, Darío Barassi and Jey Mammon (Channel 13, December 2021)

aspired to be a star in the entertainment world would have to sit at Mirtha's table (Mazzaferro 2018: 236). In 2008, Mirtha received the Martín Fierro Award after celebrating the fortieth anniversary of the talk show. Since 2020, due to COVID-19 restrictions, her granddaughter, the actress Juana Viale, has been hosting many of the lunches with various stars. Mirtha reappeared in the last show of the 2021 season at an iconic lunch where among the four guests who were invited to eat with the diva and her granddaughter was Ricardo Darín (*La Nación* 2021).

Writing in 1994, Abel Posadas claimed that the lack of industry started to impoverish Argentine cinema, not only through the lack of professional work at all levels but also because of the lack of opportunities for improvement (1994: 239). In relation to this, he even declared that besides Graciela Borges and Alfredo Alcón, not many could develop a career solely in cinema after the fall of the studios (1994: 239). No doubt the main reason behind this can also be attributed to the influx of television. Our star-in-focus, Darín, as we will explore in the following chapters, is a product of this television-driven star system, in spite of his initial scepticism towards his labelling as a star, evinced through the emphasis of his working-class upbringing and lack of interest in fame, as highlighted in statements such as the following:

> When I was eight years old I took the number 31 bus and got off in Las Heras and Salguero, and I walked eight blocks to Channel 9 whilst I was reading the script. I found that my peers arrived with their mothers, their aunts and uncles, their cousins to take a picture with famous actors
>
> [A los ocho años me tomaba el 31, me bajaba en Las Heras y Salguero y caminaba las ocho cuadras hasta Canal 9 leyendo el libreto. Y me encontraba que mis compañeros llegaban con las madres, los tíos, los primos, a sacarse fotos con los actores famosos.] (Darín quoted in *Radar* 1999: 14–15)

# Notes

1. For Abel Posadas, the poor quality of all the films that were created thanks to the film law enacted in 1947 implied a step back for the industry. Nonetheless, he considers that Peronism should not be blamed for this outcome, only for believing that more investments and protectionism would generate new talents (1994: 233).
2. All studios had to close their doors at the end of 1956 and only a few reopened when some state funding opportunities were reinstated in 1957. Those that were able to come back were: Argentina Sono Film, General Belgrano, Artistas Argentinos Asociados, Guaranteed Pictures, Producciones Sandrini and D'An Fran Productora (Kriger 2009: 91).
3. This witch-hunt took place between the *coup d'état* in 1955 and the new call for elections in 1958. Peronism was still forbidden during and after elections were held, so even though the persecution was diminished, it did not stop. Fanny Navarro was a tango singer who gained stardom in the mid-1930s, acting alongside stars like Niní Marshall and Olinda Bozán. She worked with iconic directors of the period, including Manuel Romero, Daniel Tinayre and Luis César Amadori (Maranghello and Insaurralde 1997). In Héctor Olivera's *Ay, Juancito* (2004), Leticia Brédice plays Navarro, narrating the story of her relationship with Juan Duarte, Eva Perón's brother. Navarro worked for the last time in television – Channel 9 – with Alberto Migré, who also worked, years later, with Ricardo Darín (see Chapter 5 for further details).
4. Although democratic elections were restored in 1958, Peronism was still forbidden and was not allowed on the ballot.
5. Lolita Torres started working in cinema when she was only fourteen in Luis Bayón Hererra's film *La danza de la fortuna* [*The Dance of Fortune*] (1944), with Luis Sandrini and Olinda Bozán. She worked for General Belgrano in the early 1950s and in a series of films produced by Argentina Sono Film from then on. During this period (1955–1958), she appeared mostly in films that were targeting a teenage

audience, such as *La hermosa mentira* [*Beautiful Lie*] (Saraceni 1958), starring José Cibrián, Luis Dávila and Héctor Calcagno. At the same time, she had a long and successful career as a singer (Blanco Pazos and Clemente 2008: 234–235).

6. This was the first time that full-frontal nudity took place in Argentine cinema (Mazzaferro 2018: 173). Bó not only directed the film but also starred in it, together with Ernesto Báez and Andrés Laszlo.
7. The film was written and directed by and starred Armando Bó, and it was part of a group of films made together with his muse and life-partner Sarli. Other cast members included Horacio Priani, Maruja Roig, Pablo Moret, Claudia Lapacó and Bó's own son with María Teresa Machinandiarena, Víctor Bó, who would appear in many of his films in the years to come.
8. She was then 'discovered' in the film industry by Armando Bó in 1956, who was by then a famous actor and producer, and co-founder, in 1948 with Elías Hadad, of the production company SIFA (Sociedad Independiente Filmadora Argentina).
9. The film was produced by Argentina Sono Film and Cinematográficas Tinayre-Borrás S.R.L. Cast members included Luis Sandrini, María Antinea, José Cibrián, Diana Ingro, Mirtha Legrand, Enrique Serrano, Narciso Ibáñez Menta, Malvina Pastorino, Elsa Daniel, Guillermo Bredeston, Homero Cárpena, Julio De Grazia, Héctor Calcaño and Guillermo Battaglia, many of whom later worked with Darín, in various productions.
10. Argentina Sono Film – and its CEO in particular, Mentasti – was at the centre of the corruption criticism. It was claimed that the annual film awards – the main source of funding provided by the National Film Institute to promote production – were rigged, and that Sono channelled some of that funding to incite jury members to certain opinions (Maranghello 2005: 164).
11. Cast members included the director himself in the role of Fabián, Diego Puente, Tino Pascali, Victoriano Moreira, Beto Gianola, María Vaner, María Luisa Robledo and Elcira Olivera Garcés.
12. Minghetti (2020) also considers Osías Wilensky and Hugo Santiago as belonging to this New Argentine Cinema.
13. *La tregua* was the first Argentine film nominated for Best Foreign Film at the Oscars. It was Sergio Renán's debut as director. Before embarking on this project, he had a long and successful career as an actor, working in cinema with artists like Tita Merello, Alberto de Mendoza, María Rosa Gallo, Lautaro Murúa, Graciela Borges, Alberto Argibay, María Vaner, Walter Vidarte, Jorge Salcedo, Zulma Faiad, Pepe Soriano, Alfredo Alcón, Marcela López Rey and Guillermo Battaglia. As an actor, he also worked with directors of this new wave, such as Manuel Antín and Leopoldo Torre Nilsson, as well as with some from the old generation – e.g. Mario Soffici and Lucas Demare – and with those representing the new studio trends, including Enrique Carreras, with whom Darín worked with in 1977.
14. In that same year she also worked on Fernando Ayala's *El jefe* [*The Boss*] (1958). Graciela Borges narrates her life in a podcast called *Mi vida en el cine*, available on Spotify. This podcast is revelatory in its account of the life of a true Argentine film star who experienced decades of navigating the ins and outs of the industry: https://open.spotify.com/show/6AppZEIW3Y8wY7WKYQQ5AM?si=UYu-7ATkQiuQlxKwhIwgdg&nd=1 (accessed 5 April 2022).

15. María Luisa Josefa Ángela Aleandro Robledo, known as María Vaner, was born in Spain. Her mother was the actress María Luisa Robledo, her father was the actor Pedro Aleandro, and her sister was Norma Aleandro. She worked as a model in television and as a stage designer before embarking on a successful film career within this new wave. She was married to Leonardo Favio between 1967 and 1973.
16. Other actresses who formed part of this New Argentine Cinema and who should be mentioned are Susana Freyre, Violeta Antier, María Cristina Laurenz and Mercedes Carreras.
17. Also worthy of mention is Enrique Liporace, who dared to shoot a male nude scene in the film *La terraza* [*The Terrace*] (Torre Nilsson 1963), a novelty for local audiences (Sala 2015: 12).
18. He was even considered to be the best actor of his generation (Peregil 2014; *La Nación* 2005).
19. Other cast members included Lautaro Murúa, Nelly Beltrán, Federico Luppi and Alberto Fernández de Rosa.
20. There was a defence of the figure of the director as author, above other figures such as the screenwriter and producer, and in opposition to the identification of a film by its actors, following the logic of the industrial star system (Del Valle Dávila 2021).
21. Other manifestos that formed part of the New Latin American Cinema movement included Glauber Rocha's *Aesthetic of Hunger* (1965) in the *Cinema Novo* wave in Brazil, and Julio García Espinosa's *For an Imperfect Cinema* (1969) within Cuba's revolutionary cinema (Shohat and Stam 2000: 248).
22. Grupo Cine Liberación was formed by Solanas, Getino and Gerardo Vallejos, and their seminal film, *La hora de los hornos* [*The Hour of the Furnaces*] (1968), was made of materials filmed by multiple filmmakers. *Grupo cine de la base* was formed by Raymundo Gleyzer and Álvaro Melián and was the cinematographic element of the political parties PRT-ERP (Partido Revolucionario de los Trabajadores – Ejército Revolucionario del Pueblo). The works of Fernando Birri and the school of documentary filmmakers from Santa Fé have been recognised as a strong influence for these groups.
23. Spanish scholar Sánchez-Biosca has stated that 'The Latin American filmmakers subdued the author to the collective and, to be more precise, to its leading avant-garde, although not forgetting the formal endeavour, but rejecting an artist that would re-create a personal world that was considered an expression of the *petit-bourgeois deviationisms*' (2004: 238).
24. In this film she worked with actor and singer Raúl Lavié, to whom she was married from 1965 until 1974.
25. The interview is available online at: https://www.youtube.com/watch?v=r0oAn GNfo6E (accessed 18 April 2022).
26. The '*teleteatro*' was soon transformed into *telenovelas* – i.e. soap operas.
27. The cases of Alberto Olmedo and Jorge Porcel – who worked in cinema, theatre and TV with Susana Giménez – Darín's partner for more than eight years – will be further discussed in Chapter 7. Mauricio Borensztein – aka Tato Bores – became very famous for his sarcastic political monologues on TV. His debut in cinema took place in 1947 in the film *La caraba* (Saraceni) in which he played a minor role next to Olinda Bozán, Francisco Álvarez and Armando Bó. He participated in more than twenty films after that, most of them commercial studio productions. He was the

father of Sebastián Borensztein, who has directed three films starring Darín. Carlitos Balá followed in cinema the tradition, outlined by Mazzaferro, of transferring the small screen's characters to the big screen – in roles such as Canuto Cañete. All the films he has worked on were commercial studio productions, mainly comedies, including his small role in *La carpa del amor* (Porter 1979) in which Darín had also a minor role. Altavista's case is similar, exporting his TV character Minguito to the big screen on several occasions – and working with other comedians of the time, such as Javier Portales and Juan Carlos Calabró. He participated in more than fifty films, most of them commercial studio comedies. Marrone, Biondi and the Uruguayan Verdaguer had similar career experiences.
28. Palito even decided to get married to actress Evangelina Salazar on national television in 1967.
29. In 1975, Stivel was threatened by the Argentine Anti-communist Alliance – the Triple A – and emigrated to Colombia, where he continued his work in television.
30. *El jefe*'s stars included De Mendoza, Duilio Marzio, Orestes Caviglia, Luis Tasca, Leonardo Favio and Graciela Borges. *El candidato*'s cast comprised Olga Zubarry, Duilio Marzio, Alfredo Alcón, Alberto Candeau, Guillermo Battaglia and Héctor Calcagno.
31. The long-lasting career of many of the actors and actresses of the classical-industrial period, who were still quite active in the 1960s and even 1970s, is quite unique of Argentina and Mexico. In the case of Brazil, on the other hand, Randal Johnson's analysis shows that, 'the most stable and long-lasting star system in Brazil has developed since the late 1960s and it is associated not with the film industry, but rather with television, and particularly with the Globo television network (TV Globo) and its major cultural product, the telenovela' (2017: 25).

## References

Anchou, G. (2005) 'Palito, rey de la nueva ola', in España, C. (comp.), *Cine Argentino: Modernidad y vanguardias, 1957–1983*, Buenos Aires: Fondo Nacional de las Artes, p. 248.

Avigliano, M. (2017) 'Belleza de los márgenes', in *Página 12*, 30 June. https://www.pagina12.com.ar/47244-belleza-de-los-margenes (accessed 6 April 2022).

Barreiro, N. (1974) 'Si, soy fea . . .', in *Revista Gente*, N/A.

Bazin, A. (2011) 'Cinematic Realism and the Italian School of the Liberation', in Cardullo, B. (ed.), *André Bazin and Italian Neorealism*, New York and London: Cotinuum International Publishing Group.

Bennett, J. (2008) 'The Television Personality System: Televisual Stardom Revisited after Film Theory', in *Screen*, 49.1, Spring, pp. 32–50.

Blanco Pazos, R. and Clemente, R. (2008) *Diccionario de actrices del cine argentino (1933–1997)*, Buenos Aires: Corregidor.

Cadena Nueve (2014) 'Hace 15 años fallecía el actor Héctor Pellegrini', in *Cadena Nueve Sociedad*, 1 November. https://www.cadenanueve.com/2014/11/01/hace-15-anos-fallecia-el-actor-hector-pellegrini/ (accessed 6 April 2022).

Castagna, G. (1994) 'La generación del 60. Paradojas de un mito', in Wolf, S. (comp.), *Cine Argentino: La otra historia*, Buenos Aires: Ediciones Letra Buena S.A.
Del Valle Dávila, I. (2021) 'Los nuevos cines', November. https://www.transatlantic-cultures.org/fr/catalog/los-nuevos-cines (accessed 13 April 2022).
De Marco, F. (1961) 'Entrevista con Lautaro Murúa', in *Platea*, Year 2, 48, 17 March.
De Vita, P. (2011) 'Tesoros cinematográficos y televisivos argentinos', in *40 años Museo del Cine*, Buenos Aires: Gobierno de la Ciudad de Buenos Aires/Editorial de Museos de Buenos Aires.
De Vita, P. (2017) 'Elsa Daniel: la ingenua joven que se convirtió en nuestra Ingrid Bergman', in *La Nación*, 27 June. https://www.lanacion.com.ar/espectaculos/cine/elsa-daniel-la-ingenua-joven-que-se-convirtio-en-nuestra-ingrid-bergman-nid2037236/ (accessed 6 April 2022).
De Vita, P. (2021) 'Graciela Borges: "He cumplido los suficientes años como para saber que detenerse está bien"', in *La Nación Espectáculos*. https://www.lanacion.com.ar/espectaculos/personajes/graciela-borges-he-cumplido-los-suficientes-anos-como-para-saber-que-detenerse-esta-bien-nid06062021/ (accessed 5 April 2022).
Ellis, J. (1982) 'Stars as Cinematic Phenomenon', in *Visible Fictions. Cinema. Television. Video*, New York: Routledge, pp. 91–108.
España, C. (2005) 'Modernización y censura. 1961–1966' and 'La industria no baja la guardia. Ocaso y perduración de las estrellas', in España, C. (comp.), *Cine Argentino: Modernidad y vanguardias, 1957–1983*, Buenos Aires: Fondo Nacional de las Artes, pp. 20–21, 296–302.
Fernández, R. and Nagy, D. (1999) *La gran aventura de Armando Bo: Biografía total*, Buenos Aires: Perfil Libros.
Garavelli, C. (2019) 'Experimenting with TV: *The Hour of the Furnaces* at the Crossroads of Cinematic Experimentalism and Video Art', in Campo, J. and Pérez-Blanco, H. (eds), *A Trail of fire for Political Cinema. The Hour of the Furnaces. Fifty Years Later*, Bristol: Intellect.
Getino, O. and Velleggia, S. (2002) *El cine de las historias de la revolución*, Buenos Aires: Grupo Editor Altamira.
González Acevedo, Juan Carlos (2005), *Che, qué bueno que vinisteis*, Barcelona: Editorial Diëresis S.L.
Jermyn, D. (2006) 'Bringing Out the Star in You? SJP, Carrie Bradshaw and the Evolution of Television Stardom?', in Su Holmes and Sean Redmond (eds), *Framing Celebrity: New Directions in Celebrity Culture*, London: Routledge, pp. 96–117.
Johnson, R. (2017) 'Television and the Transformation of the Star System in Brazil', in Delgado, M. M., Hart, S. M. and Randal, J. (eds), *A Companion to Latin American Cinema*, West Sussex: John Wiley & Sons/Blackwell.
King, J. (2003) 'Stars. Mapping the Firmament', in Hart, S. and Young, R. (eds), *Contemporary Latin American Studies*, London: Arnold.
Kriger, C. (2009) *Cine y Peronismo: El Estado en escena*, Buenos Aires: Siglo Veintiuno Editores.
*La Nación* (2003) 'Graciela Borges: Belleza ilustre', in La Nación Lifestyle, 27 July. https://www.lanacion.com.ar/lifestyle/graciela-borges-belleza-ilustre-nid513287/ (accessed 5 April 2022).

*La Nación* (2005) 'Alfredo Alcón: a cara limpia', in *La Nación Lifestyle*, 20 March. https://www.lanacion.com.ar/lifestyle/alfredo-alcon-a-cara-limpia-nid688540/ (accessed 7 April 2022).

*La Nación* (2021) 'El regreso de Mirtha Legrand: Ricardo Darín, muy agradecido por un gesto de "La Chiqui"', in *La Nación Espectáculos*, 20 December. https://www.lanacion.com.ar/espectaculos/television/ricardo-darin-sobre-la-vuelta-de-mirtha-legrand-estuvo-fantastica-extraordinaria-nid20122021/ (accessed 19 April 2022).

Leahy, S. (2003) 'The Matter of Myth: Brigitte Bardot, Stardom and Sex', in *Studies in French Cinema*, 3.2, pp. 71–81.

Manetti, R. (2005) 'Palito y Sandro, dos modelos para armar', in España, C. (comp.), *Cine Argentino: Modernidad y vanguardias, 1957–1983*, Buenos Aires: Fondo Nacional de las Artes, p. 429.

Manrupe, R. and Portela, M. A. (2001) *Un diccionario de films argentinos (1930–1995)*, Buenos Aires: Editorial Corregidor.

Maranghello, C. (2005) *Breve historia del cine argentino*, Barcelona: Laertes S.A.

Maranghello, C. and Insaurralde, A. (1997) *Fanny Navarro o un melodrama argentino*, Buenos Aires: Ediciones El Jilguero.

Mazzaferro, A. (2018) *La cultura de la celebridad: Una historia del star system en Argentina*, Buenos Aires: Eudeba.

Medhurst, A. (1991) 'Every Wart and Pustule: Gilbert Harding and Television Stardom', in John Corner (ed.), *Popular Television in Britain: Studies in Cultural History*, London: British Film Institute, pp. 59–75.

Minghetti, C. (2020) 'A 60 años de la generación del 60, sus mejores películas para ver en casa', in *Télam Espectáculos*. https://www.telam.com.ar/notas/202005/460347-a-60-anos-de-la-generacion-del-60.html (accessed 7 April 2022).

*MinutoUno* (2008) 'El gran dolor de Norma Aleandro: despidió a su hermana María Vaner', in *MinutoUno*, 22 July. https://www.minutouno.com/sociedad/el-gran-dolor-norma-aleandro-despidio-su-hermana-maria-vaner-n85604 (accessed 5 April 2022).

Peregil, F. (2014) 'Muere el actor argentino Alfredo Alcón', in *El País*, 11 April. https://elpais.com/cultura/2014/04/11/actualidad/1397215450_613828.html (accessed 7 April 2022).

*Platea* (1961) 'Raúl Parini. El hombre de la cara rara', in *Platea*, Year 2, 73, 7 September.

Podestá, L. (2020) 'A 30 años de la muerte de Bárbara Mujica, el recuerdo de sus compañeros y amigos', in *La Nación*, 1 August. https://www.lanacion.com.ar/espectaculos/personajes/a-30-anos-muerte-barbara-mujica-recuerdo-nid2409284/ (accessed 6 April 2022).

Posadas, A. (1994) 'La caída de los estudios ¿Solo el fin de una industria?' in Wolf, S. (comp.), *Cine Argentino: La otra historia*, Buenos Aires: Ediciones Letra Buena S.A.

*Radar* (1999), 'Ricardo Darín se confiesa', in *Página/12*, Radar supplement, 3 October, pp. 14–15.

Romano, N. (1995) *Isabel Sarli al desnudo*, Buenos Aires: Ediciones de la Urraca SA.

Ruétalo, V. (2004) 'Temptations: Isabel Sarli Exposed', in *Journal of Latin American Cultural Studies*, 13.1, pp. 79–95.

Sala, J. (2015) 'Del recambio a la consolidación de tendencias actorales en el cine moderno argentino (1957–1976)', in *Imagofagia. Revista de la Asociación Argentina de Estudios de Cine y Audiovisual*, 11, pp. 1–34.

Sala, J. (2017) 'La simbiosis actor-personaje en la configuración de textos estelares en el cine moderno argentino: Los trabajadores de cuello blanco', in *Nuevo Mundo Nuevos Mundos*. https://journals.openedition.org/nuevomundo/71430 (accessed 28 March 2022).

Sánchez-Biosca, V. (2004) *Cine y Vanguardias Artísticas: Conflictos, Encuentros, Fronteras*, Barcelona: Paidós.

Sendrós, P. (2008) 'María Vaner fue musa de Favio y de los 60', in *ámbito*, 22 July. https://www.ambito.com/espectaculos/maria-vaner-fue-musa-favio-y-los-60-n3508760 (accessed 5 April 2022).

Shohat, E. and Stam, R. (2000), 'The Third Worldist Film', in *Unthinking Eurocentrism: Multiculturalism and the Media*, London: Routledge.

Solanas, F and Getino, O (1969), 'Toward a Third Cinema', in *TRICONTINENTAL*, 14, October, pp. 107–132.

Valdéz, M. (2005) 'Las nuevas sexies', in España, C. (coord.), *Cine argentino: modernidad y vanguardias 1957–1983*, Buenos Aires: Fondo Nacional de las Artes.

Valles, R. (2014) *Fotogramas de la memoria. Conversaciones con José Martínez Suárez*, Buenos Aires: INCAA/ENERC.

Varela, M. (2005) *La Television Criolla: Desde sus Inicios Hasta la Llegada del Hombre a la Luna (1951–1969)*, Buenos Aires: Edhasa.

Vincendeau, G. (1992) 'The Old and the New: Brigitte Bardot in Fifties France', in *Paragraph*, 15, pp. 73–95.

Vincendeau, G. (2000) *Stars and Stardom in French Cinema*, London and New York: Continuum.

Vincendeau, G. (2016) 'And Bardot . . . Became a Blonde: Hair, Stardom and Modernity in Post-war France', in *Celebrity Studies*, 7.1, pp. 98–112.

# Chapter 3

# The challenges of a (non-)star system in a post-dictatorship period

In his seminal work on Stardom in Latin America, John King states that 'there is critical consensus that we can speak of stars in the 1930s and 1940s. The case is not clearly made for actors or actresses after, say, the mid-1950s' (2003: 148). In this vein, he further questions 'whether the term "star" is the right one to use for the many prominent actors working in national cinemas throughout the region in the past fifty years' (2003: 148). While there is no longer a managed or vertical system as used to be the case in Argentina during the Golden Age – hence the challenges of talking about a 'star system' in the region today – undoubtedly there are still a number of figures who possess a set of extraordinary qualities that single them out for stardom and distinguish them from other film performers (Shingler 2012: 90–91). In general, those qualities have been defined as sitting within the realm of 'glamour, charisma, and desire' (Qiong Yu 2017: 1; Shingler 2012: 90–91). Yet, as recent studies on Cult Film Stardom (Egan and Thomas 2013), Ageing Stars (Swinnen and Stotesbury 2012) and the expansion and transformation of Star Studies (Qiong Yu and Austin 2017) demonstrate, there exist different types of stardom that do not necessarily involve those characteristics.

With the aim of offering an expanded contemporary notion of stardom, Susan Hayward (2006) suggests that the star 'is representative of both normality and "acceptable" excess' (Qiong Yu 2017: 3). The actors and actresses who will be in focus in what follows negotiate the tension between these poles and, to paraphrase Qiong Yu, they '[highlight] the performativity of Stardom' (2017: 19). Informed by the 'polycentric vision' proposed by Ella Shohat and Robert Stam (1994/2014) in their groundbreaking monograph *Unthinking Eurocentrism: Multiculturalism and the Media*, this chapter moves away from a Hollywood-centric approach that would locate Latin American and, more specifically, Argentine Stardom, in the periphery – or as 'non-stardom'. As they state, 'the world has many dynamic cultural locations, many possible vantage points' and 'no single community or part of the world, whatever its economic or political power, should be epistemologically privileged' (2014: 48). My analysis builds on previous theoretical studies on stars in world cinema that have drawn from this polycentric approach (Bandhauer and Royer 2015; Nagib, Perriam and Dudrah 2012). Thus, instead of talking about 'non-stars' in a 'non-system', these pages attest to the existence of a culturally-specific star phenomena, where the symbolic capital of the star derives, as in the case of the Brazilian film industry explored by Randal Johnson, 'from two or more fields of activity rather than just the cinema' (2017: 22).

Accordingly, the following chapter will continue a chronological exploration of the history of Argentine cinema in connection to the stars – and the iconic films they have worked on – who have significantly defined its social and cultural impact and visibility. Particular attention will be paid to the last dictatorship (1976–1983) – termed by the military as the *proceso de reorganización nacional* [process of national reorganization] – and the legacy that the culture of dictatorship has in contemporary Argentine material culture, especially its cinematographic productions and key performers. As will be discussed, the New Argentine Cinema that emerged towards the end of the 1990s forms, to certain extent, part of that legacy. The relationship – or lack thereof – that New Argentine Cinema has established with stellar figures of the entertainment world will be examined with the aim of contributing to wider debates on the expansion of the notion of stardom to include, as Sabrina Qiong Yu and Guy Austin (2017) did in their edited volume *Revisiting Star Studies*, less 'glamorous, charismatic or desirable' figures.

Whereas Darín, as a 'son of the new medium of television' (Valdéz 2011), serves as a perfect springboard for the exploration of local stardom from the 1970s onwards – as subsequent chapters of this book will demonstrate – this section will focus primarily on the interconnectedness of other Argentine stars constructed in this period and their relation to industrial and socio-political changes. At a time when the industry was practically non-existent and mostly driven by the commercial and aesthetic constrictions imposed by television and the dictatorship, it is important to question how artists reached star consecration; in what ways star fame was used by the authoritarian regime, and how stars have rebelled against prevailing conservative values. Moreover, in the aftermath of the 2001 economic crisis, the Kirchnerist years (2003–2015) introduced, in Delgado and Sosa's words, 'a sharp cultural shift where grief both for the lives lost during the 1976–1983 dictatorship and the human rights abuses of the past [were] legitimised within an official national culture of mourning' (2017: 240; Sosa 2014: 1–80). Thus, the chapter will conclude with a brief analysis of how stars have been articulated in this culture of remembrance, made from a vantage point at which the New Argentine Cinema can be understood to have lost its novelty, and from where a more horizontal perspective in terms of its contemporary status is understood to be required (Chappuzeau and von Tschilschke 2016: 9–17).

The year 2023 marks forty years of democracy in Argentina. Considering that four decades have passed since the last dictatorship, it is important to question whether talking about a 'post-dictatorship period' is still a viable terminology by which to describe any contemporary production of the country's cultural field. At the time of writing, the film *Argentina, 1985*, starring Darín and directed by Santiago Mitre, is in post-production, and is considered in international circuits to be one of the 'top 100 most anticipated films of 2022' (Lavallée 2022). The film delves into the 1985 judicial trial held at the beginning of the democratic government of Raúl Alfonsín, which brought former dictators before civic judges, ultimately sentencing Jorge Rafael Videla and Emilio Massera to life imprisonment – an event considered by some scholars to be 'the most significant war crimes tribunal since Nüremberg (1945–1949)' (Delgado and Sosa 2017: 238). This demonstrates that, in spite of the country being divided politically and ideologically into Kirchnerists and anti-Kirchnerists – a Manichean reality known locally as 'la grieta' [the crack] that is particularly powerful as regards the presidential couple's politics of memory – Argentine cinema continues to evidence 'how the legacies of trauma ... produced new ways to reimagine the past, evaluate the present, and appraise the future' (Delgado and Sosa 2017: 242).

## Dictatorship and exiles

Previous chapters have outlined how different moments of political unrest and authoritarian regimes throughout the country's history have affected Argentina's star system and forced the exodus of many local stars to other latitudes. The 1976–1983 dictatorship perpetuated this trend. Most film stars of the period who found themselves on the regime's blacklist and who decided to leave chose Spain as their preferred 'sociedad de acogida' [host society] (González Acevedo 2005), in large part due to linguistic and cultural proximity. Moreover, Francisco Franco's death at the end of 1975 put an end to almost forty years of fascism on the Iberian Peninsula, slowly opening up its borders to foreign influences. According to Guillermo Mira, Spain received between 12,000 and 15,000 Argentines at the time, becoming the prime destination for those fleeing the dictatorship (2005: 191).[1] In light of this, Spanish film historian Alberto Elena explains, the national film production of the transitional period – initiated with the death of the dictator – greatly benefited from a large group of excellent professionals coming from the other side of the Atlantic. Among those were: Norma Aleandro, Héctor Alterio, María Vaner, Federico Luppi, Cecilia Roth, Luis Politti, Marilina Ross, Norman Briski, Zulema Katz, Luis Brandoni, Cipe Linkovsky, Cristina Rota, Lautaro Murúa, Martín Adjemián, Norma Bacaicoa, Sara Bonet, Raúl Fraire and Walter Vidarte (Elena 2005: 115).[2]

At first, these performers had to disguise their accents and blend in without betraying their Argentine origin (Elena 2005: 115). But soon a series of films started to give visibility to the figure of the Argentine immigrant, naturalising their presence and influence in Spanish society. Lautaro Murúa, for instance, directed the sequel to his 1975 film *La Raulito*, titled *La Raulito en libertad* [*Little Ralph is Free*] (1977) with an entirely Spanish production team, and casting once again the actress Marilina Ross in the leading role of La Raulito. Her character is, on this occasion, conveniently invited to travel to Madrid to shoot a film. Even though it did not have the commercial success of the first film, this production helped with the process of assimilation of a new hybrid community within the Spanish film industry and as an introduction of the Argentine immigrants to the wider local audience. This figure of the political exile was the focus a year later of Carlos Saura's *Los ojos vendados* [*Blindfolded Eyes*] (1978), in which Geraldine Chaplin embodied an Argentine living in Spain and experiencing the trauma of persecution, torture and the disappearance of loved ones. In fact, the effects of the Argentine dictatorship will continue to reverberate in Spanish cinema, as some dialogues in the Oscar-winning film *Todo sobre mi madre* [*All About My Mother*] (Almodóvar 1999), starring Cecilia Roth, Marisa Paredes and Penélope Cruz, seem to suggest (Elena 2005: 116).

Marilina Ross is one of those actresses who managed to give continuation to her cinematographic career in Spain, appearing in films such as *Parranda* (Suárez 1977), where she worked alongside Spanish actors of the calibre of José Sacristán, Fernando Fernán Gómez and Charo López; in *Reina Zanahoria* [*Queen Carrot*] (Suárez 1977), where Martín Adjemián had also a minor supporting role; in *Soldados* [*Soldiers*] (Ungría 1978), which included Pilar Bardem and Lautaro Murúa as cast members; in *Al servicio de la mujer Española* [*At the Service of Spanish Womanhood*] (Armiñán 1978), for which she won the Best Actress award at the Spanish *Círculo de Escritores Cinematográficos*; and in *El hombre de moda* [*Man of Fashion*] (Méndez-Leite 1980), where she played, in a self-referential manner, the role of an Argentine woman relocating to Spain due to the dictatorship. This film also included other fellow Argentine performers such as Walter Vidarte and Luis Politti, alongside renowned Spanish performers like Carmen Maura.

However, not all actors had the same luck in continuing their successful Argentine careers on the 'Old Continent'. María Vaner, for instance, once the muse of the 1960s film generation, had to make ends meet by selling handicrafts on the streets of Madrid (Fernández Irusta 1998: 175–178; Elena 2005: 115). Norma Aleandro struggled to find work, having to travel to Uruguay, Venezuela and Colombia with her play *Sobre el amor y otros cuentos sobre el amor* [*On Love and Other Stories About Love*] (Gallina 1999: 30). When director Antonio Mercero, by recommendation of his good friend Politti, offered her a part in *Tobi* (1978), he asked her to pretend to be Spanish so that they would not have any problems with the local Actors Union (Gallina 1999: 34). The following year she had an even smaller role in *Las verdes praderas* [*The Green Meadows*] (Garci 1979), starring the iconic actor of the Spanish transition, Alfredo Landa, and working with her compatriot Cecilia Roth. She recalls being treated so badly by Garci that she decided to look for work elsewhere (Gallina 1999: 35). In January 1981 she went back to Argentina and slowly started her theatre projects again. She was directing the play *Lo que vio el mayordomo* [*What the Butler Saw*] when Puenzo approached her with the idea of making *La historia oficial* [*The Official Story*], which she rejected amidst fears of suffering further terrorism and having to flee the country again.[3] After months of negotiation, she felt it was her duty to take the role, which resulted, as will be explored further in the following section, in a turning point for Argentine cinema in the international market (Gallina 1999: 35).[4]

The dictatorship's blacklists were an open secret, although their authors always denied their existence. It is calculated that more than 700 people from different professions were included on those lists

(Maranghello 2005a: 735). In 2013, in the basement of the Cóndor Building which belongs to the Air Forces, more than 200 folders were found, in which, among many important details of how the dictatorship operated, there was a list of all the artists who were considered 'dangerous' by the regime (Rebossio 2013).[5] The names of writers, journalists and intellectuals such as Julio Cortázar, María Elena Walsh, David Viñas, Rodolfo Walsh, Haroldo Conti and Osvaldo Bayer appeared next to musicians and actors such as Mercedes Sosa, Horacio Guaraní, Víctor Heredia, Federico Luppi, Héctor Alterio, Norman Briski, Marilina Ross and, justifying her fears, Norma Aleandro. In his memoirs, Luis Brandoni noted that his name appeared in these documents next to Marta Bianchi and Saulo Benavente and he recalls that during this period, when he was leading the Actors' Union:

> Curiously, in spite of the secret but evident – and very extensive – blacklist, the military dictatorship did not directly interfere with the Argentine Actors Association [...] [B]ut they did punish us by taking job opportunities away from many of us, in the hope we would then leave the country. Nevertheless, even though with the *coup* all political and unionist work ceased, we continued discussing collective work agreements and we continued holding ordinary meetings in each one of the years of the *de facto* government [...] Even Susana Giménez and Carlos Monzón came to ask for our protection when they were threatened for *La Mary*, Daniel Tinayre's film. Mirtha Legrand also came to the Actors Union in connection to this threat.[6]
>
> [Curiosamente, a pesar de la secreta pero evidente – y muy extensa – lista negra, la Asociación Argentina de Actores no fue intervenida por la dictadura militar [...] [P]ero nos castigaron a muchos de nosotros quitándonos el trabajo, con la esperanza de que abandonáramos el país. No obstante, y aunque con el golpe se congeló la actividad política y gremial, nosotros seguimos discutiendo convenios colectivos de trabajo y ajustes salariales, y fuimos la única entidad gremial del país que siguió celebrando asambleas ordinarias durante todos y cada uno de los años que duró el gobierno de facto [...] Hasta Susana Giménez y Carlos Monzón vinieron a pedir protección cuando fueron amenazados por *La Mary*, la película de Daniel Tinayre. Incluso Mirtha Legrand fue hasta Actores por ese episodio.] (2020: n.p.)

What Brandoni's statement reveals is that those film performers who stayed had to face varied challenges, mostly connected to a decaying industry that received scarce state support and that was constantly under the scrutiny of the censors. The Argentine Actors Association submitted many formal complaints, requesting not only the ceasing of the blacklists but also of the censorship of films and scripts, but none of those ended with good results (Maranghello 2005a: 735). Twenty-eight actors and actresses were disappeared, and others suffered from having to work in private theatres with no publicity, becoming deeply marginalised (Maranghello 2005a: 735). It was not only local films that were censored either, but also those coming from abroad. The reasons for this were numerous but included casting those Argentine actors and actresses in exile. As Fernando Varea states in his book on Argentine cinema during the dictatorship, many directors and film performers, such as Fernando Pino Solanas, Lautaro Murúa, Héctor Alterio, Norman Briski, Luis Politti and Marilina Ross, were winning awards and recognition abroad, but none of their films were shown in the country (2008: 83). In 2015, these blacklists were handed back to the Argentine Actors Association by the head of the Ministry of Defense, Agustín Rossi, in a highly celebrated ceremony that came in the wake of the politics of memory established by the Kirchner administrations. Alejandra Darín – Ricardo Darín's sister and president of the union – received them in conjunction with many actors, actresses and family members of those affected by these lists, and declared that the government's gesture showed a 'commitment to the truth' (cited in *télam* 2015a).

In terms of the actors who reached star consecration in this period, as mentioned in the previous chapter, probably the most significant was the king of the popular song, Palito Ortega.[7] In his study of Palito, Matt Losada declared that 'it is widely acknowledged that the films starring, directed, and produced by Ramón "Palito" Ortega between 1976 and 1982 offered ideological support to the military dictatorship of that period' (2020: 109). Ortega tends to declare that his films are 'totally innocent and there is no reason to interpret them as political propaganda of the regime' (cited in Varea 2008: 63). However, *Dos locos en el aire* [*Two Mad Men in the Air*], for instance, released only a few months after the *coup* in 1976, is plagued with references to the heroes from the Air Forces, for which he received extensive official support that infused the film with patriotic overtones.[8] In respect of this, Varea arrives at the conclusion that, because at a time of strict censorship it was not easy to gain the trust of official institutions and their censors, a level of complicity of the Tucuman artist with the regime is evident, even if only by implication through the great confidence placed in his projects (2008: 63).

Before directing his own productions, Palito had appeared in twenty films, eighteen of those directed by Enrique Carreras. In those movies, as Losada rightly states, 'Ortega functions as an avatar for a conservative bourgeois morality by delegitimising practices associated with, first, modern youth culture, then, after 1973, specific politically left-wing practices, while exalting traditional practices that support social hierarchies compatible with the Peronist conservative orthodoxy' (2020: 109). Carreras directed other films without Palito during the dictatorship which promoted the longing for a better past and traditional family values. *Así es la vida* [*That's Life*] (1977), for example, narrates the story over three decades of a bourgeois family from Buenos Aires, in a typical comedy of customs style. According to Santiago García in *El Amante* film magazine,

> Enrique Carreras contributed to the film productions of the dictatorship with the help of Luis Sandrini [...] In 1977 they managed to surpass themselves when making a conservative new version of a film from 1939, *Así es la vida* – which was already conservative by the standards of 1939! In 1977, the film adds the participation of the Patricio soldiers and a military parade in *La Rural* (the story is set in 1910) where the protagonists shout 'Long Live the Country!'
>
> [Enrique Carreras hizo sus aportes con la ayuda de Luis Sandrini [...] En 1977 lograron superarse al realizar una nueva version del film conservador de 1939 *Así es la vida*, ¡que ya era conservador en 1939! En 1977 la película agrega a los Patricios y luego, un desfile-exhibición de los granaderos en la Rural (el film transcurre en 1910) al grito de ¡Viva la patria! por parte de los protagonistas.] (2005: 27)

Besides Luis Sandrini, other cast members included Susana Campos, Adolfo García Grau, José Luis Mazza, Claudia Cárpena and Andrés Percivale. Ricardo Darín played a small role as the Chilean Rogelio González, who falls in love with one of Ernesto Salazar (Sandrini)'s daughters. Other films which were very popular during this period and in which Darín had minor roles were those made to promote commercial hit songs co-produced by Aries Cinematográfica, Estudios Baires and Microfón Argentina (Varea 2008: 59). As will be further explored in Chapter 5, they are popularly known as the 'love' films, because they tended to include that word in the title and have undertones of romantic comedy. There were similar productions in the early 1980s which aimed to promote musicians on the big screen – in which Darín was no longer participating, which were produced instead by Argentina Sono Film, such as *Ritmo, Amor y primavera* [*Rhythm, Love and Spring*] (Carreras 1981), starring Cacho Castaña, Mónica Gonzaga, Carlos Calvo and Tincho Zabala, and *Ritmo a todo color* [*Multicolour Rhythm*] (Berrondo 1980), with Alfredo Barbieri, Antonio Grimau, Jorge Barreiro and the special participation of the Spanish children's singing group *Los Parchís*, which went on to star in three films bearing their name directed by Mario Sábato under the pseudonym Adrián Quiroga.

But perhaps the most controversial film of the period in which Darín had a minor role, and whose director and cast members were somehow stigmatised for taking part – particularly under the 'culture of mourning' of the Kirchnerist era (Sosa 2014) – is *La fiesta de todos* [*Everybody's Party*] (Renán 1979).[9] It is a collage film that gathers together images from the different matches that took place in Argentina in 1978 during the FIFA World Cup. Those documentary-style sequences are linked together by a series of comedy sketches that depict various reactions to the games and Argentina's final success from the perspective of various members of the public who are played by famous actors including Luis Sandrini, Malvina Pastorino, Aldo Barbero, Ulises Dumont and Susú Pecoraro. The title, which suggests that everyone was enjoying a national party whilst thousands were being tortured and disappeared by the regime, tends to be the first target of today's criticism of this production. Varea also explains that the humour in these sketches relies mostly on different episodes of bullying of those characters who are indifferent to or critical of the World Cup (2008: 78), which is highly unacceptable under today's Equality and Diversity act. Responding to these issues, Santiago García wrote about the film in *El Amante* in a piece entitled 'Festín diabólico' [Diabolic Feast], describing

> [a] series of scenes where a homophobic, racist, and xenophobic gaze prevails – a full card at the fascist bingo! [And] a cast that involves a wide range of stars from film and television. Luis Sandrini, of course, is there, as well as Juan Carlos Calabró in his classic role of the 'negationist', on this occasion against everyone [...] Renán expressed his regret for having done the film, but stated that he does not accept the readings that were made of it in bad faith.
>
> [(...) seguidilla de escenas en donde impera una mirada por demás homofóbica, racista y xenófoba, ¡carton lleno en la lotería fascista! [Y] con un elenco que incluye una variada oferta de estrellas del cine y la televisión. No falta, por supuesto, don Luis Sandrini; así como tampoco, Juan Carlos Calabró en su clásico papel de 'el contra', esta vez virado hacia la idea de estar contra 'todos' [...] Renán manifestó su arrepentimiento por haber hecho esta película pero dijo que no acepta las lecturas de mala fe que se habían hecho sobre ella.] (2005: 26–27)

Darín himself also rejects those biased readings. He has stated that although it is valid to judge now, with the benefits of hindsight, at the time all cast members were happy to have some sort of work on the big screen, and Renán had a reputation amongst his peers of always being committed to the socio-political reality of Argentina (personal communication). In fact, in the year of the *coup d'état*, Renán released the film *Crecer de golpe* [*Grow Up Suddenly*] (1976) based on Haroldo Conti's book *Alrededor de la jaula* [*Around the Cage*]. Conti had by then already been disappeared and his colleagues were being persecuted.[10] By the time he directed *La fiesta* ... Renán was just coming off the blacklist himself and has stated that he was 'tempted by the evil metal' ['tentado por el vil metal'] – i.e. by the money (*télam* 2015b).

In connection to his own participation in these sorts of light-hearted films during this period, Darín has declared that

> I come from a time when the fact of being called to do a job was in itself a huge deal, no matter what the job was. Then came the bit of finding out if the job was worth it for your career or not, if they would pay you or not, or if the role was a juicy one or just slim pickings ... But the first and most important thing was to be able to live from your work, from your metier [...] I did so many things: horrible films, unwatchable TV programmes, things that now, looking back, I could tell myself: 'How did you dare to do such a stupid thing?' But back in the day they simply meant that I was able to support my family, simple as that [...] It was only much later that I had the luxury of choosing my roles.
>
> [Vengo de una época en la que el hecho de ser llamado para un trabajo ya era en sí mismo una gloria, se tratara de lo que fuera. Luego venía la parte de averiguar si te convenía o no te convenía, si te pagaban o no te pagaban, o si el rol que te tocaba en cuestión era jugoso o simplemente era un hueso pelado, pero en principio lo importante era poder vivir de tu trabajo, de tu oficio [...] Yo he hecho de todo: películas abominables, programas de televisión detestables, cosas que ahora, mirando hacia atrás, podría decirme: '¿Pero cómo te atreviste a hacer semejante estupidez?' Sin embargo, en su momento, significaron simple y llanamente la posibilidad de mantener a mi familia [...] A mí me llegó bastante más tarde la posibilidad de elegir.] (Quoted in González Acevedo 2005: 46)

It is worth mentioning, by way of concluding this section on stardom and the dictatorship, that there were other films that addressed children and family audiences that paradoxically evinced the ideological apparatus of the repressive regime (Varea 2008: 57). For example, Emilio Vieyra – also known as the king of the B movie – produced and directed a series of films starring Jorge Martínez, Germán Kraus and Víctor Hugo Vieyra playing police officers.[11] The exaltation of the work carried out by the paramilitary groups in the name of the cherished homeland is considered a reinforcement of the official discourse enacted by the Armed Forces (APU 2012). Vieyra himself has recognised that 'I am not a lefty, all my life I've been anti-Communist' ['no soy zurdo, toda mi vida fui anticomunista'] (cited in Varea 2008: 63), which is a political positioning evident in his productions. The super-agent films starring Víctor Bó, Ricardo Bauleo and Julio De Grazia can be included under this classification, in which a group of vigilantes – nicknamed Delfín [Dolphin], Tiburón [Shark] and Mojarrita [Little Fish] – take justice into their own hands in the name of the greater cause of the country.[12] Aries Cinematográfica Argentina continued during this period with Olmedo and Porcel's comedies, but softened them in order to appeal to a children's audience (España 2005: 680).[13] Even animation films were affected, including one of Argentina's most famous characters: Mafalda – based on the 1960s cartoonist Quino's work. The films bearing her name, directed by Carlos Márquez (1971–1979) and with drawings by Jorge Martín Catú, arrived in film theatres with one significant character missing: Libertad [Freedom] (Varea 2008: 62).

## The transition era and the industry's collapse

With the arrival of democracy in December 1983, Manuel Antín became the director of the *Instituto Nacional de Cinematografía* [INC, National Film Institute] and the Congress abolished all forms of censorship, creating instead the *Comisión Asesora de Exhibiciones* [Advisory Exhibition Commission] (Maranghello 2005b: 221). By 1985, the tax applied to 10 per cent of a film ticket value was re-applied – after being cancelled by the military – contributing to the recuperation of the INC's own income, which was then channelled into supporting new cinematographic projects. In the context of this change, some critics consider the two years from 1984 to 1986 to constitute a new wave of Argentine cinema that followed on from the 1960s film generation (López 1987), due to the large number of *operas primas* that were generated in that short period (Maranghello 2005b: 221). Indeed, the national industry experienced a period of good health between 1980 and 1987, with an average of ten million spectators choosing to watch a local film each year – although forty million were still opting for the foreign productions that continued to dominate the national market (Getino 2016: 364). Nonetheless, aside from a few exceptions, the stories created at this time tended to be conventional, featuring no exploration of the cinematographic language, and tending to use the years of the dictatorship as background. Soon, local production experienced a decline, from thirty-six films released in 1986 – representing 22 per cent of the market – to only twelve films in 1989, or 5 per cent of the market (Maranghello 2005b: 221–222).

One of those exceptions, which brought together two of the main film stars of this period – Norma Aleandro and Héctor Alterio – was the above-mentioned *La historia oficial*. As Delgado and Sosa explain,

> *La historia oficial* (...) acted as the point of departure for the construction of the cult of the disappeared within a particular mainstream cinema that could generate international audiences – and thus soft power – for Argentine exports. *La historia oficial* was the first Latin American film to win the Foreign Language Oscar, generating a series of home-grown features – as with *Muro de silencio* [*A Wall of Silence*] (Stantic 1993) and *Kamchatka* (Piñeiro 2002) – which offered crusading calls for justice at a time of increasing government indifference. (2017: 240)

Its cast members – Norma Aleandro, Héctor Alterio, Chunchuna Villafañe, Hugo Arana, Guillermo Battaglia, Chela Ruiz, Patricio Contreras, Jorge Petraglia and María Luisa Robledo – received outstanding ovations. Aleandro in particular, who announced the Oscar for Best Foreign Film at the Academy Awards ceremony, gained international recognition and multiple job offers in the USA. Her subsequent participation in the film *Gaby: A True Story* (Madoki 1987), where she plays a Mexican indigenous woman, led to her nomination in 1987 for Best Supporting Actress in the Golden Globe Awards and at the Academy Awards – better recognition than that which her two famous co-stars, Liv Ullmann and Robert Loggia, obtained. In 1990, she was offered a role alongside Anthony Hopkins in *One Man's War* (Toledo 1991), based on the true story of Joel Filártiga – Hopkins – who sought justice for his son's death at the hands of General Stroessner's secret police during Paraguay's dictatorship (1954–1989).[14] Although the film received mixed reviews, Aleandro's work was highly praised once again (Leonard 1991: 81). She continued to receive further offers of work from the USA, both in cinema and theatre, but decided instead that it was time to take a break, claiming that it was never her intention to keep working in Hollywood (cited in Gallina 1999: 41).

Héctor Alterio, as previously mentioned, managed to have a successful career in Spain from 1975. During this transitional period, he participated in a significant number of films key for the history of Argentine cinema, such as *Camila* (Bemberg 1984) (the second Argentine film to be nominated to the Academy Awards), *Yo, la peor de todas* [*I, The Worst of All*] (Bemberg 1990), *Tango Feroz: la leyenda de Tanguito* [*Wild Tango*] (Piñeyro 1993), *Caballos Salvajes* [*Wild Horses*] (Piñeyro 1995), *Cenizas del paraíso* [*Ashes of Paradise*] (Piñeyro 1997), *El hijo de la novia* (Campanella 2001) and *Kamchatka* (Piñeyro 2002), working alongside the most famous actors and actresses of this period, such as Cecilia Roth, Leonardo Sbaraglia, Susú Pecoraro, Fernán Mirás, Cecilia Dopazo, Antonio Birabent, Leticia Brédice, Dolores Fonzi, and the focus of these pages, Ricardo Darín.

Aleandro and Alterio's other co-stars also had continued successes following their work in *La historia oficial*. Chunchuna Villafañe's acclaimed performance in what was a profoundly self-referential role won her the Silver Plaque award for Best Supporting Actress at the XXI Chicago International Film Festival (Gallina 1999: 440). Having worked as a model and only occasionally as an actress, the dictatorship forced her to leave the country due to her relationship with left-wing militant director Fernando Pino Solanas.[15] She returned to Argentina after her exile in Paris in 1981 and, once democracy was restored, she was offered the role of Ana, who was also coming back to Argentina after suffering persecution. This opened the door to a rich acting career both in cinema and television. Guillermo Battaglia's career had already spanned more than five decades by this point, as he had worked on the big screen uninterruptedly since the advent of sound. After his participation in Puenzo's film he landed a role with María Luisa Bemberg in *Miss Mary* (1986), an Argentine-American co-production starring Julie Christie, Nacha Guevara and Eduardo Pavlovsky, and then in what was to be his last role – he died in 1988 – *Mirta, de Liniers a Estambul* [*Mirtha, From Liniers to Istanbul*] (Coscia and Saura 1987), a film that delved into the struggles of living in exile.

Another exception to the rule from this period that should be noted in connection to star consecration is *La noche de los lápices* [*The Night of the Pencils*] (Olivera 1986). The film launched the career of Leonardo Sbaraglia, who was only fifteen years old when he played Daniel Racero – a real-life individual who was eventually disappeared by the regime – in the film that narrates the true story of the kidnapping and torture of ten teenage activists by the Buenos Aires secret police in the first year of the dictatorship. Sbaraglia went on to work on a popular teenage TV soap opera called *Clave de Sol* [*Treble Clef*] (1987–1991, Channel 13) and after that continued to alternate between cinema and television.[16] He participated in iconic Argentine films of the 1990s, such as *Tango Feroz: La leyenda de Tanguito* (Piñeyro 1993), *No te mueras sin decirme adónde vas* [*Don't Die without Telling Me Where You're Going*] (Subiela 1995), *Caballos salvajes* (Piñeyro 1995), *Cenizas del paraíso* (Piñeyro 1997) and *Plata quemada* [*Burnt Money*] (Piñeyro 2000). After the success of this last film in Spain – in which he worked next to Spanish actor Eduardo Noriega, who was experiencing a peak in popularity at the time – he started to work more regularly in Europe. As the son of a theatre actress (Roxana Randón), Sbaraglia has also worked in several theatre productions. At only twenty-one years old he was directed by Ricardo Darín and Carlos Evaristo in the play *Pájaros in the nait* (1990) (Tolentino 2005: 71). In 2021, he was – together with Oscar Martínez – awarded the *Silver Konex Award* [*Premios Konex de Platino*] for Best Actor of the period 2011–2020.[17] In those years he worked with, among others, Ricardo Darín in *Una pistola en cada mano* (Gay 2012), in *Relatos Salvajes* (Szifrón 2014) – noted at the time as the highest-ever grossing Argentine film (*La Nación* 2014) – and in *Nieve negra* (Hodara 2017).[18] He also worked with Pablo Echarri and Clara Lago in *Al final del túnel* [*At the End of the Tunnel*] (Grande 2016) and with Antonio Banderas and Penélope Cruz in Almodóvar's *Dolor y Gloria* [*Pain and Glory*] (2019). He is considered part of a small group of actors currently driving the Spanish-language box office, both in Argentina and abroad, and, thus, forms part of what can be considered a contemporary Argentine star system – together with Darín, Adrián Suar, Oscar Martínez, Rodrigo de la Serna, Diego Peretti, Pablo Echarri, Guillermo Francella and, most recently, Peter Lanzani and Chino Darín (Vitcop 2017).[19]

In terms of other film performers who have reached various levels of stardom during this transitional period, it would be remiss not to mention Miguel Ángel Solá, who has starred in several films and television programmes, both in Argentina and Spain, including: *No habrá más penas ni olvido* [*Funny Dirty Little War*] (Olivera 1983), *El exilio de Gardel* [*Tangos, The Exile of Gardel*] (Solanas 1985), *Sur* [*South*] (Solanas 1987) and, one of the films that announced the arrival of a new Argentine cinema wave in the mid-1990s, *Picado fino* [*Fine Powder*] (Sapir 1994, released in 1998). In these films he worked with the most respected actors and actresses of this period, such as Federico Luppi, Víctor Laplace, Rodolfo Ranni, Ulises Dumont, Julio De Grazia, Ana María Picchio, Susú Pecoraro – to whom he was briefly married – and China Zorrilla. He comes from a family with a strong background in theatre – more than six generations of actors – including his aunt, the renowned Luisa Vehil, his mother, the actress Paquita Vehil, and his father, who worked for more than fifty years behind the scenes at the Maipo Theatre.

Another actor whose work marks the transition is Darío Grandinetti, who has an extensive career in theatre, cinema and television. In fact, in 2001 he received a Konex Award in the category of 'best Argentine actors of the 1990s'. His most famous films include *Esperando la carroza* [*Waiting for the Hearse*] (Doria 1985), starring Luis Brandoni, China Zorrilla, Antonio Gasalla, Julio De Grazia and Betiana Blum; *El lado oscuro del corazón* [*The Dark Side of the Heart*] (Subiela 1992), co-starring Sandra Ballesteros and Nacha Guevara; and the Oscar-winning film *Hable con ella* [*Talk to Her*] (Almodóvar 2002), in which he worked with Javier Cámara, Leonor Watling, Geraldine Chaplin and Carmen Machi. In 2018, he received the *Concha de Plata* Award for Best Actor for his work as a small-town lawyer in the film *Rojo* [*Red*] (Naishtat 2018), based on the months leading up to the start of the dictatorship. In that film, he worked alongside his own daughter, Laura Grandinetti, with Andrea Frigerio, and the renowned Chilean actor Alfredo Castro. He has also worked extensively in theatre and television since the late 1970s – his debut as an actor actually took place on the small screen in the series *Donde pueda quererte* [*Where I can Love you*] (1980 Channel 11), as was the case for most actors from this period, who had to look for an initial form of recognition first in television.

Last, but certainly not least, perhaps the star that shines the most brightly throughout this period is Cecilia Roth. She started her career in Argentina in Jusid's *No toquen a la nena* (1976) and Renán's *Crecer de golpe* (1977). She had to leave the country due to the threats that her father was receiving at the beginning of the dictatorship – he was an economist connected to the newspaper *La Opinión* (Gallina 1999: 388). Upon her relocation to Spain she started forming part of 'la movida madrileña' [the Madrilenian Scene] and became one of that group of actresses known as 'Almodóvar's girls', participating in a number of his films, including *Pepi, Luci, Bom y otras chicas del montón* [*Pepi, Luci, Bom and Other Girls Like*

Mom] (1980), *Laberinto de pasiones* [*Labyrinth of Passion*] (1982) – the first film of Antonio Banderas's career – *¿Qué he hecho yo para merecer esto?* [*What Have I Done to Deserve This?*] (1984) and *Todo sobre mi madre* [*All About my Mother*] (1999), for which she obtained several awards.[20] At the beginning of the 1990s she started working once more with Argentine directors, such as Bemberg in *Yo, la peor de todas* (1990), Aristarain in *Un lugar en el mundo* [*A Place in the World*] (1991) and *Martín (Hache)* (1997) – for which she obtained several awards for Best Actress – and Piñeyro in *Cenizas del paraíso* (1997) and *Kamchatka* (2002). Upon her return, she also started working in television, as was customary for all actors working in cinema in Argentina in those years, appearing in *telenovelas* like *Nueve lunas* [*Nine Moons*] (1994–1995 Channel 13). Her romance with popular singer Fito Páez (1992–2001) sealed her stardom status in the local tabloids. In 2022, she received the gold medal from the Spanish Film Academy in recognition of her outstanding contribution to their national cinema (WD 2022).

All of the film performers singled out in the above sections have worked at some point in their careers with Ricardo Darín, as will be explored in the following chapters. At risk of not mentioning other important names who have constituted the constellation of stars of Argentine cinema from the early 1980s to the beginning of the new millennium, this section about the transition comes to an end with the consideration that Argentine cinema was near death at the beginning of the 1990s (Maranghello 2005b: 241–256). As scholar Jens Andermann explains, 'production figures reached an all-time low in the first half of the 1990s, with only ten feature-length films produced in 1992 and a mere five in 1994' (2012: 1); the lowest production volume in the history of Argentine cinema (Getino 2016: 122). This most certainly affected film performers, leaving them as it did with limited opportunities to appear on the big screen.

## New Argentine Cinema's non-stars and its reverberations

When Carlos Menem was elected president in 1989, the country was undergoing a deep economic recession, which worsened during his ten-year administration, and culminated in the collapse of the economy in December 2001 during the short-lived government of Fernando de la Rúa. Paradoxically, considering that cinema is an expensive art form, Argentine filmmaking experienced a boom in productions in this period of economic constraints – from single figures in 1994 to sixty-six feature-length films in 2004 (Page 2009: 1). In Joanna Page's words, these filmmakers made 'aesthetic virtue out of economic necessity' and, in this, 'they demonstrate a clear affinity with cinematic productions of the 1960s in Latin America, which [...] turned poverty "into a signifier" in their representation of underdevelopment and inequality' (Page 2009: 2). Whilst the times and technology have changed, it can be claimed that this new wave of filmmakers had a similar approach to film stardom to the cases studied from the 1960s, whereby 'stars became [to a certain extent] elided' (King 2003: 143).

There has been extensive scholarly work written on the emergence of the New Argentine Cinema wave, which was generated in great part by the change in cinema law in 1994 (Falicov 2003; Aguilar 2006; Page 2009; Amatriain 2009; Pena 2009; Andermann 2012). Many scholars agree that its starting point is connected with the creation in 1999 of the Buenos Aires International Festival of Independent Film (BAFICI), and the award for Best Director given that year to Pablo Trapero for the film *Mundo grúa* [*Crane World*] (1999) (Aguilar 2006: 14; Chappuzeau and von Tschilschke 2016: 10; Pena 2009: 11). It should be noted also that at the same time that the National Film Institute – renamed in 1994 *Instituto Nacional de Cine y Artes Audiovisuales* (INCAA) – was exploring new ways of funding national productions, a series of film schools emerged in which many of the directors of this new generation were being formed (Falicov 2003: 51). In this sense, unlike the 1960s generation, who were either trained while working or abroad, these young filmmakers were educated in-house, changing the characteristics of the filmmakers' cultural frames of reference and interests.

Jaime Pena acknowledges that if we consider New Argentine Cinema as a critics' invention – thanks to the upsurge of specialised magazines that took place at this point and whose writers coined the term – certainly its origin has to be placed with the cover of the *El Amante* magazine no. 40 (from 1995), which stressed a clear break with the old generation, which for them represented the 'bad' of Argentine cinema in the figure of Eliseo Subiela and his film *No te mueras sin decirme adónde vas*, and the 'good', embodied by the new generation participating in *Historias breves* [*Short Stories*] (Burman et al. 1995) (Pena 2009: 11–12).[21] As Falicov further explains, 'without calling themselves a "movement," these filmmakers made cinema in a language that contested the imitative style of Hollywood, yet they often rejected the *auteurist* approach of the well-established Argentine film community' (2003: 49). In this sense, as Andermann states,

> Even though they caution us against misreading 'New Argentine Cinema' as a fully-fledged programmatic movement, all these critics focus their attention on a crop of young, 'independent' film-makers identified, to varying degrees, by their shared preoccupation with the national present as a time of crisis, often encountered through neo-realist chronicles of the social and geographical margins. (2012: xii)

Trapero's *Mundo Grúa* is indeed a good example of the productions grouped under this label: a debut film by a young director who studied at Universidad del Cine – known as FUC, founded by Manuel Antín in 1991. With a realist/documentary style, it portrays a micro-narrative that refers to the socio-political context, presents a strategic use of stylistic untidiness, and shows clear influence from Italian Neorealism through the tendency to shoot on location and use not-well-known or non-professional actors. With reference to this last point, the leading role in *Mundo Grúa*, for instance, is played by a non-professional actor, Luis Margani, yet throughout the film we also see quite a few familiar faces from the old guard, such as Adriana Aizemberg. Daniel Valenzuela in this film was almost new to the big screen. He comes to exemplify how the fascination for the boom of productions created by this group of directors was at first an alternative to the main industry – but then it became the norm. Actors like Valenzuela, who has an everyman look about him rather than the dashing good looks more usual of film stars, found himself in high demand throughout the first decade of the new millennium. He went on to participate in more than forty films after this, as well as acting in several TV series.

While there is no aesthetic doctrine outlined by these directors, as was the case in Italian Neorealism and the New Latin American Cinema movement, their casting choice of not-known performers lies in-between their need to cut down costs and their desire to achieve a reality effect. Nonetheless, in his seminal monograph on the emergence of New Argentine Cinema, Gonzalo Aguilar dedicates a whole section to exploring the 'actors' politics' ['la política de los actores'] (2006: 220). According to him, this new film wave has enacted a politics of face, body and name:

> In the face, there is a search for a blank page – the amateur actor has no repertoire of previously rehearsed gestures – upon which actions and affect can be inscribed. The character (a non-actor) follows

> the screenplay but also embarks upon a trajectory toward himself or herself, his or her past, what happened to him or her at some time and the emotions elicited by that experience. With the body, filmmakers pursue a possible narration. In a society that organizes the visibility of bodies on the basis of a narrow model of beauty, the new cinema shows the body as accumulation, as history, as story. [(...)] On many occasions] the names of actors and characters coincide despite the fact that the stories are invented. (2008: 209)

These casting choices and politics have been immortalised in Federico León and Marcos Martínez's film *Estrellas* [*Stars*] (2007). This documentary narrates, in a provocative way, the story of Julio Arrieta, an inhabitant of the Villa 21 slum in Buenos Aires, who decides to create his own production company with the aim of offering settings of poverty to new cinematographic ventures and representing the non-actors of the slum who, according to him, offer the true physical attributes of the poor. He thereby reasserts the importance of experience in informing performance – much to the disdain of the Actors Association (Blanco 2019). Following Gilles Deleuze's reading on Italian, French and Japanese post-war cinema, Andermann recognises the work of these new professionals as 'professional non-actors' (2012: 133).[22] And he further explains that, as was to some extent the case of the 1960s film generation, filmmakers such as

> Trapero, Caetano, Martel and Postiglione maintain the delicate balance between the real and the staged by exploiting both the professionals' capacity to contain and 'fictionalise' the non-actors' performance through their more accomplished and self-aware movement across the set and the dose of indexical realism inserted into the scene by the non-actors' spontaneity and presence. (2012: 132)

The film *La ciénaga* [*The Swamp*] (Martel 2001), for instance, demonstrates this acting dynamic very well. Andrea López, who plays the maid Isabel, and Sofía Bertolotto – one of Mecha (Borges)'s daughters – shine in their inexperience next to Graciela Borges's and Mercedes Morán's 'technical' performances in roles which took them away from what they were typically doing at the time – in tune with the tendency of New Argentine Cinema to use well-known performers in roles outside of their comfort zone (*La Nación* 2001).[23] Borges, once the face of the New Argentine Cinema of the 1960s – and a big film star of the 1970s and 1980s – became the image of this new generation, too, by participating in this film (De Vita 2021). Her capacity to adapt and envision the overturns of the industry show her nature as a timeless Argentine star – one who was even able to parody the actual image of the film stars of the Golden Era in the role of Mara Ordaz, a star in decay, in Juan José Campanella's *El cuento de las comadrejas* [*The Weasel's Tale*] (2019).

The success of this New Argentine Cinema wave in international film festivals cast new light on commercial productions – what Gustavo Aprea called 'the [parallel] renewal of entertainment cinema' (2008: 42). Marcelo Piñeyro, Juan José Campanella, Fabián Bielinsky, and younger directors such as Damián Szifrón, Lucía Puenzo, Juan Taratuto and Daniel Burman, have been creating genre films with a particular authorial gaze that establishes a recognisable star system – with Ricardo Darín as its highest representative – and whose productions benefited from the attention and prestige of the New Argentine Cinema (Aprea 2008: 43). In relation to this, Marcelo Panozzo, who was the BAFICI film programmer for six years, states that *The Son of the Bride* (Campanella 2001) 'is a film that contains two key names that by themselves sum up this not-new-mainstream: Adrián Suar and, of course, Ricardo Darín' ['*El hijo de la novia* presentaba ya dos nombres que podrían sintetizar, ellos solos, ese

**Figure 3.1** Adrián Suar, Juan José Campanella, Ricardo Darín and Norma Aleandro at the Oscar's for *The Son of the Bride* in 2002 (*Revista Gente* Archive)

no-nuevo-mainstream (…): Adrián Suar (…) y, por supuesto, Ricardo Darín'] (Panozzo 2009: 51). Other names that should be mentioned in relation to this tendency, are Pablo Echarri, Soledad Villamil, Natalia Oreiro, Leonardo Sbaraglia, Diego Peretti, Valeria Bertuccelli, and Guillermo Francella.

Twenty years have passed since the emergence of this New Argentine Cinema wave and within that time there has been a cultural shift in the way audiences are approaching and consuming local productions – natives are now indeed watching Argentine cinema, eschewing the prejudices held against it in the 1990s.[24] Thus, it is valid to question whether it is viable to still talk about a New Argentine Cinema today. Indeed, film critic Quintín stated as far back as 2009 that '[…] in ten years the situation changed considerably. Today it is well known and accepted that there was a generational change and that those new directors have been incorporated into the *establishment*. It was not a linear process and it is not over yet' (Quintín 2009: 59).

One of the clear indicators of these directors' assimilation into the new mainstream is their engagement with the issue of memory under the Kirchners' administrations. As Delgado and Sosa explore, during the transitional period, due to increasing political pressures and deepening economic crisis, Alfonsín's government introduced the so-called 'laws of impunity', which discontinued the prosecution of military personnel (2017: 239). Menem's vision for Argentina 'had no room for revisiting the past' (Delgado and Sosa 2017: 239). In the name of a politics of 'national reconciliation' all those convicted in 1985 for human rights abuses were pardoned, and a society of spectacle, individualism and consumerism was rapidly established, in which the obfuscation of history and the lack of a historical present prevailed (Sarlo 1994).[25] The New Argentine Cinema of the mid-1990s embraced this contemporaneity. In Sergio Wolf's words, 'being contemporary is the challenge of telling about the present in Argentina and the present in the lives of the characters. In almost all the films of the new generation, flashbacks or evocations of an earlier time are not to be found' (Wolf 2002: 33). And in this cult of the present – nonetheless clearly haunted by the past – the so-called 'professional non-actors' provided a level of indexicality that displaced the focus from the traditional film stars – in fact, Darín himself was highly praised in 2000 for his role of Marcos in *Nueve reinas* [*Nine Queens*] (Bielinsky 2000), which operated an estrangement effect by showing a completely different side of the famous TV personality that the public was used to, transforming him, albeit temporarily, into another not-known figure from this period.

During the Kirchnerist years, in contrast, there has been an institutionalisation of memory, which is evident in the shift made in the newer films by those New Argentine Cinema directors, such as Pablo Trapero's *El Clan* [*The Clan*] (2015) and Adrián Caetano's *Crónica de una fuga* [*Chronicle of an Escape*] (2006), both set during the dictatorship and both using famous actors in their leading roles: Guillermo Francella, Peter Lanzani, Pablo Echarri and Rodrigo de la Serna. Ricardo Darín himself has participated in a significant number of films that revisit this dark past, including *Revancha de un amigo* (Oves 1987), *El mismo amor, la misma lluvia* (Campanella 1999), *Kamchatka* (Piñeyro 2002), *El secreto de sus ojos* (Campanella 2009), *Kóblic* (Borensztein 2016) and *Argentina, 1985* (Mitre 2022). It is evident how a number of stars are once again driving sales, reinstating a solid star system.

There has also been a recent upsurge of alternative productions that continue to move away from stardom and which are receiving significant international attention. Directors such as Matías Piñeiro and Alejo Moguillansky rely on new theatrical troupes emerging in Buenos Aires's theatre circuits (Delgado and Sosa 2017: 244). Andermann also recognises that 'a different kind of actorship is flourishing in non-mainstream cinema, often through actors with a background in theatre rather than, as in the case of the commercial star performers, in television' (2012: 133). Aprea further explains that these professionals coming from the theatrical scene aim to break away from the 'realist' performance defined by television (2008: 41), which also includes a spectrum of performances of established actors, such as Julio Chávez and, to certain extent, Esteban Lamothe and Verónica Llinás.

It remains to be seen whether a new generation will end the more than twenty-year reign of Ricardo Darín, Guillermo Francella, Adrián Suar, Natalia Oreiro, Pablo Echarri, Leonardo Sbaraglia and Diego Peretti. According to Mariano Oliveros, in his analysis of cinematographic marketing,

> [the] only young figures that have emerged in the last years are China Suárez and, to lesser degree, Chino Darín. It is very difficult for cinema to generate stars. What creates stars is the television, and then they move to the cinema. The famous actors from the 1990s and early 2000s were young performers that came from television. In those years the *telenovelas* starred Natalia Oreiro and

Pablo Echarri, who were in their late twenties. Today we see Mariano Martínez and Eleonora Wexler, who are both forty. Where are the new TV personalities? You see either Disney programmes or actors and actresses in their forties. If television does not generate stars, cinema is doomed.

[Las únicas figuras jóvenes que explotaron en los últimos años fueron la China Suárez y, en menor medida, el Chino Darín. Es muy difícil que el cine genere estrellas. Lo que genera estrellas es la televisión, y después pasan al cine. Los actores famosos de los 90 y principios de los 2000 eran jóvenes que venían de la televisión. En esos años las telenovelas tenían a Natalia Oreiro y Pablo Echarri con veintipico, treinta años. Hoy están Mariano Martínez y Eleonora Wexler, que tienen cuarenta cada uno. ¿Dónde está la renovación de figuras populares en la televisión? O te vas a los programas de Disney o a actores y actrices de 40 años. Si la tele no genera, el cine está en el horno.] (Cited in Boetti 2018)

What Oliveros suggests to strengthen the current star system and guarantee its prosperity is what Hollywood has been working on in the past decade: inter-generational narratives that appeal to audiences of various ages by

cast[ing] together young on-the-rise actors such as Peter Lanzani next to an established celebrity. *You Only Live Once* and *Hypersomnia* are clear examples that he is still not ready to be the leading actor on his own, in the sense that people would still not say 'let's see the last film of Lanzani'. But it was quite clever to put him next to Francella because it really improved *El clan*. He is a very good supporting actor. If you are trying to make a film today with Natalia Oreiro, I would say that you have to add 'a teenage sister' played by Angela Torres or any of the girls from *Soy Luna* or *Violeta*.

[Lo que se podría hacer es poner actores jóvenes en ascenso al lado de una celebridad, como por ejemplo Peter Lanzani. *Sólo se vive una vez* o *Hipersomnia* mostraron que todavía no puede protagonizar solo, en el sentido de que no es un actor que la gente vaya a decir 'veamos la última de Lanzani'. Pero sí fue una movida inteligente ponerlo al lado de Francella porque levantó aún más *El clan*. Es un muy buen actor de reparto. Si hoy planteás hacer una película con Natalia Oreiro, te diría que le sumes una 'hermana adolescente' interpretada por Angela Torres o alguna de las chicas de *Soy Luna* o *Violeta*.] (Cited in Boetti 2018)

Lanzani is currently cast in Darín's latest venture: *Argentina, 1985* (Mitre 2022), whilst Oreiro continues working with big names such as Leonardo Sbaraglia, Soledad Silveyra and Gerardo Romano – in *Hoy se arregla el mundo* [*Today We Fix The World*] (Winograd 2022) – and Mercedes Morán in *Las Rojas* [*The Red Ones*] (Lucchesi 2022). Francella's latest film, *Granizo* [*All Hail*] (Carnevale 2022), has been the third most-watched film on *Netflix* around the world and across all languages for two consecutive weeks and continues to draw an audience (*Teleshow* 2022). This is certainly hopeful for the Argentine industry, but it keeps the question mark in place in terms of a potential regeneration of its star system.

## Notes

1. Mira mentions that this migration of Argentines to Spain in fact started in the early 1970s, and intensified in 1974 when the paramilitary group Triple A started a more aggressive strategy of intimidation towards those considered political dissidents (2005: 191–192). Héctor Alterio was one of those who received a death sentence from the Triple A in 1974 while he was presenting the film *La tregua* at the San Sebastian Film Festival, and so he decided to stay in Spain. His first minor role in Spanish cinema was in Carlos Saura's *Cría cuervos* [*Raise Ravens*] (1975), but it would take him arduous administrative work – and the mediation of actor Alberto de Mendoza – to become a member of the Spanish Actors Union (Gallina 1999: 45).
2. Federico Luppi's case is quite unique. He only spent a brief period of time in Spain in 1977 doing theatre, and he did not go back until 1985, to work on Mario Camus's film *La vieja música* [*The Old Music*] (1985), starring important Spanish actors and actresses such as Charo López, Antonio Resines, Francisco Rabal and Haydée Padilla (Elena 2005: 115; González Acevedo 2005: 76).
3. When the *coup d'état* took place, Aleandro was working on *Nosotros* [*Us*] in Channel 11 with Federico Luppi and was also doing theatre at Teatro Astral in Buenos Aires. On the night of 23 June a tear gas bomb was put in the theatre, leading to the evacuation of the show. In the middle of the night a bomb blew up part of Aleandro's house, and she received an 'invitation' to leave the country within twenty-four hours (Gallina 1999: 33).
4. Please refer to Mario Gallina's (1999) thorough account of the lives in exile of the most important figures of Argentine cinema during this period. It is interesting to note that, even though Spain was the most popular destination at the time, some stars did opt for different destinations. Pablo Alarcón, for example, spent the first three years of the dictatorship in Italy doing theatre with his first wife Mónica Jouvet.
5. Artists were classified into four categories according to their left-wing inclinations and whether they had 'any Marxist antecedent' (*télam* 2015a).
6. Mirtha Legrand was married to Daniel Tinayre from the age of nineteen, until his death in 1994. He was the director of *La Mary*.
7. Writing in the *El Amante* magazine, Santiago García called him 'the great Star of the dictatorship [and] his production company at the time, Chango, was also born of the dictatorship' ['la gran Estrella de la dictadura, [y] su productora del momento llamada Chango (nacida con la dictadura)'] (2005: 26).

8. This film was his debut as director. Comedian Carlitos Balá had a leading role and became a regular actor in Palito's films. Actress Evangelina Salazar, Palito's wife, also had a role. After she married Palito in 1967 the couple had six children and she started to reduce her public activities, in line with the prevailing gender politics of the regime and their conservative Catholic values.
9. The script was written by Mario Sábato and Hugo Sofovich. Adolfo Aristarain worked as production director.
10. Cast members included Cecilia Roth, Miguel Ángel Solá, Tincho Zabala, Olga Zubarry, Ulises Dumont, Elsa Berenguer, Pedro Quartucci and María Esther Podestá.
11. Titles in this series included *Comandos azules* [*Blue Commands*] (1979), *Comandos azules en acción* [*Blue Commands in Action*] (1980).
12. Films included in this series are *La aventura explosiva* [*The Explosive Adventure*] (Trucco 1976), *Los superagentes biónicos* [*The Bionic Super-Agents*] (Quiroga, aka Sábato 1977), *Los superagentes y el Tesoro maldito* [*The Super-Agents and the Cursed Treasure*] (Quiroga 1978), *Los superagentes contra todos* [*The Super-Agents Against Everyone*] (Galettini 1980) and *Superagentes y titanes* [*Super-Agents and Titans*] (Quiroga 1982/83). Other well-known cast members taking part in these productions included Carmen Barbieri, Juan Carlos Thorry, Emilio Disi, Arturo Maly, Graciela Alfano and Gianni Lunadei.
13. Please refer to Chapter 7 for further information on Alberto Olmedo and Jorge Porcel's comedies.
14. Rubén Blades played Filártiga's lawyer and Brazilian Fernanda Torres, who had just won several awards as Best Actress in various festivals, played one of the leading couple's daughters. Her mother, actress Fernanda Montenegro, is considered one of Brazil's all-time best actresses, for instance winning the Silver Bear for Best Actress at the Berlin International Film Festival in 1998, for her performance as Dora in Walter Salles' *Central do Brasil* [*Central Station*] (1998).
15. She participated in *El galleguito de la cara sucia* (Salaberry 1966) – starring Nora Cárpena – in Lautaro Murúa's *Un guapo del 900* (1971), which was the cinematographic debut of the Uruguayan actress China Zorrilla, and in *No toquen a la nena* [*Don't Touch the Girl*] (Jusid 1976), most of the leading performers of which were in exile at the time of its release – including Luis Politti, María Vaner, Norma Aleandro, Lautaro Murúa and Pepe Soriano. This work also introduced two of the eventual leading performers of the big screen: Cecilia Roth and Julio Chávez.
16. He remembers his work in the TV comedy *El gordo y el flaco* (1991–1992 Telefé) with great enthusiasm, particularly because of working alongside the 'great actor' Gianni Lunadei (Tolentino 2005: 71).
17. The Konex Awards are cultural awards given by the Konex Foundation on a yearly basis since 1980 with the aim to honour the most important personalities of different disciplines within the arts and humanities.
18. Please refer to Chapter 8 for further analysis of Hodara's film.
19. Sbaraglia has cited some of the actors that have influenced him, including Federico Luppi, Héctor Alterio, Pepe Soriano, Ulises Dumont and Alfredo Alcón (Val 2017: 89).
20. Carmen Séller and Manuel Palacio state that in her Spanish years – from 1976 until 1985 – Roth worked on seventeen films, two per year, but that she struggled in post-Franco Spain and decided to go back to Argentina (2011: 337).

21. The new legislation not only ensured a screen quota of national productions, but also provided funding opportunities for first-time filmmakers by supporting an annual competition for *operas primas* (debut films) and for the production of short films in 35 mm. In 1995 and 1997 approximately seventeen awards were given, and the end results were two feature films made up of the short films, known as *Historias breves* [Short Stories], in which many directors of the so-called New Argentine Cinema participated.
22. Names associated with this notion of 'professional non-actors' are, for example, Misael Saavedra and Argentino Vargas in Lisandro Alonso's films (Aguilar 2006: 223).
23. Other cast members included Martín Adjemián, Daniel Valenzuela, Leonora Balcarce, Silvia Baylé and Juan Cruz Bordeu – Borges's own son. The film was co-produced by, among others, Lita Stantic.
24. Mariano Oliveros's book on the local consumption of Argentine cinema states that films such as *Relatos salvajes* (Szifrón 2014) and *El secreto de sus ojos* (Campanella 2009) have re-installed Argentine cinema in the public sphere in a way that has not occurred in a long time (2017: n.p.).
25. That is to say, the lack of a present that is understood to be a result of past events was the norm.

# References

Aguilar, G. (2006) *Otros mundos. Un ensayo sobre el nuevo cine argentino*, Buenos Aires: Santiago Arcos Editor.

Aguilar, G. (2008) *New Argentine Film. Other Worlds*, translated by Sarah Ann Wells, New York: Palgrave Macmillan.

Amatriain, I. (coord.) (2009) *Una década de nuevo cine argentine (1995–2005): Industria, crítica, formación, estéticas*, Buenos Aires: Fundación de Integración, Comunicación, Cultura y Sociedad, CICCUS.

Andermann, J. (2012) *New Argentine Cinema*, London and New York: I. B. Tauris.

Aprea, G. (2008) *Cine y políticas en Argentina: Continuidades y discontinuidades en 25 años de democracia*, Los Polvorines: Universidad Nacional General Sarmiento; Buenos Aires: Biblioteca Nacional.

APU (2012) 'Cine y Golpe militar: películas al servicio del horror', in *Agencia Paco Urondo Periodismo militante*, 22 March. https://www.agenciapacourondo.com.ar/ddhh/cine-y-golpe-militar-peliculas-al-servicio-del-horror (accessed 2 May 2022).

Bandhauer, A. and Royer, M. (eds) (2015) *Stars in World Cinema. Screen Icons and Star Systems Across Cultures*, London and New York: I. B. Tauris.

Blanco, C. (2019) 'Estrellas (2007), de Federico León y Marcos Martínez', in *Página/12 Radar*, 13 October. https://www.pagina12.com.ar/224194-estrellas-2007-de-federico-leon-y-marcos-martinez (accessed 7 May 2022).

Boetti, E. (2018) 'El cine argentino en su laberinto', in *Página/12 Cultura y Espectáculos*, 26 March. https://www.pagina12.com.ar/103737-el-cine-argentino-en-su-laberinto (accessed 9 May 2022).

Brandoni, L. (2020) *Antes de que me olvide. Memorias con Marcelo Ramos*, Buenos Aires: Editorial Sudamericana.

Chappuzeau, B. and von Tschilschke, C. (2016) 'Fénix y sus cenizas: El nuevo cine en Argentina', in Chappuzeau, B. and von Tschilschke, C. (eds), *Cine argentino contemporáneo: Visiones y discursos*, Madrid: Iberoamericana-Vervuert.

Delgado, M. M. and Sosa, C. (2017) 'Politics, Memory, and Fiction(s) in Contemporary Argentine Cinema', in Delgado, M. M., Hart, S. M. and Randal, J. (eds), *A Companion to Latin American Cinema*, West Sussex: John Wiley & Sons/Blackwell.

De Vita, P. (2021) 'Graciela Borges: "He cumplido los suficientes años como para saber que detenerse está bien"', in *La Nación Espectáculos*. https://www.lanacion.com.ar/espectaculos/personajes/graciela-borges-he-cumplido-los-suficientes-anos-como-para-saber-que-detenerse-esta-bien-nid06062021/ (accessed 5 April 2022).

Egan, K. and Thomas, S. (eds) (2013) *Cult Film Stardom: Offbeat Attractions and Processes of Cultification*, London: Palgrave Macmillan.

Elena, A. (2005) 'Latinoamericanos en el cine español: Los nuevos flujos migratorios, 1975–2005', in *Secuencias. Revista de Historia del Cine*, 22, pp. 107–135.

España, C. (2005) 'La pantalla en tinieblas', in España, C. (comp.), *Cine Argentino: Modernidad y vanguardias, 1957–1983*, Buenos Aires: Fondo Nacional de las Artes.

Falicov, T. (2003) '*Los hijos de Menem*: The New Independent Argentine Cinema, 1995–1999', in *Framework: The Journal of Cinema and Media*, 44.1, Spring, pp. 49–63.

Fernández Irusta, D. (1998) 'María Vaner', in V.V.A.A. *Nuestras actrices: entrevistas (primer acto)*, Buenos Aires: Ediciones del Jilguero.

Gallina, M. (1999) *De Gardel a Norma Aleandro: Diccionario sobre figuras del cine argentino en el exterior*, Buenos Aires: Ediciones Corregidor.

García, S. (2005) 'Del brazo con la muerte', in *El Amante Cine*, 158, July, pp. 24–27.

Getino, O. (2016) *Cine argentino: Entre lo posible y lo deseable*, Ciudad Autónoma de Buenos Aires: Fundación CICCUS.

González Acevedo, J. C. (2005), *Che, qué bueno que vinisteis*, Barcelona: Editorial Diëresis S.L.

Hayward, S. (2006) *Cinema Studies: The Key Concepts*, London and New York: Routledge.

Johnson, R. (2017) 'Television and the Transformation of the Star System in Brazil', in Delgado, M. M., Hart, S. M. and Randal, J. (eds), *A Companion to Latin American Cinema*, West Sussex: John Wiley & Sons/Blackwell.

King, J. (2003) 'Stars. Mapping the Firmament', in Hart, S. and Young, R. (eds), *Contemporary Latin American Studies*, London: Arnold.

La Nación (2001) '"La ciénaga" revela el talento de una joven directora salteña', in *La Nación*, 12 April. https://www.lanacion.com.ar/espectaculos/la-cienaga-revela-el-talento-de-una-joven-directora-saltena-nid59684/ (accessed 9 May 2022).

La Nación (2014) 'Relatos salvajes, la más vista', in *La Nación espactáculos*, 26 September. https://www.lanacion.com.ar/espectaculos/relatos-salvajes-la-mas-vista-nid1730288/ (accessed 5 May 2022).

Lavallée, E. (2022) 'Annual Top Films Lists', in *ioncinema.com*. https://www.ioncinema.com/news/annual-top-films-lists/santiago-mitre-argentina-1985 (accessed 24 April 2022).

Leonard, J. (1991) 'One Half of One Man's War', in *New York Magazine*, 22 April, p. 81.

López, D. (1987) *Catálogo del nuevo cine argentino 1984–1986*, Buenos Aires: Instituto Nacional de Cinematografía.

Losada, M. (2020) 'Muchacho que vas militando: Stardom, Youth Culture, and Politics in Palito Ortega Films', in *Journal of Latin American Cultural Studies*, 29.1, pp. 109–131.

Maranghello, C. (2005a) 'Las prohibiciones del gobierno militar', in España, C. (comp.), *Cine Argentino: Modernidad y vanguardias, 1957–1983*, Buenos Aires: Fondo Nacional de las Artes.

Maranghello, C. (2005b) *Breve historia del cine argentino*, Barcelona: Laertes S.A. de Ediciones.

Mira, G. (2005) '¿Por qué se fueron, por qué se van? Migraciones y exilios en la Argentina contemporánea', in V.V.A.A. *Migraciones: Claves del intercambio entre Argentina y España*, Buenos Aires and Madrid: Siglo XXI Editores.

Nagib, L., Perriam, C. and Dudrah, R. (eds) (2012) *Theorizing World Cinema*, London and New York: I. B. Tauris.

Oliveros, M. (2017) *Yo no veo cine argentino. Cómo atraer al espectador a ver una película nacional*, Buenos Aires: Editorial Autores de Argentina.

Page, J. (2009) *Crisis and Capitalism in Contemporary Argentine Cinema*, Durham, NC and London: Duke University Press.

Panozzo, M. (2009) 'El *mainstream* que nunca estuvo', in Pena, J. (ed.), *Historias extraordinarias. Nuevo Cine Argentino 1999–2008*, Madrid: T & B Editores.

Pena, J. (ed.) (2009) *Historias extraordinarias. Nuevo Cine Argentino 1999–2008*, Madrid: T & B Editores.

Qiong Yu, S. (2017) 'Introduction: Performing Stardom: Star Studies in Transformation and Expansion', in Qiong Yu, S. and Austin, G. (eds), *Revisiting Star Studies: Cultures, Themes and Methods*, Edinburgh: Edinburgh University Press.

Qiong Yu, S. and Austin, G. (2017) *Revisiting Star Studies: Cultures, Themes and Methods*, Edinburgh: Edinburgh University Press.

Quintín (2009) 'El *mainstream* y el *off*: un mapa alternativo del cine argentino', in Pena, J. (ed.), *Historias extraordinarias. Nuevo Cine Argentino 1999–2008*, Madrid: T & B Editores.

Rebossio, A. (2013) 'Las "artísticas" listas Negras de la dictadura argentina', in *El País*, 5 November. https://elpais.com/internacional/2013/11/05/actualidad/1383624001_706481.html (accessed 26 April 2022).

Sarlo, B. (1994) *Escenas de la vida posmoderna. Intelectuales, arte y videocultura en la argentina*, Buenos Aires: Ariel/Espasa Cape Argentina S.A.

Séller, C. and Palacio, M. (2011) 'Cecilia Roth en España (1976–1985)', in *UNED. Revista Signa*, 20, pp. 335–358.

Shingler, M. (2012) *Star Studies: A Critical Guide*, London: Palgrave Macmillan/BFI.

Shohat, E. and Stam, R. (1994/2014), *Unthinking Eurocentrism: Multiculturalism and The Media*, London: Routledge.

Sosa, C. (2014) *Queering Acts of Mourning in the Aftermath of Argentina's Dictatorship: The Performances of Blood*, Woodbridge: Tamesis.

Swinnen, A. and Stotesbury, J. (eds) (2012) *Aging, Performance, and Stardom. Doing Age on the Stage of Consumerist Culture*, Zurich and Berlin: LIT Verlag.

*télam* (2015a) 'Fueron entregadas las "listas negras" de los actores prohibidos y perseguidos por la dictadura', in *télam digital*. https://www.telam.com.ar/notas/201505/105817-actores-dictadura-listas-negras-desaparecidos.html (accessed 29 April 2022).

*télam* (2015b) 'Murió Sergio Renán, figura central del cine, el teatro y la ópera', in *télam digital*, 13 June. https://www.telam.com.ar/notas/201506/108711-murio-sergio-renan.html (accessed 1 May 2022).

Teleshow (2022) 'Granizo logró posicionarse en Netflix como la tercera película más vista del mundo', in Teleshow, 13 April. https://www.infobae.com/teleshow/2022/04/13/granizo-logro-posicionarse-en-netflix-como-la-tercera-pelicula-mas-vista-del-mundo/ (accessed 9 April 2022).

Tolentino, J. (2005) *Ni delfín, ni tiburón, ni mojarrita. Diálogos con Leonardo Sbaraglia*, Madrid: Ocho y medio libros de cine.

Val, P. (2017) '¡Por fin, juntos!', in *Fotogramas*, April, pp. 86–89.

Valdéz, M. (2011) 'Ricardo Darín, más que humano', unpublished paper delivered at Festival de cine latinoamericano, Munich, 14 July.

Varea, F. (2008) *El cine argentino durante la dictadura militar 1976/1983*, Rosario: Editorial Municipal de Rosario.

Vitcop, L. (2017) 'Informe: Las estrellas impulsan la taquilla local y revitalizan la industria', in *Popular*, 8 January. https://www.diariopopular.com.ar/espectaculos/informe-las-estrellas-impulsan-la-taquilla-local-y-revitalizan-la-industria-n276932 (accessed 4 May 2022).

WD (2022) 'Cecilia Roth recibirá una medulla de oro por parte de la Academia de Cine de España', in *Clarín Espectáculos*, 19 April. https://www.clarin.com/espectaculos/cine/cecilia-roth-recibira-medalla-oro-parte-academia-cine-espana_0_dysZ07QLs8.html (accessed 5 May 2022).

Wolf, S. (2002) 'The Aesthetics of the New Argentine Cinema: The Map is the Territory', in Bernades, H., Lerer, D., Wolf, S. and Batlle, D. (eds), *New Argentine Cinema: Themes, Auteurs, and Trends of Innovation*, Argentina: Ediciones Tatanka.

PART II

# From Child Theatre Performer and TV Celebrity to Film Star

# Chapter 4

# Childhood and first performances

Children have appeared on-screen since the early days of cinema. While to begin with these child actors were nothing more than part of the ensemble cast from the audience's perspective, with time they have gained popularity to the point of becoming real film stars.[1] When analysing Scarlett Johansson's early career, Whitney Monaghan reminds us that the term 'child star' first came into use in the 1920s and 1930s classic Hollywood era (2019: 25). Back then, stars like Shirley Temple, Mickey Rooney and Judy Garland conquered people's hearts. For some scholars, that generation in the thirties was the last of the big child stars (Holmstrom 1980). Jane O'Connor argues that now the term commonly describes 'any and all children who achieve even a modicum of success in the entertainment world' and who are described as such in the media (2008: 6). What remains then from the classic Hollywood period in the general public imaginary is the negative perception of child stars as tragic figures who have been exploited by their parents and the entertainment industry (O'Connor 2008: 1). Moreover, even today, such early successes into show business continues to blur the boundaries between childhood and adulthood and to challenge the career progression of young performers beyond their prominent child roles. According to Chad Newsom, this latter point is due to the fact that 'child stars become famous for physical attributes that will rapidly change and character types they will soon outgrow' (2015: 6). Those children who manage to stay in business do so only thanks to particular circumstances, such as good transitional roles that allow the audience to grasp their coming of age and accept their inclusion in the adult world. In line with this, Monaghan concludes that 'Johansson's longevity within the film industry can perhaps be attributed to the fact that she did not attain celebrity status as a child, only gaining recognition as a star when she moved into adult roles' (2019: 24). And to a certain extent the same can be argued about Darín, whose various roles as a child did not single him out but did provide him with the necessary skills to work as a performer in different media.

Born on 16 January 1957 into a family of performers, Ricardo Alberto Darín remembers his childhood years as following the normal dynamics of a circus company – albeit without their usual nomadism (Olivera La Rosa 2019). In several interviews he has declared that 'my career move probably was no different from what happens inside a trapeze artist's family. One day, when a member of the troupe is missing, one of the children takes their place having previously observed from the sidelines' (quoted in Guerini 2016). His sister, Alejandra Darín, herself an actress and president of the Argentine Actors' Association for almost a decade, has further explained that 'for us acting was a natural thing; our bread and butter' ['Para nosotros actuar era algo natural, el alimento cotidiano'] (quoted in Ventura 2015). Although Ricardo has mentioned that he experienced some moments of tension in his family while he was growing up – particularly in the run-up to his parents' divorce in 1969 – he is not haunted by a scarred past like other so-called child stars.[2] On the contrary, in recent years, and particularly since his parents' passing, he has spoken more frequently about their careers and how proud he is of his heritage.[3] In this regard, as will be explored in the following sections, the web of social relations built by Darín's family in the entertainment world has provided the foundations for a healthy lineage of entertainers that extends for four generations, consolidating kinship patterns beyond blood ties. The study of these patterns is vital to mapping the possible existence of a star system in Argentina today.

## The Darín family's acting kinship

The study of kinship has been a central focus of anthropologists for decades. According to leading theoreticians in the field, 'kinship everywhere is based on attributing social significance to the natural facts of procreation' (Holy 1996: 1). Considering that Western family structures in the twenty-first century have altered from their previous traditional nuclear shape, it can be understood that the process of creating another being – of giving identity and social agency – goes beyond biological functions, and that there are other ways of conceptualising relationships that fall under the scope of kinship. Collier and Yanagisako highlighted in the 1980s that in Western societies the workplace and the state perform wide-ranging functions that are embedded in some definitions of kinship (1987: 3). While for them this implied that the concept of kinship was reduced to its primary function of reproduction, it can also be interpreted as an expansion. Drawing then from a more inclusive approach to the notion of kinship, where affective ties also drive who we are related to, concedes greater understanding of the foundations of Darín's stardom. Not only he was born into a family of performers, but that family also engendered a system of social ties with other artists that embraced him as part of a respected acting genealogy.

His paternal grandfather, Andrés Antonio Darín, son of an Italian immigrant, was for over twenty years co-owner of the Teatro Marconi (Darín, personal communication).[4] With its 1,073 seats (Romero 2014: 213), the Marconi theatre became, during Andrés Antonio's administration in the 1940s and 1950s, one of the biggest theatres in Buenos Aires – also known as 'el Colón del Oeste' [the Colón of the West] for its comparison with the Teatro Colón, considered one of the best theatres in the world (*La Nación* 2019b).[5] Many well-known performers crossed its stage, including Francisco Petrone,[6] Blanca Podestá,[7] Francisco Charmiello[8] and Luis Arata.[9] Tragically, Andrés Antonio died in front of the theatre at a young age, having been run over by a truck, and without leaving any property succession documents in place (Darín, personal communication). He had two sons with a woman called Oda Vita Lucía Zunino: Juan Carlos and Ricardo Andrés Darín – the latter the father of our subject, who led a fascinating life as a multifaceted entertainer.[10]

Born in 1925, Ricardo Andrés spent his life moving between radio, theatre, television and cinema. When he was eighteen years old, he travelled through Europe, Asia and Africa. It is said that on that trip he joined the French Foreign Legion, became a pilot, won a beauty contest, met Orson Welles and Louis Jourdan, and worked as one of Charles De Gaulle's bodyguards, although it is not easy to discern which parts of the story were actually embellished – according to his children he used to be quite a storyteller who liked to adorn the truth sometimes to make it more compelling (Ventura 2015; Darín, personal communication). In those years, he also wrote a book of poems, *Nuestras lágrimas: poesías* [*Our Tears: Poetry*] (1945), and a first aid manual in Portugal. Back in Argentina, he formed part of several theatre companies that belonged to acclaimed figures of the time. Among the plays he played roles in was *El conventillo de la Paloma*, in which he performed alongside Chela Ruiz.[11] In 1981, he performed in another version of the play directed by Rodolfo Graziano, where he worked with, among others, Carlos Estrada, María Rosa Gallo and Raúl Lavié – who was also working at that time with his son, our Ricardo, in the film *Abierto día y noche* (Ayala 1981).[12] That play took place at Teatro Cervantes, where he spent most of his last years working as part of the regular company.[13] In cinema, he worked in the film *La culpa* (Land 1969) with Libertad Leblanc,[14] Carlos Estrada[15] and Juan Carlos Lamas.[16] Although the film was not popular at the time, receiving terrible reviews from the critics (Manrupe and Portella 2001: 147), it paved the way to extend the family's personal connections within the cinematographic field – Juan Carlos Lamas, for instance, went on to work with our Ricardo in the film *La Rosales* (Lipszyc) in 1984, together with Héctor Alterio, Ulises Dumont, Oscar Martínez and Soledad Silveyra. Ricardo Andrés also met Renée Roxana, our star's mother, when they were both working on the radio play *Las aventuras del zorro*, at Radio el Mundo.[17]

Renée Roxana Darín (1931–2018) came to the entertainment world almost by chance. In 1952 she accompanied a friend, Elder Barber, to a radio audition at Radio El Mundo, and ended up working in the radio drama *Y sin embargo hoy muero* [*And, In Spite of Everything, Today I Die*] with Celia Juárez and Eduardo Rudy (Petti 2004). Like Ricardo Andrés, she fluctuated between radio, cinema, theatre and television, though in cinema she had more work experiences than her former partner. This included productions such as *Detective* [*Detective*] (Schlieper 1954), *La edad del amor* [*Love's Age*] (Saraceni 1954), *Pimienta* [*Pepper*] (Rinaldi 1966), *Donde duermen dos … duermen tres* [*Where Two Sleep Can Sleep Three*] (Cahen Salaberry 1979), *La canción de Buenos Aires* [*Buenos Aires Song*] (Siro 1980) – where she worked next to her son, our Ricardo – *Cuarteles de invierno* [*Winter Barracks*] (Murúa 1984), *Chechechela una chica de barrio* [*Chechechela a Common Girl*] (Kamin 1986) and *Chiche bombón* (Musa 2004). In those productions she had the opportunity to share the film set with iconic names of Argentine mass media, such as Lolita Torres, Luis Sandrini, Ulises Dumont, Ana María Picchio, Víctor Laplace, Susana Giménez[18] and Juan Carlos Calabró – many of whom also worked with her son.

In theatre, Renée played roles in important plays of the time, such as *Tu cuna fue un conventillo* [*Your Crib Was a Tenement*] – her debut on stage, at the Presidente Alvear Theatre. She worked with Luis Arata in *Mustafá* and formed part of Nelly Hering's theatre company. She shared the stage with the great Libertad Lamarque in the musical *Hello Dolly* (1967), which was co-produced by Daniel Tinayre and Luis Sandrini.[19] She also worked with the mythical Lola Membrives in *Bendita seas* [*Bless You*], with Gloria

Guzmán in *Si Eva se hubiese vestido* [*If Eva Would Had Dressed*] and with Luisa Vehil in *Un guapo del 900* [*A 900's Handsome Guy*] (Petti 2004). She wrote and performed the one-person play *La madre de . . .* [*The Mother of . . .*] under Eduardo Valentini's direction – with voice-overs by her children Ricardo and Alejandra. In addition, she had an extensive career in television, which spanned soap operas like *Muchacha italiana viene a casarse* [*Italian Girl Comes to Marry*] (Río de la Plata TV 1969),[20] *Tengo calle* [*I'm Wise*] (Channel 9, 1981)[21] and *Rincón de Luz* [*Light Corner*] (Channel 9, 2003)[22] to dramas like *Sin condena* [*Without Punishment*] (Channel 9, 1994–1995)[23] and comedies as diverse as *Su comedia favorita* [*His Favourite Comedy*] (Channel 9, 1969, 1990)[24] and *Comedias para vivir* [*Comedies to Live*] (Channel 11, 1981). In 2012, she received the Podestá Award in recognition of her career achievements from the Argentine Actors' Association and the Argentine Senate (Pacheco 2018).

As Renée herself has pointed out, when she met Ricardo Andrés at Radio El Mundo in 1954, radio was still the most popular media available (Petti 2004). The premieres of a new show were marked by glamourous events at special venues where participants attended in black tie and walked a red carpet. In the mid-1930s, specialised magazines like *Antena* were already claiming that young people were no longer looking to Hollywood in search of fame but to the radio, which was becoming the artistic medium par excellence by which to generate 'stars' (Mazzaferro 2018: 46; *Antena* 1934: 25). Although they usually worked at different stations – Excelsior and Porteña – Renée remembered working with Ricardo Andrés in a radio play written by a very young Alberto Migré, *Un viaje de ensueño hacia el Líbano en la historia* [*A Dreamy Journey to Lebanon in History*] (Petti 2004). (Migré, as will be explored in Chapter 5, went on to become one of the most prolific *telenovela* screenwriters and producers of the country, having a significant impact on Ricardo Darín's career – as well as on that of many other performers.) The couple experienced first-hand the rise of television and its rivalry with radio throughout the 1960s (Ulanovsky et al. 2009). They worked together on a television programme called *Las mujeres y su mundo, visto por el abuelito* [*Women and Their World, As Seen by Grandad*] in conjunction with Pedro Aleandro – Norma Aleandro's father – who became a very good friend of Ricardo Andrés (Darín, personal communication).[25] According to Renée, that TV show, broadcast on Channel 7, was our star's debut as an actor, when he was only twenty-two months old. However, Darín laughs at that assumption, emphasising that 'it was not acting, just appearing in a scene' (Riera 2000).

Renée and Ricardo Andrés separated in 1969.[26] They continued with their individual, very busy, careers in different media, liaising with well-known personalities of Argentina's celebrityhood, but they always struggled to get by financially. In fact, it has been suggested that lack of financial stability was the main issue underpinning the tensions that led to the breakdown of the relationship (*Pronto* 2018). Ricardo has mentioned on several occasions that his parents were never lucky in show business, and how their struggles taught him to be respectful of the profession.[27] Regardless of how much revenue they generated in their careers, though, the couple's passage through radio, theatre, cinema and television over time consolidated extensive relationships, creating invaluable ties that undoubtedly had an impact on their son Ricardo's career. When Renée passed away in 2018, for instance, the close family friends who attended the funeral included Gerardo Romano, Pablo Codevilla, Selva Alemán, Nora Cárpena, Ana María Picchio, Dolores Fonzi, Santiago Mitre, Andrea Pietra and Germán Palacios (*Pronto* 2018). All these actors, and the director, Mitre, worked with our star – in many cases on more than one occasion – and have been the main supporters of Darín's career and reputation.

Anthropological perspectives on kinship inform us that 'the study of kinship, from its very inception, has been based on the assumption that kinship creates divisions in society by conceptually separating those who are genealogically related to each other from those who are not so related' (Holy 1996: 143). The same can be inferred from the bloodless affective ties constructed around the Darín name. He has mentioned, when talking about his son's first steps into acting, that he was worried because he felt the surname was a 'big anchor' and people in the business could pigeonhole him (quoted in Olivera La Rosa 2019). His sister, Alejandra, has tried to dismantle the myth around the family name, stating that it is by no means a magic key that opens doors: 'there is this fantasy narrative, as if I say my surname or mention that my parents were actors and that's done. Everybody in this family has had to work very hard to earn our successes' ['Hay mucha fantasía, como si pusiera mi apellido o el de mis padres actores y listo. Todos en esta familia somos gente que se ganó las cosas con mucho esfuerzo'] (Ventura 2015). Although it cannot be denied that this is the case, being part of this lineage of performers grants power through access to certain opportunities and knowledge that are difficult to obtain for those outside that sphere. Ricardo 'Chino' Darín, our star's son, confirmed this when he declared that, 'yes, it is true, I found out that they needed people [to work in the production of the film *El secreto de sus ojos*] thanks to my dad, but they had me doing all the grunt work, and I didn't care. I didn't want them to think I expected anything handed to me on a plate' ['Sí es cierto que me enteré que buscaban gente por mi viejo, pero me tenían para el cachetazo y no me importaba. No quería que pensaran que era un ñoqui'] (Ventura 2015).

In our Ricardo Darín's case, there are some specific family connections that have been key in his career. Cases in point are Norma Aleandro, Luis Sandrini, Alberto Migré, Daniel Tinayre and Arturo Puig. When the Bertuccelli affair became public, in which Darín was accused of mistreatment by the actress – please refer to Chapter 11 for further information – she pointed out the close network of connections between all those working at the theatre. She even emphasised that she was not surprised that Norma Aleandro did not support her, nor anyone else from the group, which had worked as a team for almost fifty years, and which had a close relationship with Ricardo Darín and his family (Montfort 2018). It was once also suggested that Ricardo Darín ate meals more frequently on Mirtha Legrand's TV programme – called, precisely, *Comiendo con Mirtha Legrand* [*Eating with Mirtha Legrand*] – than he did at home (Molero 1998). The actor explained that he used to have a close relationship with Mirtha's husband, director Daniel Tinayre, and that Mirtha had helped him on many difficult occasions, so he feels it is his duty to be there for her any time he is needed (Molero 1998). Another good example of this kinship camaraderie is the case of Arturo Puig. He was a good friend of Renée's. When the film *He nacido en la ribera* [*I Was Born in the Riverbank*] was in the making, he was the one who suggested that Ricardo should screen test for one of the roles, which ultimately was Darín's debut in cinema (Darín, personal communication). After that first collaboration, Ricardo and Arturo worked together on many projects.

## First appearances: radio, tv, dubbing

Although Darín's first appearance in the entertainment world, as mentioned, was on Channel 7's TV programme *Las mujeres y su mundo, visto por el abuelito*, one of the first experiences he remembers as a true performer took place in a radio novel at Radio El Mundo – where his parents met – when he was eight years old.[28] Alfredo Alcón and Norma Aleandro played a married couple – they were together in real life at that time as well – and Darín played their son. What remained with him from that experience, besides a long-lasting relationship with both stars, was the feeling of amusement he felt when looking at the person doing all the special sound effects, creating the rain out of pieces of metal and rice, and a whole new universe from coconut shells and boxes (Riera 2000). He also remembers that he felt at ease reading those lines, as if it were just another everyday activity. This ability to submerge himself in the imaginary world of the story being told, following the particular pace of a radio programme's production, is what helped him to succeed as a dubbing actor. He won an award in that field while working at Laboratorios Alex when he was still a child.[29]

In relation to this, he has declared that, at the time, 'it was not easy to find a kid that was able to do dubbing: for the little ones it was very hard to get into the pace of the story . . . I worked a lot in dubbing, while I was waiting for other opportunities to arise in television, radio or publicity' ['No era nada fácil encontrar un chico que hiciera doblaje: para los pibes era muy difícil meterse en los mismos tiempos . . . Laburé muchísimo en doblaje, mientras aparecían cosas nuevas en televisión, en radio, alguna publicidad'] (Riera 2000). In fact, in an interview carried out by the tabloid magazine *Revista Gente* in 1987 with both Susana Giménez and himself, at the peak of their media exposure as a couple and their work in theatre with the play *Sugar*, it was mentioned that he was very busy at that time with a dubbing project – more than twenty years on from his first experiences in the field (Parrotta 1987: 7).[30] It is interesting to note that, when he started at Laboratorios Alex, Nelly Hering, Renée's colleague at the theatre, was one of the leading figures at the dubbing laboratory, which could have certainly eased the transition for our young star into that world.[31]

Between the end of the 1960s and the beginning of the 1970s, Darín worked in several TV programmes. Perhaps one of his most bizarre roles was in the programme called *La mesa redonda de los niños prodigio* [*The Round Table of the Gifted Children*] (1967), hosted by Héctor Coire – who was a very popular TV presenter at that time, with more than ten films and several radio shows to his name.[32] According to Ricardo, most of the children attending were gifted, except for him and Pablo Codevilla, both of whom were invited as professional child actors (Riera 2000).[33] Zuretti was a twelve-year-old egiptologist, Daniel Melero a promising musician, and Claudio María Domínguez was there to comment on Homer and the Illiad – and then went on to become, at only nine years old, the winner of the questions-and-answers programme *Odol pregunta* in 1970, which was at that time one of the most popular shows on Argentine television.³⁴ Darín has since reflected on how embarrassing it is for him that he tried to talk constantly on the show, in an attempt to hide that he was not gifted, and said, to the astonishment of Coire, that 78 per cent of the country was illiterate – only to correct himself, on seeing the host's pale reaction, by noting that it was in fact 7.8 per cent (Riera 2000). He also recalls one occasion when he took his mother's dog, Pichipilú, to the programme, in an attempt to make him sing live and thereby himself participate a little bit more in the show (Darín, personal communication).

From that experience came other roles in fictional programmes, such as his participation in *La pandilla del tranvía* (Channel 9, 1968). The archives of Channel 9 are scarce, but we know that this show, aimed at young audiences, used to follow the lives and adventures of a group of children from the outskirts of the city. Members of the cast included the twin sisters Noemí and Liliana Serantes, who were well known at that point for winning, at only six years old, the contest organised by Alejandro Romay to become the face of Channel 9 – an image that gave them the nickname of 'Nu and Eve' (*La Nación* 2011).³⁵ The programme seems to have followed a similar format from a previous children's show broadcast on that channel in 1964 called *La pandilla One and Two* [*The One and Two Gang*] – renamed after a few episodes as *La pandilla Uanantú* (*La Nación* 1964) – that was very popular at the time. In 1971–1972 came Darín's work in *Estación Retiro* (Channel 9). This daily *telenovela* narrated the love affair between a girl from the provinces and an actor returning from a successful tour in Europe, who have a chance encounter as they both arrive at Buenos Aires's Retiro train station. The main story was mixed with single episodes about different characters also connected to the train station. Regular members of the cast included Luis Dávila, Beatriz Día Quiroga, Susana Campos, Irma Roy, Víctor Laplace and Antonio Grimau. Darín participated in the single episodes, every time they needed a child for a scene – hence the absence of his name from the credits (Darín, personal communication).

In 1970, he worked on the limited series *Las grandes novelas* [*The Great Novels*] (Channel 7), where literary classics were adapted to the small screen. Darín participated in several episodes, although he was only credited for the one based on Charles Dickens's story *Tiempos difíciles* [*Hard Times*]. That was directed by Sergio Renán and included as cast members many regular colleagues of our star, such as Héctor Alterio,

Luis Brandoni, Pablo Codevilla and María Valenzuela. The beginning of the 1970s was also the start of *Alta comedia* in which, according to the publicity of the time, 'more than 100 stars of the highest caliber' were gathered together – it consisted of one episode per week with a rotating cast, it ran from 1970 to 1975, and it was relaunched from 1990 to 1996. Darín participated in an episode directed by Alejandro Doria entitled 'Ayer fue primavera' [Yesterday was Springtime], in conjunction with Pablo Alarcón, Graciela Araujo, Carlos Estrada, and a very young but already promising star, Andrea del Boca, with whom our Ricardo would work later in his career when both were popular soap opera celebrities – see Chapter 5 for further details.[36]

## *He nacido en la ribera* (Catrani 1972)

Darín's first role in cinema was playing the younger version of a character called Miguel Notari, whose adult self was played by Arturo Puig – who had made four other films and several TV shows by that time. Described as a *costumbrista* film, *He nacido en la ribera* depicts the career of the character of Notari, a professional football player, from his humble origins in the La Boca neighbourhood, an area on the outskirts of Buenos Aires, to playing in the top leagues. How people live, work and share their aspirations and passion for football is shown in a fairly moralistic way, stressing working-class values of good behaviour. Throughout the film, the naturalistic paintings of Benito Quinquela Martín are intertwined with real images of the port, the fisherman's boats and the characteristic, colourful houses of the neighbourhood. Nostalgic extra-diegetic tango music blends with the diegetic music of El Greco who, throughout the film, sings several new songs from his repertoire. To an extent, the film serves as an introduction to this artist's music, in the same fashion as other films of the time that were partly produced by recording companies, like the 'love' series that Darín worked on at the end of the 1970s – discussed in more detail in Chapter 5.

The film also stars Susana Giménez as a woman who has a brief love affair with Notari. She had worked regularly throughout the 1960s as a model, and towards the end of the decade she started appearing in minor roles in film and television – by the time she joined Darín in *He nacido en la ribera* she had participated in more than a dozen films. Her participation in the advertising campaign for Cadum soap in 1969, where the

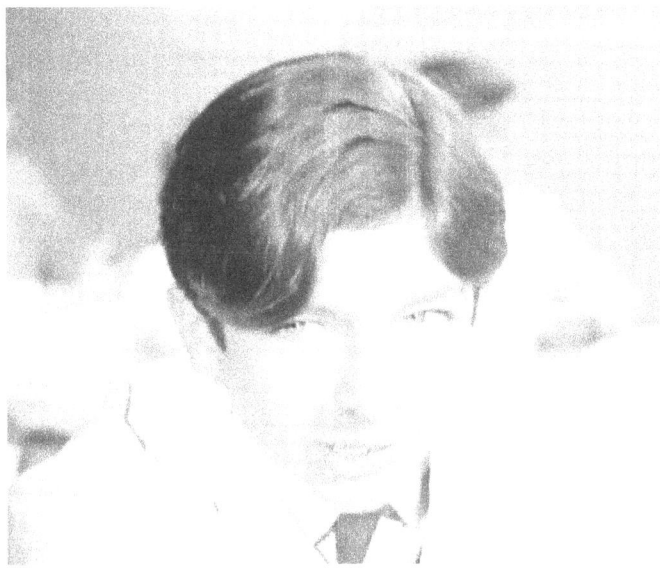

**Figure 4.1**  Ricardo Darín in *He nacido en la ribera* (Catrani 1972)

half-naked model is first seen from the distance standing in a waterfall using the soap, before turning to face the camera and pronouncing the word 'shock', has been widely recognised as the turning point in her career (Mauri and Lastreto 1999: 63; Kriger 1995: 18–22). From that moment came the success of the TV comedy show *Matrimonios y algo más* [*Marriages and Something Else*] (Channel 13, 1968–1972), which garnered her a Martín Fierro Award for Best Emerging Actress in 1970, and a long-lasting career of more than five decades in the spotlight. *He nacido en la ribera* was read by Miriam Kriger in her study of Susana's rise to stardom as a film in which parts of the script almost literally reproduce fragments of her life – the girl of modest upbringing who makes it to the big city's catwalks (1995: 31). In this respect, it is interesting to note the scene in the film when Notari and his friends stare at the poster of the soap campaign made by the girl with whom he is infatuated. It was that scene which slightly delayed the release of the film due to copyright disputes for its remarkable resemblance to the Cadum campaign (*Crónica* 1972).

This production was director Catrano Catrani's penultimate film. His first film was a comedy entitled *En el último piso* [*On the Top Floor*] (1942) starring one of Argentina's big stars, Zully Moreno, and actor Juan Carlos Thorry. Trained at the Centro Sperimentale di Cinematografia di Roma in Italy, across his career Catrani worked with several of the big names of the Argentine entertainment world, including Juan Carlos Altavista, before his famous character Minguito Tinguitella, Olga Zubarry, who appeared in more than 80 films from 1943 to 1997, Juan Carlos Lamas, who, as mentioned, worked with Ricardo Darín in 1984 in the film *La Rosales*, Sandro, before his extraordinary success as a singer, and Luis Landriscina. He also worked with several other performers who worked with Renée, Darín's mother, such as Luis Arata, Luisa Vehil and Guillermo Bredeston – the last in the film *Las Furias* (1960), directed by Catrani's wife, Vlasta Lah, where the director appeared in a minor secondary acting role in what is considered the first sound film directed by a woman in Argentina.

Even though Ricardo Darín did not become a child star as an outcome of *He nacido en la Ribera*, the experience certainly demonstrated that he knew how to behave in front of the camera and how to handle the different timings involved in a cinematographic production – in contrast to those of the theatre, radio, television and dubbing industries that he was so used to. This work also helped him to consolidate and nurture his family's acting kinship, particularly with Arturo Puig and Susana Giménez. But it would be another five years after this first experience in cinema before he was involved in another film, *Así es la vida* (Carreras 1977), starring Luis Sandrini and Susana Campos, both of whom had worked with Renée Roxana Darín in the past and went on to perform alongside our Darín in other projects.

## Notes

1. For further information on the construction of children's subjectivity and agency in Latin American film please consult Rocha and Seminet (2012 and 2014).
2. Chapter 11 provides some details of Darín's remarks on his experience of domestic violence during his childhood.
3. His father, also called Ricardo Darín, passed away in January 1989, a week before the birth of his grandson, Ricardo 'Chino' Darín. At the time, the media captured Ricardo's words about the strong integrity of his father, who died with no possessions, which was a clear life lesson for him (Brando 2013). His mother, Reneé Roxana Darín, passed away in September 2018. In a press conference in 2019, when asked about her, he declared, on the verge of tears, that she was always there for him (*La Nación* 2019a).
4. The surname 'Darín' is of Germanic origin – meaning 'those who come from the Rin'. They settled by Lago di Cadore, in the north of Italy, many centuries ago, which is where Ricardo's great-grandfather came from. Every 23 July there is a gathering of all the 'Daríns' in that region.

5. The theatre was located in Rivadavia 2300. Created under the name of Doria in 1887, it was a popular neighbourhood theatre mainly targeting working-class Italian immigrants. In 1903, it was bought by Geronimo Bonomi, who commissioned its refurbishment and reopening, under the administration of Miguel Gea (*La Nación* 2019b; González Velasco 2010). Ricardo Darín does not know the exact years but does know that his dad and uncle debuted in a play there when his dad was ten years old (1935) and that his grandfather ran the theatre for about twenty-five years (Darín, personal communication). We discovered it was actually run by four partners: Darín's grandfather, Ricardo Marturet, Enrique Sartori and Atilio Predazzi, who passed away in 1957, leaving the other three partners in charge (Carlos Predazzi, personal communication 2020). The theatre was demolished in 1967 (*La Nación* 2019b).
6. In 1940, he played the leading role at the Marconi in the play *Un guapo del 900*, which was adapted for the big screen in the 1960s by Leopoldo Torre Nilsson (Eichelbaum 1999: 105). He was a prolific theatre and cinema actor who worked in, among others, *Prisioneros de la tierra* [*Land's Prisoners*] (Soffici 1939) and *La guerra gaucha* [*The Cowboy's War*] (Demare 1942).
7. She was known for playing historical roles in films such as *Camila O'Gorman* (Gallo 1910) and *Manuelita Rosas* (Villarán 1925).
8. Charmiello was a film, theatre, radio and television actor. In cinema, he participated in films such as *Mosquita muerta* [*Little Bitch*] (Amadori 1946) with Niní Marshall, and *Tren internacional* [*International Train*] (Tinayre 1954) with Mirtha Legrand.
9. Arata worked with Tita Merello and Alfredo Alcón in *La morocha* (Pappier 1958) and received an award for Best Supporting Actor from the Argentine Film Institute for the film *Cinco gallinas y el cielo* [*Five Chickens and the Sky*] (Cavallotti 1957), on which he worked with Narciso Ibáñez Menta. In 1942, he appeared next to Libertad Lamarque in *Ceniza al viento* [*Ashes in the Wind*] (Saslavsky), which was a very popular film at the time.
10. Although both his father and uncle worked in a play at the Marconi when they were children, Ricardo's uncle eventually entered into a career as a pilot and mechanic. Oda Vita fell in love with another man and separated from Andrés Antonio during these years. At a time when Argentina was a highly conservative, patriarchal and religious society, she lost the battle for custody of her sons, spending part of her long life in Perú and Tucumán, Argentina, with her lover, Saturnino (Darín, personal communication).
11. Chela Ruiz (1921–1999) was popularly known for her role as the grandmother who was searching for her disappeared daughter and grandchild in the film *La historia oficial* [*The Official Story*] (Puenzo 1985). She also worked for many well-known Argentine directors, such as Marcelo Piñeyro, Eliseo Subiela and Fernando Ayala. She also had parts in several popular *telenovelas*, sharing the small screen with important local celebrities like Arnaldo André, Luisa Kuliok, Pablo Alarcón, Leonor Benedetto, Carlos Calvo, China Zorilla and Pepe Soriano.
12. Further information is available at: https://www.teatrocervantes.gob.ar/obra/el-conventillo-de-la-paloma/ (accessed 15 July 2020).
13. Ricardo's sister, Alejandra, also spent many years of her career working at Teatro Cervantes.

14. In the 1960s she was considered 'the rival of Isabel Sarli' (Dillon 2004). She became a sexual icon thanks to her audacious nude scenes and extremely feminised style.
15. Demetrio Jorge Otero Logares, known as Carlos Estrada, was a renowned theatre, cinema and television actor, both in Argentina and Spain. He worked in several of Enrique Carreras's films, sharing the screen with key names of the Argentine entertainment arena, such as Tita Merello, Rodolfo Bebán and Soledad Silveyra. He also worked on other productions in close collaboration with actors and directors who were in contact with the Darín family, such as Daniel Tinayre, Raúl Taibo, Ulises Dumont and Héctor Alterio.
16. Born as Rafael Velázquez, he was a tango singer as well as a film and television actor. Our Ricardo mentioned that his father worked in other films, such as *Pobre mariposa* [*Poor Butterfly*] (De la Torre 1986), in uncredited roles (Darín, personal communication).
17. It seems that Ricardo Andrés was a real character with a great sense of humour, appearing in the radio studio on a horse when interpreting *El zorro* (Darín, personal communication).
18. This took place just a couple of years before Susana Giménez became our Darín's girlfriend and a few years after they worked together in *He nacido en la ribera* (Catrani 1972).
19. With the participation of, among others, Arturo Puig, who had worked with Ricardo Darín on several occasions, and who was directing the new version of this musical at the beginning of 2020 at the Ópera Theatre.
20. It was a resounding success that was exported to 200 countries worldwide. Cast members included Rodolfo Ranni, María Valenzuela and Gabriela Acher, who have all worked with our Ricardo Darín at some point in their careers.
21. Alicia Aller, Alfonzo De Gracia and Óscar Martínez formed part of the cast and have all also worked with Ricardo Darín in other productions.
22. This was a spin-off of the famous children's *telenovela*, *Chiquititas* [*Little Girls*] (Telefé 1995–2006). The main protagonists were Soledad Pastorutti and Guido Kaczka, although Alejandra Darín also had a leading role.
23. In each episode the series recreated different infamous police cases. Some of the actors involved were Norman Briski, Ulises Dumont, Germán Palacios, Alejandra Darín, Leticia Brédice and Alicia Aller.
24. Originally created by Alberto Migré. The 1969 version included Soledad Silveyra, Pablo Codevilla and Susana Campos. The 1990 version was done mostly by Georgina Barbarossa, Germán Kraus and Eleonora Wexler.
25. It seems they also worked together in other TV shows, such as *Nosotros tres ... y alguien más* [*The Three of Us and Someone Else*] and *Boleta de empeño* [*Pawn Ballot*], although there is not much information on either programme.
26. He had another daughter who now lives in Madrid (Spain), Daniela Darín, with a partner outside the entertainment world.
27. Interview by Andrés Parra via Instagram Live, 31 May 2020. For further information see: https://novedadcultural.com/2020/06/02/ricardo-darin-en-tiempos-de-cuarentena-vi-sufrir-a-mis-padres-por-este-oficio-y-eso-me-ha-permitido-de-no-creerme-las-cosas/ (accessed 21 July 2020).

28. As told by Darín in a personal communication. This first experience in radio was further discussed in a radio interview with Cristina Pérez on 9 July 2020 – for more information see: https://cristinaperez.cienradios.com/ricardo-darin-recuerdos-radio-cruzada-seamos-uno-llamado-respeto-base-todo/ (accessed 27 July 2020). We know that it was 1965 when Radio El Mundo announced the participation of Alfredo Alcón in their programming (Ulanovsky et al. 2009: 59).
29. He said that among the adults who won this Latin American award was the broadcaster Leopoldo Costa and among the children was him (Riera 2000).
30. When asked about this project, Ricardo was unsure what it was. He mentioned that, because the sound in Argentine cinema was of such bad quality during the shooting process, it was common that you had to dub yourself in post-production (Darín, personal communication).
31. Ricardo does not remember her involvement at Laboratorios Alex. He talked about Nelly Hering as one of the greatest artists of the radio world who worked with his mother (Darín, personal communication). We know from several interviews with different people working on dubbing that Hering was indeed a key figure in that area.
32. The exact year when this programme was aired is uncertain. Ricardo remembers that it lasted almost a year and that Claudio María Domínguez was around nine or ten years old, so it could have been in 1970 instead of 1967.
33. Pablo Codevilla and Andrea del Boca were two of Argentina's most popular and prolific child stars.
34. Claudio María Domínguez is now a spiritual leader, with eighteen self-help books to his name, and a best-selling autobiography – *Por qué cambié mi vida* [*Why I changed My Life*] (Planeta 2016) – in which he explores how winning *Odol pregunta* changed his life, and how tormented he was as a child star.
35. Ricardo remembers working with them in *La familia Superstar* [*The Superstar Family*] rather than *La pandilla del tranvía* (Darín, personal communication).
36. Ricardo said that he worked for the first and only time with Andrea del Boca in the *telenovela*, *Estrellita mía* (1987). Although he does not remember, several sources confirm that they also crossed paths in *Alta comedia*.

# References

*Antena* (1934) 'La ruta de las estrellas', *Antena*, Year IV, 151, 13 January, p. 25.
Brando (2013) 'Ricardo Darín: Somos un país niño', in *La Nación Brando*, 8 January. https://www.lanacion.com.ar/lifestyle/ricardo-darin-somos-un-pais-nino-nid1542781 (accessed 22 June 2020).
Collier, J. F. and Yanagisako, S. J. (eds) (1987) *Gender and Kinship. Essays Toward a Unified Analysis*, Stanford, CA: Stanford University Press.
Crónica (1972) Short critique of *He nacido en la ribera*, 22 May.
Dillon, M. (2004) 'Siempre libre', in *Página/12*, 23 January. https://www.pagina12.com.ar/diario/suplementos/las12/13-974-2004-01-23.html (accessed 3 July 2020).
Eichelbaum, S. (1999) *Un tal Servando Gómez*, Buenos Aires: Ediciones Colihue S.R.L.

González Velasco, C. (2010) 'Una pandilla de truhanes y un cándido público: el negocio de los espectáculos teatrales, Buenos Aires, 1920', in *Nuevo Mundo Mundos Nuevos*. https://journals.openedition.org/nuevomundo/60069 (accessed 29 June 2020).

Guerini, E. (2016) 'Ricardo Darín: "I'm fine filming in Spanish thank you"', in ScreenDaily. https://www.screendaily.com/features/ricardo-darin-im-fine-filming-in-spanish-thank-you/5107036.article (accessed 19 June 2020).

Holmstrom, J. (1980) 'Babes in Hollywood: The Juvenile Giants Who Took Hollywood by Storm', in *The Movie: The Illustrated History of the Cinema 11*, London: Orbis Publishing, pp. 218–212.

Holy, L. (1996) *Anthropological Perspectives On Kinship*, London: Pluto Press.

Kriger, M. (1995) *Susana Giménez: Una estrella en la superficie*, Buenos Aires: Ediciones Colihue S.R.L.

La Nación (1964) 'La pandilla del barrio en TV', in *La Nación*, 15 March. http://hijituslogia2.blogspot.com/2010/03/uanantu-la-pandilla-del-barrio-en-tv.html (accessed 29 July 2020).

La Nación (2011) 'Falleció Liliana Serantes, la recordada "Nu" de la televisión', in *La Nación Espectáculos*, 10 October. https://www.lanacion.com.ar/espectaculos/fallecio-liliana-serantes-la-recordada-nu-de-la-television-nid1413309#comentarios (accessed 29 July 2020).

La Nación (2019a) 'En una conferencia de prensa Ricardo Darín se emocionó cuando le preguntaron por su madre', in *La Nación Espectáculos*, 28 June. https://www.lanacion.com.ar/espectaculos/personajes/la-pregunta-su-madre-descoloco-ricardo-darin-nid2262757 (accessed 22 June 2020).

La Nación (2019b) '10 teatros que Buenos Aires perdió', in *La Nación Lugares*. https://www.lanacion.com.ar/turismo/10-teatros-buenos-aires-perdio-nid2243890 (accessed 27 June 2020).

Manrupe, R. and Portela, M. A. (2001) *Un diccionario de films argentinos (1930–1995)*, Buenos Aires: Editorial Corregidor.

Mauri, F. and Lastreto, R. (1999) *Susana Giménez: Retrato íntimo de su vida*, Buenos Aires: Editorial Atlántida S.A.

Mazzaferro, A. (2018) *La cultura de la celebridad. Una historia del star system en la Argentina*, Ciudad Autónoma de Buenos Aires: Eudeba, Universidad de Buenos Aires.

Molero, M. (1998) 'Ricardo Darín, con proyectos sin fronteras. El hombre orquesta', in *La Nación*, 10 August. https://www.lanacion.com.ar/espectaculos/el-hombre-orquesta-nid106448/ (accessed 25 July 2020).

Monaghan, W. (2019) 'Young Scarlett Johansson and the Liminal Perspective', in Loreck, J., Monaghan, W. and Stevens, K. (eds), *Screening Scarlett Johansson: Gender, Genre, Stardom*, Switzerland: Palgrave Macmillan.

Monfort, F. (2018) 'Escenas de la vida patriarcal', in *Página/12*, 28 September. https://www.pagina12.com.ar/144887-escenas-de-la-vida-patriarcal (accessed 16 July 2020).

Newsom, C. R. (2015) 'Temple of Youth', in *Film Criticism*, 39.3, Spring, pp. 6–25.

O'Connor, J. (2008) *The Cultural Significance of the Child Star*, New York and London: Routledge.

Olivera La Rosa, M. (2019) 'Desde Buenos Aires: Entrevista exclusiva en casa de Ricardo Darín', *Cosas*, 17 June. https://cosas.pe/personalidades/158980/entrevista-exclusiva-ricardo-darin/ (accessed 21 July 2020).

Pacheco, C. (2018) 'Murió la mamá de Ricardo Darín, la actriz Reneé Roxana Darín', in *La Nación Espectáculos*, 13 September. https://www.lanacion.com.ar/espectaculos/personajes/murio-mama-ricardo-darin-actriz-renee-roxana-nid2171666 (accessed 22 June 2020).

Parrotta, R. (1987) 'Susana y Darín ¿Separados?', in *Revista Gente*, Year 21, 1142, 11 June, pp. 4–9.

Petti, A. (2004) 'Volver a las fuentes/Roxana Darín. Una vida al frente del micrófono', 27 June. https://www.lanacion.com.ar/espectaculos/radio/una-vida-al-frente-del-microfono-nid613545/ (accessed 16 July 2020).

*Pronto* (2018) 'Falleció Renee Roxana, madre de Ricardo y Alejandra Darín', in *Espectáculos Pronto*, 13 September, available at: https://www.pronto.com.ar/espectaculos/2018/9/13/fallecio-renee-roxana-madre-de-ricardo-alejandra-darin-47983.html (accessed 20 August 2022).

Riera, D. (2000) 'El golpe perfecto. Ricardo Darín', in *Rolling Stones, La Nación Espectáculos*, 1 October. https://www.lanacion.com.ar/espectaculos/ricardo-darin-nid585078/ (accessed 28 July 2020).

Rocha, C. and Seminet, G. (eds) (2012) *Representing History, Class, and Gender in Spain and Latin America: Children and Adolescents in Film*, New York: Palgrave Macmillan.

Rocha, C. and Seminet, G. (eds) (2014) *Screening Minors in Latin American Cinema*, Plymouth: Lexington Books.

Romero, C. (2014) *La murga porteña. Historia de un viaje colectivo*, Ciudad Autónoma de Buenos Aires: Fundación CICCUS.

Ulanovsky, C. et al. (2009) *Días de radio 1960–1995*, Buenos Aires: Emecé.

Ventura, L. (2015) 'Una dinastía de artistas', in *La Nación Espectáculos*, 28 June. https://www.lanacion.com.ar/espectaculos/una-dinastia-de-artistas-nid1805569 (accessed 22 June 2020).

# Chapter 5

# *Telenovelas* and music-based youth films

Television was imported from the USA to Argentina in 1951 by media tycoon Jaime Yankelevich, who made a deal with the government to broadcast the first transmission on 17 October, as part of the national commemoration day known as 'Loyalty Day', which marks Perón's release from prison in the wake of massive labour strikes and the origin of Peronism (Taquini and Trilnick 1993: 11). The fact that Darín appeared in a TV programme for the first time just a few years after this date, when he was still a baby, makes him a true 'television native', who has observed almost literally from the cradle the challenges that the new medium represented for established actors and actresses (Valdéz 2011). By the time he reached his twenties, he had spent most of his life in television studios and was very comfortable in that environment, surpassing any of the challenges experienced by his predecessors. It was in those years, at the end of the 1970s and the beginning of the 1980s, when he became a TV celebrity, and when his small-screen fame and personality started to feed into his film and theatre performances. In relation to this should also be noted – as Tierney, Ruétalo and Ortiz do in their study on new Latin American Stardom (2017) – the important role played by television in determining stardom in national contexts. And, as they correctly explain, 'this is particularly the case' when it comes to 'Latin American television's most popular format, the *telenovela*' (2017: 165).

Most performers in Latin America who have reached a high level of public recognition and have crossed over to become big film stars have passed through the rite of passage of *telenovelas*.[1] In recent decades, with the upsurge of Latino demographics in the USA, this tendency has also had a strong impact in Hollywood. In 2013, *NBC Latino* reporter Nina Terrero explained that 'over the last ten years, *novela* exports from Mexico, Venezuela, Colombia and other Latin American countries have dominated the U.S. Hispanic television market, creating an avenue for scheming villains, lovelorn hunks and poor maids to become

Hollywood heavyweights'. Darín himself declared that he used to do *telenovelas* because back in the day it was believed that they 'guaranteed access to the international market' (Darín in Fantino 2013). This idea that *telenovelas* inform the stardom system for Latin American actors is not new (Mazziotti 1993; López 1995; Matelski 1999; Acosta-Alzuru 2003). Many scholars have pointed out how the genre has 'catalysed the development of the Latin American television industry, and, at the same time "cross-bred" new audiovisual technologies' (Martín-Barbero 1995: 276; Mazziotti 1993). As Ana M. López rightly states, 'in nations that are continuously struggling to sustain cinematic production (and often fail to do so), *telenovelas* produce indigenous star systems of great cultural (and economic) significance, for the great mass media icons are not movie stars but *telenovela* stars' (1995: 258).

The cultural value of television has been contested ever since its inception, and even more so the fame that is generated within its sphere. As James Bennett explains in his analysis of stardom and the small screen, 'television has been understood as a purveyor of "personalities"; a term the academy has subsequently gone on to understand in contradistinction to stars: ordinary rather than extraordinary, an authentic rather than unattainable image' (2011: 1). Thus, television stardom has been considered by the so-called 'founding fathers' of studies in television fame as inferior to cinema's star system (Bennett 2011: 1). In more contemporary bodies of work in media and celebrity studies, however, the TV star has acquired a higher esteem – one that goes hand-in-hand with the process of mutation of television towards a more prestigious cinematographic domain in the 'on demand' culture. Bearing this in mind, Bennett warns us to distinguish between television personalities – those who play themselves – and television actors who 'can be understood in relation to the paradigm of stardom' (2011: 2). Nevertheless, and although the notion of stardom is indeed increasingly used to refer to TV performers, Redmond and Holmes explain that 'outside of film studies, the term "celebrity" has [still] more commonly been employed', and that 'academia has to some extent persisted with boundaries which are not always reflected in *public* discourse' (2007: 8).

Thus, it should be noted that the discourses of power at play in the analysis of fame demonstrate that fame is a highly politicised concept (Braudy 1986; Marshall 1997; Redmond and Holmes 2007: 4). The distinction between stardom and celebrity speaks of a hierarchical status within the audio-visual arts – albeit one that is gradually disappearing.

Whilst 'celebrity' once was the least-valued term for its implied decline of talent, merit and achievement, it cannot be denied that today's film stars occupy – and to a certain extent depend on – the realm of celebrity culture for the perpetuation of their careers. The following sections aim to explore how Darín became a TV celebrity through a series of roles in *telenovelas* and how that fame, to borrow the words of Martín-Barbero, 'cross-bread' his big screen performances at the time. In so doing, the chapter acknowledges the terminological distinctions operating in the 1970s and 1980s, whereby Darín became a TV celebrity for being publicly recognised and not because his talent was popularly valued at that time.

## *Telenovelas* and the influence of Alberto Migré

*Telenovelas* have long been one of the most devalued and criticised audio-visual genres and yet, as expert in the field Nora Mazziotti has pointed out, people establish very strong connections with their actors and narrative (1993: 20). When analysing the differences between *telenovelas* and soap operas, Carolina Acosta-Alzuru states that the genres share precisely the paradox of being successful and disdained at the same time. Nonetheless, she emphasises the fact that the Latin American *telenovela* differs from the US soap opera in important ways, including how the former are financed by television networks and broadcast both in prime-time slots and in the afternoon block – which contributes to their success – how they drive the stardom system, and how the identities of actors are not tied to the characters they portray because they perform in various *telenovelas* (2003: 193–194; Matelski 1999). Another distinctive characteristic that should be mentioned, particularly during the decades of the 1960s to 1980s, is the important role played by scriptwriters.

Ana M. López states that 'throughout Latin America, telenovela writers, not directors, are as respected, well-known, and well-paid as telenovela stars and often better known than their literary counterparts' (1995: 260–261). This is the case of the screenwriters who were working with Darín during this period. The first *telenovela* he worked on, for instance, was called *Ayer fue mentira* [*Yesterday Was a Lie*] (Channel 9, 1975) and was written by Nené Cascallar, who at the time was one of the leading names in the genre (Ulanovsky, Itkin and Sirvén 2018).[2] Born Alicia Inés Botto (1914–1982), she had more than twenty years of experience as a stellar radio melodrama writer before her resounding success in TV.[3] By the time she worked with Darín in 1975, she had written *El amor tiene cara de mujer* [*Love Has the Face of a Woman*] (which ran on Channel 13 for eight consecutive years, from 1964 to 1971),⁴ *Cuatro hombres para Eva* [*Four Men for Eve*] (Channel 9, 1966) and *Cuatro mujeres para Adán* [*Four Women for Adam*] (Channel 9, 1966), which shot many Argentine stars to fame – including Norma Aleandro, Rodolfo Bebán, Ana María Picchio, Federico Luppi, Arnaldo André, Soledad Silveyra, Rodolfo Ranni and Evangelina Salazar. She was so well known and respected that she was given the privilege of requesting in her contracts the right to choose her own actors for the roles she created – a requirement shared by other famous *telenovela* screenwriters of the time (*Urgente24* 2009). Since radio and TV studios were so familiar for Darín that they were like 'an extension of his own house' (Darín, personal communication), and as Cascallar had coincided with Darín's parents in Radio El Mundo and Radio Splendid in the past, his choice for this *telenovela* seems to have followed the course of his family's acting kinship – reinforced, of course, with a strong audition.⁵

The story of *Ayer fue mentira* was based on a love triangle between a father, a son and a stepmother. Atilio Marinelli – Alberto Migre's preferred *galán* in the 1960s, also known as the Argentine Humphrey Bogart – played the father. Cristina Alberó, who had until then only played minor roles in cinema and TV but became a TV celebrity at the end of the 1970s – and surprised the Argentine public at the beginning of the 1990s with her cover in the Argentine edition of *Playboy* magazine – played the character of the stepmother. Darín played the son who pursued her love, in a fairly perverse turn of events (Darín, personal communication). After working with Marinelli for almost a year on this *telenovela*, and given the growing friendship between Darín's mother and Alberto Migré from their time together at Radio El Mundo (Viola 2017: 371), it is not surprising that his next step in this world was in one of Migré's *telenovelas*, called *Los que estamos solos* [*Those of Us Who Are Alone*] (Channel 13, 1976). A role he has always been grateful for (Viola 2017: 371).

Born Felipe Alberto Milletari (1931–2006), the writer, producer and director popularly known as Alberto Migré started his prolific broadcasting career working in radio when he was only a teenager (Mazziotti and Migré 1993). His greatest success took place in 1972–1973 with *Rolando Rivas, taxista* [*Rolando Rivas, Taxi Driver*] (Channel 13) – starring Claudio García Satur, Soledad Silveyra and Nora Cárpena. Many Argentine television historians consider that *telenovela* a turning point in the genre's local history (Ulanovsky, Itkin and Sirvén 2018; Viola 2017; Stiletano 2008). It had such a significant popular impact that the taxi from this *telenovela* appeared in a cameo in the film *El secreto de sus ojos* (Campanella 2009), more than thirty years on from its TV heyday (Viola 2017: 210).[6] In a recently published book on Migré's life, Darín explained that he was seventeen years old when he heard that the writer was planning to do *Los que estamos solos* with Arnaldo André and Nora Cárpena and called him for an audition:

> We were two candidates: Raúl Padovani, already a famous music star, and me. Migré put me in front of the camera and said: 'Talk to me as if I were your mother'. An unconventional request that I tried to do in my own way – in other words, I played the clown a bit. He came back and said: 'I am serious, Mr Ricardo Darín'. With that warning we started again and he seemed satisfied. But before I had left he asked me one more thing: 'I want you to go out the door, and then come back in as if you are just back from looking at the sun.' How on earth do I do that?! I don't remember how I did it, but it seems he liked it. He gave me a leading role and it was the role that made me famous. The first time I realised that someone was looking at me on the bus and thinking 'I recognise that face' was because of this *telenovela*. I laughed a lot during my *galán* period. Not at or because of the genre, but because of what they asked me to say in many *telenovelas*. But I swear that I never found any part of Migré's ridiculous.[7]
>
> [Éramos dos candidatos: Raúl Padovani, que ya era una estrella de la canción, y yo. Me puso frente a la cámara y me dijo: 'Te pido que le hables como si fuera tu madre'. Un pedido poco convencional que yo intenté a mi manera, es decir, haciéndome el payaso. Viene de nuevo y me dice: 'Estoy hablando en serio, señor Ricardo Darín'. Con ese correctivo recomienzo y aparentemente queda satisfecho. Pero antes de irme me pide otra cosa: 'Quiero que salgas por la puerta, vuelvas a entrar y me demuestres que venís de ver el sol'. ¡¿Cómo se hace eso?! No me acuerdo cómo lo resolví pero se ve que le gustó. Me dio un protagónico y ese es el papel que me dio a conocer. La primera vez que me di cuenta de que alguien me miraba en el colectivo y decía 'Esta cara la conozco', fue por esta novela. Me he reído mucho en mi etapa de galán, no del género sino de lo que me hacían decir en muchas telenovelas, pero te aseguro que no me reí jamás de las de Migré.] (Interview in Viola 2017: 371–372)

*Los que estamos solos* was also based on a love triangle, between the characters of Arnaldo André, already a big *telenovela* star, Nora Cárpena, who was also a famous TV and theatre performer by then and who had worked with Migré on several occasions, including on *Rolando Rivas*, and Darín. The *telenovela*, which was lost in the fire that hit the Channel 13 building at the beginning of the 1980s, touched upon some controversial topics for a TV programme that aired during the first year of the military dictatorship. Most significantly, the main protagonist, Jimena Casabó (Nora Cárpena), was raped, and spent the entire series recovering from the trauma, but eventually became an empowered figure, able to face her abuser and achieve justice.

After this role, which, albeit important for his celebrity status, still left him in the shadows of the two star protagonists, Darín participated in another three *telenovelas* written by Migré: *El tema es el amor* [*The Topic is Love*] (Channel 13, 1977), *Pablo en nuestra piel* [*Pablo in Our Skin*] (Channel 13, 1977) and *Vos y yo, toda la vida* [*You and Me, Always and Forever*] (Channel 13, 1978). *Pablo en nuestra piel* told the love story of a secondary school history teacher, Pablo – played by Arturo Puig – and his student, Micaela, who was played by María del Carmen Valenzuela. The pressing tension between the lovers was their class difference – she was a rich girl and he was from a humble background – rather than the fact that she was a minor and he was in a position of power as her tutor; a storyline which illuminates the moral contradictions and gender politics of the time. This was the first leading role for Valenzuela, who like Darín had been acting since she was a little girl – including performances in very popular programmes such as *Jacinta Pichimahuida* (Channel 9, 1966–1968) and *Estación Retiro* (which Darín also worked on). Darín had a secondary role with other very popular actors of this period such as Pablo Codevilla, Beba Bidart, Carlos Artigas, Susy Kent, Guillermo Rico and Antuco Telesca. All of them participated in other *telenovelas* written by Migré, including ones where Darín had a part. In fact, Arturo Puig and María del Carmen Valenzuela became the must-see couple by the end of the 1970s, and they were the leading protagonists of all three remaining *telenovelas* of what we can call 'the Migré period' in Darín's career.

Although we can trace in these works a tight network of acting kinship that has certainly contributed to an ongoing presence on the small screen for Darín during the challenging first years of the dictatorship, he was also slowly gaining the respect of his peers. Alberto Migré himself emphasised his talent when he exclaimed that Darín 'was undisciplined; he arrived at the time he wanted, he laughed a lot during the shooting process; when he got together with Pablo Codevilla we had to separate them because they were unbearable. But I put up with it because I knew he was good' ['Era indisciplinado, eso sí. Llegaba a la hora que quería, se reía mucho en las grabaciones, cuando se juntaba con Pablo Codevilla había que separarlos porque se ponían insoportables, pero yo lo toleraba porque sabía que era bueno'] (quoted in Riera 2000). Nonetheless, as will be seen in the following sections, it was going to take a few more years for the general public to recognise this talent and to see beyond the amenable and comedic face of a 'minor' *telenovela* actor.

## Other TV series and *telenovelas* from this period

Alberto Migré continued working with both Arturo Puig and Maria del Carmen Valenzuela, who were successfully paired with other partners. Nonetheless, by 1979 Darín was at a standstill with Migré, so he moved on to work on other projects. *Una escalera al cielo* [*A Stairway to Heaven*] (Channel 9, 1979) was written by Gerardo Galván, who belonged to a new generation of *telenovela* writers (less visible in the media than Cascallar or Migré). This *telenovela* is described by Darín as of the 'costumbrista barrial' genre – one that depicted the way of life of a local neighbourhood (personal communication) – and is considered by some critics as another

**Figure 5.1** Ricardo Darín and Alicia Zanca in *Una escalera al cielo* (Channel 9, 1979, Grandes de la Escena Nacional Archive)

turning point in Darín's rise to celebrity status (Zuliani 2001; Pablo 2018), even though the actual success of the programme was moderate (Nielsen 2006: 254). It followed the love story of Elena (Selva Alemán) and Damián (Jorge Mayorano), a couple who dreamed of having a house with stairs that led to a terrace where you could see the sky – hence its title. In parallel to the leading couple's story, other relationships were explored, including the dramas faced by the couple played by Darín and Alicia Zanca. Cast members included an array of established performers, such as Pablo Alarcón, Luis Aranda, Carmen Vallejo and Luisa Kuliok.

According to Darín, the success of this *telenovela* and the popular acceptance of the couple he formed with Alicia Zanca led director Juan David Elicetche to create a new *telenovela* with them as leading protagonists: *Me caso con vos* [*I Will Marry You*] (Channel 13, 1981) (personal communication; Zuliani 2001). Part of the couple's popular recognition was also due to the fact that they appeared together in yet another secondary role in a 1980 *telenovela* called *Un día 32 en San Telmo* [*A Day 32 in San Telmo*] (Channel 9), which was written, like *Me caso con vos*, by the acclaimed *telenovela* screenwriter Delia González Márquez.[8] In his history of Argentine television, Jorge Nielsen states that *Me caso con vos* was a remake of a prior success written by González Márquez called *Muchacha italiana viene a casarse* [*An Italian Girl Arrives to Get Married*] (1969) – which Darín's mother worked on – and that it was scheduled at the very inopportune time slot of 12.30 in the afternoon (2007: 20). Darín describes that *telenovela* as such a resounding failure – it only lasted three months – that both him and Zanca used to laugh at the prospect of being kicked out of the studio (Darín, personal communication).

Amidst the ups and downs of these series of *telenovelas*, Darín appeared in a five-episode mini-series entitled *Casa de muñecas* [*Doll's House*] (Channel 13, 1980). Eduardo Rozas of IMDb explains that the series was 'based on Henrik Ibsen's famous play and produced at the centenary of his work. [It was] a free version of the original play that extended and re-elaborated the conflicts of its characters. The first mini-series ever produced in color [sic] television in Argentina, [which] certainly represents one of the most important projects of that country's television serving the best of universal literature.'[9] The production company behind the project, RZS – owned by the brothers Fernando, Eduardo and Gustavo Rozas[10] – started working on this programme at the beginning of the military dictatorship in 1976. Columbia Pictures Television was in charge of its distribution and initiated long negotiations to show the programme in

Argentina. The constant struggles to try to sell the series to the channels controlled by the military led to its delayed broadcast in 1980, and it was then only accepted for scheduling at the unpopular time of Sunday at midnight.[11] It was directed by Diana Álvarez, and played by Dora Baret, who had an extensive career in cinema and television – including working with Susana Giménez and Carlos Monzón in the famous film *La Mary* (Tinayre 1974) – and Alberto Argibay, one of the most important actors of the '1960s generation'.

The year 1980 proved to be quite a prolific year for our star. Jorge Nielsen has explained that one of the best programmes on TV that year was the one written by Sergio De Cecco called *Vivir con todo* [*To Live Fully*] (2006: 291), in which Darín played a surgeon. There is almost no evidence of this programme in any database connected to Darín. Nielsen described the story as that of four young men raised in the same neighbourhood and who had shared life experiences – the other three characters were a truck driver (Pablo Codevilla), a lawyer (Adrián Ghio) and an architect (Germán Krauss). The critic Alfredo Andrés noted in the newspaper *La Opinión* at the time that 'the most important aspect of De Cecco's work is its authenticity ( ) It is about people from the Buenos Aires of today, diverse in terms of the cultural differences that separate one personality from the other, but the same when it comes to the place and time they are living in' ['Lo fundamental de esta presentación de la obra de De Cecco es la autenticidad ( ) Se trata de gente de Buenos Aires de hoy, distinta en cuanto a las diferencias culturales que median entre un carácter y otro, pero unificables en cuanto al lugar y el tiempo en que viven'] (quoted in Nielsen 2006: 291).

Diana Álvarez, the director of *Casa de muñecas*, would also direct Darín's next two projects: the *telenovela Juan sin nombre* [*Juan Without a Name*] (Channel 9, 1982) and the series *Nosotros y los miedos* [*Us and Fears*] (Channel 9, 1982–1983). The former was written by another star writer of the period, Abel Santa Cruz, who worked with Migré and Cascallar in radio and had an impressive curriculum in different media – most significantly his success in TV with series like *Jacinta Pichimahuida* (1970), and *telenovelas* of the caliber of *Había una vez un circo* [*Once Upon a Time there was a Circus*] (1972) and *Andrea Celeste* (1979), starring the great child star Andrea del Boca. *Juan sin nombre* had Carlos Calvo and Luisina Brando as the leading couple. This was the second time Calvo and Darín coincided on the small screen, having previously worked together in 1978 in a short-lived family series called *La familia*

*Super Star* [*The SuperStar Family*], in which they both had minor roles.¹²
Even though their work on TV in this period was neither outstanding nor
unforgettable, Darín and Calvo managed to use their modest visibility
on TV to become big celebrities on the theatre stage in Mar del Plata
under the label of '*galancitos*' – as will be explored in the next chapter.

## Love is in the air: youth films

While he was busy working on TV, Darín also started a very active period
on the big screen: he participated in five films released in 1979 and three
shown in 1980. All these films built on his roles as a *telenovela* actor and
profited from his constant off-screen presence in the tabloids due to his
new relationship with big Argentine star Susana Giménez. Some critics
have declared that their romance – which started in 1978 and ended in
1987 – was the most talked-about topic in the 1980s tabloids (Sarasqueta
2016; *La Nación* 2000).¹³ In this respect, Darín's career seems to have

**Figure 5.2**   Cover of the satirical magazine *Humor Registrado*, nº 65, September 1981, courtesy of *Revista Humor*.

followed a similar path of other Latin American stars of the period. Olivia Cosentino, for instance, has analysed the trajectory of Mexican star Lucerito in the 1980s, and emphasises that the film industry of the time in that country was transitioning to 'a more horizontally integrated structure firmly tied to other types of media' (2016: 39). Accordingly, Lucerito's stardom in youth films depended on her work on TV – *telenovelas* in particular – the music industry, and her off-screen romances.[14] Both of Cosentino's conclusions can be applied to Darín's career and the Argentine industry of the time.

Continuing to highlight the connections between different media and creative platforms, scholars Pablo Piedras and Sophie Dufays state that in the 1960s–1980s Latin America was going through a period whereby the relationship between cinema and popular music was being re-articulated (2018: 246). In tune with what was happening in the USA, 'the common cross-promotion of films and records [was intended to benefit] both industries in almost equal measure' (Reay 2004: 95; Piedras and Dufays 2018: 246). These were the years before the emergence of MTV – established in 1981 – and the upsurge of the videoclip. While Mexico's youth films contracted pop stars like Luis Miguel, Lucero and Gloria Trevi (Podalsky 2008: 144–145), in Argentina the industry included artists like Sandro, Palito Ortega, Leonardo Favio – mostly in the 1960s and 1970s – and Cacho Castaña. This last was one of the leading figures in the films in which Darín appeared, which are popularly referred to as 'the love films', not only because they include the word in the title, but also because they are about romantic relationships and love songs. In this sense, *Los éxitos del amor* [*Love's Hits*] (Siro 1979), *La carpa del amor* [*Love's Tent*] (Porter 1979), *La playa del amor* [*Love's Beach*] (Aristarain 1980) and *La discoteca del amor* [*Love's Disco*] (Aristarain 1980) follow the same theme of the *telenovelas*, but in a light-hearted and comedic way.[15]

These music-driven youth films were part of the conservative cultural project that supported the neoliberal economic strategies being implemented by the dictatorship at this time. One of the aims of the films was indeed to promote a group of singers and songs to the general public to boost sales. Cacho Castaña, for instance, always had a dedicated part of the plot where he sang one of his songs. In *Los éxitos . . .* the disco song 'Love is in the air', sung by John Paul Young, is constantly played in the portable cassette recorder carried by one of the protagonists. At one point he challenges a street kid and accuses him of having no idea how important the song is, and the kid replies with a rehearsed speech giving all of the details behind the song, which was distributed by one of the film's producers. In this regard, it should be noted that these films were produced between film companies Aries Cinematográfica Argentina – owned by Héctor Olivera and Fernando Ayala – Estudios Baires Films S.A., and the record label Microfón, in a clear attempt to cross-promote and integrate other media in their film productions.

As mentioned above, these types of films were produced in other parts of Latin America at that time too, with various levels of engagement from TV conglomerates and record companies (Piedras and Dufays 2018). The renewal that cinema experienced due to the incorporation of TV celebrities and personalities was accompanied in Argentina by the prerogative of promoting the family values and moral standards of the dictatorship. It was not only the laid-back comedic 'love films' that echoed this tendency, however, but also the other films in which Darín participated during this period, including: *La rabona* [*Truancy*] (David 1979), *La fiesta de todos* [*Everybody's Party*] (Renán 1979), *Juventud sin barreras* [*Youth Without Limits*] (Montes 1979), and *La canción de Buenos Aires* [*Buenos Aires Song*] (Siro 1980). Darín once stated that performers of the time were instructed to keep to a certain light-hearted comedic style: 'I listened to directors, both in cinema and television, that said to me "no, lighter, lighter, not heavy. . . ." And I replied: "Well, but this character has lost his mother and. . . ." "Yes, yes, but that's not important" ['Yo he escuchado a directores, tanto en cine como en televisión, que me decían "no, livianito, livianito, que no pese . . ." Y yo: "Bueno, pero resulta que a este personaje se le murió la madre y. . . ." "Sí, sí, pero eso no es lo importante"'] (*La Nación* 2000).

The exception to this style – or rather its parodying – seems to be *La discoteca del amor*. Adolfo Aristarain had the experience of directing *La playa . . .* and wanted to upgrade the love series as much as possible within the limitations imposed by producers. On this matter, Darín explains how staff members used to gather in the mornings of the shooting of *La discoteca . . .* to rewrite parts of the script. Aristarain told them 'OK, we have to promote some singers, fine, but let's do it in the best possible way. It is not necessary that a character says: "Let's listen to this song while we have a drink"' ['Ok, hay que promocionar unos cantantes, perfecto, pero hagámoslo de la mejor manera posible. No es necesario que un personaje diga: "Escuchemos este tema mientras tomamos una copa"'] (*La Nación* 2000). While the music performances remained almost intact, the connecting plot was undoubtedly more compelling: an old private detective was hired to solve the upsurge in music piracy that was threatening the survival of a record company. Darín played the role of a radio journalist, Eddie Ulmer, who, together with his radio partner (Stella Maris Lanzani), helped the private detective and his associate to disclose the corrupt network led by a dangerous gang. In 1980 the newspaper *La Opinión* described the film as different within its genre, but no less funny and with no betrayal of the regular audience of the series.

In order to make the most of the success of these films, one executive from the music label offered Darín the chance to record his own long play. They hired a music teacher, but the producer then suggested Darín could instead recite poems with background music. That was the origin of the record entitled *De a dos* [*In Pairs*] released in 1979 (*La Nación* 2000). It included songs/poems on topics related to Darín's everyday life, such as *Mamá hoy soy otro* [*Mother, Today I Am Different*], dedicated to his mother Renée, *Soy un buen tipo* [*I Am a Good Guy*] and *Eramos tan lindos* [*We Were So Beautiful*], all related to an old girlfriend, Martita (*La Nación* 2000). The musical arrangements were done by Emilio Kauderer, an award-winning Argentine composer, who worked on *La discoteca*... and years later composed the music of several acclaimed films, including *El*

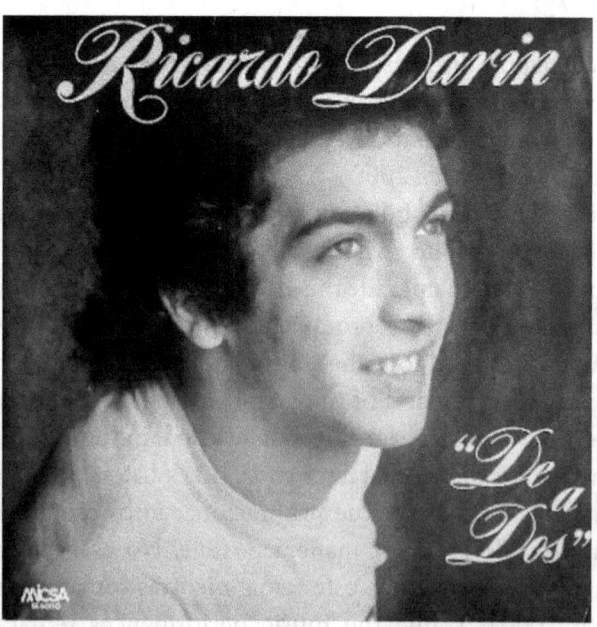

**Figure 5.3** Record cover *De a dos* (1979)

*secreto de sus ojos*. Other actors were also following this trend for recording long plays alongside the release of their films or TV programmes. Arturo Puig, for instance, had already recorded four LPs by the time he worked again with Darín in the play *Sugar* (1986–1987), and Andrea del Boca had six singles out when she worked with Darín in the *telenovela Estrellita mía* [*My Little Star*] in 1987.

## More than a TV celebrity

Although he followed producers' advice on market tendencies, and accepted multiple job offers in roles that were far from memorable – a period that could be called, to borrow a phrasing from Luis Buñuel, 'alimenticio' [alimentary] – Darín started to gain peer recognition by the beginning of 1980s. As discussed, *telenovelas* gave him public visibility, and his off-screen relationship with Susana Giménez sealed his celebrity status for the media. Nonetheless, it was his participation in 1982 in the TV programme *Nosotros y los miedos* that showed his star quality to a general audience. Directed by Diana Álvarez, the programme consisted of a series of single episodes focusing on a revolutionary idea for TV at the time: 'Our Fears' (Nielsen 2007: 48). Cast members included an array of established and respected performers such as Miguel Angel Solá, Aldo Barbero, Rodolfo Ranni, Olga Zubarry, Graciela Dufau, Ana María Picchio and Cristina Murta.

Darín is convinced that he owes his participation in *Nosotros . . .* to Diana Álvarez, who fought with the directors of Channel 9 to include him. Up until then he was considered a second-hand '*galancito*'/*telenovela* actor, and they could not see him fitting in with the concept of the show nor with those 'serious' actors. Darín has previously said that 'the episode where I played a drug addict' was very important for him. 'It was expected that I would play that part as some sort of seething amoeba [. . .] But instead I played it like a real person. It was then when people in the street started looking at me differently, to respect me a little bit more' ['Para mí fue muy importante un capítulo en el que hice de drogadicto. Se esperaba que hiciera una especie de ameba pululante (. . .) y no hice eso, sino una persona de verdad. Ahí me empezaron a mirar de otra manera, a respetarme un poco más'] (quoted in Riera 2000). Indeed, in his history of Argentine television, Jorge Nielsen (2007) acknowledged this period of Darín's career as a moment when 'a *galancito* tries to stand out' ['un "galancito" intenta imponerse'] and signalled *Nosotros y los miedos* as a steering moment: 'Until then considered a *"galancito"*, Ricardo Darín started to be respected' ['Hasta entonces un "galancito", Ricardo Darín comenzó a ser respetado'] (2007: 50).

Darín's approach to the character of *Nosotros* . . ., which went against what was expected of him, showed his love for the profession more than the spotlight. He continued with a few more roles in *telenovelas*, most significantly next to Andrea del Boca in the popular *Estrellita mía* (Channel 11, 1987),[16] and then coupled with the highly successful Venezuelan actress Grecia Colmenares in *Rebelde* [*Rebel*] (Channel 9, 1989), but continued mixing those rather formulaic roles with more art-house productions. It was in this last *telenovela* that critics of the time recognised Darín's wealth of experience. Néstor Gutiérrez Mónaco at the newspaper *Diario Popular* said that the 'expressionless Colmenares sometimes infects Darín, who still manages to show his expertise' (quoted in Nielsen 2008: 204). *Telenovelas* would continue to provide income and celebrity status for another decade, but Darín was already demonstrating that fame and money were not really his primary aim. As Nielsen declares, Darín was far from being an established *telenovela* actor as were figures such as Bebán, García Satur, André, Bermúdez, Corrado, or the more contemporary Pablo Echarri and Facundo Arana (2007: 20). Darín was diversifying his career, moving away from the comfort of the *telenovela*-celebrity personality label.

## Notes

1. Examples include the cases of Salma Hayek, Gael García Bernal, Sônia Braga, Diego Luna, Wagner Moura, Diego Boneta and Sofía Vergara.
2. There are two other *telenovelas* prior to this one that tend to be wrongly associated with Darín: *Soledad Monsalvo* (Channel 11, 1960) and *Abelardo Pardales* (Channel 9, 1969). We know from Darín himself that it was his father who worked on those two programmes and not him (personal communication).
3. Further information on Cascallar's broadcasting years can be found in Ehrick (2015).
4. Considered to be the most successful *telenovela* of the 1960s (Viola 2017: 37; Ulanovsky, Itkin and Sirvén 2018).
5. Darín remembers that all staff members working on this *telenovela* knew his parents for years, so much so that he felt he was treated as if he were the nephew or son of many of them, blurring the lines of professionalism (Darín, personal communication).
6. According to Liliana Viola, Migré's signature style also appears in the most famous scene of this film, when Irene (Soledad Villamil) is standing on the platform and runs towards the train that is taking away the love of her life (Ricardo Darín). The extra-diegetic music composed by Federico Jusid is inspired by the Chopinesque

style used by Migré and, according to the author, that run and the facial expressions of both protagonists are 'totally Migré's style' (Viola 2017: 210).

7. In a personal interview Darín mentioned that the role was actually meant to go to Raúl Taibo, who was gaining popularity at that time, but that Migré had some sort of disagreement with him and so started the 'pruebas' – castings – through which he was selected (Darín, personal communication).

8. The leading couple was played by Miguel Ángel Solá and Gabriela Gilli. The story was based in a bar in San Telmo – a neighbourhood in Buenos Aires – where different love stories took place, including that of Darín and Zanca. Jorge Nielsen states that González Márquez wrote four mini-series for Channel 9 in 1980, with three of those including Darín as a member of the cast: *Daniel y Cecilia* [*Daniel and Cecilia*], which ended abruptly when the leading actor, Claudio Levrino, passed away; *Casados ayer* [*Married Yesterday*], with Luisina Brando and Aldo Barbero; *Un día 32 . . .* [*A Day 32*], which according to the scholar was not very popular. The fourth programme was called *De profesión ama de casa* [*My Profession: Housewife*], which González Márquez herself decided to end in spite of its growing popularity (Nielsen 2006: 290).

9. See the IMDb webpage for further details: https://www.imdb.com/title/tt0498422/ (accessed 7 August 2020).

10. This company was the first to produce and export colour TV in Argentina. For further information on their history, see: https://www.facebook.com/rztelevision/ (accessed 21 August 2020).

11. Darín has mentioned that the Rozas brothers had to face the difficulty of a newly established state colour production company, EAM '78 – created to broadcast the FIFA World Cup of 1978 – that did not want any competition. The constant struggles to get their products across made it impossible for them to cover the costs of equipment and they were soon bankrupt (Darín, personal communication).

12. Darín does not remember working with Calvo on this programme. He mentioned that the important figure there was Carlos Estrada (personal communication). He also coincided in this series with the Serantes sisters, with whom he worked in *Estación Retiro* [*Retiro Station*].

13. When it comes to the couple's visibility in the media Darín said, 'in our case, there were even street surveys being done about us (. . .) For me she was never "Susana Giménez". She was Susana, a girl with whom I played cards (. . .) maybe she felt comfortable with me, free from that burden . . . We were both lonely and we fell in love; as simple as that . . . And maybe our romance lasted many years because the fact that everyone felt uncomfortable with it united us' ['En nuestro caso, llegaron a hacer encuestas callejeras (. . .) para mí ella jamás fue "Susana Giménez". Era Susana, una mina con la que jugaba al truco (. . .) quizá se sentía cómoda conmigo, liberada de esa carga . . . Los dos estábamos muy solos y nos enamoramos; es así . . . Y tal vez nuestra pareja duró tantos años porque nos unía que a todo el mundo le molestara'] (*La Nación* 2000).

14. The youth films in Mexico were produced by the giant media conglomerate Televisa. Lucerito married singer Miguel Mijares – her co-star in the film *Run Away with Me* – in a televised wedding that attracted 40 million viewers (Cosentino 2016: 38).

15. One of the last titles in the series was the film *Ritmo, amor y primavera* [*Rhythm, Love and Spring*] (Carreras 1981), which included most of the cast of the previous films, such as Cacho Castaña, Mónica Gonzaga and Tincho Zabala, but Carlos Calvo took Darín's place.
16. It was also directed by Diana Álvarez.

# References

Acosta-Alzuru, C. (2003) 'Tackling the Issues: Meaning Making in a *Telenovela*', in *Popular Communication*, 1.4, pp. 193–215.

Bennett, J. (2011) *Television Personalities. Stardom and the Small Screen*, Abingdon: Routledge.

Braudy, L. (1986) *The Frenzy of Renown. Fame and Its History*, New York: Vintage Books.

Cosentino, O. (2016) 'Televisa Born and Raised. Lucerito's Stardom in 1980s Mexican Media', in *The Velvet Light Trap*, 78, pp. 38–52.

Ehrick, C. (2015) *Radio and the Gendered Soundscape: Women and Broadcasting in Argentina and Uruguay, 1930–1950*, Cambridge: Cambridge University Press.

Fantino, A. (2013). *Animales Sueltos*, 18 September, Buenos Aires: America TV. https://www.youtube.com/watch?v=30SH75EtxcM (accessed 6 August 2020).

*La Nación* (2000) 'Ricardo Darín', in *La Nación espectáculos*, 1 October. https://www.lanacion.com.ar/espectaculos/ricardo-darin-nid585078 (accessed 6 May 2020).

*La Opinión* (1980) 'La discoteca del amor', *La Opinión*, 5 August.

López, A. M. (1995) 'Our Welcomed Guests: Telenovelas in Latin America', in Allen, R. C. (ed.), *To Be Continued... Soap Operas Around the World*, London and New York: Routledge.

Marshall, P. D. (1997) *Celebrity and Power. Fame in Contemporary Culture*, Minneapolis and London: University of Minnesota Press.

Martín-Barbero, J. (1995) 'Memory and Form in the Latin American Soap Opera', in Allen, R. C. (ed.), *To Be Continued... Soap Operas Around the World*, London and New York: Routledge.

Matelski, M. (1999). *Soap Operas Worldwide: Cultural and Serial Realities*, Jefferson, NC: McFarland.

Mazziotti, N. (comp.) (1993) *El espectáculo de la pasión. Las telenovelas latinoamericanas*, Buenos Aires: Colihue.

Mazziotti, N. and Migré, A. (1993) *Soy como de la familia: Conversaciones de Nora Mazziotti con Alberto Migré*, Buenos Aires: Editorial Sudamericana.

Nielsen, J. (2006) *La magia de la television Argentina 3, 1971/1980*, Buenos Aires: Ediciones del Jilguero.

Nielsen, J. (2007) *La magia de la television Argentina 4, 1981/1985*, Buenos Aires: Ediciones del Jilguero.

Nielsen, J. (2008) *La magia de la television Argentina 5, 1986/1990*, Buenos Aires: Ediciones del Jilguero

Pablo, J. (2018) 'Una escalera al cielo (1979)', in *recordaresvivir* blog. https://www.tapatalk.com/groups/recordaresvivir/una-escalera-al-cielo-1979-selva-aleman-jorge-mayo-t76327.html (accessed 20 August 2020).

Piedras, P. and Dufays, S. (2018) 'Espacios nocturnos y canción popular en el cine latinoamericano de los años 70', in Piedras, P. and Dufays, S. (eds), *Conozco la canción. Melodías populares en los cines posclásicos de América Latina y Europa*, Ciudad Autónoma de Buenos Aires: Libraria.

Podalsky, L. (2008) 'The Young, the Damned, and the Restless. Youth in Contemporary Mexican Cinema', in *Framework: The Journal of Cinema and Media*, 49.1, pp. 144–160.

Reay, P. (2004) *Music in Film: Soundtracks and Synergy*, London and New York: Wallflower Press.

Redmond, S. and Holmes, S. (2007) 'Introduction: What's in a Reader?', in *Stardom and Celebrity: A Reader*, Los Angeles and London: SAGE Publications.

Riera, D. (2000) 'El golpe perfecto. Ricardo Darín', in *Rolling Stones, La Nación Espectáculos*, 1 October. https://www.lanacion.com.ar/espectaculos/ricardo-darin-nid585078/ (accessed 28 July 2020).

Sarasqueta, A. (2016) 'Susana Giménez y Ricardo Darín: Detalles del romance más comentado de los "80"', in *Guioteca*, 20 April. https://www.guioteca.com/espectaculo-argentino/susana-gimenez-y-ricardo-darin-detalles-del-romance-mas-comentado-de-los-80/ (accessed 22 August 2020).

Stiletano, M. (2008) 'Desde mañana, a las 22, por Volver. Rolando Rivas, un taxista de regreso en las calles', in *La Nación*, 31 March. https://www.lanacion.com.ar/espectaculos/television/rolando-rivas-un-taxista-de-regreso-en-las-calles-nid999951/ (accessed 18 August 2020).

Taquini, G. and Trilnick, C. (1993) 'Una memoria del video en Argentina', in *Buenos Aires Video V*, Buenos Aires: ICI.

Terrero, N. (2013) 'For Latino Stars, *Novelas* Can be Fast Track to Hollywood Crossover success', in NBC Latino. https://nbclatino.com/2013/01/02/for-latino-stars-novelas-can-be-fast-track-to-hollywood-crossover-success/#s:ermenegildo-zegna-ny-passion-for-silk-event-hosted-by-gildo-zegna (accessed 6 August 2020).

Tierney, D., Ruétalo, V. and Ortiz, R. C. (2017) 'New Latin American Stardom', in D'Lugo, M., López, A. M. and Podalsky, L. (eds), *The Routledge Companion to Latin American Cinema*, London and New York: Routledge Taylor and Francis Group.

Ulanovsky, C., Itkin, S. and Sirvén, P. (2018) *Estamos en el aire: Una historia de la televisión en la Argentina*, Ciudad Autónoma de Buenos Aires: Ediciones B, Libro Digital, EPUB.

*Urgente24* (2009) 'De Jorge Barreiro a Nené Cascallar: Aquellas tardes de canal 13 . . .', in *Urgente24*, 25 March. https://archivo.urgente24.com/49381-de-jorge-barreiro-a-nene-cascallar-aquellas-tardes-de-canal-13 (accessed 17 August 2020).

Valdéz, M. (2011) 'Ricardo Darín, más que humano', unpublished paper delivered at Festival de cine latinoamericano, Munich, 14 July.

Viola, L. (2017) *Migré. El maestro de las telenovelas que revolucionó la educación sentimental de un país*, Ciudad Autónoma de Buenos Aires: Sudamericana.

Zuliani, S. (2001) 'Con éxito garantizado', in *La Voz del Interior*, 10 September. http://archivo.lavoz.com.ar/2001/0910/suplementos/temas/nota54410_1.htm (accessed 20 August 2020).

## Chapter 6

# Theatre performances

The complex relationship between acting and stardom depends, according to Barry King, on the mediation of the labour market (1985: 27). Acting as a discursive practice in film and television produces a particular kind of performance strategy that must continually 'negotiate a way through the forcefield of other practices' (King 1985: 27). In Richard Dyer's words, in order to become a star those other practices are located 'at the point of intersection of public demand (the star as a phenomenon of consumption) and producer initiative (the star as a phenomenon of production)' (1998: 10). While the applicability of the term 'star' to both stage and screen performers is contested,[1] it is widely accepted among actors that 'stage acting provides a yardstick against which to evaluate acting on screen' (King 1985: 28). Darín himself is of this opinion. For him, 'theatre is the place of resistance for the actor. It provides time to experiment, research, to make mistakes, and it is there where great things are created' ['El teatro es un lugar de resistencia del actor. Aquí hay tiempo para experimentar, investigar, para la equivocación, donde nacen cosas muy buenas'] (quoted in Paredes 2019).

King further explored this assumption that it is on the stage that the actor is best placed to realise her/his creative potential as a result of multiple factors, including the performer's desire to be associated with an 'elite institution' – the 'great' tradition of the stage – and the claim of the profession's autonomy (1985: 28). With respect to this he said that 'it is in the theatre that actors have the greatest degree of direct control over the signifying direction and grain of their performance – even if this control is only unevenly realised in practice' (1985: 33). Darín also praises the power of self-control granted by a live performance in front of an audience when he explained that 'in cinema, in television and in other formats you have the possibility of cutting and doing it again; in theatre you can't. That is what it makes it something unique, and for actors this becomes a blessing' ['En cine, en televisión y otros formatos tienes la posibilidad de cortar e ir de nuevo, en el teatro no, eso lo convierte en algo único y para los actores deviene una bendición] (Redacción digital

2019). Moreover, as Grotowski (2002) states, the preference for stage over screen responds to a perceived centrality of the actor in theatre, to the belief that the theatre relies on his/her body, voice and gestures to fulfil the process of representation (King 1985: 35).

Grotowski's 'poor' theatre principles are mentioned here because they are similar to Darín's approach to the stage: 'Theatre can be done with nothing: a good idea, a good play at hand, a group of actor friends and you can put on a play in your backyard, while other formats require many other things' ['el teatro se puede hacer sin nada: una buena idea, una buena obra entre manos, un grupo de amigos actores y puedes hacer una función teatral en un patio, mientras los demás formatos necesitan muchas otras cosas'] (Redacción digital 2019). When Susana Giménez interviewed Darín in 2010 in her TV programme on Telefé, she could not understand why he was reviving the play *Art* in Buenos Aires at a moment when he was having so much success in cinema.[2] He simply replied that 'it is theatre that makes me happy (...) And, besides, we also love seeing each other, laughing, eating out together after the rehearsals ...' ['es el teatro lo que me hace feliz (...) Además nos gusta encontrarnos, juntarnos, ir a comer juntos después ...']. These ludic aspects of live performances, the sense of camaraderie and sociality, were not mentioned by King and Grotowski, but they are clearly also pivotal to Darín's inclination towards the stage, as is the case for many other contemporary performers. In a more recent interview, he also declared that 'theatre is the most vivid form of communication I have' ['El teatro es la forma más viva que yo encuentro para comunicarme'] (Barbeta 2019).

While Darín's love for and commitment to the theatre is evident in the above statements, not much has been written on the topic. Even though the list of plays he has participated in is not as extensive as his works in film and television – please refer to the Appendices for further information – theatre has been a constant presence throughout his career, unlike other practices.[3] Bearing this in mind, the following sections will explore different plays and performance strategies implemented by Darín on the stage in order to negotiate his journey through theatre, television and cinema. His constant movement from stage to screen shows his capacity for 're-skilling', as King would say (1985: 33), demonstrating his great versatility as an actor. It also demonstrates his ability to interpret the demands of the market when it comes to using his own image. Thus, particular attention will be paid to those plays that have contributed to the construction of his stardom, thanks to his negotiation of the maze of different practices.

## The 'galancito' period

Although Darín comes from a family of performers and he has been on a stage since he was a baby, the first actual performance in a play that he recalls as being of significance – and most likely his 'debut' as stage performer – was the romantic comedy *El tema es el amor* [*The Topic is Love*] (1978), written by Alberto Migré and directed by Diana Álvarez (*La Nación* 2000).[4] Bearing the same title of the *telenovela* shown on Channel 13 the year before – where Darín also had a role – the play starred, like its TV counterpart, Arturo Puig and María del Carmen Valenzuela in the leading roles. It appeared in several theatres in Buenos Aires that year, but the most iconic performances took place in a theatre located in the neighbourhood of Las Flores called Teatro Fénix (Darín, personal communication).[5] According to the testimony of a café owner near the theatre, the area was deserted. One day Alberto Migré had a coffee there and started asking a few questions about the Fénix. When they told him that the place was dead, he replied: 'Start buying food because you'll get very busy' – and so they did. He ended up resuscitating not just the theatre, but the whole neighbourhood thanks to this play (Viola 2017: 374).

Darín's next venture on stage was in the hectic year of 1980. Amidst his work in three films of the 'love' series and three TV programmes, he participated in *La vida fácil* [*The Easy Life*]. According to Darín, the play itself was a purely commercial attempt to launch '*los galancitos*' [the little gentlemen] (personal communication). In an interview at the newspaper *La Capital*, Raúl Taibo, who belonged to the *galancitos*, explained that:

> The group of *los galancitos* was originated thanks to a play called *La vida fácil* (in which, among others, Ricardo Darín performed), and it was from that moment in the theatre season in Mar del Plata where the label of '*los galancitos*' was born, because we were competing with the senior *galanes* that were performing in the theatre around the corner. Those *galanes* at the time were (Guillermo) Bredeston, (Rodolfo) Bebán, and (Claudio) García Satur.
>
> [El grupo de los galancitos se originó gracias a una obra que se llamó 'La vida fácil' (en la que entre otros actuaba Ricardo Darín), y a partir de ahí en la temporada de teatro en Mar del Plata nació el rótulo de 'Los galancitos' porque estábamos en competencia con los galanes que estaban en el teatro de la vuelta. Los galanes en ese entonces eran (Guillermo) Bredeston, (Rodolfo) Bebán, (Claudio) García Satur.] (*La Capital* 2015)

According to the magazine *TV Semanal*, which reported the challenges faced by the group during the rehearsals, the play was directed by Fernando Siro and written by Alberto Alejandro for Ricardo Darín, Alicia Zanca – with whom Darín was working at the time as a sweetheart couple on TV – Raúl Taibo, Gustavo Rey, Virginia Falad and Pablo Codevilla (*TV Semanal* 1980).[6] Darín, in a TV interview by José De Zer in 1984, stated that they did not mind the nickname of *galancitos* at the beginning, since it was a way to differentiate them from the other group of actors that were on the stage in Mar del Plata, but then with time he said the title became derogatory. In fact, the interviewer said with surprise at some point that the *galancitos* have demonstrated that it is possible to be actors and not just a pretty face – a comment sparked most likely by the play *La extraña pareja* [*The Odd Couple*] (1984), which Darín was doing at the time with Carlos Calvo.[7] What this interview evinced, as well, is that the label of *los galancitos* was a useful marketing strategy that lasted for a few years, partly fuelled by the off-stage and off-screen media presence of its members' private lives.[8] When remembering that upsurge in celebrity status, Darín declared that

> It was crazy, a sudden state of visibility in the public scenario, incited by a certain kind of press that was interested in the reunion of a series of young actors and actresses, some of them not so novice, because the truth is that Carlos Olivieri, Raúl Taibo, Gustavo Rey and me, who constituted that initial group, we were very young but also senior in the profession.
>
> [Eso fue una locura, un estado de súbita aparición en la escena pública, motorizado por cierta prensa ante la reunión de una serie de actores y actrices jóvenes, en algunos casos no tan noveles, porque en realidad Carlos Olivieri, Raúl Taibo, Gustavo Rey y yo, que éramos los que conformábamos aquel primer grupo, éramos muy jóvenes pero a la vez veteranos dentro del oficio.] (Quoted in González Acevedo 2005: 53)

As we will explore in more depth in Chapter 11, this visibility allowed them to participate in other public events – which certainly contributed to the lasting impact of the group – such as the charity football and tennis games that were generally attended by screaming fans of *los galancitos* across the country. But the *galancito* label was not always a guarantee of success. The next play Darín participated in, *Hasta mañana, si Dios quiere* [*See you Tomorrow, if it be God's Will*] (1982) was a 'resounding failure' that only lasted one summer in Mar del Plata (Darín, personal communication). It was a comedy starring Raúl Taibo, Gachi Ferrari, Virginia Hanglin, directed by Rodolfo Ranni, which took place in a theatre outside the commercial circuit called Teatro Alberdi. Darín recalls that the only time they managed to gather a good crowd was when they decided to put the prices of the tickets up, only to go back to the normal fairly empty theatre for the very next show (personal communication).

Conversely, as José De Zer's interview suggested, *La extraña pareja*, the play written by Neil Simon shown in Mar del Plata in 1984 and, the following year, *Taxi* (1985), the adaptation of the English play *Run for your Wife* written by Ray Cooney and directed by Carlos Moreno, were extremely successful. Both plays starred Carlos Calvo and Ricardo Darín, who were considered at one point to be the foremost figures of the *galancitos* (Ladrón de Guevara 2019; *La Nación* 2020). According to the press, *Taxi* began quite slowly, with low attendance, but thanks to favourable reviews it soon became one of the most popular plays of the season in Mar del Plata. This allowed them to move the show to Buenos Aires once the summer was over (*Clarín.com* 2003).[9] The play has been put on in Argentina on several occasions since, with different actors in the leading roles. Carlos Calvo, for instance, worked on one version called *Taxi 1. El original* [*Taxi 1. The Original*] twenty years after his stage performance with Darín (Cruz 2005). But none of those versions of the play attracted the audience that the pairing of Darín and Calvo did in 1985.[10] Moreno, the director, has said that it is quite a difficult play to perform: 'In general, with pieces of this sort, the actors want to be more important than the author' ['En general, con piezas de este tipo los actores quieren ser más importantes que el autor'] (*La Nación* 2004). Darín has affirmed that there is the misconception that in comedies everything is valid, when that is not the case, and that with plays like Cooney's it is easy to shift in the wrong direction (personal communication). Carlos Calvo also mentioned the demands of the play for performers, particularly those coming from a TV comedy background:

> For me that work meant the realization that comedy could be done seriously and well. Up until that point being funny was enough. When we started with Ricardo we were afraid. Then we realised that people were laughing and that response was wonderful. In my case, after that play I forbade myself to use television catchphrases.
>
> [Para mí aquel trabajo significó pensar que una comedia se podía hacer en serio y bien. Hasta ese momento, con hacerse el gracioso estaba. Cuando comenzamos con Ricardo teníamos mucho miedo.

Luego nos dimos cuenta de que la gente se reía y esa respuesta fue maravillosa. En mi caso, a partir de esa obra me prohibí usar un latiguillo televisivo.] (Cruz 2006)

The Darín-Calvo pairing was also meant to appear in the musical *Sugar* in 1986. Nonetheless, as reporter Pablo Gorlero (2016) explained in the newspaper *La Nación* in 2016 – when the new version of the play was in the making – that first edition of *Sugar* took place against all odds. One of the first problems it faced was precisely the altercation between Darín and Calvo, which ended with 'Carlín' leaving the rehearsal and being replaced by Arturo Puig. There was much speculation in the press about this disagreement, including the suggestion that Calvo had an affair with Susana Giménez, co-star in the play and Darín's girlfriend at the time (*Redacción LA* 2018). Others suggested that Calvo had had an argument with Carlos Perciavalle, the producer, and that he was not happy that Darín did not support him in the discussion (*El trébol digital* 2013).[11] Whatever the reason for them going their respective ways, that moment of separation of the most popular acting pair signified the end of an era for the *galancitos* – with the exception of the sporadic charity events that they agreed to participate in from time to time.[12]

Other disagreements which challenged *Sugar* in 1986 included the dispute between producer Perciavalle and the Spadone brothers' production company; it was they who owned the Lola Membrives theatre where the musical was taking place (Gorlero 2016). Perciavalle

**Figure 6.1** Ricardo Darín and Carlos Calvo (*Clarín* Archive)

ended up abandoning the play, in spite of the fact that he was one of the main promoters of the musical, and regardless of the direct contact with Peter Stone, author of the musical that premiered on Broadway in 1972 (which was based on the 1959 Billy Wilder film *Some Like It Hot*, starring Marilyn Monroe, Tony Curtis and Jack Lemmon (Gorlero 2016)). On the night of the premiere, with 1,500 people waiting outside the theatre in Corrientes street – including many celebrities such as Niní Marshall, Teté Coustarot, Graciela Borges and Pinky – a technical problem with the sound system delayed the opening by several hours and ultimately caused the postponement of the show to the following day (*futuro digital* 2017). The final blow for *Sugar* was the separation of Darín and Susana as a couple after a year on stage, and his new romance with Florencia Bas, to whom he has been married ever since.[13] In *Gente* magazine in June 1987 it was suggested that perhaps Susana and Darín had only stayed together 'to keep the image of *Sugar* alive' ['para mantener la imagen de *Sugar*'] (Parrotta 1987: 5). But in more recent studies on Susana Giménez, it was proposed that the couple knew very well how to transform their relationship into a friendship that kept the show successfully running until the end of that year's season (Kriger 1995: 63).[14]

## Theatre producer and director

After *Sugar*, and following changes in Darín's personal life – he got married in April 1988 after a four-month-long courtship with Florencia Bas (Ballan 1988: 6–13), it was another three years before the actor was involved in a play again. And this time he was working behind the scenes, as director of *Pájaros in the nait* [*Birds in the Night*] (1990–1991). The play was the stage debut of actor/singer Diego Torres and of Adrián Suar, and was one of Leonardo Sbaraglia's first attempts at comedy. It was written by Korovsky-Hermida, Carlos Evaristo was in charge of staging and Eduardo Celasco was the executive producer. The play toured several cities in Argentina, although Diego Torres had to be replaced by Pablo Codevilla in some of those shows due to other commitments. It was in fact a unique historical moment for those leading actors. Torres and Suar were about to start the TV teenage show *La banda del Golden Rocket* [*The Golden Rocket Gang*] (Channel 13, 1991–1993), after which their careers sky-rocketed. Torres also released his first solo album the following year, becoming an award-winning Latin pop singer, and Suar funded *Pol-ka producciones* in 1994 with Fernando Blanco, becoming 'the producer of the decade' – according to Fundación Konex.[15] Sbaraglia, albeit quite young, was already a respected and popular actor, after having worked in films such as *La noche de los lápices* [*The Night of the Pencils*] (Olivera 1986) and in TV teenage programmes like *Clave de sol* [*Treble Clef*] (Channel 13, 1987–1991), from where some of the most famous performers of his generation emerged.[16] He always remembers this work with Darín and Evaristo as a 'very nice experience' ['una muy linda experiencia'] at a time when he was only twenty-one years old (Sbaraglia interviewed in Tolentino 2005: 71).

In 1990, Darín also performed on stage in the play *Rumores*, which was, like *La extraña pareja*, another successful adaptation of a Neil Simon play. Cast members included Mirta Busnelli, María Valenzuela, Alejandra Majluf, Roxana Randón, Roberto Fiore, Adriana Salgueiro and José Luis Mazza (Gorlero 2009). When Darín was interviewed in Jorge Guinzburg's popular TV chat show *Peor as nada* [*Nothing is Worse*] (Channel 13, 1990–1994), it was jokingly mentioned that the play was a success because they did not have to pay an expensive director – a position that, undoubtedly, had to be filled by the actors at some point or another during the rehearsals, including Darín himself.[17] Anecdotically, years later, Carlos Calvo agreed to bring the play back to Mar del Plata – in the 2009–2010 season (Gorlero 2009) – playing the role that Darín previously played, and declaring that back in the day he had passed on the opportunity to do the play, which was the reason Darín had taken the role, mildly refuelling the old rivalry between the two.

The following year Darín embarked on both activities: acting and directing the play *Necesito un tenor* [*Lend me a Tenor*] (1991). The comedy, written by Ken Ludwig, was produced on both the West End in London (1986) and on Broadway (1989), winning several Tony Awards. In Argentina, the play took place for the first time at the old Blanca Podestá theatre, although other versions soon followed due to its success (*La Nueva* 2008).[18] Theatre critic Luis Mazas (1991: 3) praised Darín's work as director and interpreter. Most significantly, even though over a decade had passed since the label of *galancito* was used to talk about Darín, Mazas emphasised how the actor wanted to show that he was much more than that: 'Ricardo Darín, as the leading figure, plays the character of Max with ease, reaffirming his intention of becoming something else besides the institutionalised image of the *galán*' ['Ricardo Darín como protagonista resuelve a Max con frescura, confirmando su intención de buscar algo más que su institucionalizada imagen de galán'] (Mazas 1991: 3). Mazas also stated that in this play, as director, Darín looked more in control and experienced than in *Rumores* and *Pájaros in the nait*, suggesting that Darín was responsible for part of the directorial work of Neil Simon's play (Mazas 1991: 3).

*Pizzaman* (1994–1995) was Darín's next work behind the curtain, at a time when his role as a comedy actor on TV with the show *Mi cuñado* [*My Brother-in-law*] was booming (Channel Telefé, 1993–1996). The play, shown at Teatro Picadilly in Buenos Aires, was an adaptation of Darlene Craviotto's book that was first shown in Los Angeles (USA) in 1982, winning both the LA Dramatist Award and Dramalogue Award as best new play of the season. Cast members included Pablo Novak, Patricia Echegoyen and Mariana Briski. The comedy was one more production along the lines of Darín's previous works, but not as successful with the public as it could have been if it had had him on the stage. The breaking point in his stage career came after this play, when Darín decided to move away from comedy to drama in the play *Algo en común* [*Something in Common*] (1995–1996). With respect to this, in a recent interview in the newspaper *La Nación* he said that:

> The first time I did a hard, a tough play, was a very intense moment. It was then that I felt an enhanced public acceptance. It was in 1995 with *Algo en común*, which I did together with my beloved Ana María Picchio, a very young Nico Cabré and the well-remembered Silvina Bosco, directed by Emilio Alfaro. Up until that point, 90 per cent of all I had done – including cinema, theatre and television – was comedy. I did dramatic comedies, yes, but never a fully-fledged drama. This expanded my acting range. I experienced something like this before, when I was tempted to try the musical with Susana (Giménez) and Arturo (Puig) in *Sugar*.
>
> [La primera vez que hice una obra teatral dura, áspera, fue un momento fuerte, ahí sentí que la aceptación se había potenciado. Fue en 1995 con *Algo en común*, junto a mi querida Ana María Picchio, Nico Cabré que era un niño y la recordada Silvina Bosco, dirigidos por Emilio Alfaro. Hasta entonces el 90 por ciento de todo lo que había hecho (tanto en cine como en teatro y televisión) era comedia. Había hecho comedias dramáticas, sí, pero nunca un drama puro. Esto me amplió el rango de acción. Algo así me había pasado antes, cuando fui tentado a probar la comedia musical con Susana (Giménez) y Arturo (Puig) en *Sugar*.] (Lladós 2020)

**This role was not only important for him on a personal level, it was also a final recognition from the press and his peers that he could be a 'serious'**

performer (Urien 1995: 10–15). He won the ACE – Asociación de Cronistas del Espectáculo [the Argentine Association of Entertainment Press] – Award for Best Dramatic Actor (Gaffoglio 1998: 14). He also obtained the Estrella de Mar Award for Best Leading Actor – Argentina's highest theatre accolade – and the play itself, an adaptation of Harvey Fierstein's book, also won the Best Drama award, together with Nicolás Cabré, who earned the Best Newcomer award (Balmaceda 1996).[19] Nonetheless, accounts of Darín's performance which praised his acting in the play also kept returning in their narrative to a derogatory image of the *galancito* – indeed, many of them were already emphasising that he was 'an ex-*galancito*' (Muñoz 1996: 33; Urien 1995: 10) – an image that was starting to be replaced by the new label of Chiqui Fornari, the cheeky 'brother-in-law' of the TV programme that was starting to define him (Baduel 1996: 8).

Up to this point, Darín had only worked informally as a producer on some plays. It was in 1998 when he decided to embark on the role more professionally, not because he was interested in producing, but because he found the perfect project to do so (personal communication, Molero 1998). Both him and José Luis Mazza – with whom he had worked on several plays, including *Extraña pareja*, *Necesito un tenor* and *Rumores* – got hold of the text of *El submarino* [*The Submarine*] which they wanted to put on stage (Molero 1998).[20] They thought that the best way to do so was with their own production company, and that is how El Tenor SRL was created. Casa del Teatro offered them the space of Teatro Regina, which they had to reconstruct for the occasion, after a few years of being closed to the public. The critics said that the comedy, directed by Víctor García Peralta, was a turning point in the careers of Diego Peretti and Verónica Llinás who, since then, have become renowned performers in Argentina (*Clarín.com* 1998). Nonetheless, for Darín, as producer, the play was not a defining moment. He has said that they never recovered the money invested, but they nonetheless enjoyed doing it (personal communication).

He has participated as producer in some other projects since then, but always as a partial payment method for his work on the play in question (personal communication). What *El submarino* subtly revealed is Darín's love for intimist plays. The scene of a couple in bed discussing their everyday chores and ventures, which was typical of the play he produced, was also the basis of the adaptation of Bergman's *Escenas de la vida conyugal* [*Scenes From a Marriage*], which became Darín's recurrent play from 2013 until 2022, replacing his long-standing work on stage in the play *Art*.

## *Art* and *Scenes from a Marriage*

French playwright Yasmina Reza's play *Art* tells the story of three friends whose relationship comes apart over a white-on-white painting that one of them acquires at a very high price. In various interviews Darín has declared that the play is a profound reflection on friendship and tolerance more than a discussion on modern art (Cabrera 2007). It was premiered in 1994 in Paris and was soon translated to different languages. In Argentina, the original cast included Darín, Germán Palacios and Óscar Martínez, but subsequent versions replaced Martínez for José Luis Mazza, until then the executive producer, with whom Darín has worked on multiple occasions – in fact, it was recently suggested that their close friendship was the reason behind Valeria Bertuccelli's and Darín's dispute when working together in *Scenes from a Marriage* (*Clarín.com* 2018).[21] Luis Brandoni briefly replaced Mazza in the 2000–2001 summer season, although cast members tended to remain in place over the years doing the same roles. In some interviews it was suggested that this was due to the fact that there were specific character's features that did not go with the personality of all actors (Hopkins 2010) and that switching roles would take a lot of time for adaptations that they did not tend to have (Bravo 2005).

Darín worked in *Art* almost uninterruptedly for twelve years. He started with the play in the Argentine summer season of 1997–1998. In 2003, amidst his transnational success in cinema, he decided to perform it in Spain. As the Spanish newspaper *El País* explained at the time, the play was successfully performed in Madrid for a number of years by Josep María Flotats, José María Pou and Carlos Hipólito, which made Darín's enterprise quite risky (García 2003). Nonetheless, Darín's 'moments of glory in the Spanish billboards' (García 2003), with films like *El hijo de la novia*, *Nueve reinas* and *Kamchatka*, soon proved to be the lucky charm. Whilst they only planned to be on stage in Madrid for three weeks (García 2003), the play soon toured other cities in Spain and was brought back to the peninsula in 2005–2006. His love for the play is such that he gave it priority over other works. In 2002, for instance, he declared that: 'It hurt me to reject Achero Mañas's last film project' ['Y me dolió rechazar el proyecto de la última película de Achero Mañas'] (quoted in Fernández-Santos 2002), but the theatre was retaining him in Buenos Aires at the time and for him 'theatre is the exercise of methodology that I am most interested in. It is the best workshop for an actor' ['El teatro es el ejercicio de metodología que más me interesa. Es el mejor taller para un actor'] (quoted in Fernández-Santos 2002).

In 2020, Darín was meant to go back to *Art* again, this time as director, with a 'winning' cast: Pablo Echarri, Mike Amigorena and Fernán Mirás (*TBO Argentina* 2020), but the COVID-19 crisis put the project on hold. He also had to cancel his Spanish tour of *Scenes From a Marriage*, which he was going to perform alongside Andrea Pietra in several cities for a few months – which took place in the summer of 2022. Ingmar Bergman's play, which narrates the ups and downs of a married couple, has been replacing *Art* in Darín's annual stage schedule since 2013. The first season took place in Buenos Aires, thanks to the adaptation by Fernando Masllorens and Federico González del Pino. It was directed by Norma Aleandro, who acted alongside Alfredo Alcón in a previous version of the play staged in 1992. It was she who suggested to Darín that he was at the right age to do this play (*Página/12* 2013) – a suggestion that he embraced with ease:

> There are characters, histories and structures that fit better at some points than others ... I had the need to do theatre. People have the wrong idea about cinema; they think it is great fun. It isn't really like that. Actors, we enjoy being on stage a lot. There is a process of work and preparation that can be tedious and painful, but the moment when you step out on the stage to do your job next to your colleagues has no parallels.
>
> [Hay personajes, historias y estructuras que calzan mejor en una época que en otra ... Tenía necesidad de hacer teatro. La gente tiene una idea equivocada del trabajo en cine; creen que hacer cine es divertidísimo. No es necesariamente así. Los actores disfrutamos mucho, mucho, el hecho de estar sobre el escenario. Hay un proceso de trabajo y preparación, que puede ser tedioso y doloroso, pero el momento de entrar al escenario a hacer tu trabajo junto a tus compañeros no se parece a ninguna otra cosa.] (Quoted in *Página/12* 2013)

As a play that relies mostly on the acting couple to work, Darín's partners over the years have been instrumental in his successes. Valeria Bertuccelli first, followed by Erica Rivas, have made headlines, not only for their polemic discussions with Darín – see Chapter 11 for further details – but also for their talent and ability to take this play to a new level. The newspaper *Clarín*, for instance, talked about the opening of the play in 2013 as a reunion of 'three of the greats' – referring to Aleandro, Darín and Bertuccelli (*Clarín.com* 2013). When the play was taken to Madrid in 2015, the critics not only praised Darín's performance and magnetism for Spanish audiences, but also Rivas's expertise: 'It is, undoubtedly, Erica Rivas who steals our hearts. Darín's partner in *Relatos salvajes* represents a huge surprise, and her performance is not only of the calibre of the

Argentine but, most significantly, she steals his leadership on several occasions with her brilliant work' ['Es, sin duda, Érica Rivas la que nos roba el corazón. La compañera de Darín en *Relatos salvajes* ha supuesto una enorme sorpresa y, no solo está a la altura del argentino, sino que además, le roba el protagonismo en muchas ocasiones con su brillante actuación'] (Ruíz 2015).

## All the world's a stage

Famously, in *As You Like It*, William Shakespeare compared the world to a stage and life to a play and said that in his life a man plays many parts. Darín's relationship with the stage can be read in those terms. Paraphrasing Shakespeare's play, he had his exits and entrances, both on stage and behind the curtain, but he has always been a faithful player – even choosing the stage over other art forms. He has gone through most of the so-called 'seven ages of man' on stage, from being an 'infant' and 'schoolboy', through a period of being the 'lover', as the *galancito*. He has also been a 'soldier', who fought to keep a play on in spite of many challenges. It remains to be seen what the years ahead will represent for his stage career. In an interview almost twenty years ago he declared that 'what I'm not going to say is that common phrase that I will die on a stage . . . I think it would be embarrassing. At the end of my life I see myself by a barbecue, with a bottle of wine and friends. But I confess that, as a *galancito*, I find very hard to picture myself as an old *galancito*' ['no te voy a decir un lugar común del tipo Moriré sobre un escenario . . . Creo que sería un papelón. En el final de mi vida me veo cerca de una parrilla, con una botellita de vino y amigos. Pero te reconozco que, como galancito, me cuesta imaginarme como galancito anciano'] (quoted in Urtizberea 2003).

## Notes

1. In his seminal work on stars, Edgar Morin stated that an actor has never reached a level of popularity that could be described as stardom in theatre, and that cinema 'invented and revealed the star' (1972: 15). Yet, for Richard Dyer, Christine Gledhill (1991: xi) and other Star Studies scholars, 'the star system was already a well-developed feature of the popular theatre' (Dyer 1998: 10).
2. Please refer to Susana's interview: https://www.youtube.com/watch?v=m9DrtiNlB-k (accessed 23 September 2020).
3. He has reduced his participation in TV programmes in the last few years, only appearing in small roles, many of them as a cameo, as in the programme *Para vestir*

santos [*To Dress Up Saints*] (Channel 13, 2010), where one of the protagonists, Malena (Celeste Cid), dreamt that she met her father and it was Ricardo Darín. In a recent interview he explained that he is not doing television because he has spent years on TV sets since he was a little boy and feels he already had his share of it (*La Capital* 2020). He also stopped doing dubbing work.

4. It is 'most likely' because Darín himself is unsure if this was his debut and the theatre archives for this period are not reliable. The web page 'amordarín' contains a section on theatre productions where you can consult logs of various plays that in theory included Darín as cast member. According to that webpage, he participated in previous plays, including: *Recuerdo del viejo Buenos Aires* [*Memories of old Buenos Aires*] (1968) and *Martín Fierro* (1978). However, the web page includes many plays as part of Darín's CV that in fact were done by his father – such as *Edipo Rey* [*King Oedipus*] (1979) and *El conventillo de la Paloma* [*Conventillo of the Dove*] (1981). For further information please refer to: https://www.amordarin.com/teatro (accessed 16 October 2020).

5. During the summer they did the play in a public square in Necochea, which is an unlikely place to perform a play according to Darín, mainly due to its small capacity in comparison to the theatres in Mar del Plata (personal communication).

6. As discussed in Chapter 5, Fernando Siro directed several of the 'love' films series. The challenges faced by the group of performers were mainly in terms of the competing schedules of those involved in the play, which were so great that some rehearsals had to be scheduled at 3 a.m. (*TV Semanal* 1980).

7. Please refer to the interview for further details: https://www.youtube.com/watch?v=bE--YAvFvm4 (accessed 28 September 2020).

8. Not only did Darín's relationship with Susana Giménez appear constantly in the tabloids at the time, but also the love affairs and scandals of other actors considered *galancitos* did too. Carlos Calvo, for instance, appeared in *TV Semanal* (1982) due to a possible secret child he might have had. His love affair with Luisina Brando constantly appeared in the tabloids, and Darío Grandinetti's relationship with veteran *telenovela* actress Silvia Montanari also shocked the public (Martínez 2018).

9. Marta González, Alberto Fernández de Rosa, Carlos Olivieri, Mario Alarcón, Carlos Evaristo and Linda Peretz completed the cast (*Nuestros Actores* 2010).

10. According to director Carlos Moreno, that first show in 1985 with Darín and Calvo was the most successful version of the play, attracting 115,000 people to the stage (*La Nación* 2004).

11. In the press there were several reports of various confrontations between the two actors, to the point that it was suggested that their rivalry became a folkloric event (*El trébol digital* 2013; *Diarioveloz.com* 2009).

12. Carlos Calvo passed away on 11 December 2020 after suffering the consequences of two strokes for many years. On his official Twitter account, Darín paid his respects to the actor stating how they had argued for twenty years and laughed for another twenty: 'Please allow me to die a little bit with you today' ['hoy dejame que me muera un poco con vos'] (*La Nación* 2020).

13. They met while Darín was doing *Sugar*. He was eating a pizza outside the theatre when she passed by. The following day she went to have a coffee at a place near the theatre and they met again and started talking (*La Nación* 2000).

14. In Miriam Kriger's words: 'The friendship Darín-Susana, in this new period, is offered to the public in Sugar as a last act in the history of GOOD LOVE, demonstrating that the most important thing is not broken' ['La amistad Darín-Susana, en esta nueva etapa, se ofrece a la gente nuevamente en Sugar, como último acto de una historia de BUEN AMOR, y mostrando que lo esencial no se quebró'] (1995: 63).
15. Please refer to Fundación Konex's web page for further details on Suar's award: https://www.fundacionkonex.org/b2300-adrian-suar (accessed 4 October 2020).
16. Including Pablo Rago, Cecilia Dopazo, Julián Weich, Florencia Peña and Federico D'Élía.
17. In an interview given in 1995 for the cultural magazine of the newspaper *La Nación*, Darín declared that he gathered the strength to direct the play *Rumores* only when his son Chino Darín was born (Urien 1995: 12–13).
18. The Blanca Podestá theatre, located on Corrientes Street in Buenos Aires, received its name when its director, actress Blanca Podestá, passed away in 1967 – before that date it was called Cine-Teatro Smart. It is known that many famous personalities trod that stage, including Carlos Gardel, who sang a tango there to Spanish poet Federico García Lorca (Mecca 2019). Another version of the play was, for instance, *El tenor* [*The Tenor*], 2008, which took place at Teatro Don Bosco and starred Emilio Disi, Fabián Gianola, Germán Kraus, Melina Petriella, Cristina Alberó, Darío Lopilato, Mimí Ardú and Sabrina Rojas (*La Nueva* 2008).
19. Other versions of the play followed, including one with Julián Vena, Viviana Saccone, Ricky Aielo and Romina Yan, in 2008 and 2010, respectively.
20. One of the slogans of the play was 'el submarino es como el matrimonio: puede flotar, pero esta hecho para hundirse' ['the submarine is like marriage: it can float, but it is made to sink'] (*Clarín.com* 1998). The text was written by María Carmen Barbosa and Miguel Falabella (Ruffo 1998).
21. Please refer to Chapter 11 for further information on this dispute.

# References

Baduel, G. (1996) 'Ricardo Darín-Alex Benn, su cuñado', in *Clarín: Espectáculos, Arte & Estilo*, 19 February, p. 8.

Ballan, R. (1988) 'Susana. La fiesta. Los chimentos. Todo el casamiento de Darín', in *Gente*, 1187, 21 April, pp. 6–13.

Balmaceda, O. (1996) 'Se entregaron los premios Estrella de Mar. Ricardo Darín y Ana Acosta los mejores actores', in *La Nación Espectáculos*, 14 February. https://www.lanacion.com.ar/espectaculos/ricardo-darin-y-ana-acosta-los-mejores-actores-nid176068/ (accessed 17 October 2020).

Barbeta, A. (2019) 'Ricardo Darín: "El teatro es mi vávula de escape"', in *Urban*, 20 September 2019. https://www.levante-emv.com/urban/2019/09/20/ricardo-darin-teatro-valvula-escape/1923288.html (accessed 18 September 2020).

Bravo, J. (2005) 'Vuelve a Madrid el fenómeno teatral "Art" de la mano de Ricardo Darín', in *ABC Cultura*, 15 March. https://www.abc.es/cultura/teatros/abci-vuelve-madrid-fenomeno-teatral-mano-ricardo-darin-200503150300-201213911570_noticia.html (accessed 31 December 2020).

Cabrera, H. (2007) 'El centro no es el arte modern sino las emociones', in *Página/12*, 31 December. https://www.pagina12.com.ar/diario/suplementos/espectaculos/10-8782-2007-12-31.html (accessed 29 December 2020).

*Clarín.com* (1998) 'Teatro: Se estrenó El Submarino. Dos personajes en mar turbulento', in *Clarín.com*, 14 August. https://www.clarin.com/espectaculos/tripulantes-mar-turbulento_0_HylgkoeJ8ne.html (accessed 30 October 2020).

*Clarín.com* (2003) 'Con Calvo y Darín', in *Clarín*, 24 June. https://www.clarin.com/espectaculos/calvo-darin_0_SkZbaxWlAFg.html (accessed 30 September 2020).

*Clarín.com* (2013) '"Escenas de la vida conyugal": un clásico con tres grandes', in *Clarín.com*, 2 June. https://www.clarin.com/espectaculos/teatro/Escenas-vida-conyugal-clasico-grandes_0_rJIu2cDjDQg.html (accessed 1 January 2021).

*Clarín.com* (2018) 'Un conflicto en crecimiento: Se supo quién fue el actor de la Discordia entre Valeria Bertuccelli y Ricardo Darín', in *Clarín.com*, 14 June. https://www.clarin.com/espectaculos/fama/trascendio-actor-discordia-valeria-bertuccelli-ricardo-darin_0_S1Ph5yg-7.html (accessed 29 December 2020).

Cruz, A. (2005) '"Taxi": un clásico que no perdió el humor', in *La Nación*, 9 January. https://www.lanacion.com.ar/espectaculos/teatro/taxi-un-clasico-que-no-perdio-el-humor-nid669727/ (accessed 1 October 2020).

Cruz, A. (2006) 'Mar del Plata: mañana se estrenará la obra de Neil Simon. Extraña pareja de amigos', in *La Nación Espectáculos*, 14 December. https://www.lanacion.com.ar/espectaculos/teatro/extrana-pareja-de-amigos-nid867290/ (accessed 3 October 2020).

*Diarioveloz.com* (2009) 'Tristezas, peleas y sonrisas en la vida de Carlín', in Infoveloz.com, 9 October. https://www.infoveloz.com/post/tristezas-peleas-y-sonrisas-en-la-vida-de-carlin_29209 (accessed 3 October 2020).

Dyer, R. (1998) *Stars*, London: BFI and Palgrave Macmillan.

*El trébol digital* (2013) 'El 21 de febrero de 1953', in *El trébol digital*, 21 February. http://www.eltreboldigital.com.ar/2013/02/21/el-21-de-febrero-de-1953/ (accessed 2 October 2020).

Fernández-Santos, E. (2002) 'Actores argentinos, estrellas españolas', in *El País*, 11 August. https://elpais.com/diario/2002/08/11/revistaverano/1029016801_850215.html (accessed 23 September 2020).

*futuro digital* (2017) 'Las lágrimas de Susana Giménez por el estreno fallido de "Sugar", en 1986', in *futuro digital*. http://www.futuro-digital.com.ar/espectaculos/54654-las-lagrimas-de-susana-gimenez-por-el-estreno-fallido-de-sugar-en-1986 (accessed 2 October 2020).

Gaffoglio, L. (1998) 'Deberían pedirme perdón', in *La Nación*, 29 November, p. 14.

García, R. (2003) 'La versión argentina de "Art" se estrena en Madrid gracias al éxito de Ricardo Darín', in *El País Espectáculos*, 4 January. https://elpais.com/diario/2003/01/04/espectaculos/1041634801_850215.html (accessed 29 December 2020).

Gledhill, C. (1991) 'Introduction', in *Stardom. Industry of Desire*, London: Routledge, pp. xi–xix.

González Acevedo, J. C. (2005), *Che, qué bueno que vinisteis*, Barcelona: Editorial Diëresis S.L.

Gorlero, P. (2009) 'Bambalinas', in *La Nación Espectáculos*, 21 October. https://www.lanacion.com.ar/espectaculos/teatro/bambalinas-nid1188638/ (accessed 14 October 2020).

Gorlero, P. (2016) 'Sugar: un verdadero clásico, 30 años después. Sugar, el regreso de una comedia musical que hizo historia en la calle Corrientes', in *La Nación*, 14 November. https://www.lanacion.com.ar/espectaculos/el-regreso-de-una-comedia-musical-que-hizo-historia-en-la-calle-corrientes-nid1955927/ (accessed 2 October 2020).

Grotowski, J. (2002) *Towards a Poor Theatre*, New York: Routledge.

Hopkins, C. (2010) 'Va a convertirse en un clásico', in *Página/12*, 10 January. https://www.pagina12.com.ar/diario/suplementos/espectaculos/10-16596-2010-01-10.html (accessed 31 December 2020).

King, B. (1985) 'Articulating Stardom', in *Screen*, 26.5, September–October, pp. 27–51.

Kriger, M. (1995) *Susana Giménez: Una estrella en la superficie*, Buenos Aires: Ediciones Colihue S.R.L.

La Capital (2015) 'No estamos tan dominados por la tevé como en décadas atrás', in *LaCapital*, 14 February. https://www.lacapital.com.ar/edicion-impresa/no-estamos-tan-dominados-la-teve-como-decadas-atras-n659154.html (accessed 29 April 2020).

La Capital (2020) 'Ricardo Darín explicó los motivos por los que no hace televisión', in *La Capital*, 12 May. https://www.lacapital.com.ar/escenario/ricardo-darin-explico-los-motivos-los-que-no-hace-television-n2583771.html (accessed 26 September 2020).

Ladrón de Guevara, F. (2019) 'Carlos Calvo, cómo es la vida hoy del galán que vio la muerte de cerca', in *Clarín*, 12 November. https://www.clarin.com/espectaculos/carlos-calvo-hoy-vida-galan-vio-muerte-cerca_0_psI--uWw.html (accessed 29 September 2020).

La Nación (2000) 'Ricardo Darín', available at: https://www.lanacion.com.ar/espectaculos/ricardo-darin-nid585078 (accessed 6 May 2020).

La Nación (2004) 'Moreno, un experto en la obra de Cooney', in *La Nación Espectáculos*, 11 December. https://www.lanacion.com.ar/espectaculos/teatro/moreno-un-experto-en-la-obra-de-cooney-nid662054/ (accessed 30 September 2020).

La Nación (2020) 'El conmovedor mensaje de Ricardo Darín a Carlín Calvo: "Hoy dejame que me muera un poco con vos"', in *La Nación Espectáculos*, 12 December. https://www.lanacion.com.ar/espectaculos/personajes/el-conmovedor-mensaje-ricardo-darin-carlin-calvo-nid2537399 (accessed 2 January 2021).

La Nueva (2008) 'Se necesita un tenor y toda la comicidad', in *La Nueva Cartelera Teatro*. https://www.lanueva.com/nota/2008-11-7-10-0-0-se-necesita-un-tenor-y-toda-la-comicidad (accessed 14 October 2020).

Lladós, G. (2020) 'Ricardo Darín: "He tenido mucha suerte en mi carrera, siempre encontré manos extendidas para defenderme"', *La Nación Espectáculos*, 25 April. https://www.lanacion.com.ar/espectaculos/personajes/ricardo-darin-nid2356508 (accessed 20 July 2020).

Martínez, S. (2018) 'Parejas desparejas: ¡Es un escándalo!', in *Agencia Nuevas Palabras*, 12 February. https://nuevaspalabras.com.ar/parejas-desparejas-escandalo/ (accessed 1 October 2020).

Mazas, L. (1991) 'Un tenor que cumple con las reglas de la comedia', in *Clarín Espectáculos*, 17 October, p. 3.

Mecca, D. (2019) 'El día que Carlos Gardel le canto "Caminito" a Federico García Lorca en Buenos Aires', in *Clarín Cultura*, 26 May. https://www.clarin.com/cultura/dia-carlos-gardel-canto-caminito-federico-garcia-lorca-buenos-aires_0_BNkPcgDhK.html (accessed 16 October 2020).

Molero, M. (1998) 'Ricardo Darín, con proyectos sin fronteras. El hombre orquesta', in *La Nación: Espectáculos*, 10 August. https://www.lanacion.com.ar/espectaculos/el-hombre-orquesta-nid106448/ (accessed 25 October 2020).
Morin, E. (1972) *Las Stars. Servidumbres y mitos*, Barcelona: Dopesa.
Muñoz, O. (1996) 'Ricardo Darín y su público, un diálogo con elogios y reclamos', in *La prensa: Espectáculos*, 21 January, p. 33.
*Nuestros Actores* (2010) 'Taxi (1985)', available at: http://www.nuestrosactores.com.ar/index.php/component/content/article/23-obras/1216-taxi-1985 (accessed 30 September 2020).
*Página/12* (2013) 'En el teatro, uno es su propio instrumento', in *Página/12 Espectáculos*, 16 June. https://www.pagina12.com.ar/diario/suplementos/espectaculos/10-28958-2013-06-16.html (accessed 1 January 2021).
Paredes, B. (2019) 'Ricardo Darín: "El teatro es un lugar de resistencia del actor"', in *Diario Correo*, 27 June. https://diariocorreo.pe/cultura/ricardo-darin-el-teatro-es-un-lugar-de-resistencia-del-actor-895169/ (accessed 18 September 2020).
Parrotta, R. (1987) 'Susana y Darín ¿Separados?', in *Revista Gente*, 1142, 11 June, pp. 5–9.
Redacción digital (2019) 'Ricardo Darín en Cuba habla de la bendición del teatro para el actor', in *Trabajadores, órgano de la central de trabajadores de Cuba*, 7 December. http://www.trabajadores.cu/20191207/ricardo-darin-en-cuba-habla-de-la-bendicion-del-teatro-para-el-actor/ (accessed 18 September 2020).
*Redacción LA* (2018) 'Romance bomba: Carlín y Susana Giménez fueron novios', in *Los Andes*. https://www.losandes.com.ar/romance-bomba-carlin-y-susana-gimenez-fueron-novios/ (accessed 2 October 2020).
Ruffo, E. (1998) 'Historias alrededor de la cama', in *La Nación Espectáculos*, 22 August. https://www.lanacion.com.ar/espectaculos/historias-alrededor-de-la-cama-nid107859/ (accessed 30 October 2020).
Ruíz, A. (2015) 'Ricardo Darín y Érica Rivas nos enamoran con sus *Escenas de la vida conyugal*', in *El Teatrero*, 27 October. https://elteatrero.com/2015/10/27/escenas-de-la-vida-conyugal-ricardo-darin/ (accessed 1 January 2021).
TBO Argentina (2020) 'Vuelve Art: la obra teatral más exitosa de los últimos años con tres protagonistas súper', in TBO Argentina, 4 March. https://www.telebajocero.com/oscar-martinez/vuelve-art-la-obra-teatral-mas-exitosa-los-ultimos-anos-tres-protagonistas-super-convocantes-n8885 (accessed 2 November 2020).
Tolentino, J. (2005) *Ni delfín, ni tiburón, ni mojarrita. Diálogos con Leonardo Sbaraglia*, Madrid: Ocho y Medio.
*TV Semanal* (1980) '¿Qué pasó en "La vida fácil"?', in *TV Semanal*, December, p. 32.
*TV Semanal* (1982) 'El extraño caso del hijo secreto de Carlos Calvo', in *TV Semanal*, Year II, 102, 10 April, Buenos Aires.
Urien, P. (1995) 'Darín: Días de cambio', in *La Nación Revista*, 18 June, pp. 10–15.
Urtizberea, M. (2003) 'Entrevista. Ricardo Darín: "Mi felicidad no depende del trabajo"', in *La Nación*, 13 July. https://www.lanacion.com.ar/lifestyle/ricardo-darin-mi-felicidad-no-depende-del-trabajo-nid509840/ (accessed 2 January 2020).
Viola, L. (2017) *Migré. El maestro de las telenovelas que revolucionó la educación sentimental de un país*, Ciudad Autónoma de Buenos Aires: Sudamericana.

# Chapter 7

# Comedy roles and 1980s–1990s work in cinema

As discussed in previous chapters, television and film stardom have been defined in opposition, generally undervaluing the former for the sense of familiarity it generates with the star instead of the distance produced by film (Leppert 2018; Bennett 2011; Ellis 1991; Langer 1981). But the ordinary/extraordinary binary that has thus far defined these forms of stardom (Dyer 2001: 89) is slowly becoming obsolete. Both the changing nature of television and film regimes in the new on-demand virtual culture and the expansion of social media platforms have undermined the notion of stars as unreachable figures, altering the mediated identities that are promoted, consumed and commodified (see Chapter 11 for further discussion of this issue). Back in the 1980s and 1990s, before the impact of the internet and social media, the interplay between star text and star character depended to a great extent on mediated discourses that were less volatile and more impersonal than those allowed by today's media. Star comedians were generally typecast, and mainstream media rarely constructed a star text that moved them away from the specific significance of their comedy roles.

Generally speaking, comedy stardom can be fairly idiosyncratic (Patterson 2012: 232). It blurs the boundaries of the above-mentioned ordinary/extraordinary opposition that tended to dissociate television and film stardom. The case of Argentine comedians Alberto Olmedo and Jorge Porcel, for instance, demonstrate how the extraordinary can be ordinary. In spite of having thirty-six films to their credit – between 1973 and 1988 (Fidanza 2019) – and their undeniable popularity, they were never really defined as film stars by scholars and critics. This is due to several factors: their films were generally regarded as low-brow; their constant participation in other media, including variety shows, radio and television, created a sense of familiarity with the performers that was removed from the unattainable aura generated by traditional film stardom; and they tended to play variations on the same characters that were constructed with a television performance criteria in mind (López 2005: 610–619). Darín's comedy stardom, however, as will be discussed in the following sections, demonstrates how the perceived ordinariness of comedy and television performance can coexist with and inform the alleged extraordinariness of film stardom, if performers are willing to take risks and move beyond the characters that define them when they are at the peak of their celebrity status.

## Federico 'Chiqui' Fornari

In her analysis of Tina Fey, Eleanor Patterson emphasises that comedy stardom is not only 'distinct from other categories of celebrity but that it is configured through cultural identity (gender, race, sexuality) and tied to material means, namely the cultural and economic power of a comedy star's brand' (2012: 236). Darín's comedy stardom is certainly tied to specific Argentine tropes, having played many characters that fit within the stereotype of the '*chanta*' – the friendly, local wheeler-dealer – which reconfigured the cultural and economic power of his star text in the 1990s.[1] It was during those years that he managed to slowly move away from the '*galancito*' figure of the public eye, and to become more widely recognised as a comedian, as the character of Federico 'Chiqui' Fornari – the cheeky brother-in-law of Roberto Cantalapiedra, played by Luis Brandoni, in the 1993–1996 sitcom *Mi cuñado* [*My Brother-in-law*] (Channel Telefé).[2]

The character of 'Chiqui' consolidated the '*chanta*' performance Darín had begun developing in a previous TV show called, precisely, *Mi chanta favorito* [*My Favourite Chanta*], shown on Channel 13 in 1983 (Darín, personal communication). Jorge Nielsen has discussed this programme as one of the successes of Hugo Moser, who presented Darín in another important turn in his career, in the role of the twenty-something depoliticised son of a Peronist family who has a love affair with the daughter of an anti-Peronist family (played by María del Carmen Valenzuela) (2007: 100).[3] The show was such a success that Hugo Mosser wanted to take it to the theatre in Mar del Plata during the summer season. When Darín requested to see a proposal for the play before signing the contract, Mosser got offended, bringing to an end both the working relationship between the two and the programme (Darín, personal communication). In spite of its single season, though, Darín's interpretation of the *chanta*

**Figure 7.1** Luis Brandoni and Ricardo Darín in *Mi cuñado* (1991, *Clarín* Archive)

was so convincing that a decade later it became an inherent element of his star brand.

The character of Chiqui was so deeply engrained in the popular imaginary that, as María Valdez explained at the 2011 Festival of Latin American Cinema in Munich (Germany), character and actor fused into one.[4] This is common with situation comedy performers. According to David Marshall, 'the stars produced through the television situation comedy have several clear-cut tendencies. The familiar characteristics of the star, because of the seriality of the form, determine the way in which his or her public personality is decoded by the audience. [And] the character's name often dominates over the actor's name in public memory' (2014: 130). When reviewing the case of the *Friends* actors, Alice Leppert goes a step further with this idea, concluding that 'situation comedies freeze stars in time, limiting their abilities to work outside the bounds of their character type' (2018: 741). Yet, in spite of Chiqui taking over Darín's star brand in the 1990s, he managed to move beyond the limitations imposed by the role. Argentine film critic Diego Lerer finds that:

> For a long time Darín was associated with the 'cheeky wheeler-dealer' type, a stigma that he managed to overcome when he realised that: 'I used to take it as an insult. Then I realised that, in fact,

it was a hidden compliment: if they mistakenly associate you with the character it means that you are doing it well.'

[Durante mucho tiempo, Darín fue asociado al 'chanta simpático', un estigma que le costó sobrellevar hasta que espantó los fantasmas razonando de esta manera: 'Lo tomaba como un insulto. Después me di cuenta de que, en realidad, era un elogio encubierto: si te confunden con el personaje quiere decir que te sale bien.'] (2001: 27)

The idea that, in situation comedies, performer and character become interchangeable contributes to the perception that television stardom is of lesser quality – i.e. that it requires a less skilful actor than film. But Darín's words show, as does Mills's analysis of situation comedy, that 'comedians can perform as themselves – even in texts which are quite clearly signalled as fiction – which means that versions of themselves can multiply across texts, resulting in a version of themselves which, while seemingly repeatedly confessional, may be nothing more than a performance' (2010: 189). The risk of being potentially typecast and not being able to escape the character is high for performers of situation comedies, then, but not unavoidable. In the aftermath of *Mi cuñado*, during the promotion campaign of the film *Nueve reinas*, Darín declared that:

Every month I receive at least ten comedy projects for TV, film and theatre. Clearly, people see me as a comedian. It is a bit of a paradox: there is nothing more difficult than doing comedy right. So this is quite flattering. But I have to take on other things, too, for my own personal satisfaction.

[Por mes recibo diez proyectos de comedia para TV, cine y teatro. Evidentemente, me visualizan más como comediante. Y es como una paradoja; no hay nada más difícil que la comedia – para hacerla bien. O sea que por un lado es halagador. Pero tengo que cargarme de otras cosas; además, por una cuestión de satisfacción personal.] (Quoted in Montesoro 2000: 2)

*Nueve reinas*, Fabián Bielinsky's opera prima, released in August 2000, was the turning point that allowed him to choose more roles in cinema and leave Chiqui behind. Throughout the 1980s and early 1990s he was laying the groundwork for that moment of superseding the imposed labels of his television characters by choosing roles in cinema that were aligned neither with the *galancito* nor with the *chanta* stereotypes. By the time he started working on Bielinsky's production, *Mi cuñado* had ended and he was reducing his appearances on TV. He took a minor role as the father of one of the child protagonists in the popular teenage *telenovela Chiquititas* [*The Little Ones*] (Channel Telefé, 1998), appearing only sporadically in season 4.[5] The following year, he accepted what was up until now his last leading role in a mini-series, playing Agustín Moyano, a wrongly-accused businessman in the weekly suspense programme *La mujer del presidente* [*The President's Wife*] (Channel Telefé, 1999).[6] And in the year 2000, at the time *Nueve reinas* was gaining recognition on the big screen, he participated in a single episode of the Borenzstein brothers' *Tiempo final* [*The Final Moment*] (Channel Telefé, 2000), playing an electrician called Juan. The show consisted of a series of one-off episodes. It was popular for casting well-known performers in roles that were in opposition to their usual character types – for instance, Gabriel Corrado, usually seen in 'Prince Charming' roles, played a corrupt policeman, and Antonio Gasalla, a queer comedian, was a grey bureaucrat (Andisco 2020).[7] This presence on TV, at a time when he was being praised for his interpretation of the detestable Marcos in cinema, served as the perfect combination by which to change popular perception and propel his star text and career prospects into the new millennium.

In 2013, much to Darín's chagrin, Telefé decided to air *Mi cuñado* again. He declared that re-releasing the show at that juncture was anachronistic and that: 'I would have preferred that it was not re-programmed because that programme meant a lot to me. I worked so much for that and I don't want a distorted image of it to prevail' ['Hubiera preferido que no lo repusieran porque ese programa significó mucho para mí. Dejé la piel trabajando ahí y no quiero que quede una imagen distorsionada'] (*Ciudad Magazine* 2012). The fear of reinstating in the public imagination a label he had finally managed to surpass, or of exposing a new generation of viewers to a comedy whose humour had by then become cliché – thus risking becoming a cliché himself – is visible in Darín's statements on the matter. But as Leppert has demonstrated in her analysis of *Friends*, the re-circulation of programmes that has come with the multiplication of streaming platforms is an inherent part of today's television's intertextual world (2018: 754–755). Even though earlier accounts of television stardom dismissed its stars as simply 'ordinary', the interest over time in looking back at the past successes of a particular performer, albeit evidencing the vulnerability of humour to the effects of the passing of time, consolidates his/her fandom and, hence, the extraordinary qualities that single them out from simple celebrities. Since Darín had moved on from Chiqui-like roles during the decade-long period between its initial run and this new re-programming of *Mi cuñado*, he was not at risk of being '[frozen] in time', as Leppert suggested was the case of the *Friends* performers and other situation comedy stars.

## Moving away from typecasting roles

At the beginning of the 1980s, Darín decided to leave the series of 'love films' behind in favour of film projects with more substantial plots. During this transition, he still accepted a minor role in a light erotic comedy of the like of Olmedo and Porcel's trademark productions: *Abierto día y noche* [*Open Day and Night*] (Ayala 1981).[8] The film belonged to a so-called tradition of 'hotel films', known for placing the action in 'love hotels' – short-stay motel-style establishments, typically understood as being for brief sexual encounters – where the protagonists experience all sorts of humorous entanglements. Within that tradition we also find *La Nueva Cigarra* [*The New Cicada*] (Siro 1977), which is usually wrongly attributed as part of Darín's filmography in popular media.[9] *Abierto día y noche* is a remake of Fernando Ayala's 1966 film called *Hotel Alojamiento* [*Love Motel*], which experienced a box-office success unprecedented for a local production.[10] With the aim of replicating the same commercial revenue, the new production resorted to updating the cast with popular performers of the time, including comedians Juan Carlos Calabró and Tincho Zabala, singer Cacho Castaña, and *telenovela* stars such as Mariquita Valenzuela – many of whom often formed part of other Aries Cinematografica's projects.[11] Darín, together with Alicia Zanca, formed one of the new couples attending the hotel – in the roles previously played by Rodolfo Bebán and Marilina Ross – making the most of his recognisably *galancito* features and of the success the duo was then experiencing on TV, as explored in Chapter 5.

Darín's next adventure on film was as a supporting actor in the thriller *El desquite* [*Retaliation*] (Desanzo 1983). Rodolfo Ranni, the usual leading actor in those years, played Juan Parini, a frustrated middle-aged editor who inherits his friend Celco's nightclub emporium after he is suddenly killed.[12] Most of the film deals with Parini's quest to find his friend's killers whilst changing his 9-to-5 job at a publishing house for the alluring night life, full of dangers and sexy women. Darín's character, Silvio, one of Celco's nightclub managers, is a social climber whose shady alliances lead Parini to finally grow disenchanted with his chosen pathway. This is one of the first times we see Darín in a role that does not respond to the *galancito* or to the funny *chanta*. In light of this, the *Heraldo*, a weekly international journal dedicated to show business, said Darín's choice in taking this role showed that 'the young actor wants to finally bury his image of handsome fellow destined to accept roles of little note' ['(el ...) joven actor que quiere definitivamente sepultar su imagen de galán dedicado a asumir papeles de poca monta'] (1983: 206).

A year later, amidst the feelings of freedom caused by the transition to democracy, he took part in *La Rosales* (Lipszyc 1984), a historical drama based on the 1892 sinking of the Argentine navy ship of the same name, known for the trial of its captain and senior officers, who allegedly sacrificed the crew to save their lives. In line with the films that were being made at the time – such as the Oscar-winning *La historia oficial* [*The Official Story*] (Puenzo 1985), which was released a year later – Lipszyc's work was plagued with metaphors of the dictatorship, uncovering the impunity of the navy and the injustices suffered by those who decided to challenge the official discourse. Ulises Dumont, for instance, a regular actor in the main productions of those years, played the Italian immigrant Battaglia, a survivor of *La Rosales*, who was sent to jail after talking with a reporter about the events that unfolded on the night of the tragedy. Darín, continuing with his choice of non-typical TV characters, plays Lieutenant Jorge Victorica, the second officer in charge, who did not hesitate to shoot those who mutinied in order to save himself and the high-ranking officers, and who unscrupulously claimed in the trial that he was following orders.[13]

At the time *La Rosales* was released, there were negative responses from several military officers who claimed the film distorted the facts (Ruiz 1985: 18–19; Zaratiegui 1984; Pitt Villegas 1984; *La Nación* 1984: 4). Lipszyc, though, insisted on the need to return to this polemical story at that particular historical moment, because it would 'show how the mechanisms of power begin to reveal themselves' ['mostraremos como empiezan a evidenciarse los mecanismos de poder'] (interviewed by Vinelli 1984). Captain Funes, for example, was a relative of soon-to-be President Roca, and Victorica was the nephew of Benjamín Victorica, President of the Supreme Court. In this vein, other articles also supported the timely release of the film and posed the question as to whether 'any justice can come out of a military trial' ['¿Hay justicia en un juicio militar?'] (Couselo 1984), in a tacit reference to the court hearings that were taking place in connection to the dictatorship.

**Figure 7.2** Darín in *Expreso a la emboscada* (Béhat 1986)

What these heated reactions demonstrate is Darín's growing participation in politically committed films, which created the foundations of different casting pathways when it came to his roles in cinema. Another case in point is his performance in 1986 in the Franco-Argentine co-production *Les Longs Manteaux* – released in Argentina under the title *Expreso a la emboscada* [*The Long Coats*] (Béhat 1986).[14] The story takes place in 1982, at the end of the military dictatorship in Bolivia, when writer and political prisoner Juan Mendez is liberated, and a group of Argentine military officers embark on a mission to repatriate him to Argentina. A French Geologist, Loïc Murat – played by popular French actor Bernard Giraudeau – finds himself helping Mendez's daughter when a fascist group called 'The Long Coats' takes over the town through which Mendez's train will pass, with the aim to intercept it and kill him. Darín's role seems quite heroic: he plays Lieutenant Lamas, who is in charge of protecting Mendez on his train journey. He has to fight against the betrayal of one of his men – a role played by Darío Grandinetti – and dies protecting his senior officer. In spite of these honourable gestures, however, we soon find out through Coronel García – played by Federico Luppi – that the writer was dead all along and the journey was taking place only to maintain good political relationships between the two countries, thereby making Lamas an accomplice in the charade. Although Darín's performance was not singled out by the press at the time, his role was not constructed on the *galancito* nor the *chanta* characters he was then playing on TV – contradicting the occasional reporter's suggestion that the Argentine cast did not make any effort to construct characters outside their usual works (J.A.M. 1986).

That same year he accepted another supporting role in the film *Te amo* [*I Love You*] (Calcagno 1986), which had fewer political ambitions than Béhat's or Lipszyc's films, but still managed to subtly criticise a conservative society and the Others it seeks to establish. Ulises Dumont leads the cast, on this occasion taking the role of the bohemian uncle of a pregnant teenager – played by the emerging actress Valentina Fernández de Rosa – who decides to have the baby on her own, supported by the performers of her uncle's low-brow cabaret. Ricardo Darín plays Germán, a dog walker who becomes the teenager's confidant and her brother figure. He adapts the *galancito* features from his *telenovela* roles to a friendly guy-next-door charisma that we would soon be seeing again in future productions. Nonetheless, as Jorge Abel Martín stated in the newspaper *Tiempo Argentino*, in this film 'Darín gets lost in the fray of a badly-scripted character' ['Darín se desdibuja en un personaje descuidado desde el guión'] (1986).[15]

Continuing with these more politically committed stories, Darín finally had a leading role in 1987 in the film *Revancha de un amigo* [*Revenging a Friend*] (Oves 1987). Santiago Carlos Oves's *opera prima* narrates the story of Ariel Llanarte – Darín's character – a reporter in exile who decides to return to Argentina towards the end of the dictatorship due to his mother's ill health. The disappearance of one of his closest friends and his father's mysterious death leads Ariel to a series of dangerous investigations, reconnecting him with former acquaintances and love affairs. Luisa Kuliok plays the old girlfriend and reporter Marta, who helps Ariel in his quest, and is eventually brutally murdered. Manrupe and Portela defined the film as a 'standard police thriller from the 1980s, with a minor political flavour' ['Policial estándar de los '80s, con algún toque político'] (2001: 504).[16] Darín's performance was usually described as borderline-adequate by critics of the time (Fernández 1987; DL 1987; Martínez 1987). With regards to this, it is interesting to note how, in their criticism, they tended to blame Oves's inexperience in directing leading actors, instead of Darín himself for not further developing the complexities of the character. As experienced *telenovela* actors, both Darín and Kuliok were familiar with romantic scenes, but in this example they took their characters a step forward in an erotic love-making sequence that was not customary for television performers at the time, thus signalling a renewed commitment on Darín's part towards his cinematographic career.

In that same year he had another supporting role in *The Stranger* (Aristarain 1987), an Argentine-American thriller starring Bonnie Bedelia, Peter Riegert, Barry Primus, Cecilia Roth, Julio de Grazia and

Federico Luppi (also to be analysed in more depth in Chapter 10). Darín's character, Clark Whistler, draws on a few typical *galancito* tropes from his *telenovela* performances, particularly in some of the flashback sequences when Bedelia's character, who is suffering from post-traumatic amnesia after witnessing a crime, remembers having a romantic relationship with him. There are a series of mid-shots of Darín looking at the camera with a picaresque smile and an inviting tilted head, showing the friendly openness and body posture of his TV roles. As discussed in Chapter 5, it was in this year that his work with Andrea del Boca in the *telenovela Estrellita mia* saw him reaching new heights of popularity (see Chapter 5), and it was also in this year that his private life experienced an important turning point, with the end of his relationship with Susana Gimenez. Partly due to the many changes that were taking place at a personal level, and partly due to the struggles that Argentine cinema was going through in those years, it would take Darín another six years to get back to the big screen.[17]

So it was in 1993 that he landed his second leading role in Alberto Lecchi's *opera prima* as director: *Perdido por perdido* [*Nothing to Lose*] (1993). He had worked with Lecchi in the past, when the director acted as Aristarain's Assistant Director in both *La playa del amor* and *The Stranger*, and this had brought them closer together.[18] When writing for *TV Guía* Magazine, Sandra López (1993) said about Darín's role in this film that he 'was once the *galancito*. Then he was the *chanta*, a renowned actor, and he fulfilled his aim to become a theatre director. Now he will be a loser. This job has nothing to do with his personal life, only with the roles he had to play' ['(...) fue alguna vez el "galancito". Después un "chanta", un actor reconocido, y cumplió su propósito de ser director teatral. Ahora será un perdedor. Esta profesión no tiene que ver con su vida personal, sino con los roles que le tocó realizar']. There is already an indication in these words that Darín's film performances were by then beginning to develop specific character types that, even though they built on the *chanta* and *galancito* features, created a new casting trend in his career: the everyday guy-next-door – a tendency that has led recent definitions of Darín as the Argentine Tom Hanks (Delgado and Sosa 2021). It is also interesting to note that these comments were made before Darín's outstanding success in *Mi cuñado*, which is the role that consolidated his *chanta* stereotype, demonstrating that the typecasting actually predates 'Chiqui' Fornari.

In *Perdido* ... Darín plays Ernesto Vidal, a middle-class *'porteño'* – a man born and bred in Buenos Aires – who is struggling to make ends meet and, in an attempt to make the last payment on his mortgage, becomes a victim of usury. Together with his wife, played by Carolina Papaleo, and the detective who is investigating the robbery of his car, played by Enrique Pinti, they embark on a plan to steal half a million dollars from the company profiting from these illegal deals. Matesutti (Pinti) is killed in the process, and the leading couple escape to Brazil with the money, but not before trying to convince Clara (Ana Maria Picchio) – Matesutti's partner – to escape with them. Pinti's performance was paid the most attention in the media at the time, for being so opposite to his comedic public persona – indeed, he received a standing ovation at the San Sebastian Film Festival (Batlle 1993: 2). Darín's and Papaleo's casting was more associated with a 'commercial cinematic' choice by some critics (Giménez 1993: 14). Lecchi has said that when he chose Darín for the role he was certainly not a prestigious actor in cinema and was experiencing a difficult moment in his career – a likely reference to Darín's unsuccessful TV programme Mi otro yo [My Other Self] broadcast on Channel 13 in 1992 and taken off air after just a few episodes.[19] By the time the film was released, Darín was experiencing a revival of his media popularity with the success of the sitcom Mi cuñado, thus associating his participation in Perdido ... with an arguably opportunistic commercial decision on the production's part (M.S. 1993: 79).

From 1993 until 1996 the role of Chiqui Fornari took over most of Darín's professional life, winning him a Martín Fierro award and outstanding popularity. Given his commitments in theatre – see Chapter 6 for discussion of this – it was going to take him another few years to return to cinema, when he joined the cast of Eduardo Mignogna's El faro [The Lighthouse] (1998). This Argentine-Spanish co-production had Ingrid Rubio as its main protagonist – a Spanish cinema sensation at the time, having won a Goya in 1996 for Best Emerging Actress.[20] El faro narrates the story of two sisters, Carmela (Rubio) and Aneta (played by Jimena Barón and Florencia Bertotti, respectively), who become orphans after their parents die in a car accident which also leaves Carmela with a permanent limp. We follow their lives for a few years and encounter the people they meet along the way, until Carmela's health finally deteriorates and she dies. Among their new acquaintances is Dolores (Norma Aleandro), an old friend of their mother, and Andy, played by Darín, who even becomes Carmela's love interest at one point.[21] Other cast members included Norberto Díaz, Jorge Marrale, Boy Olmi, Mariano Martínez and Paola Krum. Even though Darín's role is rather small, it is nonetheless charged with symbolic strength: he is caring and protective, taking the girls to spend time at a lighthouse so that Carmela could recover from a miscarriage, providing the guidance and support that gives meaning to the film's title. The role imbues Darín with a special fraternal aura that remained with the audience – and particularly with the Spanish audiences that were starting to become familiar with him.

## The turning point: *Nueve reinas* [*Nine Queens*] (Bielinsky 2000)

In September 2000, right after *Nueve reinas* was released, the last page of Argentina's top film magazine at the time – *El Amante* – was entirely dedicated to highlighting how Bielinsky's film had become 'the work that has consecrated Ricardo Darín' ['El trabajo consagratorio de Ricardo Darín'], thanks to his being awarded the Silver Condor Award for Best Actor by the Argentine Film Critics Association.[22] In that article, Gustavo Noriega also stated that

> Prejudice towards his work should have long vanished, but in some circles it is still said: 'A Darín film? I won't see that!' The primary mistake is the following: it is not that after starting in silly roles Darín became a serious actor. He was always serious. As a heartthrob he had to deal with the most ridiculous scripts and, in spite of that, he never failed.
> 
> [El prejuicio debería haberse disipado ya hace bastante tiempo pero sigue flotando en algunos ambientes: '¿La de Darín? Ni en pedo.' El error primitivo es el siguiente: no es que luego de iniciarse en el mundo de la pavada Darín se hizo serio: siempre lo fue. Como galancito tuvo que ponerles el hombro a los parlamentos más imposibles y, sin embargo, nunca falló.] (2000: 64)

The newspaper *La Nación*, following Noriega's remarks, spelled out this prejudice: 'Ex-*galancito*, TV star, Susana Giménez's ex-partner, friendly by nature. Darín's career to date seems to be a cluster of contradictions: a person like that cannot by a great actor' ['Ex galancito, estrella de la tevé, ex pareja de Susana Giménez, simpático profesional. Los antecedentes de Ricardo Darín parecen una acumulación de contrariedades: una persona así no puede ser un gran actor'] (*La Nación* 2000). Darín gallantly faced those who were surprised by his performance, declaring that 'it is not a bad thing to be seen as a constant promise, it is better than being a consecrated actor' ['No está tan mal ser una promesa permanente, es mejor que ser un actor consagrado'] (*La Nación* 2000). In his analyses of *Nueve reinas* in the same issue of *El Amante*, Gustavo Castagna begs Darín to work in cinema 'at least once a year' (2000: 7), clearly articulating a desire that would become mainstream: as Panozzo explained a decade later in his analysis of New Argentine Cinema: 'if there is a new mainstream in Argentina it is called Ricardo Darín' (2009: 51). A tendency that arguably originated with Bielinsky's film.

Also in the year of *Nueve reinas*'s release, Argentine film critic Quintín pointed out the commercial aspects that contributed to its popularity when he stressed that: 'It seems that the best film this year will be a genre film, a type of film that is never done very well here. Most importantly, *Nine Queens* is produced by Patagonik, a company made up of the Clarín Group, Disney and Telefónica. In other words, it is a multinational and corporate industrial product' ['Por lo que parece, la mejor película del año será un film de género, una clase que no suele producir obras valiosas entre nosotros. Además, *Nueve reinas* está producida por Patagonik, sociedad en la que intervienen el grupo Clarín, Disney y Telefónica. Es decir, es un producto industrial de factura multinacional y corporativa'] (2000: 7). Yet, when the director started to circulate the script under the title *Farsantes* [*Phonies*], no one wanted to invest in it. It took an author's nickname and a rebranding for the film to win the 1998 script contest co-organised by Patagonik Film Group that led to its eventual production – most likely due to Bielinsky's reputation in the industry after having worked in publicity and as assistant director, and thus benefiting from the anonymity of the process.[23]

*Nueve reinas* has been analysed by a myriad of scholars and critics over the past twenty years, being one of those films understood to mark the beginning of the so-called New Argentine Cinema boom that occurred at the end of the 1990s (Copertari 2005; Andermann 2012; Oyarzabal 2020).[24] The roles of Marcos (Darín) and Juan (Gastón Pauls), two conmen who decide to work together and forge a plan to swindle stamps – the 'Nine Queens' – to a foreign investor, were originally written with Gabriel Goity and Leonardo Sbaraglia in mind. The proposal came to the latter right after the shooting of *Plata quemada* [*Burnt Money*] (Piñeyro 2000) had come to an end, when the actor decided it was time to have a break. As Darín himself has stated, Bielinsky's proposal arrived just at the time when he was trying to move away from working in television.

Initially, Bielinsky did not want Darín for the role of Marcos, because he thought Darín was too nice and did not want the public to have any empathy with the character (Squillaci 2020). The amoral and sleazy features of Marcos were opposite to the type of roles Darín was working on – but it was precisely this contrast that made Darín's performance skills stand out for critics. In the end, the audience identified with both characters, in spite of Marcos's well-developed unlikeability, since they were both seen as victims of a wider, corrupt system. Other cast members included Leticia Brédice, in the role of Marcos's sister (Valeria) and, as we find out in the eye-opening ending, Juan's girlfriend and ally. Tomás Fonzi is Federico, their younger brother, Elsa Berenguer is Berta, one of Juan's associates, Rolando 'Roly' Serrano is Castrito, and Ignasi Abadal, Oscar Núñez and Alejandro Awada all contribute to the con-the-con plot perpetrated by Juan.

In the special TV programme shown on national television dedicated to celebrating the twentieth anniversary of *Nueve reinas*'s release, it was emphasised once again that this film marked a 'before and after' moment in Darín's international film career. *Nueve reinas* was released in Spain almost at the same time as *El hijo de la novia* [*The Son of the Bride*] (Campanella 2001), which gave foreign spectators the chance to see him in different roles and plots and appreciate his acting ability. He won the Sant Jordi Award for Best Actor and shared the same award with Gastón Pauls at the Biarritz International Festival of Latin American Cinema. The film reached such an international dimension that is considered to be one of the national films with the widest distribution in Europe and the USA (Copertari 2005: 280), and in 2004 a Hollywood remake appeared – *Criminal* (Jacobs) – with John C. Reilly as Richard (Marcos) and Diego Luna as Rodrigo (Juan).[25] Some scholars have blamed the lack of success of this American adaptation to the replacement of the original setting – Los Angeles for Buenos Aires – which resulted in a depoliticisation of the narrative (Oyarzabal 2020: 98; Squillaci 2020). However, as other critics were more open to admitting, John C. Reilly was 'miscast in Darín's role' (Beatriz 2005).

## Final reflections

Darín's work in the domain of the familiar and the intimate – i.e. situation comedies and *telenovelas* (Marshall 1997: 131) – continued informing his film performances throughout the 1990s, but a change in direction in his career path becomes visible from the beginning of the new millennium. As has been discussed in this chapter, Darín's star text is a site of contradictions. Beginning as a typecast comedy star and a *galancito*, this phase of his career sees him become the unscrupulous Marcos, pimping out his sister to close a fraudulent deal without any sign of remorse. With the boom of Argentine cinema at the end of the 1990s and his intention to move away from television, Darín went from having only two leading film roles in ten years – in Oves's and Lecchi's films – to becoming a regular of the big screen. It was also during the period of *Nueve reinas* when he started his association with Juan José Campanella; a connection which, as will be explored in more depth in the next chapter, would translate into four leading characters and his questioning of the power of Hollywood's Academy to define the star system.

## Notes

1. According to *Diccionario de argentinismos* (De Santillán 1976: 133), the stereotype of the '*chanta*' comes from the Italian *ciantapuffi*, which is a term used to identify those individuals who avoid formal work and get into debt, having to resort to a series of tricks to get out of trouble. Lucía Rodríguez Riva further explains that one of the main features of the Argentine *chanta* as a publically-known character is that, even though his actions – these roles are commonly associated with men – are not completely legal or morally positive, he tends to enjoy the sympathy of the audience (2020: 4).
2. There were new episodes released in 1998, making a total of 248 episodes. The sitcom narrates the story of Roberto Cantalapiedra – a widower with one daughter, Lili, played by Cecilia Dopazo – who remarries Andrea Fornari (Patricia Viggiano), who, in turn, brings her brother Federico 'Chiqui' Fornari into their lives. Episode plots revolve around Chiqui driving Roberto mad for different reasons each time. It was a remake of an older TV programme called *Mi cuñado y yo* (Channel 13, 1976), starring Osvaldo Miranda and Ernesto Bianco.
3. Darín's Peronist family was played by Perla Santalla, Tino Pascali, and Claudia Rucci as his sister. María del Carmen Valenzuela's anti-Peronist family included Enrique Fava and Julia Sandoval as her parents, and José Luis Mazza as her brother (Nielsen 2007: 100).
4. Courtesy of María Valdez, from an unpublished presentation delivered on 14 July 2011 to open a special series of screenings at the festival celebrating Darín's career.
5. *Chiquititas* was a highly successful *telenovela* for children that ran for seven seasons, from 1995 until 2001. It was produced by Cris Morena for Telefé, although in 2003 there was a spin-off called *Rincón de luz* [*A Corner of Light*] that was shown on Channel 9, starring Soledad Pastorutti, Guido Kaczka and Alejandra Darín. Regular

cast members included Romina Yan, Gabriel Corrado, Fernán Mirás, Facundo Arana, Grecia Colmenares, Darío Grandinetti, Romina Gaetani, Iván Espeche, Agustina Cherri and Gastón Ricaud. Many stars participated in the show, including Hilda Bernard, Alicia Zanca, Jorge Martínez, Sergio Denis, Pablo Echarri, Celeste Cid and Andrea del Boca.

6. *La mujer del presidente* lasted sixty episodes. It was directed by Eduardo Ripari. Cast members included Natalia Lobo, Franklin Caicedo, Ángel Molina, Fernán Mirás, Andrea Pietra, Carolina Papaleo, Andrea Politti, Carlos Santamaría, Alicia Aller, Osvaldo Bonet and Julio Riccardi.
7. The series included various A-list stars in different episodes, such as Norma Aleandro, Catherine Fulop, Norman Briski, Leticia Bredice, Guillermo Francella, Luisa Kuliok, Gaston Pauls and Facundo Arana, as well as other celebrities, such as dancer Julio Bocca and singer Alejandro Lerner. It lasted sixty-nine episodes, coming to an end in October 2002 (Andisco 2020).
8. Also produced by Aries Cinematográfica Argentina.
9. This film is based on Dante Sierra's book, which also served as inspiration for Daniel Tinayre's previous film in the tradition of 'hotel films', *La cigarra no es un bicho* [*The Dragonfly is Not an Insect*] (1963), starring Luis Sandrini, Mirtha Legrand, Pepe Cibrián and Guillermo Bredeston. Cast members included Olga Zubarry, Enrique Pinti, Claudio Levrino, María Aurelia Bisutti, Alberto Martín and Marta Albertini.
10. *Hotel alojamiento* opened in Mar del Plata in February 1966. It was then released in Buenos Aires, where it stayed on the billboards for twenty-two weeks at the Trocadero, and ran at forty film theatres around the country for five weeks – something which had never happened with any prior national film (*La Semana* 1982: 57). Its cast members included Atilio Marinelli, Marilina Ross, Rodolfo Bebán, Pepe Soriano, Tincho Zabala, Alberto Olmedo and María Aurelia Bisutti.
11. Other well-known actors appearing here included Nelly Beltrán, Pablo Alarcón, Julio De Grazia and Jorge Martínez.
12. The character of Emilio Celco was played by Gerardo Sofovich, who was also a co-producer of the film.
13. Other cast members included Héctor Alterio in the role of Funes, the captain of the frigate. Oscar Martínez is the anarchist Italian reporter, Soledad Silveyra played Darín's fiancé, Alicia Bruzzo was Battaglia's girlfriend Renata, Arturo García Buhr was the prosecutor and Raúl Rizzo was the defendant.
14. A co-production between Les Films de la tour (Francia) and Aries Film Internacional, this was the second film to follow a cooperation treaty signed between the two countries in 1984 – the first was Fernando Solanas's *El exilio de Gardel* [*Gardel's Exile*] (1986) (*La Razón* 1984a: 30). Originally, the casting included Isabelle Huppert in the role of Mendez's daughter, but the actress was ultimately replaced by the Brazilian Claudia Ohana (*La Razón* 1984b: 2).
15. Other cast members included Betiana Blum, Pepe Soriano, Perla Santalla, Gogó Andreu, Víctor Laplace, Eleonora Wexler, Mónica Galán, Guillermo Rico, Germán Palacios, Georgina Barbarossa, Renée Roxana and Willy Lemos. Darín himself has declared that the film deserved a better public reaction than it received (quoted in Saavedra 2002: 15).

16. Ariel's mother was played by Adriana Aizemberg, and his father, who faked his death and reappears briefly to talk to Ariel about the military's dirty business with his company, was played by Rodolfo Ranni. Other cast members included Juan Leyrado, Alicia Aller and Marcela Ruiz. The film was produced by Victor Bó Producciones.
17. The early 1990s were difficult times for Argentine cinema, with some scholars even declaring its near death (Andermann 2012: 1). Moreover, in 1991, Darín was briefly put in jail for the acquisition of a car that was brought into the country without the required legal process. Even though he was later absolved of all charges, the negative publicity haunted him during this period.
18. In an interview a propos the film, Lecchi mentioned that, in terms of actor selection, 'I looked for friends: with Darín I had worked twice; I had directed Enrique Pinti in a video called "Full Pinti" and I had worked with Carolina Papaleo and Alberto Segado' ['Busqué amigos: con Darín había trabajado dos veces; a Enrique Pinti lo había dirigido en un video ("A todo Pinti") [...] y había trabajado con Carolina Papaleo y Alberto Segado'] (quoted in España 1993: 10).
19. In this series, Darín played 'Pablo', a driver, detective and womaniser. It was directed by Juan José Castro, and cast members included Rubén Ballester, Adriana Castro, Daniel Freire, Pablo Iemma and Villanueva Cosse. Its authors stated that the programme combined humour with the police thriller genre (quoted in Lamazares 1992: 4). In 1992 and 1993, Darín made two TV commercials for the cigarette brand Derby which kept him in the public eye, but he has also stated that Lecchi contacted him at a difficult professional moment (Rodríguez 1993: 25).
20. In fact Rubio won several awards for this film, including the Condor de Plata Award for Best Actress and the same category at the Montreal International Film Festival.
21. There were more scenes from this film which did not make it to the final cut in which Darín had a more prominent presence. In those, it was made more obvious that his character was homosexual and his partner, Boris, who is mentioned a few times in the film as the old owner of the lighthouse, was played by Federico Luppi, although his participation was never shown in the end (Boido 1999: 14).
22. An award he would receive eleven more times after this.
23. Please refer to Damián Kirzner's testimony, Bielinsky's nephew and one of the first producers of the film, in the special TV show dedicated to celebrating the twentieth anniversary of the film, available at: https://www.youtube.com/watch?v=H8HrVt7QSkg (accessed 8 August 2021).
24. Although the fact that this is a genre film produced by multinational corporations somewhat excludes it from the canon of films grouped under the label of New Argentine Cinema (Copertari 2005: 280).
25. Produced by Steven Soderbergh. Other cast members included Maggie Gyllenhaal, Jonathan Tucker and Peter Mullan.

# References

Andermann, J. (2012) *New Argentine Cinema*, London and New York: I. B. Tauris.
Andisco, P. (2020) 'A 20 años de "Tiempo final", el programa que reivindicó el unitario y le hizo frente a los reality shows', in *Teleshow*, 19 March. https://www.infobae.com/

teleshow/2020/03/19/a-20-anos-de-tiempo-final-el-programa-que-reivindico-el-unitario-y-le-hizo-frente-a-los-reality-shows/ (accessed 16 May 2021).
Batlle, D. (1993) 'Aplausos para Enrique Pinti', in *Clarín*, 23 September, p. 2.
Beatriz, M. (2005) 'Nueve Reinas y Criminal', 6 November. http://veoypienso.blogspot.com/2005/11/nueve-reinas-y-criminal.html (accessed 20 August 2022).
Bennett, J. (2011) *Television Personalities; Stardom and the Small Screen*, Abingdon and New York: Routledge.
Boido, J. I. (1999) 'El hombre que fue Batman', in *Página/12-Radar*, 3 October, pp. 14–15.
Castagna, G. (2000) 'Un milagro argentino', in *El Amante Cine*, 102, September, pp. 4–7.
Ciudad Magazine (2012) 'El enojo de Ricardo Darín: "Hubiera preferido que no repusieran Mi cuñado"', in *Ciudad magazine espectáculos*, 30 December. https://www.ciudad.com.ar/espectaculos/101322/enojo-ricardo-darin-hubiera-preferido-no-repusieran-mi-cunado (accessed 9 May 2021).
Copertari, G. (2005) '*Nine Queens*: A Dark Day of Simulation and Justice', in *Journal of Latin American Cultural Studies*, 14.3, December, pp. 279–293.
Couselo, J. M. (1984) '*La Rosales*: esclarecimiento y polémica', in *Clarín*, 31 August.
Delgado, M. and Sosa, C. (2021) '10 Great Argentinian Films of the 21st Century', in *BFI*, 8 April. https://www.bfi.org.uk/lists/10-great-argentinian-films-21st-century (accessed 24 July 2021).
De Santillán, D. A. (1976). *Diccionario de argentinismos*, Buenos Aires: Editora Argentina.
DL (1987) 'Apasionante policial de Oves', in *La Razón*, 12 June.
Dyer, R. (2001) *Stars*, London: BFI Publishing.
Ellis, J. (1991) 'Stars as a Cinematic Phenomenon', in Butler, J. (ed.), *Star Texts: Image and Performance in Film and Television*, Detroit. MI: Wayne State University Press.
España, C. (1993) 'Alberto Lecchi: Un flamante director para quien nada está aún perdido', in *La Nación*, 17 July, p. 10.
Fernández, M. (1987) 'Anodino film local bien intencionado', in *El Cronista Comercial*, 12 June.
Fidanza, F. N. (2019) 'Humor apto todo público. El cine de entretenimiento de Alberto Olmedo, Jorge Porcel y Enrique Carreras', in *Questión: Revista Especializada en Periodismo y Comunicación*, 1.63, pp. 1–19.
Giménez, N. (1993) 'Alberto Lecchi filma Perdido por perdido: Un lugar en el cine', in *Revista Clak*, 10, August, pp. 14–15.
*Heraldo* (1983) 'El Desquite de Juan Carlos De Sanzo', in *Heraldo*, 2662, 25 March, p. 206.
J.A.M. (1986) 'Despliegue de producción con magro resultado', in *Tiempo Argentino*, 1 August.
Lamazares, S. (1992) 'Ricardo Darín: El mismo pero otro', in *Clarín*, 19 April, p. 4.
*La Nación* (1984) 'Circula entre oficiales navales un volante sobre la Rosales', in *La Nación espectáculos*, 8 September, p. 4.
*La Nación* (2000) 'Ricardo Darín', in *La Nación espectáculos*, 1 October. https://www.lanacion.com.ar/espectaculos/ricardo-darin-nid585078 (accessed 6 May 2020).
Langer, J. (1981) 'Television's Personality System', in O'Sullivan, T. and Jewkes, Y. (eds), *The Media Studies Reader*, London: Arnold, pp. 165–167.
*La Razón* (1984a) 'Importante coproducción: El francés Gilles Béhat filmará en Buenos Aires', in *La Razón*, 22 December, p. 30.

*La Razón* (1984b) 'Isabelle Huppert: un filme en Buenos Aires', in *La Razón espectáculos*, 26 November, p. 2.

*La Semana* (1982) 'De Hotel alojamiento a albergue transitorio', in *La Semana*, pp. 54–57.

Leppert, A. (2018) '*Friends* Forever: Sitcom Celebrity and Its Afterlives', *Television & New Media*, 19.8, pp. 741–757.

Lerer, D. (2001) 'Confesiones del actor del momento', in *Revista Viva*, 4 November, pp. 20–28.

López, D. (2005) 'Erotismo y humor en Aries. Olmedo y Porcel. Noventa minutos de pura risa', in España, C. (ed.), *Cine Argentino: Modernidad y vanguardias 1957–1983*, Buenos Aires: Fondo Nacional de las Artes.

López, S. (1993) 'Ricardo Darín dice que para hacer este filme se acordó de cuando le tocó perder en la vida', in *TV Guía*.

Manrupe, R. and Portela, M. A. (2001) *Un diccionario de films argentinos (1930–1995)*, Buenos Aires: Editorial Corregidor.

Marshall, P. D. (1997) *Celebrity and Power. Fame in Contemporary Culture*, Minneapolis and London: University of Minnesota Press.

Marshall, P. D. (2014) *Celebrity and Power: Fame in Contemporary Culture*, Minneapolis and London: University of Minnesota Press.

Martín, J. A. (1986) 'Válida incursión en el mundo adolescente', in *Tiempo Argentino*, 4 May.

Martínez, A. (1987) 'Una revancha poco vigorosa y entretenida', in *La Nación*, 12 June.

Mills, B. (2010) 'Being Rob Brydon: Performing the Self in Comedy', *Celebrity Studies*, 1, pp. 189–201.

Montesoro, J. (2000) 'Darín, el malo de la película', in *La Nación espactáculos*, 29 April, p. 2.

M.S. (1993) 'Alberto Lecchi: Corrupción hubo siempre pero ahora está legalizada', in *Revista Humor*, 368, p. 79.

Nielsen, J. (2007) *La magia de la televisión argentina 4: 1981–1985*, Buenos Aires: Del Jilguero.

Noriega, G. (2000) 'Ricardo Darín', in *El Amante Cine*, 102, September, pp. 4–7.

Oyarzabal, S. (2020) *Nation, Culture and Class in Argentine Cinema*, Woodbridge: Tamesis.

Panozzo, M. (2009) 'El mainstream que nunca estuvo', in Pena, J. (ed.), *Historias extraordinarias: Nuevo Cine Argentino 1999–2008*, Madrid: T&B Editores.

Patterson, E. (2012) 'Fracturing Tina Fey: A Critical Analysis of Postfeminist Television Comedy Stardom', in *The Communication Review*, 15.3, pp. 232–251.

Pitt Villegas, J. (1984), 'Cartas de lectores. *La Rosales*', in *La Nación*, 29 October.

Quintín (2000), 'Ahora y entonces', in *El Amante Cine*, 102, September, p. 7.

Rodríguez, D. (1993) 'Ricardo Darín habla de su nuevo film', in *La Razón*, 27 July, p. 25.

Rodríguez Riva, L. (2020). 'Humor gráfico, radio, cine: la configuración del estereotipo del *chanta* en *Avivato* y *El Gordo Villanueva*', in *Dixit*, 32, pp. 1–15.

Ruiz, E. (1985), 'Temas para un mejor cine argentino', in *Tiempo argentino*, 2 March, pp. 18–19.

Saavedra, G. (2002) 'Darín a cara lavada', in *La Nación Revista*, 5 May, pp. 14–20.

Squillaci, P. (2020) 'Ricardo Darín: "A los argentines nos gustan los turros"', in *La Capital*, 30 August. https://www.lacapital.com.ar/escenario/ricardo-darin-a-los-argentinos-nos-gustan-los-turros-n2606382.html (accessed 11 August 2021).

Vinelli, A. (1984) 'Un drama urticante', in *La Opinión*, 10 June.

Zaratiegui, H. (1984) 'La Rosales. Carta al director', in *La Nación*, 16 October.

# Chapter 8

# Contemporary productions and the ageing star

Film stars must continuously negotiate their stardom status as they grow older in a highly mediated world where youth is considered a prime value – particularly in Western cultures. Whether a star is able to 'age successfully' has been a growing area of investigation in Film and Media Studies, under the banner of what has become known as 'Ageing Studies' (Basting 1998; Gullette 2004; Harrington, Bielby and Bardo 2014). Early scholars in the field have drawn from theories on feminism and gender to move away from a biological approach to ageing – gerontology – and instead to emphasise how we learn to act one's age. In other words, age, like gender and other markers of identity, is understood as a cultural construction (Gullette 2004; Lipscomb and Marshall 2010: 2; Swinnen 2012: 7). Mark McKenna's analysis of Sylvester Stallone for the *Celebrity Studies* journal, for example, explores how certain stars, like Stallone, have a rare level of iconicity that is indicative of a significant moment of cultural resonance which 'often brings with it a refusal in popular culture to allow the iconic image to change, grow or evolve' (2019: 501). Since that image inevitably does change, there is a perception that stars become redundant. However, some artists, like Stallone, have been able to capitalise on this narrative of redundancy and reconceptualise ageing as transition (McKenna 2019: 501). Even though Darín has never reached that level of iconicity in the public sphere, the typecasting he experienced at particular points in his career – mainly the *galancito* and the *chanta* imagery explored in previous chapters – have threatened him with an expiration date. In light of these realities, the following pages will explore whether he has also been able to reconceptualise his ageing as career transition.

Sabrina Qiong Yu states in her introduction to *Revisiting Star Studies* that 'there is a common perception that ageing is less an issue for male stars than female stars, since appearance weighs much more in a female star's career. This explains why researchers focus heavily on ageing and female stars [...]' (2017: 5).[1] However, as Gates claims, 'the assumption – on the part of stars and society in general – is that aging lessens a man's masculinity' (2010: 279). Holmlund further explains that 'in most cases aging is experienced and regarded as deformation, disintegration, and fragmentation rather than, more neutrally, as transformation' (2002: 145). In Hollywood, this translates into the age of forty being the critical turning point for actors (Guo 2016). In contrast, the majority of the best-known contemporary Argentine actors are over forty years of age. And in Darín's specific case, besides already being over forty when his big screen break happened, his film stardom has mainly been constructed through characters that are based on masculinities in crisis, as a result of the expansion of global capitalism that, as Rocha (2012: 11), Hearn (1987), Horrocks (1994) and Harris (1995) all outline, 'undermines patriarchy and men's status in society'. The fact that he managed to move away, in the process of consolidation of his cinematographic career, from stereotypical roles that could have encapsulated him as an epitome of youthful masculinity seems to have granted Darín the opportunity to revalue age as wisdom.

## Reaching maturity on the big screen

When Fabián Bielinsky's *Nueve reinas* [*Nine Queens*] was released at the beginning of the new millennium, Darín was forty-three years old, with more than three decades of experience in show business. By that time, his roles as *telenovela* heart-throb were coming to an end, and the sitcom *Mi cuñado* [*My Brother-in-law*] completed a successful cycle of four seasons, with the last remaining episodes airing in 1998. Although he had worked on twenty films, including two leading roles, he was still popularly considered a television personality – fluctuating between a *galancito* and the shameless Chiqui Fornari. He was also seen as a theatre performer, who danced in *Sugar* with old girlfriend Susana Giménez, and who romanticised a white canvas in the famous play *Art*. He was even considered a regular family guy, who in a television advert goes with his wife and son to 'Casa tía' to do his Christmas shopping.[2] But what he was not regarded as was a cinema actor. So while the over-forties tend to be cast away from Hollywood's star system, with a sharp decline in the number of lead roles for performers who pass that threshold (Fleck and Hanssen 2016: 37), Darín's film career went in the opposite direction.

The role of the veteran con artist Marcos in *Nueve reinas*, the role which started to bring visibility to Darín as a cinema actor, came to him at a moment when Argentine cinema was experiencing a revival. As explored in Chapter 3, the emergence of the new cinema law in 1994, and the upsurge of a new generation of young directors and film critics, repositioned national productions as a viable popular option for an audience eager to engage with a cutting-edge aesthetic, local realities and relatable faces – albeit those from the street and not from a local star system. In spite of its severe economic crisis, the country went from producing fourteen feature-length films in 1994 to almost five times that number by 2004 (Page 2009: 1).³ With an increase in production came more working opportunities for film performers. Even though there was a tendency to hire non-professional actors to reduce costs and infuse a sense of neo-realist authenticity, experienced artists still secured regular job opportunities (Aguilar 2006: 220). Darín, for instance, embarked on multiple projects in a short period of time, which allowed audiences and peers to appreciate his versatility. In only four years, between 1998 and 2002, he acted in seven films, six of those as the protagonist.⁴

It is interesting to note that the only film of this period in which he did not play a leading role was in the historical drama *La fuga* [*The Escape*] (Mignogna 2001), which also happens to be the only film in which he was playing neither a middle-aged man in crisis nor a veteran. His character, Domingo Santaló, was nicknamed '*el pibe*' [the kid], the youngest of a group of seven inmates from the National Penitentiary in Buenos Aires who manage to escape by tunnelling their way out of prison. Based on true events from 1928, the story is narrated by the brains behind the operation, ex-con Laureano Irala, who is played by prolific actor Miguel Ángel Solá. We follow each one of these men as they part ways. Belisario 'Pampa' Zacarías (Oscar Alegre) dies in the tunnel. His partner in crime and love interest, Omar 'the Turkish' Zajur, goes to visit Pampa's widow (Norma Aleandro) to come to terms with his own loss and relationship. Camilo Vallejo (Alberto Jiménez), 'the anarchist', dies in an attempt to bomb a government car. We learn of the tragic love story of bookie Julio 'the Professor' Bordiola (Gerardo Romano), who discovers that his wife, Rita, has committed suicide. The wrongly imprisoned airplane pilot, Tomás Opitti (Alejandro Awada), embarks on a revenge mission to kill commissioner Duval (Patricio Contreras), the man tasked with capturing the inmates, who was also responsible for killing Opitti's family.

Darín's character is constructed from a puzzle of features that would become signature tropes in other roles he would play in those years. As an expert poker player and forger, there are elements of skilful trickery that we will meet again in Marcos in *Nueve reinas*. The idealistic lover who escapes prison and aims to get back together with his old girlfriend, Tabita (Inés Estévez), even though she is married to his old boss, the dangerous Escofet – played by regular television villain Arturo Maly – shows a romantic side that will reappear in *El baile de la Victoria* [*The Dancer and the Thief*] (Trueba 2009). Yet, the film-noir aesthetic of his story dominates, influencing his performance. The encounter with a femme fatale who deceives Santaló, leading to his death, and inflicting a double wound: that to his heart and that to the ego of the swindler who gets conned, is a topic that will reappear in exacerbated form in *La señal* [*The Signal*] (2007).[5] Written, precisely, by the director of *La fuga*, Eduardo Mignogna was also meant to direct *La señal*, until his sudden death resulted in Darín and Hodara taking up the task of seeing the project through.[6] The leading character, Corvalán, is the archetypal private detective who struggles to make ends meet, until the beautiful and mysterious Gloria (Julieta Díaz) hires him to take on a case. Corvalán's smart period clothes and confident sex appeal builds on Darín's *galancito* years. In spite of being called 'el pibe', like Santaló in *La fuga*, Corvalán shows signs of being a more mature man with a tormented past, and we can physically see in his face and body postures the marks of the passage of time.

In terms of the six leading roles played in this period, it was at the end of the 1990s and during the upsurge of New Argentine Cinema when Darín began a very fruitful alliance with director Juan José Campanella. A number of scholars have linked Darín's rise to stardom precisely with his successful collaborations with this director (Andermann 2012: 132; Oyarzabal 2020: 117). It started with the film *El mismo amor, la misma lluvia* [*Same Love, Same Rain*] (1999), followed by *El hijo de la novia* [*The Son of the Bride*] (2001), *Luna de Avellaneda* [*Avellaneda's Moon*] (2004) and the Oscar-winning film *El secreto de sus ojos* [*The Secret in their Eyes*] (2009). In all these films, we see characters coming to terms with the passing of time. *El mismo amor* defies the exteriorisation of the ageing process by following the character of Jorge Pellegrini for almost two decades, without physically changing anything about Darín himself. From a promising twenty-eight-year-old writer who falls in love with a waitress – Laura Ramallo, played by Soledad Villamil – to a middle-aged man in crisis recovering from a suicide attempt after years of moral disintegration and lack of love, the film relies heavily on the identification of Jorge's ageing process to social, cultural and historical changes. The body is not, in this film and as it otherwise tends to be (Van den Bulck 2014: 59), the vehicle through which discourses of ageing are articulated. Instead, lifestyle choices and socio-political shifts determine the audience's acceptance of the passing of time, showing that ageing parameters are blurring (Jermyn 2012).[7]

*El hijo de la novia* portrays a middle-class man going through a classic middle-age crisis. Consumed by the financial difficulties of keeping the Italian family restaurant afloat, Rafael Belvedere (Darín) suffers a heart attack at the beginning of the film that forces him to re-evaluate his life. While showing clear signs of fragility and deterioration at first, by the end of the film we experience the transformation of the middle-aged body into a youthful one, still able to wait in the rain to declare his unconditional love to his younger lover Naty – played by Natalia Verbeke. Moreover, the reunion with his childhood friend, Juan Carlos (Eduardo Blanco), reminds Rafael of his youthful courage and the ideals of a life full of possibilities, causing a rejuvenating effect.[8] Besides exposing age as a cultural and psychological construction rather than a biological determination – albeit by touching on a Peter Pan syndrome – the film also attempts to romantically desacralise some of the misconceptions about love in old age. Rafael's parents, the elderly couple played by Héctor Alterio and Norma Aleandro, offer an inter-generational sub-narrative that subtly challenges discourses of decline, vulnerability and dependency in Nino's (Alterio) unconditional infatuation with his wife Norma.[9] He is willing to sacrifice the beliefs of his youth in order to fulfil her desire to have a religious wedding ceremony and get married in a church, before Alzheimer's disease takes her mind. He enjoys being the groom and being treated as a younger version of himself because of that status, which is normally associated with the beginning of a life together as a couple. In terms of third-age defying moments, Norma, for her part, has rare instances of clarity, but when she does, she tends to see beyond exterior appearances, as when she sees Juan Carlos as the kid who used to steal her *polvorones* [cookies] and warns him not to do it anymore. In those moments, she ceases to be a fragile, disoriented, older woman, and becomes a young mother full of life and determination.

In *Luna*, we also witness the tribulations of a middle-aged man in crisis who has to hit rock bottom to rediscover life's 'true values' (Andermann 2012: 40–42). Román Maldonado (Darín) together with Amadeo

Grimberg (Eduardo Blanco) and Graciela Fernández (Mercedes Morán) are fighting to keep their social and sports club open – the *Luna de Avellaneda* – amidst one of its worst economic crisis; one that threatens to close it down for good and see it turned into a casino.[10] The film has generally been read as another depiction of the social effects of Argentina's 2001 crisis, and as an exercise in nostalgia (Oyarzabal 2020: 114–115). It is in this longing for a better past that the film navigates the position of old age in a fractured postmodern society. The character of Aquiles, the founder of the club played by veteran Spanish actor José Luis López Vázquez, embodies the deterioration of a past that has arguably become obsolete. After he passes away, the club's partners discuss the need to 'move with the times' and more than half of the members vote to sell. In doing so, they adhere to the chronological view of ageing as degeneration, and also in the same spirit as it was portrayed by Beatriz Sarlo (1994) in her *Scenes from Postmodern Life*, in which time was no longer experienced as 'historical time' in the Argentina of the 1990s. To a certain extent, Román's final suggestion to Amadeo to open a new club betrays Campanella's previous inter-generational appeal, as it suggests that it is the responsibility of the new generations to build a renewed project and there are no seniors at hand to guide it through. Yet, the fact that the new club would build on *Luna*'s old principles imbues as an ever-present reality the wisdom that comes only from maturation, timidly reinstating in the public imaginary the importance of ageing.

The plot of *El secreto de sus ojos* begins at the end of the 1990s, at the point of the retirement of Benjamin Espósito (Darín), ex-judiciary agent, when he decides to start writing an autobiographical novel about the unresolved 1974 case of the rape and murder of Liliana Colotto de Morales (Carla Quevedo). In this venture, he reconnects with his old boss and love interest, judge Irene Menéndez-Hastings, played by Soledad Villamil. The film goes back and forward in time, alternating between the old investigation and Espósito's new quest to find out what happened to the main protagonists of his novel. In the end, we discover that Gómez (Javier Godino), the presumed murderer, who was aligned with the emerging counter-revolutionary militia, was kept captive for twenty-five years by Liliana's grieving widower (Pablo Rago). Espósito comes to terms with the death of Pablo Sandoval, his old partner, played by Guillermo Francella.[11] And we finally witness the long-awaited reunion between Irene and Espósito, who are now free from societal pressures and embrace the possibility of a romantic affair in their senior years. The work with the mise-en-scène, particularly with hair, make-up and costuming, drives temporality, alongside the socio-political changes portrayed – particularly the pre- and post-dictatorship years. In this sense, the film combines several of the strategies of Campanella's previous works, but further emphasises physical changes in the main protagonists as signs of fulfilment rather than decay.[12] This supports Campanella's statement that he chose Darín on several occasions because he became more attractive over time, showing signs of a life well-lived in his face (cited in Jara 2010: 25).

Considered an 'industrial author' (Bernades, Lerer and Wolf 2002: 120), Campanella's last film at the time of writing, *El cuento de las comadrejas* [*The Weasel's Tale*] (2019), tackles precisely the topic of ageing on the big screen. It narrates, in a darkly comic vein, the story of a retired film star from the Golden Age – played by Graciela Borges in a self-referential mode – who shares a big mansion with her husband, old scriptwriter Pedro de Córdova (Luis Brandoni), her former director Norberto Imbert (Oscar Martínez) and past actor Martín Saravia (Marcos Mundstock). Although the film is an adaptation of a 1976 film called *Los muchachos de antes no usaban arsénico* [*Yesterday's Guys Used No Arsenic*] (Martínez Suárez 1976), there are clear influences of previous, classic Hollywood films about the decline of film stars, such as *Sunset Boulevard* (Wilder 1950), and its remake forms part of the 'longevity revolution' that popular Western culture is currently experiencing, in view of the change of demographic composition produced by the ageing population (Cox 2012; Dolan 2018; Casado-Gual 2019). The three old men, played by three prolific veteran actors, become the anti-heroes with whom the audience identifies, while the villains of the story are the slick young city couple that aims to buy the house – played by Clara Lago and Nicolás Francella, Guillermo Francella's son.

The other fruitful alliance that started in this period for Darín, as referred to in previous chapters, was with director Fabián Bielinsky. Although short-lived due to Bielinksy's sudden death in 2006, the two films they made together remain iconic masterpieces in the history of Argentine cinema (Courau 2021). In addition to playing a versed con artist in *Nueve reinas*, Darín embodied another mature character in *El Aura* [*The Aura*] (2005). Esteban Espinosa is a middle-aged, introspective taxidermist who suffers from epileptic attacks – which he describes as 'auratic' moments – and who fantasizes about committing the perfect crime thanks to his photographic memory. After his wife leaves him, his friend Sontag (Alejandro Awada) invites him to Bariloche to go hunting. While in Patagonia, he has the opportunity to execute one of the crimes he has always dreamt of.[13] Following Marcos's steps in *Nueve reinas*, Esteban shows a pusillanimous yet surprisingly seductive personality (Batle 2005), which granted Darín the opportunity to keep exploring characters outside his usual charming guy-next-door roles. The sombre atmosphere of the forest dominates, transforming most characters into ghosts that have only a spectral presence in Esteban's life (Bielinsky, quoted in Letelier 2021). Moreover, his work as a taxidermist causes an allegorical effect that permeates the film, infusing the illusions of life with the realities of a barren existence. In this regard, even though there is no specific reflection on ageing, *El Aura* provides an existential view of life at the margins.

There are two other roles that Darín took on at the turn of the century that have contributed to showing his versatility and to consolidating him as a cinema actor whose characters are beyond the age of forty: *Samy y yo* [*Sammy and Me*] and *Kamchatka*, both released in 2002. The former was directed by Eduardo Milewicz.[14] Before embarking on this project with Darín, he directed *La vida según Muriel* [*Life According to Muriel*] (1997), working alongside Soledad Villamil and Inés Estévez, who had participated with Darín at that time in other films. *Samy y yo* is a Woody Allen-esque romantic comedy that explores the relationship between a neurotic television scriptwriter, Samy Goldstein (Darín), and the sexy, young, new girlfriend of the boss of the TV network, played by Colombian actress Angie Cepeda.[15] Anxious about his upcoming fortieth birthday, Samy contemplates leaving everything behind and dedicating his life to writing his long-awaited novel, in a classic middle-age crisis. The encounter with Mary (Cepeda) and their subsequent TV project together destabilises but rejuvenates him, adding to Darín's filmography another story where love conquers time and challenges the ageing process.

*Kamchatka* sees Darín working again with Cecilia Roth after their brief shared experience in 1987 in Aristarain's film *The Stranger*. On this occasion, they play a couple whose life is turned upside down by the military dictatorship. The disappearance of their close friends forces them to leave their careers behind and relocate temporarily to the countryside. While in *Samy y yo* we witness Darín in his old comedy style, in this film – with its dramatic ending – we meet an endearing character, a human rights lawyer persecuted by the regime. Marcelo Piñeyro, the director whose career skyrocketed with the teenage sensation *Tango Feroz* [*Wild Tango*] (1993), presented here a reflection on the end of childhood and the importance of legacies. The title of the film, *Kamchatka*, is the country depicted in the strategy board game TEG that the father (Darín) plays with his ten-year old son Harry (Matías Del Pozo), which becomes the film's metaphor: a place of resistance hidden in our souls (Piñeiro quoted in Fernández-Santos 2002). Ageing becomes an impossibility for the leading couple, who disappear at the end of the film, but it turns out to be a site of aspiration for Harry, who only comes to terms with his parents' fate and their legacy of resistance as he grows older and recounts their story for us.[16]

There is a curious reference in some filmographies attached to Darín to a 2001 film by Mario Sábato called *Porque te quiero* [*Why I Love You*]. The director himself has said of this film that it was never made in the end due to the economic constrains he suffered during Menem's administrations and also because he could not convince Darín that the role was perfect for him.[17] Indeed, this proposal came at a time when Darín had started working with Campanella, Mignogna and Bielinsky, and when the play *Art* was reaching new heights of popularity, both in Argentina and Spain. It was also a particular breaking point in his career when, as discussed in this section, he was embracing more mature characters that tended to be in opposition to his common television appearances. In this respect, the turn of the century was a hinge moment for Darín that opened the door to opportunities to delve into anti-hero and sombre personalities in his future work.

## Fifty shades of gray? Exploring darker characters

It is well known that a star's appearance, particularly his/her face and body, are 'the most important and identifiable property possessed by any film star' (Qiong Yu 2017: 6). Following Girelli's (2017) chapter on Montgomery Clift, Qiong Yu explores the idea of appearance as masquerade and concludes that 'a star's image can go against the pleasure of the spectator and be disturbing rather than pleasurable' (2017: 7). When a star transforms their image into a worse-looking self, in other words when s/he challenges the established norms of stardom, this tends to be either to overcome disadvantages or to regenerate one's star image (Qiong Yu 2017: 7). Moreover, as Pam Cook observes in her analysis of Nicole Kidman, 'actors are more likely to achieve award nominations if they display dedication to their craft by making themselves almost

**Figure 8.1**   Ricardo Darín in *Nieve negra* (Hodara 2017)

unrecognizable in portraying character' (2012: 62). Although Darín has not played any disfigured character yet, many of his roles in the past few years have been disturbing and even disagreeable, testing the image spectators have had of this Argentine actor. A good example of this is when he played Salvador in *Nieve negra* [*Black Snow*] (Hodara 2017).

Martín Hodara's solo directorial debut, after working as co-director with Darín in *La señal* and as assistant director in Bielinsky's *Nueve reinas*, is a thriller that narrates the complex relationship of two siblings. Salvador, who lives in a bleak snowy cottage in Patagonia is visited by his brother Marcos (Leonardo Sbaraglia) and his pregnant sister-in-law Laura (Laia Costa) to discuss their inheritance after their abusive father passes away. They have not seen each other since they were teenagers, when their younger brother Juan was shot dead and their sister Sabrina (Dolores Fonzi) ended up in a psychiatric ward as a result. While throughout the film we assume Salvador was responsible for Juan's death – an assumption derived undoubtedly from the way he looks and behaves – towards the end it transpires in a series of flashbacks that it was in fact Marcos who committed fratricide after Juan caught him and Sabrina in an incestuous act. Darín's screen presence in this film has been described by some critics as 'worn and world-weary' yet possessing an indistinguishable 'guarantee of quality' (Moore 2020). Appearance, thus, becomes a powerful masquerade that holds the plot's tension. As Jonathan Holland stated in

*The Hollywood Reporter* at the time, part of the film's dramatic suspense relies on the fact that 'the shaggy-bearded, trigger-happy Salvador, looking and behaving like someone who got lost on his way to *The Revenant*, is anything but amicable' (Holland 2017). It is the impact of Salvador's appearance on others, his surly expression and savage way of living, that ends up causing his death and its cover up by the family's lawyer Seppia – played by old-timer Federico Luppi.

How appearance and masquerade become indistinct in the high spheres of power is the central focus of the political thriller *La cordillera* [*The Summit*] (Mitre 2017), which is another project Darín embarked on whilst involved in *Nieve negra*. Set during a summit of Latin American presidents at a remote resort in the Andes, Hernán Blanco (Darín), the new president of Argentina, has to prove his value on the international scene whilst struggling with his daughter's mental health problems.[18] Presented to the public as a 'regular guy', we slowly discover in every encounter with different political leaders that the concessions Blanco has to make to show his strength take away part of his humanity.[19] Santiago Mitre consciously plays in this film with the dialectical indexical relationship between Darín's star image and the good-guy façade of the character to expose appearance as masquerade. In an interview, the director declared that Darín was the perfect casting choice for the role as he is loved by the public and has the aura of a commoner whilst being nothing short of extraordinary.[20] Hence, the character implies in its indexical parallelism that there is more to Darín the actor than his appearance and star image reveal at first glance.

This exploration of a darker side of his screen persona tends to be considered as Darín's 'new phase' (Andermann 2012: 133). Nonetheless, this period has yet to be associated with the process of the ageing star. Even in the two cases discussed, which are the most extreme instances of unsympathetic/scoundrel characters he has played at the time of writing, his filmography continues to be rooted in his lovable everyman characters. Both Salvador and Hernán Blanco have qualities we can relate to as men living on the edge. Accordingly, this phase is not a distinct period that marks a career shift per se but rather a natural development of his star persona as he grows older. Ageing becomes a performative act by which to re-position his 'niceness' within the romantic image of non-conformity that is embedded in the mature outlaw figure. In *Séptimo* [*The Seventh Floor*] (Amezcua 2013), for instance, he plays a deceitful lawyer, Sebastián Roberti, who frees criminals for a living. The fact that his ex-wife – played by Spanish actress Belén Rueda – orchestrates the kidnapping of their own children to obtain more money from him with a fake ransom makes the audience empathise with Sebastián in spite of knowing he is untrustworthy.

This is the same reaction provoked by his character Héctor Sosa in *Carancho* [*The Vulture*] (Trapero 2010). An ambulance-chasing lawyer – known as a '*carancho*' in Argentina – who lost a friend in an accident he orchestrated to scam the insurance company, his character here is not an audience-pleaser. Yet Sosa's relationship with the young new paramedic Luján Olivera – played by Trapero's wife and muse Martina Gusmán – leads to Sosa questioning his own integrity and encourages him to look for a way out. His attempt to make amends and stop his association with the corrupt firm behind the frauds culminates in a violent persecution that ironically leads to his death in a car accident. The audience, thus, ends up relating to the renegade who is looking for a second chance in life.[21] These types of chiaroscuro characters have been recurrent for Darín in the past decade. *Un cuento chino* [*Chinese Take-Away*] (Borensztein 2011), Darín's first work with Borensztein after *Carancho*, shows an unsympathetic Falklands/Malvinas war veteran working in a hardware store. He is obsessive-compulsive, prejudiced and disagreeable. Nonetheless, he finds himself reluctantly helping a Chinese immigrant, Jun (Ignacio Huang), who is thrown out of a car in front of him. In the process, he learns to connect with others, including the spectators. In *Tesis sobre un homicidio* [*Thesis on a Homicide*] (Goldfrid 2013), he plays Roberto Bermúdez, a retired lawyer turned university lecturer. He is cynical, arrogant, alcoholic, a cheater. But his quest to find the killer of his student resonates with the public, who admires his perseverance.[22]

Probably one of his most iconic roles within this new trend of bittersweet characters is '*bombita*' [little bomb] in *Relatos salvajes* [*Wild Tales*] (Szifrón 2014). Damián Szifrón's portmanteau film features six stand-alone shorts interconnected by the common theme of violence and revenge and drawn from everyday encounters of people on the edge. Darín's segment narrates the story of Simón Fischer, a demolition expert whose car gets towed on the day of his daughter's birthday, for no apparent reason. This act sparks a series of events, including his wife – played by Nancy Dupláa – demanding a divorce, and him losing his job and possibly the custody of his daughter. Upon unsuccessfully applying for another job and getting his car towed again, he retrieves it from the pound, loads it with explosives, and waits for it to be towed again in order to detonate it and blow up the impound office. He becomes a sudden hero on social media under the motto 'we are all *bombita*', whilst a seemingly happy ending shows Fischer being visited by his wife and daughter in prison, where he is cherished by all the inmates as a national hero. Many critics have acknowledged that the film's success lies in the tales being quite cathartic for the audience (Blanes 2016). Darín himself declared that 'this Latin reaction to injustices can be liberating' and that 'we are all *bombitas* in one way or another' (Blanes 2016). It was, precisely, the release of *Relatos salvajes* that incited the actor to join Twitter – with the handle '@BombitaDarin'. The emphasis on the proximity of his persona to the character who is reflected in that choice denotes this fearless – or at least less politically-correct era – throughout which he is revealing that, in the terms of Gilleard and Higgs (2005), 'ageing' can be liberated from 'old age'.

The fact that Darín is now accepting roles that desacralise his established sweetheart appearance in favour of showing a darker side reveals a process of repositioning his star image in the public imaginary as he lives out his sixties. In this sense, ageing becomes the masquerade that disguises any possible misreading of a star's decay. Keeping secrets, exposing failures, manifesting unethical behaviours, being involved in dubious practices are all accepted by the audience as caveats of old age. And, thus, because of his age and long-standing career, these features are perceived as less threatening to Darín's consolidated star image. Instead, they evince a greater depth of character whereby Mr Nice comes of age. In this vein, following Qiong Yu's (2017) analysis, these roles form part of a conscious process of regenerating Darín's own star image, promoting a particular vision of successful ageing.

## Silvering screen

As several scholars have pointed out (Dolan 2018; Jermyn 2012; Holmlund 2010), we now live with an ageing demographic whose impact on contemporary mainstream cinema is evident in both audience composition and in the proliferation of popular films starring older stars and which tell stories about old age (Dolan 2018: 1). As was discussed in the previous sections, Darín is negotiating the realities of ageing by accepting darker characters that add layers of complexity to his typical guy-next-door roles. Moreover, he is also extending his stardom status by embracing the recent trend of mature love stories (Hobbs 2013), which has even been identified – rather controversially – as a new sub-genre, now named the 'gerontocom' (Casado-Gual 2019). This is particularly evident in his participation in films like *El amor menos pensado* [*An Unexpected Love*] (Verá 2018), the first production of his new company, Kenya Films. It narrates the story of a couple, Marcos (Darín) and Ana (Mercedes Morán), who, after twenty-five years of marriage, decide to separate.[23] In a comic vein, we follow each one of them as they navigate the world of dating in their senior years, struggling with social media platforms and unreasonable expectations of passionate encounters on the contemporary dating scene.

In spite of this tendency towards silvering the screen, ageing remains contentious in popular culture and, as Jerslev and Petersen have pointed out, 'celebrity culture by and large remains a culture of youth' (2018: 159). The political economy of the male and female celebrity body is threatened by signs of ageing. Therefore, growing old in a youth-centred world means that stars need to break away from a limelight of a frenzied celebrity status towards a redefinition of stardom as long-standing professional recognition and ongoing casting opportunities for leading roles. Darín is succeeding in this reconceptualisation of his star image. For him, this instance of reaching maturity on the big screen has taken an opposite direction from the connotations of impairment and social immobility associated with old age. In Gilleard and Higgs's terms, he has indeed managed to liberate ageing from old age – stepping into what they recognise as a Third Age paradigm shift in cultural representation (2005: 161).

In an interview, upon being asked if he was scared of the passing of time, Darín confessed he was not scared but anxious (quoted in Corbacho 2020). Nonetheless, in one of the last films he worked on at the time of writing, *La odisea de los giles* [*Heroic Losers*] (Borensztein 2019), he embraces his six decades with grace. There are several scenes in the first half of the film when we see Fermín Perlassi (Darín) dying his hair while his friends, Belaúnde (Daniel Aráoz) and Antonio Fontana (Luis Brandoni) mock him for his poor attempt at disguising his age. When his wife – played by Verónica Llinás – dies in a car accident, he lets himself go. But the prospect of gaining justice by planning a heist against Manzi (Andrés Parra), the lawyer who stole all their cooperative's money during the 2001 crisis, gives him the opportunity to accept his grey hair as a sign of wisdom and maturity. Ageing is not to be hidden anymore, but instead to be praised and exposed as a demonstration of a successful life. Accordingly, the happy ending shows Perlassi with all the perks of a sexagenarian.[24] He is holding a baby, presumably his grandchild, after his son Rodrigo – played by Darín's son in real life – reunites with Manzi's secretary (Ailín Zaninovich), who kept their plan a secret. Both character and actor reflect on what it means to be 'aged by culture' (Gullette 2004) and, as Holmlund concluded in her analysis of Jackie Chan's ageing process, they reaffirm that 'we all need to make it possible to think, feel and act "ageing" as something other than planned obsolescence' (2010: 108).

## Notes

1. There are several studies that delve into the age-specific gender gaps of Hollywood actors (Fleck and Hanssen 2016; Lincoln and Allen 2004; Lauzen and Dozier 2005). The Geena Davies Institute on Gender in Media provides important quantitative data on the subject – available at: https://seejane.org/wp-content/uploads/frail-frumpy-and-forgotten-report.pdf (accessed 28 December 2021).
2. 'Casa tía' was a chain of superstores owned by Francisco de Narváez (Melo 2020). In the mid-1990s, Darín did a commercial with his wife, Florencia Bas, in which they go to the supermarket to do their Christmas shopping and, as in the film *Home Alone* (Columbus 1990), they forget their son in the store – available at: https://www.youtube.com/watch?v=xPwvtynaPMY (accessed 9 September 2021). In those years he also did another commercial with Luis Brandoni for the Brahma beer label, where both play similar roles as in *Mi cuñado* – available at: https://www.youtube.com/watch?v=LGhGAGwXiuM (accessed 9 September 2021).
3. According to Andermann, 'only ten feature-length films were produced in 1992 and a mere five in 1994 [...] Overall production figures have steadily risen since 1994, effectively breaking through the ceiling of 100 feature films per year in 1997 (now putting Argentina just below France in terms of quantity of cinematographic output' (2012: 1–2).
4. Please refer to the Appendices for a full filmography.
5. Santaló decides to play poker on behalf of Escofet, gambling in a no-limit game against Víctor Ganz, played by famous *telenovela* star of the time, Facundo Arana. Santaló gives up and falls asleep. Escofet thinks he was tricked by Santaló and shoots him, only to be shot back by Tabita. It is then revealed that Tabita made an arrangement with Ganz, who turned out to have an identical twin who took turns during the game. She flees with the brothers and the money, leaving Santaló to die.
6. This was Darín's and Hodara's debut as directors, although Hodara had worked as assistant director on several occasions, many of those on productions where Darín was involved in front of the camera, which consolidated their friendship and long-standing partnership.
7. The film included many well-known performers such as Ulises Dumont, Eduardo Blanco, Alfonzo De Grazia, Alicia Zanca, Graciela Tenembaum, Rodrigo de la Serna, Magela Zanotta and Mariana Richaudeau.

8. Other characters and cast members included: Claudia Fontán as Rafael's ex-wife Sandra; Atilio Pozzobon as Francesco, one of the Belvedere restaurant's employees; Humberto Serrano as the priest Mario; and Adrián Suar as the director of the film shot within the film.
9. It can be claimed that it is precisely due to this inter-generational approach that the film was so successful at home and abroad – being released in more than thirty countries (Getino 2016: 321). In recent studies on ageing on the big screen, some scholars have signalled appeal to all age groups as the business's pre-eminent aspiration (Jermyn 2018: 167; Cox 2012).
10. Other characters defending the club are the dance teacher, played by Valeria Bertuccelli, Román's wife (Silvia Kutika), and the club's partner Emilio (Atilio Pozzobon). The character who brings the dissenting voice is played by Daniel Fanego, who won a Cóndor de Plata for Best Supporting Actor for this role.
11. In the film, Sandoval takes Espósito's place when two *sicarios* come looking for him, resulting in his death. This role was crucial in Francella's career, who until then was considered mainly a comedy actor (Medios 2020). He won several awards, including Best Supporting Actor in the Premios Clarín, Premios Cóndor de Plata and Premios Sur, which also granted this award to Pablo Rago for his performance as Ricardo Morales.
12. Other cast members included Mario Alarcón, José Luis Gioia and Mariano Argento.
13. Dolores Fonzi plays Diana Dietrich, the young wife of abusive Carlos Dietrich (Manuel Rodal), the owner of the cabin where Esteban and Sontag spend the night, who is killed by mistake by Esteban while hunting a deer. Other cast members included Pablo Cedrón, Jorge D'Elía, Rafa Castejón, Walter Reyno and Nahuel Pérez Biscayart.
14. It was released as *Un tipo corriente* [*A Regular Guy*] in Spain.
15. Alejandra Flechner, Cristina Banegas, Henny Trayles, Carolina Peleritti, Alejandra Darín, Roberto Pettinato and Rita Cortese complete the cast.
16. The film included other well-known actors, such as Héctor Alterio, Fernanda Mistral, Tomás Fonzi and Leticia Brédice.
17. According to Sábato, 'I invited Darín to participate in the project when he was still an actor working in insignificant comedies. I believed in his talent when nobody did, not even himself. But neither his manager nor myself could convince him that he could take on this leading role' ['Yo lo había convocado a Darín, cuando aún era un actor que solo trabajaba en comedietas sin importancia. Y confiaba en su talento cuando nadie lo vislumbraba, ni siquiera él mismo. Pero ni su representante ni yo logramos convencerlo que podía enfrentar el protagonista'] (conversation exchange courtesy of Adrián Muoyo, personal communication).
18. Role played by Dolores Fonzi.
19. The film features an array of Latin American stars, such as Alfredo Castro, Paulina García, Daniel Giménez Cacho, Hernán Romero, Rafael Alfaro and Leonardo Franco. Erica Rivas plays Blanco's personal secretary, Spanish actress Elena Anaya is the journalist covering the summit, Gerardo Romano is one of Blanco's Ministers, and nineties Hollywood box-office sensation Christian Slater plays the US representative who buys off Blanco to accept the energy deal discussed at the summit.

20. Interview done by *Canal-e.com* and available at: https://www.youtube.com/watch?v=IU24hl3GOrM (accessed 19 December 2021).
21. The film also featured Darío Valenzuela, Carlos Weber, José Luis Arias, Fabio Ronzano, Loren Acuña and Gabriel Almirón.
22. Other cast members included Alberto Ammann as the presumed killer, Calu Rivero as Laura Di Natale, Arturo Puig, Fabián Arenillas, Mara Bestelli, José Luis Mazza, Antonio Ugo, Mateo Chiarino and Natalia Santiago.
23. Other cast members included Juan Minujín, Claudia Fontán, Luis Rubio, Andrea Pietra, Norman Briski, Jean Pierre Noher, Andrea Politti, Andrés Gil and Gabriel Corrado.
24. We will also see Darín playing a minor role as Alex's (Junio Valverde) deceased grandfather in the film *Violet* (Berdejo 2013).

# References

Aguilar, G. (2006) *Otros mundos. Un ensayo sobre el nuevo cine argentino*, Buenos Aires: Santiago Arcos Editor.
Andermann, J. (2012) *New Argentine Cinema*, London and New York: I. B. Tauris.
Basting, A. D. (1998) *The Stages of Age: Performing Age in Contemporary American Culture*, Ann Arbor: The University of Michigan Press.
Batle, D. (2005) 'Impactante film con un Darín prodigioso', in *La Nación*, 15 September. https://www.lanacion.com.ar/espectaculos/cine/impactante-film-con-un-darin-prodigioso-nid738772/ (accessed 21 November 2021).
Bernades, H., Lerer, D. and Wolf, S. (eds) (2002) *El nuevo cine argentino: Temas, autores y estilos de una renovación*, Buenos Aires: Ediciones Tatanka/Fipresci.
Blanes, P. (2016) 'Ricardo Darín: "En Hollywood Relatos salvajes va a resultar más liberadora"', in *Cambio16 Actualidad y Cultura*. https://www.cambio16.com/ricardo-darin-en-hollywood-relatos-salvajes-va-a-resultar-mas-liberadora/ (accessed 24 December 2021).
Casado-Gual, N. (2019) 'Ageing and Romance on the Big Screen: The "Silvering Romantic Comedy" *Elsa & Fred*', in *Ageing & Society*, 40.10, pp. 2257–2265. DOI: https://doi.org/10.1017/S0144686X19000643
Cook, P. (2012) *Nicole Kidman*, London: Palgrave Macmillan.
Corbacho, L. (2020) 'Ricardo Darín: La odisea de ser argentino', in *El Planeta Urbano*, April. https://elplanetaurbano.com/2020/04/ricardo-darin-%C2%B7-la-odisea-de-ser-argentino/ (accessed 10 May 2020).
Courau, G. (2021) 'Fabián Bielinsky: a 15 años de la muerte del joven director que dejó huella en el cine nacional', in *La Nación*, 28 June. https://www.lanacion.com.ar/espectaculos/cine/fabian-bielinsky-a-15-anos-de-la-muerte-del-joven-director-que-dejo-huella-en-el-cine-nacional-nid28062021/ (accessed 20 November 2021).
Cox, D. (2012) 'How Older Viewers are Rescuing Cinema', in *The Guardian*, 8 March. https://www.theguardian.com/film/2012/mar/08/older-viewers-rescuing-cinema (accessed 24 October 2021).
Dolan, J. (2018) *Contemporary Cinema and 'Old Age': Gender and the Silvering of Stardom*, Glasgow: Palgrave Macmillan.

Fernández-Santos, E. (2002), 'El territorio de la resistencia', in *El País*, 29 November. https://elpais.com/diario/2002/11/29/cine/1038524404_850215.html (accessed 6 December 2021).

Fleck, R. K. and Hanssen, A. (2016) 'Persistence and Change in Age-specific Gender Gaps: Hollywood Actors from Silent Era Onward', in *International Review of Law and Economics*, 48, pp. 36–49.

Gates, P. (2010) 'Acting His Age? The Resurrection of the '80s Action Heroes and Their Aging Stars', in *Quarterly Review of Film and Video*, 27.4, pp. 276–289.

Getino, O. (2016) *Cine argentino: entre lo posible y lo deseable*, Buenos Aires: Fundación CICCUS.

Gilleard, C. and Higgs, P. (2005) *Contexts of Ageing: Class, Cohort and Community*, Cambridge: Polity.

Girelli, E. (2017) 'In your Face: Montgomery Clift Comes Out as Crip in *The Young Lions*', in Qiong, S. and Austin, G. (eds), *Revisiting Star Studies: Cultures, Themes and Methods*, Edinburgh: Edinburgh University Press.

Gullette, M. M. (2004) *Aged by Culture*, Chicago: The University of Chicago Press.

Guo, J. (2016) 'Why the Age of 40 is So Important in Hollywood', in *The Washington Post*, 19 September. https://www.washingtonpost.com/news/wonk/wp/2016/09/19/these-charts-reveal-how-bad-the-film-industrys-sexism-is/ (accessed 2 September 2021).

Harrington, L., Bielby, D. and Bardo, A. (eds) (2014) *Aging, Media, and Culture*, Lanham, MD: Lexington Books.

Harris, I. (1995) *Messages Men Hear: Constructing Masculinities*, London: Taylor & Harris.

Hearn, J. (1987) *The Gender of Opression: Men, Masculinity, and the Critique of Marxism*, New York: St. Martin's Press.

Hobbs, A. (2013) 'Romancing the Crone: Hollywood's Recent Mature Love Stories', in *The Journal of American Culture*, 36.1, March, pp. 42–51.

Holland, J. (2017) 'Black Snow (Nieve negra): Film Review', in *The Hollywood Reporter*, 28 April. https://www.hollywoodreporter.com/movies/movie-reviews/black-snow-review-998533/ (accessed 14 December 2021).

Holmlund, C. (2002) *Impossible Bodies*, London and New York: Routledge.

Holmlund, C. (2010) 'Celebrity, Ageing and Jackie Chan: Middle-aged Asian in Transnational Action', in *Celebrity Studies*, 1.1, pp. 96–112. DOI: 10.1080/19392390903519107

Horrocks, R. (1994) *Masculinity in Crisis. Myths, Fantasies and Realities*, New York: Palgrave Macmillan.

Jara, L. (2010) 'Ricardo Darín, el elegido', in *.dom*, 16 May, pp. 21–26.

Jermyn, D. (2012) '"Get a life, ladies. Your old one is not coming back": Ageing, Ageism and the Lifespan of Female Celebrity', *Celebrity Studies*, 3.1, pp. 1–12. DOI: 10.1080/19392397.2012.644708

Jermyn, D. (2018) '"Grey is the new green"? Gauging Age(ing) in Hollywood's Upper Quadrant Female Audience, *The Intern* (2015), and the discursive construction of "Nancy Meyers"', *Celebrity Studies*, 9.2, pp. 166–185. DOI: 10.1080/19392397.2018.1465296

Jerslev, A. and Petersen, L. N. (2018) 'Introduction: Ageing Celebrities, Ageing Fans, and Ageing Narratives in Popular Media Culture', in *Celebrity Studies*, 9.2, pp. 157–165.

Lauzen, M. M. and Dozier, D. M. (2005) 'Maintaining the Double Standard: Portrayals of Age and Gender in Popular Films', in *Sex Roles*, 52, pp. 437–446.

Letelier, J. (2021) 'Fabián Bielinsky, Director de El Aura', in *Revista de cine Mabuse*, 3 December. https://www.mabuse.cl/entrevista.php?id=72022 (accessed 4 December 2021).

Lincoln, A. E. and Allen, M. P. (2004) 'Double Jeopardy in Hollywood: Age and Gender in the Careers of Film Actors, 1926–1999', in *Sociological Forum*, 19, pp. 611–631.

Lipscomb, V. B. and Marshall, L. (2010) 'Introduction', in *Staging Age*, New York: Palgrave Macmillan.

McKenna, M. (2019) 'Sylvester Stallone and the Economics of the Ageing Film Actor', in *Celebrity Studies*, 10.4, pp. 489–503. DOI: 10.1080/19392397.2019.1672999

Medios (2020) 'Por qué Campanella buscó a Francella para El secreto de sus ojos', in *El Sol*, 6 August. https://www.elsol.com.ar/el-motivo-por-el-que-campanella-busco-a-francella-para-el-secreto-de-sus-ojos (accessed 12 November 2021).

Melo, S. (2020) 'A más de 20 años del cierre de Casa Tía, Vuelve De Narváez a las gondolas olavarrienses', in *El Popular*, 15 November. https://www.elpopular.com.ar/nota/151234/a-mas-de-20-anos-del-cierre-de-casa-tia-vuelve-de-narvaez-a-las-gondolas-olavarrienses (accessed 9 September 2021).

Moore, R. (2020) 'Netflixable? Siblings try to keep the secret of "Black Snow (Nieve negra)"', in *Movie Nation* blog, 12 August. https://rogersmovienation.com/2020/08/12/netflixable-siblings-keep-the-secret-of-black-snow/ (accessed 14 December 2021).

Oyarzabal, S. (2020) *Nation, Culture and Class in Argentine Cinema: Crisis and Representation (1998–2005)*, Woodbridge: Tamesis.

Page, J. (2009) *Crisis and Capitalism in Contemporary Argentine Cinema*, Durham, NC: Duke University Press.

Qiong Yu, S. (2017) 'Introduction; Performing Stardom: Star Studies in Transformation and Expansion', in Qiong Yu, S. and Austin, G. (eds), *Revisiting Star Studies: Cultures, Themes and Methods*, Edinburgh: Edinburgh University Press.

Rocha, C. (2012) *Masculinities in Contemporary Argentine Popular Cinema*, New York: Palgrave Macmillan.

Sarlo, B. (1994) *Escenas de la vida posmoderna. Intelectuales, arte y videocultura en la argentina*, Buenos Aires: Ariel/Espasa Cape Argentina S.A.

Swinnen, A. (2012) 'Introduction', in Swinnen, A. and Stotesbury, J. (eds), *Aging, Performance, and Stardom. Doing Age on the Stage of Consumerist Culture*, Zurich and Berlin: LIT Verlag.

Van den Bulck, H. (2014) 'Growing Old in Celebrity Culture', in Harrington, C. L., Bielby, D. and Bardo, A. R. (eds), *Aging, Media, and Culture*, Lanham, MD: Lexington Books.

PART III

# A 'Hispanic' Star

## Chapter 9

# Spanish *conquistador*

If there is one country in which Darín's stardom and popularity reached the same dimension as in Argentina, that country is Spain. Darín appeared for the first time in Spanish film theatres in 1994 with *Perdido por perdido* [*Nothing to Lose*] directed by Alberto Lecchi. At that time, Argentine films were slowly starting to gain more attention, thanks to the success of *Un lugar en el mundo* [*A Place in the World*] (1992), a film directed by Adolfo Aristarain which attracted the outstanding number of half a million spectators in commercial theatres (Colmena 1994; Elena 2011: 42). Inspired by those figures, and given that Lecchi was one of the scriptwriters of Aristarain's film, *Perdido* was destined to be one of only two Argentine films that made it to the Spanish big screen that year. Although Darín's presence in this film was not singled out by the critics at the time, who preferred to focus on the plot and the connections between Lecchi and Aristarain, the seed of Darín's Spanish stardom was being sown in many positive reviews of the film's performances (such as Torreiro's in 1994). Moreover, his character, an ordinary middle-class fellow in crisis who cleverly manages to run away with the money and the girl, marked a precedent for his lovable future characters.

Four years later, a co-production with Spain, *El faro del sur* [*The Lighthouse*] (1998),[1] brought Darín back to Spanish shores. On that occasion, the 1997 Goya Award-winning director Eduardo Mignogna and the promising young Spanish actress Ingrid Rubio caught the press's attention (Villena 1998; Rivera 1998; Torreiro 1998). Highly favoured by the presence of renowned cast and crew from both countries, *El faro* increased the number of spectators of *Perdido* by almost sevenfold and in 1999 won what was Mignogna's second Goya Award for Best Foreign Film in Spanish. Overshadowed by the presence of Norma Aleandro and the popularity of Rubio, Darín's work eluded the headlines once again. Nonetheless, his sympathetic middle-aged character stayed in the Spanish audience's imaginary not only thanks to the film's success and its highly visible presence in the media, but also because of his role as a soap opera heart-throb in *Rebelde* (shot in 1989), which was shown on national TV at that time (on Channel 5 from 1997 to 1998). This was a role that placed him among the *galán* actors who were rising stars of the 1980s and 1990s Spanish film industry, such as Imanol Arias, who was also working in both countries and who contributed to the implementation of a shared star system.[2] Accordingly, Darín's third appearance in Spanish film theatres proved to be the charm. For many film historians and critics, *Nueve reinas* [*Nine Queens*] (2000) by Fabián Bielinsky represents the turning point in Darín's Spanish career (Herbera 2012). Released at the end of August 2001, it was accompanied by an increase in Argentine migrants to the Iberian Peninsula and the constant presence of Argentina in the news, due to its deteriorating socio-political circumstances. Two months later, in October 2001, another film by Mignogna put Darín back in the theatres: *La fuga* [*The Escape*] (which won yet another Goya); and in November came the overwhelming success of *El hijo de la novia* [*The Son of the Bride*], arguably the true turning point in Darín's rise to stardom in Spanish film culture.

As the film scholar Alberto Elena has pointed out, Campanella's film *El hijo de la novia* changed the history of cinematographic relations between Spain and Argentina (2011: 43). With more than €7 million in box-office earnings and with more than 1.5 million spectators, the film enjoyed an uninterrupted run in theatres for an entire year (González Acevedo 2005: 17). Its enormous success made possible the release of a former Campanella film starring Darín, *El mismo amor, la misma lluvia* [*Same Love, Same Rain*], a few months later (Ginart 2002). Along with the constant presence of Darín's face on the billboards came the local awards, accompanied by critical acclaim: for three years in a row he received the Sant Jordi Award for Best Foreign Actor (for his performances in *Nueve reinas*, *La fuga* and *El hijo de la novia*), and he also won the Leading Character of the Year Award (granted by *Onda Cero* in 2002). Since then, he has had a spot reserved on the Spanish big screen almost every year, and his public recognition has continued to grow. He won the Best Actor Award at Valladolid's International Film Festival for *Luna de Avellaneda* [*Avellaneda's Moon*] (2004) and was nominated twice for the Goya Awards in 2009 – for Best Leading Actor in *El secreto de sus ojos* [*The Secret in Their Eyes*] (2009) and Best Supporting Actor in *El baile de la Victoria* [*The Dancer and the Thief*] (2009). In 2015 he received the Silver Shell for Best Actor at the 63rd San Sebastian Film Festival for *Truman* (Gay 2015) – for which he also obtained his first individual Goya Award and the *Círculo de escritores cinematográficos*'s medal in 2016 – and in 2017 the same festival granted him the Donostia Award for his outstanding career, naming him one of the best Latin American contemporary actors.[3]

This rise to film stardom in Spain paved the way for Darín's transnational stardom. Such a crossover brings to the fore questions on the postcolonial nature of the film industry's power relationships and legitimising strategies; and on whether a performer from Latin America needs the old colonial – i.e. European – recognition to transcend local familiarity, or not. As will be explored in more depth in Chapter 10, Darín claims to have rejected Hollywood's proposals because he did not want to be boxed in stereotypical *Latino* roles. Yet, his constant appearance in Spanish films as the 'Argentinian', performing with a peculiar accent and body movements, speaks of a commonplace stereotype in a shared Hispanic geopolitical community. This chapter explores the existence of this stereotype. It will do so by analysing Darín's reception in both Spanish specialised film literature and the general public media, taking into consideration not only the films that have been shown in Spain but also his participation in major cinematographic events in that country, such as the Goya awards and the San Sebastian film festival. The growing network of friends, family members and colleagues working in the Spanish film industry will also be considered, alongside the assumption of a dual nationality and role as a member of the Instituto Cervantes' patronage. By analysing the treatment of Darín's public image in Spain, this chapter ultimately aims to question how the impact of socio-economic circumstances and the dynamics of the Spanish cinematographic industry on the reception of foreign actors reflects and refracts the collective Hispanic imaginary at times of intense migration on both sides of the Atlantic.

## Migratory flows, co-productions and the Ibermedia programme

Darín's prominent position in the shared Spanish-Argentine star phenomenon is the product of a changing socio-political and cultural context informed by the constant emigration of Argentines from the turn of the century onwards, and by the shared past of social, political, cultural and economic relationships. Migration played a central role in the increased representation of Latin American characters in Spanish cinema and in the arrival of foreign films to the peninsula. The exodus caused by the various dictatorships throughout Latin America during the twentieth century was followed by the incorporation of Spain into the European Union in the mid-1980s, with the subsequent freedom of movement of European citizens. The Argentine crisis of 2001 also played an important part in this equation, bringing hundreds of Argentines to the country (Schmidt 2010; Actis 2005). The Spanish and Argentine film industries were both transformed not only by this ongoing circulation of people but also by the development of government policies and industrial collaborations in the form of financial support for production and/or distribution and co-production programmes such as Ibermedia, founded in 1998 (Lara 2011: 274–286; Sanz 2019: 128).[4] As the Spanish film historians Carmen Ciller and Manuel Palacio have pointed out, before the emergence of these programmes the Argentine and Spanish industries were barely connected (2011: 339).

The first wave of Argentine performers to arrive to Spain took place in the 1940s. As discussed in Chapter 1, this was a consequence of the emergence of Peronism and its restrictive policies, and later on due to the various dictatorships that overthrew Peronism and its supporters. During those years, the Francoist's National Entertainment Union demanded special permits for work in Spain, which restricted participation and forced many performers to request dual nationality (Ciller and Palacio 2011: 339). Franco's dictatorship ended in 1975, opening up a long transitional process that welcomed foreign cultural influences.

Whilst Spain was slowly becoming more inclusive, in 1976, on the other side of the world, the National Reorganization Process took its toll on the local Argentine entertainment industry, bringing to Spain a new wave of artists – as discussed in Chapter 3. At the end of the dictatorship in Argentina, the new democratic government tried once more to promote the circulation of national productions abroad. Between 1986 and 1990 the Argentine National Film Institute ran a sales office in Madrid to that end (Getino and Schargorodsky 2008). Spanish Television (*Televisión Española*, TVE) also had an ambitious co-production policy in place between 1985 and 1995, but only a few films were produced with Argentina at first, in comparison with those produced with Mexico and other Latin American countries (Elena 2009: 295; Hoefert de Turégano 2004: 17).

It was with the creation of the Ibermedia programme at the end of the 1990s that the circulation of performers between both countries was significantly increased.[5] According to Alberto Elena, since the emergence of this programme, all the co-production initiatives that have appealed to a shared star system were more prone to box-office success, which encouraged more producers to invest in these sorts of enterprises. It was precisely this shared star system that dethroned Mexican productions in Spain and located Argentina as the main Latin American country with which to co-produce and show films in Spanish theatres from the 1990s onwards.[6] In Elena's words, with the exception of Gael García Bernal for Mexico, and the Cuban Jorge Perugorría, the plethora of Argentine artists familiar to Spanish audiences, including Federico Luppi, Cecilia Roth, Héctor Alterio, Darío Grandinetti and, more recently, Leonardo Sbaraglia, Miguel Ángel Solá and, very specially, Ricardo Darín, have become the most attractive strategy to lure audiences to the theatres, even more so than the 'universality of the stories', 'the common socio-cultural connections' or the 'similarity of artistic sensibilities', which according to representatives of Casa de América were the key audience drivers of co-productions (Elena 2009: 295).

The configuration of Darín as a star in Spain depended a great deal on this industry's dynamics. At the time of writing, thirty-two films including Darín as cast member – out of fifty-two films he has worked on to this day – have made it into Spanish theatres, and twenty-seven of them are co-productions (see Table 9.1 in Appendix 2).[7] In other words, almost 80 per cent of the films that brought Darín to Spanish audiences managed to do so thanks to co-production entrepreneurship. Most significantly, of those twenty-seven co-productions, twenty-one of them were produced with Spanish resources, demonstrating the close relationship that Argentina and Spain have been co-developing since the year 2000. They also indicate the complex financial structure behind filmmaking in Latin America, whereby multiple funding awards and sources of income from around the world are required to successfully generate any single production (Tierney 2019: 4, 16). This challenges the very concept of a national cinema (García Canclini 1997; McClennen 2018) and, in many cases, shapes narratives – and cultures – based on casting choices that have to fulfil the 'technical-artistic' requirements of co-productions (Falicov 2012). These requirements all contributed, to a certain extent, to consolidating the so-called 'Darín effect' in Spain (Sanz 2019: 137).

Darín has insisted that while co-productions have accelerated and facilitated the process, they were tried in the past and did not influence the success of any specific star, 'that's why I like to believe that it is directly related to the simplicity of the stories ... I think they were able to go a bit further, to the people's hearts' ['por eso me gusta creer que está directamente relacionado con la simplicidad de las historias ... me parece que se ha conseguido llegar un poco más lejos, al corazón de la gente'] (Darín quoted in González Acevedo 2005: 43). The kind of stories depicted is certainly an important factor in terms of attracting an audience, as will be analysed in the next section, but considering that almost all of these co-productions fall in the post-*El hijo de la novia* period, and that many excellent films from Argentina never reached the same level of exposure in Spain as in their home country, it cannot be denied that industrial and socio-political changes that occurred at a particular moment in Darín's career have benefited his Spanish conquest. In this respect, Álvaro Martín Sanz emphasised that Argentine cinema in general remains almost unknown in Spain today, with the exception of films made with Spanish funding by specific directors – such as Campanella – or those including Ricardo Darín in the cast (2019: 137–140).

As previously mentioned, his role in *Nueve reinas* and, shortly after, his performance in *El hijo de la novia* marked a turning point for Spanish audiences. Throughout 2002, one could go to the cinema and choose between five different films starring Darín – an unprecedented situation that put him right in the spotlight (González Acevedo 2005: 41). Despite his not living in Spain, in contrast to other Argentine actors who found success in the country, such as Federico Luppi or Héctor Alterio, he managed to shine by taking careful advantage of this sudden public exposure. In the Spanish newspaper *El País*, Darín himself recognised at the time that it was only thanks to this auspicious moment that he dared to appear then in a play in Madrid – and the title of the article actually stated that this new version of *Art* was taking place in Spanish theatres at that particular moment precisely due to Darín's success at the billboards (García 2003).[8]

Towards the end of 2002, when the impact of *El hijo* in the press and public opinion was starting to wane, two more films were released in theatres. The first one, *Un tipo corriente* [*Sammy and Me*] (released in Argentina as *Samy y yo*), portrayed a Woody Allen-esque character who has an unlikely romantic venture with the sexy Colombian actress Angie Cepeda, who was quite famous in Spain for her participation in popular soap operas such as *Luz María* or *Pobre Diabla* [*Poor Crazy Girl*] – which were two of the most successful soap operas shown on Spanish TV over the last few decades. A month later, *Kamchatka*, which told the story of a family living clandestinely due to the arrival of the Argentine military regime, brought Darín back to the big screen once again, together with two other Argentine actors well known to Spanish audiences, Cecilia Roth and Héctor Alterio. Roth was experiencing the peak of her career after the overwhelming international success of *Todo sobre mi madre* [*All About my Mother*] (Almodóvar 1999),[9] and Alterio was appearing on Spanish TV in one of the most popular series of the time, *Cuéntame cómo pasó* [*Tell Me How It Happened*] (TVE), which undoubtedly caught the general public's attention and placed Darín among those recognisable faces from abroad who were respected by Spanish cinemagoers.

As mentioned by Elena in his review of the migratory flows that have contributed to an ongoing presence of Latin Americans in the Spanish film industry, the relationships between Spain and its former colonies confer upon the national audio-visual productions a certain specificity that is yet to be properly analysed (2005: 111). Darín's growing presence in films directed by Spanish filmmakers, such as *La educación de las hadas* [*The Education of Fairies*] (Cuerda 2006), *El baile de la Victoria* (Trueba 2009), *En fuera de juego* [*Offside*] (Marqués 2012), *Una pistola en cada mano* [*A Gun in Each Hand*] (Gay 2012), *Séptimo* [*7th Floor*] (Amezcua 2013), *Torrente 5: Operación Eurovegas* (Segura 2015) and *Truman* (Gay 2015) shows an increased transnational flow of cast and crew members that speaks to a common, mixed imaginary community. Nonetheless, as Chris Berry has rightly stated, no transnational cinema exists without encountering and negotiating national spaces and cultures (Berry 2010: 112; Dennison 2013: xv). In these cases, we can arguably state that Darín's roles, instead of embracing a hybrid global – or 'Hispanic' – quality, are deeply rooted in local recognisable tropes of 'the Argentinians'. Thus, they negotiate the space that migrants from the South American country occupy in the contemporary Spanish imaginary. A critical interplay of identity, where Darín is at the same time one of them – the Spanish residents – and the Other – the Argentinian. This stereotype of the Argentinian in Spanish cinema is an area that, according to Carmen Ciller and Manuel Palacio, has not been studied yet (2011: 338) and, undoubtedly, the case of Darín is the best point of departure for such an exploration.

## Darín 'the Argentinian'

The stories and the types of characters that brought Darín to Spain, as mentioned above, are also important factors in the construction of Darín's star image. I have previously stated, in an article written for the

*Bulletin of Hispanic Studies* and following Rafael Miret's criticism of *El hijo de la novia* in the Spanish film magazine *Dirigido por* ... (2001: 40), that these are simple stories that have captured the audience's attention due to their thematic proximity and as apertures to easy self-identification and, when it comes to Darín's own personal success, charming characters who speak to people's emotions (Garavelli 2015: 417–418). Nonetheless, in that article I did not delve into the tensions in interpretation of the star persona based on whether he was located at home or abroad – in other words, whether he was acting in a film directed by an Argentine director or by someone from overseas. As the paragraph that closed the previous section affirmed, when Darín appeared in films directed by Spanish filmmakers, he played fairly stereotypical roles of what can be described as the male 'Argentinian figure'.

In *La educación de las hadas* (Cuerda 2006), he plays Nicolás, a toy inventor living in Barcelona, who was brought up in Argentina and had a tormented relationship with his father. The story is set in the countryside near Barcelona, and tells the love quadrangle between Nicolás, Ingrid – played by French actress Irène Jacob – her son Raúl, and the supermarket cashier, Sezar, played by Spanish singer/actress Bebe Rebolledo. When Ingrid decides suddenly to break up with Nicolás, he is devastated by the prospect of losing both her and Raúl, and finds in Sezar a confidant. Raúl sees in Sezar the fairy that will save them all from a possible life in solitude. *El baile de la Victoria* (Trueba 2009), is also a dramatic love story. Darín once more plays the hopeless romantic Argentinian, Vergara Grey, who upon being released from prison in Chile due to the general amnesty law at the end of the dictatorship, goes in search of his ex-wife – played by Spanish actress Ariadna Gil – and his son. The young prisoner Ángel Santiago – Argentine actor Abel Ayala – is also released from prison on the same day and follows the famous bank robber Vergara to convince him of a last heist. Whilst waiting for Vergara to come around, Ángel meets a street girl, a mysterious dancer called Victoria – Chilean dancer Miranda Bodenhöfer – and falls in love with her. Moved by their romance and lost after discovering that his ex-wife and child are living a very good life with another man, Vergara decides to proceed with the robbery to help them out, which will end with the tragic death of Ángel whilst Vergara and Victoria escape through the Andes to Argentina.

In a more comic vein, *En fuera de juego* (Marqués 2012) sees Darín playing a minor role – for which he did not receive on-screen credit– of an Argentine footballer's representative. After having a heart attack, he sends his nephew Diego – a gynaecologist who hates football, played by Diego Peretti – to Madrid to protect his interests in the transaction with the Real Madrid football club that wants to acquire the promising young football star who was under his protection, Gustavo César – a role performed by Darín's son, 'el chino', in his big-screen debut. Fernando Tejero, in the role of the Spanish agent, and Diego Peretti form the perfect comic duo that face multiple adversities to seal the deal. *Una pistola en cada mano* (Gay 2012), is a portmanteau film where one of the eight tragi-comic stories brings together Darín and the Spanish actor Luis Tosar,[10] in a dialogue in which Darín's character defines himself as 'a cuckold fifty-something year-old South American' ['Sudaca, cornudo, cincuentón'] wanting explanations from the guy who was sleeping with his wife.[11] Another minor role, also in a comedy, is his appearance in *Torrente 5: Operación Eurovegas* (Segura 2015) as a pilot performing an online tutorial of how to fly a 747, with a distinctive Argentine accent, gesture and intonation.

*Séptimo* (Amezcua 2013) is a suspense film based in Buenos Aires. Darín interprets the role of an Argentine criminal defence lawyer, Sebastián Roberti, whose children are kidnapped inside the building from which he was picking them up to go to school. Delia, his soon-to-be ex-wife – played by Spanish actress Belén Rueda – describes him as a liar who cheated on her with her best friend. Her constant pressure to take the children back to Spain with her after the divorce turns out to be the driving force behind the pretend kidnapping. The scam is discovered by Sebastián at the end of the film who, in order to protect his children, lets her go unpunished. *Truman* (Gay 2015), in turn, has been defined as a comedy-drama. Darín plays Julián, an Argentine actor dying of cancer living in Madrid who decided to stop his chemotherapy treatment. The arrival from Canada of his best friend Tomás – Javier Cámara – gives him the strength to say goodbye to his dog, Truman, and put his other business in order before the eminent departure.

We can also include in this cartography of Darín's performances in 'Spanish' films the latest film shot in Spain, *Todos lo saben* [*Everybody Knows*] (2018) by Iranian director Asghar Farhadi, with Javier Bardem and Penélope Cruz.[12] Darín plays Alejandro, Laura (Cruz)'s Argentine husband, who has to return from Argentina to Spain when their daughter is kidnapped. We discover, as the tension mounts, that their daughter was not actually his, but Paco's (Bardem), and that her birth helped him recover from alcoholism.

As can be appreciated from these plot descriptions, all these characters share similar characteristics. The Spanish critic Torreiro explained this in *Fotogramas*: '(Darín) plays very well characters that fluctuate between being defeated and full of hope, bowled over by life, but not willing to indulge in demagoguery in connection to their weaknesses' ['tan bien se mueve con personajes entre derrotados y portadores de esperanzas, desarbolados por la vida pero no dispuestos a hacer demagogia con sus debilidades'] (2008). Moreover, all these characters are connected in one way or another to Argentina, prompting a debate on identity that plays on the perception of the 'Other'. In this vein, the first feature that distinguishes them is the accent. When analysing Almodóvar's films, Mark Allinson explained the importance of accents in the identification of Spanish national identity and how they are a 'highly political and cultural subject' in Spain (2001: 44). During Franco's dictatorship it was forbidden to show films in any language other than Spanish, so the dubbing industry flourished. Even some Argentine films at the time were dubbed to peninsular Spanish to avoid any perception of foreign intrusion.

Although the Argentine accent today in Spain is cherished as one of the most attractive (Europa Press 2012), there are certain idioms that still ostracise the general Spanish population and that can be challenging when attracting an audience. Santiago Segura (quoted in Soto 2017), when analysing the lack of interest in Spain in the film he shot in Argentina, declared that 'It doesn't work over here, except when Ricardo Darín is in it. I was speaking to a friend not long ago: "Tell me an Argentine film that worked and that didn't include Darín." "Wild Tales." "Darín is in it." A lot of good films are made in Argentina and in films like this one not even the accent is an issue' ['Aquí no funciona, salvo cuando está Ricardo Darín. Hace poco hablaba yo con un amigo: "Dime una película argentina que haya funcionado en la que no salga Darín." "Relatos salvajes." "Sale Darín." Se hacen muy buenas películas en Argentina y en cintas como esta ni siquiera el acento es un problema']. Not only does he demonstrate here the importance of Darín's presence to guarantee box-office success, he also reveals how accents and idioms can be challenging when it comes to marketing a Latin American film in Spain.

Anne Walsh's study on Antonio Banderas's career in Spain and Hollywood delves into the importance of accents in stardom. She rightly notes how accents as an identification of nationality can be contradictory, since they could be interpreted as signs of multiculturalism that rejuvenate the host culture (2015: 99). Darín's own son, el Chino, had to face constant scrutiny of his Argentine accent in Spain, particularly when he played Spanish characters. The host of the popular Spanish TV programme *El Hormiguero 3.0*, Pablo Motos, in an interview with Penélope Cruz and el Chino at the end of 2016, challenged him to reproduce the right accent on live TV – to el Chino's dismay. In April 2019, the issue of his accent generated stronger reactions from the actor, who publicly condemned a Twitter comment that, albeit celebratory of his skills to hit the right Spanish tone, showed a chauvinistic attitude towards local immigrants.[13] El Chino's reaction caused a strong impact in the local media, which tended to praise his upfront response (JA 2019). Most importantly, the whole dispute revealed the general perception that the boundaries are blurred when it comes to distinguishing between fiction and reality – where the character ends and the actor begins. In this sense, even though Darín's characters in Spanish films are bound up in the perception that they are from an Other culture – he has never played Spanish roles as his son has done – this 'Otherness' does not alienate the audience. Darín's Argentine characters work because the stereotypes they are based on speak a common vocabulary adopted by the dominant/Spanish culture as part of an accented cinema that is constantly negotiating between global tendencies and local features. Darín's on-/off-screen persona consolidates this accepted multiculturalism, rejuvenating a Spanish cinema that, from the turn of the century, has strategically emphasised the vernacular to gain attention abroad (Pohl and Türschmann 2007: 19).

Accordingly, the 'guy-next-door' charisma portrayed in the above-mentioned films seems to be, for the Spanish audience, Darín's own likeable off-screen personality. Christine Gledhill in her anthology on stardom said that 'actors become stars when their off-screen life-styles and personalities equal or surpass acting ability in importance. Stardom enacts the power and material success of individual lives' (1991: xii). This is only partly the case of Darín in Spain. In contrast to what happens in Argentina where his personal life constantly appears in the tabloids, on the other side of the Atlantic it is rarely mentioned in the press. On the very few occasions that his lifestyle surpassed his acting ability in importance, such as in 2008 when the news that a group of burglars had broken into his house in Buenos Aires received much media attention, Spanish newspapers and magazines covered this information not as a way of revealing his private drama or of focusing on his personal matters in a voyeuristic vein, as they would in the case of other stars, but rather as a means to describe the socio-political context of Argentina. That notwithstanding, this media emphasis on external issues instead of his persona, when he appeared in the headlines for reasons other than promoting a new film, has slowly been changing over the past year. The case of his son, el Chino, is different. He constantly appears in Spanish tabloids, even more so since he started a relationship with Spanish actress Úrsula Corberó – the star of the popular TV show *La casa de papel* [*Money Heist*]. This had an impact on Darín's public exposure in the local media, as he appears now as the golden 'father-in-law'.

Certainly, as Gledhill suggests in her analysis of the construction of Hollywood's star system, stardom has the possibility to narrativise the real lives of stars. In Darín's case, the actor has been turned into a character, which is also an aspect of his star image that has developed over time. He started to appear steadily on TV chat shows such as *Buenafuente*, *Salvados* and *El hormiguero*,[14] and specific programmes dedicated to cinema such as *Versión Española* and *Días de cine*. The fact that the latter programme selected Darín as one of 'the best Spanish actors of 2012' demonstrates the high level of acceptance he has gained within Spanish film culture, up to the point of being considered one of Spain's own actors. This situation was partly triggered by the 'special circumstances' mentioned in the royal decree which in 2006, after a few more successful releases following *El hijo*, granted Darín, in conjunction with director Juan José Campanella and the producer Jorge Eliécer Estrada Mora, Spanish citizenship (EFE 2006). Those 'special circumstances' then shifted the focus from his characters to Darín himself, someone worthy of distinction for his work as a cultural promoter. This recognition was recently ratified by the Instituto Cervantes, which at the end of 2018 pronounced him a member of the Board of Trustees – *vocal del Patronato*.

It has been suggested that Darín not only plays an Argentinian but, more specifically, those from the city of Buenos Aires – a *porteño*. This is not a label that Darín appreciates. In fact, he has declared that: 'I feel some sort of discomfort and it makes me laugh somewhat when sometimes people tell me that I represent the prototypical *porteño*, precisely a character that for me does not have the best of reputations. The thing is that on certain occasions I have happened to play these types of roles and I'm then directly connected with the image that is produced' ['Me causa una cierta desazón y una cierta gracia cuando a veces me dicen que represento al prototipo del porteño, precisamente un personaje que para mí no goza de la major de las reputaciones. Lo que pasa es que en ocasiones me ha tocado en suerte componer ese tipo de personajes y estoy directamente relacionado con la imagen que se produce'] (quoted in González Acevedo 2005: 50). His discomfort is understandable, since the stereotype of the *porteño*, outside Buenos Aires, in Latin America, and Spain, is associated with argumentative, arrogant and egotistical people who distill an air of superiority. With quite a xenophobic tone, the Spanish philosopher Julián Marías tried to capture the essence of this stereotype as a general Argentine trope when he said

> The Argentines are like Italians that speak Spanish. They aim to have North American salaries and live like the English. They cite French speeches and vote like the Senegalese. They think like left-wing activists and live like bourgeois. They praise Canadian entrepreneurship and follow Bolivarian organizational strategies. They admire Swiss order and practice Iraki disorder.
>
> [Los Argentinos son Italianos que hablan Español. Pretenden sueldos norteamericanos y vivir como ingleses. Dicen discursos franceses y votan como senegaleses. Piensan como zurdos y viven como burgueses. Alaban el emprendimiento canadiense y tienen una organización boliviana. Admiran el orden suizo y practican un desorden iraki.][15]

There are no real traces of these qualities in the fictional characters played by Darín. In the instances where they seem to be implied, the characters are captured at a particular juncture when they are embracing their flaws and limitations – such as Sebastián in *Séptimo*, or Julián in *Truman* – and, thus, instead of focusing on discriminatory aspects of the stereotype, they emphasise their conciliatory potential.[16]

In Darín's defence as well, there are other scholars who do not read these performances' local specificities, but rather associate Darín with sensitive middle-class characters in crisis that are easily recognised from everyday life around the world. In this regard, Argentine researcher Carolina Rocha, when discussing masculinities in contemporary Argentine cinema, asserted that 'it has become de rigueur to refer to masculinities as experiencing a crisis resulting from the expansion of global capitalism, which undermines patriarchy and men's status in society' (2012: 11). Hence, according to this reading, the inner struggles generally experienced by the male characters played by Darín are not related exclusively to an Argentine context, but to the global crisis of masculinities that affects the 'Hispanic macho' without discrimination. If we add to this shared broken patriarchy the common cultural background between Argentina and Spain, we can fully comprehend how these 'Argentine' characters and stories are 'mediators between the real and the imaginary' (Hayward 1996: 344) that reflect not only particular elements of Argentine nationhood but also the concomitant construction of desires and identifications in contemporary Spanish popular culture.

## Notes

1. Shown in Argentina simply as *El faro*.
2. Imanol Arias first appeared in Argentine film theatres in 1984 in the film *Camila* (María Luisa Bemberg). He played the role of a Catholic/Jesuit priest during Rosas's time – in the nineteenth century – who has a romantic relationship with an upper-class lady, Camila O'Gorman – played by the popular Susú Pecoraro – resulting in the execution of the two lovers by the regime. *Camila* was one of the most popular films of that decade – with more than 2 million spectators in the year of its release, and it became an unprecedented success still remembered today (Neifert 2009). Arias was also very well-known by then both at home and in Argentina for his role in *Laberinto de pasiones* [*Labyrinth of Passion*] (Almodóvar 1982) and *La colmena* [*The Beehive*] (Camus 1982).
3. The Donostia Award dates from 1986 and, at the time of this writing, Ricardo Darín has been the only Latin American personality to receive this distinction.
4. Among those government policies put in place during these years we should mention the Miró Law in Spain (Triana-Toribio 2003: 111–121) and, in Argentina, the New Cinema Law of 1994 (Falicov 2003).
5. All member countries that comprise the multicultural agreement of Ibermedia can compete via production companies to receive funds from the shared pot, to which Spain remains the main contributor (Tierney 2019: 17; Falicov 2007; Villazana 2008).
6. See the charts by Elena (2011: 46–49). Also, consult the research coordinated by Rufo Caballero (2014), Nora de Izcue (2009), Villazana (2008), Carmen Ciller and Sagrario Beceiro (2013) and Leandro González (2018) for further information about the rise in co-productions between Spain and Argentina since the year 2000.
7. All films including Darín as member of the cast were checked against the data available at the Spanish Film Institute ICAA (*Instituto de la Cinematografía y de las Artes audiovisuales*). The thirty-three films mentioned are those that have a file number and were classified and assigned an age rate for exhibition in local theatres.
8. The play written by Yasmina Reza was put on in Madrid only a few years before this performance, in 1998, casting three well-respected Spanish actors: Carlos Hipólito, José María Flotats and José María Pou. Darín relocated temporarily to Spain between 2004 and 2005 to perform on stage (González Acevedo 2005: 42) together with Argentine actors Óscar Martínez and Germán Palacios. During that time, the play was regularly in the news thanks to the active presence of famous

personalities in the audience (including members of the royal family, politicians and distinguished celebrities from the arts).
9. Almodóvar's film won an Academy Award in 1999 for Best Foreign Film, a Golden Globe for Best Film in a Foreign Language, and won awards at Cannes, San Sebastián, and the Goyas, among others. Cecilia Roth won a Goya for Best Leading Actress.
10. Tosar was at the peak of his career at this particular time, after the enormous success of *Celda 211* [*Cell 211*] (Monzón 2009), which won him a Goya for Best Leading Actor, among other awards.
11. This film included a vastly popular cast from both sides of the Atlantic, including Javier Cámara, Leonardo Sbaraglia, Cayetana Guillén Cuervo, Eduard Fernández, Leonor Watling and Eduardo Noriega.
12. The film tends to be considered as 'Spanish'. Penélope Cruz stated in *The Washington Post* that 'When you see it, you forget that it is an Iranian director. You just see a Spanish film and somebody that doesn't play with clichés' (quoted in Izadi 2019).
13. The twitter comment read: 'El Chino Darín talking in Galician accent, ha ha ha ... That's how we, the Argentinians, are. 5 minutes in Spain and we sound like Sabina. There are Venezuelans over here that have been living here for 40 years and still when they speak it's like they are singing *Cachita*' ['El Chino Darín hablando con acento gallego. Ja, ja, ja, ja, ja ... Así somos los argentinos, estamos 5 minutos en España y hablamos como Sabina. Acá hay venezolanos que viven hace 40 años y cuando hablan parece que estuvieran cantando Cachita'].
14. In September 2019 he became a member of the *Club Platino* [Platinum Club], which is formed by guests who have appeared on the show ten or more times.
15. For a full text that explores this controversial stereotype of the Argentinians in Spain please refer to: https://www.grijalvo.com/America_Argentina/Argentinos_estan_entre_vosotros.htm (accessed 17 February 2020).
16. When analysing Hispanic identities and the concept of the stereotype, Nadia Lie and Dagmar Vandebosch explain that stereotypes may have discriminatory effects, but they also contribute a shared vocabulary from which it is possible to formulate agreements and disagreements (2012: 15).

# References

Actis, W. (2005) 'Las políticas migratorias y su impacto en las formas de inserción de la población inmigrante en España', in *Migraciones: claves del intercambio entre Argentina y España*, Buenos Aires: Siglo XXI, pp. 135–155.

Allinson, M. (2001) *A Spanish Labyrinth: The Films of Pedro Almodóvar*, London and New York: I. B. Tauris.

Berry, C. (2010) 'What is Transnational Cinema? Thinking From the Chinese Situation', in *Transnational Cinemas*, 1.2, pp. 111–127.

Caballero, R. (2014) 'Producción, coproducción e intercambio de cine entre España, América Latina y el Caribe', in *Avances de Investigación*, Madrid: Fundación Carolina CeALCI. https://www.fundacioncarolina.es/wp-content/uploads/2014/07/Avance_Investigacion_5.pdf (accessed 27 January 2020).

Ciller, C. and Beceiro, S. (2013) 'Coproducciones cinematográficas en España: Análisis y catalogación', in *Revista Eptic Online*, 15.2, May, pp. 234–246.
Ciller, C. and Palacio, M. (2011) 'Cecilia Roth en España (1976–1985)', in *UNED, Revista Signa*, 20, pp. 335–358.
Colmena, E. (1994) 'Perdido por perdido. Un envite siniestro', *Criticalia.com*. http://www.criticalia.com/pelicula/perdido-por-perdido/471 (accessed 4 July 2019).
De Izcue, N. (coord.) (2009) 'Producción, coproducción, distribución y exhibición del cine latinoamericano en América Latina y otras regions, 2005–2007', in *Cuadernos de estudios*, Habana: Fundación del Nuevo Cine Latinoamericano.
Dennison, S. (2013) 'Preface', in *Contemporary Hispanic Cinema. Interrogating the Transnational in Spanish and Latin American Film*, Woodbridge: Tamesis.
EFE (2006) 'El cineasta Juan José Campanella y el actor Ricardo Darín obtienen la nacionalidad española', in *El País*, 10 March. http://elpais.com/elpais/2006/03/10/actualidad/1141976933_850215.html (accessed 11 February 2020).
Elena, A. (2005) 'Latinoamericanos en el cine español: Los nuevos flujos migratorios, 1975–2005', *Secuencias. Revista de Historia del Cine*, 22, pp. 107–135.
Elena, A. (2009) 'Medio siglo de co-producciones hispano-mexicanas', in De la Vega Alfaro, E. and Elena, A. (eds), *Abismos de pasión. Una historia de las relaciones cinematográficas hispano-mexicanas*, Madrid: Cuadernos de la Filmoteca Española 13, pp. 279–297.
Elena, A. (2011) 'Difusión y circulación del cine Argentino en España', in *Imágenes compartidas: Cine Argentino–Cine Español*, ed. De CCEBA/AECID, Buenos Aires: CCEBA Apuntes, pp. 28–50.
Europa Press (2012) 'Un 45% de españoles se rinden ante el acento argentino seguido del italiano y del francés', in *Epturismo*, Madrid, 1 June. https://www.europapress.es/turismo/nacional/noticia-45-espanoles-rinden-acento-argentino-seguido-italiano-frances-20120601153716.html (accessed 15 February 2020).
Falicov, T. L. (2003) 'Los hijos de Menem: The New Independent Argentine Cinema, 1995–1999', in *Framework: The Journal of Cinema and Media*, 44.1, Spring, pp. 49–63.
Falicov, T. L. (2007) 'Programa Ibermedia. Co-Production and the Cultural Politics of Constructing an Ibero-American Audiovisual Space', in *Spectator*, 27.2, Fall, pp. 21–30.
Falicov, T. L. (2012) 'Programa Ibermedia: ¿Cine transnacional Ibero-americano o relaciones públicas para España?', in *Rev. Reflexiones*, 91.1, pp. 299–312.
Garavelli, C. (2015) 'Conquering the Conquerors: Ricardo Darín's Rise to Stardom in Spanish Film Culture', in *Bulletin of Hispanic Studies*, 92.4, pp. 411–428.
García, R. (2003) 'La versión argentina de "Art" se estrena en Madrid gracias al éxito de Ricardo Darín', in *El País*, Madrid, 4 January. https://elpais.com/diario/2003/01/04/espectaculos/1041634801_850215.html (accessed 28 January 2020).
García Canclini, N. (1997) 'Will there be Latin American Cinema in the Year 2000? Visual Culture in a Postnational Era', in Stock, A. M. (ed.), *Framing Latin American Cinema – Contemporary Critical Perspectives*, London and Minneapolis: University of Minnesota Press.
Getino, O. and Schargorodsky, H. (2008) *El cine argentino en los mercados externos*, Buenos Aires: FCE-UBA.

Ginart, B. (2002) 'Ricardo Darín dice que la falta de recursos "puede estimular la creación"', *El País*, 9 April. https://elpais.com/diario/2002/04/09/espectaculos/1018303203_850215.html (accessed 8 July 2019).

Gledhill, C. (1991) 'Introduction', in *Stardom. Industry of Desire*, London: Routledge, pp. xi–xix.

González, L. (2018) 'Cruzando el Atlántico: Cine argentino en España', in *Imagofagia: Revista de la Asociación Argentina de Estudios Cine y Audiovisual*, 17, pp. 41–70.

González Acevedo, J. C. (2005) *Che, qué bueno que vinisteis. El cine argentino que cruzó el charco*, Barcelona: Editorial Diéresis.

Hayward, S. (1996) *Key Concepts in Cinema Studies*, London: Routledge, pp. 337–348.

Herbera, J. (2012) 'Ricardo Darín: idilio interminable', *RTVE.es* online blog, 12 July. https://blog.rtve.es/estrenos/2012/07/ricardo-darín-idilio-interminable.html (accessed 8 July 2019).

Hoefert de Turégano, T. (2004) 'The International Politics of Cinematic Coproduction: Spanish Policy in Latin America', in *Film & History: An Interdisciplinary Journal of Film and Television Studies*, 34.2, pp. 15–24.

Izadi, E. (2019) 'How an Iranian Oscar Winner Made a Film That Feels So Thoroughly Spanish', in *The Washington Post*, 15 February. https://www.washingtonpost.com/arts-entertainment/2019/02/15/how-an-iranian-oscar-winner-made-film-that-feels-so-thoroughly-spanish/ (accessed 13 February 2020).

JA (2019) 'En las redes: Se quiso burlar del Chino Darín y le salió mal: él le contestó y la dejó sin palabras', in *Clarín.com*, 4 April. https://www.clarin.com/espectaculos/fama/quiso-burlar-chino-darin-salio-mal-contesto-dejo-palabras_0_-fOGEDcHJ.html (accessed 14 February 2020).

Lara, F. (2011) 'Nada es igual sin Ibermedia', in *Imágenes compartidas: Cine Argentino–Cine Español*, ed. De CCEBA/AECID, Buenos Aires: CCEBA Apuntes, pp. 272–288.

Lie, N. and Vandebosch, D. (2012) 'El estereotipo y las identidades hispánicas. Pautas para un debate', in Lie, N., Mandolessi, S. and Vandebosch, D. (eds), *El juego con los estereotipos. La redefinición de la identidad hispánica en la literatura y el cine postnacionales*, Berne: Peter Lang.

McClennen, S. A. (2018) *Globalization and Latin American Cinema: Toward a New Critical Paradigm*, Switzerland: Palgrave Macmillan.

Miret, R. (2001) 'El hijo de la novia', in *Dirigido por...*, December, p. 40.

Neifert, A. (2009) 'A 25 años del estreno de "Camila"', available at: https://www.lanueva.com/nota/2009-8-1-9-0-0-a-25-anos-del-estreno-de-camila (accessed 10 February 2020).

Pohl, B. and Türschmann, J. (eds) (2007) *Miradas glocales. Cine español en el cambio de milenio*, Madrid and Fráncfort: Iberoamericana and Vervuert.

Rivera, A. (1998) 'Ingrid Rubio logra el premio a la mejor actriz en Montreal', *El País*, 8 September. https://elpais.com/diario/1998/09/08/cultura/905205612_850215.html (accessed 8 July 2019).

Rocha, C. (2012) *Masculinities in Contemporary Argentine Popular Cinema*, New York: Palgrave Macmillan.

Sanz, A. M. (2019) 'No sos vos, soy yo. Impacto del Nuevo Cine Argentino en España en el período 2002–2018', in *Archivos de la Filmoteca*, 76, April, pp. 125–144.

Schmidt, S. (2010) 'Miradas sobre la migración Argentina en España: Fuentes orales, periodísticas y cinematográficas', in *El Futuro del Pasado*, 1, pp. 557–581.

Soto, A. (2017) 'La reinvención de Santiago Segura', in *El Comercio*, Madrid, 4 May. https://www.elcomercio.es/culturas/cine/201705/04/santiago-segura-casi-leyendas-20170504195625-rc.html (accessed 14 February 2020).

Tierney, D. (2019) *New Transnationalisms in Contemporary Latin American Cinemas*, Edinburgh: Edinburgh University Press.

Torreiro, C. (1994) 'Ganar alguna vez', in *El País*, 3 June. https://elpais.com/diario/1994/06/03/cultura/770594413_850215.html (accessed 8 July 2019).

Torreiro, C. (1998) 'Hermanas argentinas', in *El País*, 6 June. https://elpais.com/diario/1998/06/06/cultura/897084012_850215.html (accessed 8 July 2019).

Torreiro, M. (2008) 'Luna de Avellaneda', in *Fotogramas*. http://www.fotogramas.es/Peliculas/Luna-de-Avellaneda/Critica> (accessed 11 February 2020).

Triana-Toribio, N. (2003) *Spanish National Cinema*, London and New York: Routledge.

Villazana, L. (2008) 'Hegemony Conditions in the Coproduction Cinema of Latin America: The Role of Spain', in *Framework: The Journal of Cinema and Media*, 49.2, pp. 65–85.

Villena, M. Á. (1998) 'Mignogna insiste en "El faro del sur" en un cine de sentimientos', in *El País*, 15 May. https://elpais.com/diario/1998/05/15/cultura/895183211_850215.html (accessed 8 July 2019).

Walsh, A. (2015) 'Spanish Stars, Distant Dreams: The Role of Voice in Shaping Perception', in Bandhauer, A. and Royer, M. (eds), *Stars in World Cinema. Screen Icons and Star Systems Across Cultures*, London and New York: I. B. Tauris.

## Chapter 10

# Transnational mobility and cross-cultural exchanges

Darín's international stardom is in many respects a contested construction. The question that persists in Star Studies is whether star consecration necessarily involves Hollywood's recognition or not. Leah Kemp, whilst insisting that Darín cannot be compared to Gael García Bernal in international reach, begins her analysis of stardom in Spanish America with the assumption that Darín is a star, and by trying to demonstrate that 'the perception of Hollywood as a sort of finish-line in the race to stardom' (2017: 38) for Hispanic American actors needs to be challenged when considering how the global south operates. Albeit a promising start, she eventually concludes (with some nuances) that indeed it is participation in Hollywood films that makes these actors transnational stars (2017: 46).[1] When discussing Darín's transnational recognition, Nahuel Ribke and Jerome Bourdon arrive at a similar conclusion, privileging the use of the term 'peripheral stardom' when talking about stars outside the Hollywood system who transcend their own cultural specificity.[2] They further explain that 'peripheral stardom cannot have the global or international reach of Hollywood stardom and is dependent on specific reception processes in various geopolitical areas, while simultaneously influencing the self-image of the nation of origin' (2017: 713).

Contrasting these assumptions, Darín has eluded working in the giant of the north and yet, as discussed in the previous chapter, it cannot be denied that his star status goes beyond his country of origin. Therefore, instead of looking at Darín as a 'peripheral star', or as having appeal only to Spanish-speaking audiences, this chapter aims to explore his international and transnational reach by considering that other centres exist within the Western world and that it is possible to talk about 'stars' beyond a Hollywood-centric and even Eurocentric perspective.

There are conceptual blurrings between the terms 'global', 'transnational' and 'international' which ought to be considered when exploring Darín's transnational mobility and cross-cultural exchanges.[3] Nataša

Durovicová has marked a distinction between 'global' – a category that implies totality – 'international', whose prefix implies a sort of parity between nations, and 'transnational', which acknowledges the agency of the state but where the prefix implies both unevenness and mobility (2010: ix–x).[4] According to Meeuf and Raphael, what is at stake in Durovicová's definition of the transnational is 'the ability of media, such as cinema, to produce cultural meaning in relation to (but not dictated by) the existing power structures of nations and states, to remain mobile, flexible, and open to multiple avenues of meaning and pleasure in different contexts of politics, social relations, and cultural assumptions' (2013: 3). This reading of the transnational encompasses the view expressed at the end of Chapter 9, whereby Darín's characters would be general reflections of the masculinities in crisis in the neoliberal world. The potential problem with the unevenness and flexibility of the transnational brought about by globalisation, though, is the flattening out of differences between different geopolitical regions (Miller et al. 2001). Joanna Page, when challenging the concept of the transnational, goes a step further in suggesting that 'there is little evidence to suggest, either to Argentine filmmakers or to cinemagoers, that the globalization of the film industry means anything other than its Americanization' (2009: 12). Once again, the spectre of Hollywood seems unavoidable when examining the international flow of stars, and so this chapter aims to demystify its haunting presence by looking at Darín's US reach and disputed relationship with that nation/culture.

Paul Julian Smith, following Chris Berry's analysis on transnational Chinese cinema, explores the differences between the notions of 'globalising' and 'transnational' and brings to the fore another term, 'transborder cinema', which he explains is not so much a network or system, as 'a Deleuzian "assemblage" of multiple plateaux that are interconnected and mutually affecting' (Smith 2011: 68). For some scholars, this characteristic would be another form of transnationalism (Shaw 2013: 58; Hjort 2010: 12–33). Regardless of their limitations, what these terms do come to demonstrate are the difficulties of abiding the notion of the national in the current global context of film production and distribution.[5] Without a doubt, in the case of Darín's films, John King's defence of the national is more than valid and, as the previous chapter's analysis of the stereotype of the Argentinian demonstrated, 'an awareness of the culturally specific is all important and an approach that considers the pressures on *national* cinemas in a changing international order would still seem the best way to keep the picture in focus' (2000:

255). Indeed, some of Darín's films produced for the domestic market are inherently national, like *Delirium* and *El destino del Lukong*, whilst others, as discussed in Chapter 9, can be considered transnational for their modes of production, distribution and exhibition. It could be argued also that there are transnational elements in all of his films, since they present intertextual influences and cross borders on many levels (Shaw 2013: 65). Thus, at the risk of generalising due to the pervasiveness of the term, instead of using transnational as a descriptive label, this chapter embraces its potential as a critical methodology (Higbee and Lim 2010). It is not thus connected to whether Darín's films are conceived in national or transnational terms, but rather provides a tool with which to review Darín's star status at an international level, considering the complex interplay at work when a star text negotiates cultural tensions.[6]

In their monograph on transnational stardom, Meeuf and Raphael affirm that 'stars attain transnational resonance at very particular moments of historical crisis or transition' (2013: 6). Kemp further specified that the transition to the transnational sphere depends on many factors, including 'the actor's willingness and ability to work in languages other than Spanish, particularly English, and to work far from home for extended periods; the reception of the actor's body of work at festivals and award ceremonies, and relationships with agents and directors' (2017: 47). If we add to these factors what Kemp called 'the network of cinematic kingship' (2017: 37), we can appreciate that Darín meets most of these categories. The question remains whether or not language – and, more specifically, the US and Hollywood – is a determining factor in transnational stardom. It is difficult not to think about this emphasis on the supremacy of the English language as anything other than imperialist. It is known that major industries like Nollywood, Bollywood and Chinawood, to name but a few, experience a very healthy life, without the need to recur to the English language.[7] In Darín's case, as previously discussed, in many respects he has become a transnational star already by conquering the Spanish market, where he spends a considerable part of his time. Whether he can surpass his linguistic community – and on what terms – to become in Kemp's words 'truly' transnational, is also part of the focus of the following pages.

Because he has become such an important figure in Brazil, France and Italy – three non-Spanish speaking territories – Darín does not belong to the category of the 'transregional' and 'transcommunity' stardom that Deborah Shaw recognises, for instance, in Bollywood stars (2013: 60). Nor is he a 'global' star of the calibre of actors such as Brad Pitt and George

Clooney – or Al Pacino, with whom he has been compared on several occasions (Hemardinquer 2012). While Darín on- and off-screen was tied to a sense of national identity and a rooted homeland in Spain – albeit via the stereotype of 'the Argentinian' – when it comes to his reception and popularity in other parts of the world, such as the UK and the USA, the culturally specific becomes more diluted. In transnational terms, Darín could be viewed in those places as belonging to a Hispanic tradition – a loaded term that needs some revisiting. Whether the imaginary of the 'Hispanic' applies to Darín would determine the kind of transnational stardom he has been constructing abroad. The ability to move beyond the national, and even beyond his linguistic community, places him in a more difficult conceptual territory to explore than other Latin American or Hispanic stars.

When analysing the 2012–2016 period, Leandro González explained that Argentina's National Film Institute (INCAA) reviewed the circulation of Argentine cinema in seven foreign markets considered of prime importance – Brazil, Chile, Colombia, Mexico, Spain, France and Italy – and concluded that, in terms of spectators, Spain represents 35 per cent of the tickets sold in those regions, followed by Brazil (15 per cent) and France (14 per cent) (González 2018: 18–19; González 2021). Accordingly, besides examining Darín's relationship with Anglo-Saxon communities – Hollywood/USA, the UK – the next sections will explore his transnational reach in Brazil, France and Italy. In order to do so, various media texts are examined. A distinction will not be made, as Dyer (2011) proposes, between promotion, publicity, criticism and commentaries, but rather will consider all of these together as media texts aimed precisely at attracting public attention to the films starring Darín and, therefore, ones which have also contributed to his star status and visibility in an international market. How Darín as a star circulates between and beyond national borders, how this circulation implies a 'transnational gaze' that is increasingly mobilised by new media technologies, how different historical contexts and systems of knowledge are negotiated in a cinematic world where unequal power relations prevail – under the long shadow of Hollywood and its neocolonialist/imperialist domain – are some of the questions explored here.

## Good neighbours: the challenges of the 'Hispanic' star

In Chapter 1 we briefly explored some of the flows of performers from Latin America – and, more specifically, from Argentina – to the USA in the 1930s and 1940s, as part of Roosevelt's Good Neighbour Policy (GNP). What the policy implied for the North American film industry was the proliferation of a representation of Latina/os and Hispanics as positive otherness, breaking with the negative connotations of the past. This change did not diminish, however, the stereotyping process and the existence of a 'racialized politics of casting' (Shohat and Stam 1994; Berry 2000: 110) that has historically limited acting opportunities for the performers associated with this group – and others deemed non-white (Beltrán 2009: 11) – and which has continued until this day.

In her analysis of Latina/o stars in Hollywood, Mary Beltrán, drawing on Shohat and Stam (1994: 138), explained that 'in time periods when Latina/os have been promoted as stars, [such as during the GNP period], the utilization of "tropicalist" tropes, neocolonialist associations with Latin America as always involving "heat, violence, passion, and spice," has often flavoured their promotion to U.S. audiences' (2009: 10).[8] Moreover, the 'negligent undifferentiation of the continent' that Ana M. López (1993: 70) recognised in the GNP era's productions, whereby there is no ethnical or cultural distinction between the different Latin American countries portrayed, finds also its parallelism in the roles played by 'Hispanic' stars in Hollywood today. If we look, for instance, at the cases of Benicio del Toro, Penélope Cruz and Diego Luna, they have played Mexican, Argentinian, Italian and various 'undifferentiated "Latins" on screen' (Dennison 2013: 9). In this vein, one of Darín's most solid offers to work in a Hollywood production was to play the role of a Mexican drug dealer in Tony Scott's *Man on Fire* (2004) – a role played in the end by the Italian Giancarlo Giannini.[9]

It should be noted that this 'undifferentiation' is Hollywood's way to capitalise, as Hershfield has argued, 'on the economic possibilities of difference' (2000: xi) that involves a complex process of cultural racialisation. Under this process, the underlying agenda is Euro-American superiority. Someone like Darín, with white skin and blue eyes, would not normally fit in terms of appearance with a 'Latin look'.[10] Nonetheless, he is typecast under the stereotype of 'Hispanic' in US eyes because he fulfils other markers of Latinness, including cultural practices, social class, language and accent (Sánchez 1995: 285).[11] These borderline identity tropes – which go beyond the scope of this study – shape the fluctuating terminology. Hence, 'Latin', 'Hispanic', 'ethnic', are some of the terms used in the USA to refer to these performers which continue stoking tensions today, due to their inherent labelling of an 'ethnic other' (Dennison 2013: 4; Beltrán 2009: 8). Beltrán, for instance, explains that 'Antonio Banderas and Penélope Cruz have been among the most heavily hyped Latina/o stars, despite the fact that many U.S. Latinos do not include Spaniards in their definition of Latina/o identity because of their European status' (2009: 9). In this sense, the term 'Hispanic' would be more inclusive, but nonetheless problematic.[12] The Ulmer Scale's top ten list of 'Hispanic' stars includes,[13] for example, the names of Cameron Diaz and Marisa Tomei, who only remotely have some Latin ancestry – a characteristic that could arguably be found in most of Hollywood's stars.[14]

According to Nahuel Ribke and Jerome Bourdon, 'while many foreign stars have experienced racial profiling or undergone self-exoticization as a result of pressure from Hollywood managers and audiences, Darín succeeded in establishing an international reputation as an excellent performer, representing the "average middle-class guy"' (2017: 719). This 'ordinariness' masks, nonetheless, Hollywood's whiteness strategy according to which white racial imagery represents the whole of humankind (Dyer 1997; Barrueto 2014). Ribke and Bourdon (2017) acknowledge this impact of racialisation on stardom and continue their analysis by exploring the many articles from US and French media that have focused on Darín's Caucasian features. They conclude, in fact, that 'Darín's experience shows that an actor from a peripheral country who can physically pass as European has a chance at mainstream assimilation' (2017: 720).[15] There is certainly an issue of language barrier, about which Darín is conscious and the authors mention: 'the fact that Darin is not fluent in English means he is relegated to ethnic roles in Hollywood' (2017: 722).

In a panel discussion on transnational stardom, Corey Creekmur, when talking about the problems of cross-cultural sharing of stardom between the USA and India, gave an example of one of India's major stars, Amitabh Bachchan, when he was asked, a number of years ago, '"Why haven't you tried to make the crossover to a Hollywood film?" [...] He said, "why would I want to be the brown sidekick, when I'm the leading man to a billion fans?"', from which Creekmur concluded that 'it would almost be an embarrassment for these idolized stars to move into a Hollywood film and play a sidekick role' (quoted in Meeuf and Raphael 2013: 22). In a widely cited interview by Alejandro Fantino (2013) for the Argentine TV show *Animales sueltos*, Darín agreed with Bachchan's idea, with humility, when he said that he has everything he needs: people kiss him in the streets and he has never been out of work, so 'Why would I want to go to Hollywood?' (Darín cited in Fantino

2013). To the astonishment of his host, Darín stressed the importance of not being consumed by ambition and the false belief that Hollywood is a panacea. He also mentioned the difficulties of performing in a language he does not dominate well.

In the previous chapter we explored how Darín's accent placed him within the stereotypical role of the Argentinian and, thus, gave him a desirable quality for the local audience perspective. Certainly, the notion of what constitutes charismatic and sensual is culturally bound. When transposed to Anglo-Saxon latitudes, this particular sign of his public attraction in Spain disappears, thus bringing to the fore other qualities connected more to his performance and cinematic kingship. Andrea Vaucher wrote in a 2001 article in *Variety* that 'for foreign talent looking to orchestrate a U.S. breakthrough, landing the right agent – one with a sense of the artist's strengths and eventual potential – is de *rigeur* after compulsory speech lessons to lessen or lose the accent'. This is not always the case in Hollywood today. Accents are important signifiers of Hispanic stardom – as shown by Anne Walsh when discussing Antonio Banderas's leading role in *Puss in Boots* (DreamWorks Animation 2012), and the works written on Sofia Vergara's characters, which follow the lead of Carmen Miranda's heavy accent (Milian 2017; Rosa and Flores 2017). But to benefit from this, actors/actresses need to be willing to play with the 'Hispanic' stereotypes, and to attempt to say a few words in English.

In the *Animales sueltos*'s interview, Darín explains that, contrary to popular belief, he did not reject the opportunity to work in Hollywood for what Hollywood represents, but because he is at a particular stage in his career when he does not need Hollywood anymore – subtly underscoring: 'unless you are over ambitious'. He also explains how, when he was younger, the general idea among Argentine performers was that you had to act in *telenovelas*, 'because it was believed that they guaranteed the international market' (Darín in Fantino 2013). It was precisely when he was doing just that, in his late twenties, that he performed in an Argentine-US co-production directed by Adolfo Aristarain and distributed by Columbia Pictures Entertainment, called *The Stranger* (1987), which was shot entirely in English. In most Argentine press articles that mention the shooting process of this film in 1986 – known at that stage as 'Deadly' – reporters described it as a Hollywood production (Coire 1986; López 1986; García Oliveri 1986).[16] All of them also explored the challenges posed by shooting and performing in English. In this respect, Aristarain said that he selected cast members who were able to speak the language well and were working very hard to soften the accent. In an interview for the newspaper *La Razón* he was convinced that this was going to work:

> Barone (B) – En la película hay actores argentinos que tendrán que hablar en inglés, ¿serán doblados? [In the film there are Argentine actors that will have to speak in English. Are they going to be dubbed?]
>
> Aristarain (A) – No, y será en sonido directo. [No, and it will be done in synchronous sound.]
>
> (B) – ¿No los traicionará la fonética? [Isn't phonetics a problem?]
>
> (A) – De Grazia y Cecilia Roth lo hablan perfectamente. Luppi y Darín están practicando intensamente, cuando eso no pueda corregirse, veremos de darle al personaje una referencia extranjera que justifique su acento. [De Grazia and Cecilia Roth speak English perfectly well. Luppi and Darín are practising a lot, if that cannot be fixed, we will have to think of a foreign reference for the character in order to make the accent work.] (Barone 1986)

In other articles at the time Aristarain contradicted himself and said that the Argentine performers who did not speak English would be dubbed (*Clarín* 1986). In either case, he did not have the rights over the final cut (López 1986). We know now that the film was dubbed and sound was mixed back in the USA. *The Stranger* was indeed a strange film in terms of its target audience. It was meant to be released in 1,400 theatres in the USA, but in the end it did not perform as expected – neither there nor at home.[17] To this day, it remains Darín's first and last work in English. In this sense, it can be claimed that it was the closest experience he had of working in a Hollywood production, with some of the key Hollywood performers of the time, such as Bonnie Bedelia, and at a key moment in his career, when internationalisation was part of his interests.[18] It remains to be explored whether the fact that he, and the other Argentine performers in the film, did not play a role that was stereotypically 'Hispanic' had an impact or not on the film's performance in the USA – he played Clark Whistler, a DEA agent, who had a romantic relationship with the protagonist. Certainly, language was a barrier for local commercialisation. Argentine audiences, accustomed to seeing many of those performers on TV, could not relate to their different voices nor to the foreign dialect.

In terms of his cinematic kingship and the industry's dynamics, Darín has had several other encounters with Hollywood. As Ribke and Bourdon rightly explain in their analysis of Fantino's interview,

> despite Darin's [theoretical] anti-Hollywood rhetoric, much of his international career has been made possible by multinational Hollywood entertainment financiers and distributors. His first and most successful film, *Nine Queens*, was a crime film in the Hollywood tradition, and his work under American-trained director Juan Jose Campanella gave him wide international exposure as a result of the film's Academy nominations and awards. (2017: 722)[19]

Indeed, many of his films which reached international markets were produced by Pol-ka and Patagonik, two Argentine companies that are partially owned by Buena Vista International, the distribution arm of Disney (Falicov 2008: 272). Additionally, Darín became a member of The Academy of Motion Picture Arts and Sciences in 2018, in a move from the institution to change its policies and increase the number of members from minorities (Kilday 2018) – thus gaining direct influence in Hollywood's mecca, the Oscars. In that year, he received the Gloria Award at Chicago's *Festival de cine latino* and participated in a series of red-carpet events with two A-list Hollywood stars, Bardem and Cruz, receiving media attention and the treatment of an international star.[20] This transnational star system and cinematic kingship has been structurally possible as a result of the work of shared agents, personal managers and independent publicists. As Paul McDonald correctly specifies when reviewing the construction of stardom in Hollywood, 'acknowledging the importance of the roles played by these intermediaries and advisors invites attention to the overall structural conditions in which stardom is now produced' (2013: 100). In this respect, Darín's agents, the Asturians Pedro and Facundo Rosón and his representative, Jesús García Ciordia, have also worked with many other actors who were part of the cast in various Argentine films released in Spain – and vice versa – demonstrating a thriving network of performers that has contributed to Darín's continuous ability to draw a crowd.

Besides Campanella's Oscar-winning film *El secreto de sus ojos*, which generated US$6.4 million – and a remake with Julia Roberts and Nicole Kidman[21] – and *El hijo de la novia*, which grossed US$625,000, Darín's other major successes in the USA in terms of box-office revenue were Bielinsky's *Nueve reinas*, which made an astounding, for the time, figure of US$1.2 million,[22] *Todos lo saben*, with US$2.7 million, and the unprecedented case of Szifrón's *Relatos salvajes*, with US$3.1 million. As Appelo (2014) explained in *The Hollywood Reporter*, when reviewing this film's success, 'putting all those stars on one poster was a very powerful sales tool in Argentina, and it helped *Wild Tales* smash all local box-office records'. It also contributed to attracting foreign distributors, such as Sony Pictures Classics. Their co-president, Michael Barker, explained that the appeal of the film to the US lay primarily within an older audience, but also 'the younger audience, attracted by that new energy they don't necessarily get from American movies. It's broad-based, and on top of that, there's the Latino audience' (Appelo 2014). His words demonstrate the importance of good 'classical' stories told well in a genre style, but not the existence of a transnational star system big enough to make a difference in sales. They also suggest a cultural stereotyping at work 'which allows no space in the commercial sphere, particularly oversees, for films that break away from preconceptions of what a sellable film is' (Ross 2010: 68).

## Crossover appeal in the UK, France, Italy and Brazil

Based on population estimates by McIlwaine, Cock and Linneker (2011), Nicola Astudillo-Jones, in her PhD thesis on the consumption of Latin American cinema in the ¡Viva! Film Festival in Manchester, concluded that 'Latin Americans form a relatively small-scale ethnic community in contemporary Britain in comparison with official estimates for other groups' (2016: 10). If in the USA Latin Americans represent the largest ethnic group and yet, as a study done by the USC Annenberg Inclusion Initiative demonstrated, 'the prevalence of latino leading actors is vastly out of step with U.S. population', in the UK this presence is almost non-existent.[23] Astudillo-Jones further explains that 'historically, the UK has primarily profited from a commercial relationship with Latin America and has had less direct colonial involvement in Central and South America than in other areas of the world. For this reason, Latin America has traditionally assumed an aura of exoticism and intrigue, as well as one of danger and the unknown in the British cultural imagination' (2016: 12). This aura is, to certain extent, in tune with the depiction of Hispanics in Hollywood (Barrueto 2014), but it is not one that tends to be associated in the UK with the blue-eyed Caucasian Darín.

According to the British Board of Film Classification (BBFC), eleven films from Darín's filmography were released in the UK – most of them post-*Nueve reinas*, except for *The Stranger*.[24] However, statutory powers over film remain with local councils, which can overrule the BBFC's decisions. In the British Film Institute (BFI) there are in fact references and archive documents for twenty-five of his films.[25] When Darín is mentioned in specialised and general public media, he tends to be praised for his performances. In *Sight & Sound*, for instance, he has been described as 'formidably charismatic' (Diestro-Dópido 2015). In *The Guardian*, he has been complimented for his 'outstanding and nuanced performance' (Felperin 2016). Nonetheless, most comments on his performer appeal tend to appear in reviews of film festivals, which address specialised audiences. Outside the arthouse/film festival circuit, Darín's persona is not really singled out. With the exception of Gael García Bernal, who studied drama in the UK and has London-based representatives, and, back in the 1980s and 1990s, the Cubans Mirtha Ibarra and Jorge Perugorría, Latin American actors in the UK do not tend to 'sell' a film. Channel 4 has a long-standing healthy relationship with Latin American film industries, but its interest lies in what Miriam Ross sums up as those films that are 'sellable ... abroad' (2010: 68) – i.e. films that come out of Latin America have to encapsulate the required aura of exoticism, intrigue, danger and the unknown described by Astudillo-Jones.[26]

As mentioned in previous chapters, Argentine cinema has always experienced a close connection with French audiences. Darín has been called 'the Argentine Depardieu' (Gomez 2014) and the 'Argentine George Clooney' (Godin 2018) in the local press, and many of his films have reached French theatres, but directors and stories are still the audience drivers there, rather than a popular transnational star system or a particular Latin American star such as Darín. In terms of other European countries, Darín has had significant visibility in Germany and Italy. In 2011, the Cervantes Institute in Munich hosted a special screening and series of talks by professor María Valdéz about his films and career.[27] In the newspaper *La Repubblica*, Chiara Ugolini (2016) stated that Darín has only become known internationally thanks to the Oscar success of *El secreto de sus ojos*, and later on because of *Relatos salvajes*, suggesting, as other critics have, that he was not known in Italy before then. Nonetheless, in 2011, Sebastián Borensztein's *Cuento chino* – known in Italy as *Cosa piove dal cielo?* – obtained the Marc'Aurelio Award for Best Film at the fourth

**Figure 10.1**  Ricardo Darín and Andrea del Boca in *Estrellita Mia* (1987)

edition of the Festival Internazionale del Film di Roma, and films such as *Nueve reinas*, *La fuga* and *XXY* were very well received. This suggests that Darín has been on the critics' radar for a while. Additionally, his *telenovela* *Stellina* – mentioned in Chapter 5 as *Estrellita mía* – was quite popular on Italian national TV in the early 1990s and enjoyed a re-run in 2019 on cable TV. This *telenovela*, and the association with Andrea del Boca, who was popular in Italy for other *telenovelas* shown there, allowed him to gain a degree of celebrity recognition in spite of the comments made by a few film critics – in fact, some of his 'fan clubs' on social networks like Facebook are run, or are well attended, by Italians.

It is beyond the scope of this work to explore the reception of his image in all of Latin America. Nonetheless, for the purposes of this chapter, it is important to stress Darín's recognition in the biggest non-Spanish speaking country of the region, Brazil, as this further demonstrates his transnational mobility and cross-cultural influence. In popular media in Argentina and other Latin American countries, the reaction to Fantino's interview, as Ribke and Bourdon also note, 'had the impact it did because it connected with deep-rooted cultural and ideological assumptions about the subcontinental identity' (2017: 722). In Brazil, where the effects of postcolonialism are as vivid as in the rest of the continent, Darín's willingness to call out corporate/imperialist powers has also generated admiration (Claudio 2010). Moreover, and most importantly for our debate, Darín's name tends to be read as a synonym for contemporary Argentine cinema in general. In the press, reference is made to the 'Darín effect', whereby he can be solely responsible for driving 300,000 spectators to go and see a film (Góes 2017), and the question is posed as to what his secret is (Medeiros 2019). When it comes to actual figures, the truth is that only *Relatos salvajes*, with 467,062, and *El secreto de sus ojos*, with 328,219, gained those kinds of numbers of spectators, and this in comparison with the millions who attended Hollywood blockbusters in those years. They are, however, impressive figures for Latin American productions. An award-winning film like *Zama* (Martel 2017), for instance, did not manage to attract more than 9,000 spectators.[28]

## International dimension: final remarks

In a 2001 article in *Variety* – one of North America's oldest entertainment magazines – Berney explained that 'with all the cross-border culture, there's lots of awareness in the States of popular Mexican film stars and singers' (Vaucher 2001). However, when it comes to other Latin American stars and productions, the relationship with the US is more challenging. Whether stars are able to compromise and play 'Hispanic' roles or not seems to have been determining the Hollywood connection and their transnationalism. Darín's case is different. The international written responses to his films' performances, whether in specialised or general public media, have crystallised Darín's image by distinguishing him as someone we should notice for his acting ability. US critic John Hopewell (2013) has said on several occasions that 'Ricardo Darín has a big marquee value in his native Argentina, but clearly has a big following in other countries'. Vicente Canales, managing director of Film Factory Entertainment,[29] also confirms that 'Ricardo Darín's presence in a film helps spark pre-sales. He's one of South America's only actors who can open a film in territories abroad' (quoted in Hopewell 2013). Thus, without falling into the Hispanic stereotypes, he has managed a significant level of transnationalism.

Meeuf and Raphael remind us that 'the power and resonance of transnational stars have been increasing as systems of media distribution become more international and inch toward becoming truly global. This is, perhaps, the case, but since the early 1900s, with the emergence of film stars and the modern star system as we know it, the culture of celebrity has always been transnational [...]' (2013: 7). As has been discussed, there are indeed different perspectives in Film Studies regarding transnationalism and stardom. In 2004, John King emphasised that 'the nation remains the principle site for both the production and the reception of movies' (2004: 304). In Darín's case, in spite of the fact that Hollywood films dominate up to 85 per cent of the Argentine market (Appelo 2014), his productions find in that nation their main audience, just as King suggested. This does not mean his star image is not transnational. On the contrary, his widespread national success has opened the door to cross-cultural exchanges and transnational mobility. The impact of digital and social media in the flow of stars internationally remains to be explored. There is now more access to films produced outside the dominance of Hollywood. A film like *Nieve negra*, for instance, was not released in theatres in the US, yet is available to watch on the Netflix platform there. In 2013 Shaw asserted that the topic of audiences selecting these sorts of films in Anglo-Saxon countries was too niche to consider. However, at the time of writing these words, the COVID-19 pandemic is keeping people at home in an unprecedented way. With film theatres closed around the world and productions of popular series cancelled, new research into these virtual platforms and how people are starting to watch older and foreign films will need to be carried out. For as Miriam Ross has rightly stated: 'while traditional distribution and exhibition patterns appear to work against South American cinema there is optimism that this situation can be readdressed by new screen technologies' (2010: 85).[30]

## Notes

1. In her article, she developed the cases of Gael García Bernal, Ricardo Darín and the Chilean actor Alfredo Castro.
2. Although it should be pointed out that they also mention in their article that 'while most studies of international stars focus on their transition to and reception by Hollywood, Darín's case is interesting because it points to the emergence of an international stardom set apart, at least in some respects, from the U.S. film industry' (Ribke and Bourdon 2017: 723).
3. For a literature review and an explanation of the concept of transnationalism in Film Studies please refer to Villazana (2013), Higbee and Lim (2010), Durovicová and Newman (2010), Ezra and Rowden (2006). In Latin American film scholarship, please refer to Barrow and Dennison (2013), Shaw (2013), and Smith (2011).

4. According to Corey Creekmur, the term transnational has largely been created to displace 'global', 'in part because global did have more negative connotations in Western hegemonic globalisation and transnational tries to loosen that up a bit, but it does seem to me that so often, what we are talking about is the pressure of stars from around the world to speak English [...] it is a little curious when changes are enforced, when at the same time, what's being marketed is exotic difference' (Creekmur et al. 2013: 26).
5. Dolores Tierney explains that many scholars believe in the retention of the concept of the national for exploring Latin America's national cinemas – such us King (2004) and Page (2009). She says that 'for these critics, the transnational is masking the very real difficulties of film production in Latin America and creating an apolitical form of criticism that finds value in commercial success and ignores the very specific conditions of economic exploitation currently threatening Latin American filmmaking endeavours' (2019: 7).
6. For a further explanation of the importance of using critical transnationalism as a methodology and what it implies, please see Deshpande and Mazaj (2018).
7. Except of course the fact that their names all bow to Hollywood's dominance.
8. These characteristics have been recognised by several scholars working on the construction of film stereotypes and the Hispanic community, such as Ramírez Berg (2002) and, more recently, Barrueto (2014).
9. The film cast included A-list Hollywood stars like Denzel Washington, Christopher Walken, Mickey Rourke and Dakota Fanning. It also included the performance of well-known 'Hispanic' stars, such as Marc Anthony, Jesús Ochoa and Carmen Salinas.
10. Please refer to Clara Rodríguez's book (1997) for further information about the term 'Latin look' and what it involves.
11. These markers, in Diana Negra's words, come to challenge the process of stereotypisation. She discusses the idea of 'border agents', 'such as white ethnic stars whose qualified whiteness can trouble the security of a white identity whose power has historically derived from its status as the normative unnamed' (2001: 5). We can argue that Darín, to certain extent, would be such a 'border agent'.
12. This would refer to those of Latin origin living in the US – Latina/os and Chicana/os – those from various countries of Latin America and the Republic of Equatorial Guinea.
13. The Ulmer Scale is one of Hollywood's 'powerbases for tracking, measuring and ranking the star power of more than 1,400 actors worldwide'. Please refer to: http://www.ulmerscale.com/TopTen.html (accessed 16 March 2020).
14. Tom Hanks, for example, is the embodiment of Hollywood and its star system today, and his mother is of Portuguese descent.
15. A similar conclusion to that reached by other scholars when analysing other Latin American performers in the US, such as the Brazilian actor Rodrigo Santoro (O'Brien 2017; Shaw and Dennison 2007).
16. R.P. (1986) said in *Tiempo Argentino* that it was a North American production, written by a North American, with a plot line taking place in the US. Nonetheless, the film was shot in Buenos Aires.

17. Johnny Web said that 'it was barely released to theatres and never made it to DVD at all, thus indicating that the studio which filmed it had just about abandoned it'. Please refer to: http://www.scoopy.com/stranger.htm (accessed 17 March 2020).
18. A year after the release of this film, Bonnie Bedelia became the on-screen wife of Bruce Willis in the popular *Die Hard* film series, and acted in several well-known films of the time, such as *Presumed Innocent* (Pakula 1990) with Harrison Ford. The cast of *The Stranger* also included three other Hollywood actors: Peter Riegert, Barry Primus and David Spielberg.
19. It should be noted that Campanella was not only trained in the US – he graduated from the NYU Film School – but he had also been working there as director of several popular TV shows, such as *House, M. D.* and *Law and Order: Special Victims Unit*, which undoubtedly tightens the web of cinematic connections he has in Hollywood, paving the way for his acceptance and recognition.
20. In previous years he also received second place in the Golden Space Needle Award at the Seattle International Film Festival for his performance in *Truman*. In 2013, he obtained the Grand Jury Prize at the Miami Film Festival for *Una pistola en cada mano*. He was nominated in 2009 for the Chlotrudis Awards – a non-profit US organisation that honours outstanding achievement in independent and world cinema – for *XXY*.
21. The remake had the same title as the Argentine original, *Secret in Their Eyes* (2014). It was directed by Billy Ray, and the actor Chiwetel Ejiofor took on the role originally played by Darín.
22. And another remake called *Criminal* (2004), directed by Gregory Jacobs, produced by George Clooney and Steven Soderbergh, with Diego Luna in the role played by Gastón Pauls, and John C. Reilly in the role played by Darín.
23. For further reference: http://assets.uscannenberg.org/docs/aii-study-latinos-in-film-2019.pdf (accessed 15 April 2020).
24. These films were: *The Stranger; Nueve reinas; El hijo de la novia; El aura; XXY; El secreto de sus ojos; Carancho; Elefante blanco; Relatos salvajes; Truman; Todos lo saben*. We are omitting from this list *Argentina, 1985*, to be released at the time of this publication.
25. In addition to the above-mentioned films, the BFI also references the following: *La discoteca del amor; El desquite; La Rosales; Perdido por perdido; El faro; El mismo amor, la misma lluvia; La fuga; Samy y yo; Kamchatka; Luna de Avellaneda; La educación de las hadas; La señal; Amorosa soledad; El baile de la Victoria*.
26. An interesting exception here, perhaps, would be the documentary on Diego Maradona by Asif Kapadia (2019), shown in prime time on the UK's Channel 4, in March 2020. It seems that Maradona's name is still popular enough to grant him transnational celebrity status in the UK, which, albeit stating the obvious, seems to be a level only reached by Latin American footballers, and not performers.
27. For further information on these screenings and Valdéz's talk, see: https://munich.cervantes.es/FichasCultura/Ficha71541_25_4.htm (accessed 11 April 2020).
28. My sincere thanks to Natalia Christofoletti Barrenha for her assistance with Brazilian box-office figures and for liaising with Ancine and FilmeB.
29. Film Factory Entertainment is an independent international sales agency based in Barcelona, Spain. It has established itself in the market as a sales agent capable of

taking on projects at an early stage and ensuring that they achieve pre-sales. For further information visit their website: https://www.filmfactoryentertainment.com/about-us/ (accessed 24 February 2020).
30. At the end of March 2020 the 'Tropical on demand' platform was launched in the UK, and according to Guy Lodge (2020) is already giving visibility to films otherwise unlikely to reach British cinemas.

# References

Appelo, T. (2014) 'How "Wild Tales" Director Damian Szifron Wrote a Foreign-Language Oscar Contender in His Bathtub', in *The Hollywood Reporter*, 12 September. https://www.hollywoodreporter.com/news/how-wild-tales-director-damian-755131 (accessed 9 April 2020).

Astudillo-Jones, N. (2016) *Consuming Latin America: The ¡Viva! Film Festival and Imagined Cosmopolitan Communities*, unpublished PhD Thesis, The University of Manchester. https://www.research.manchester.ac.uk/portal/files/73361984/FULL_TEXT.PDF> (accessed 8 April 2020).

Barone, O. (1986) 'Adolfo Aristarain: Cuatro millones de dólares estilo Hollywood', in *La Razón*, 19 June.

Barrow, S. and Dennison, S. (eds) (2013) 'Latin American Cinema Today: Reframing the National', in *Transnational Cinemas*, 4.2, pp. 143–145.

Barrueto, J. (2014) *The Hispanic Image in Hollywood: A Postcolonial Approach*, New York and Germany: Peter Lang Publishing.

Beltrán, M. C. (2009) *Latina/o Stars in U.S. Eyes*, Urbana: University of Illinois Press.

Berry, S. (2000) 'Hollywood Exoticism: Cosmetics and Color in the 1930s', in Desser, D. and Jowett, G. S. (eds), *Hollywood Goes Shopping*, Minneapolis: University of Minnesota Press.

*Clarín* (1986) 'Otra película de Adolfo Aristarain', in *Clarín*, 16 June.

Claudio, I. (2010) 'O astro que diz não a Hollywood', in *Istoé*, 26 November. https://istoe.com.br/112394_O+ASTRO+QUE+DIZ+NAO+A+HOLLYWOOD/ (accessed 15 April 2020).

Coire, L. (1986) 'Aristarain: otro filme y, siempre, la polémica', in *Clarín*, 13 May.

Creekmur, C. et al. (2013) 'A Panel Discussion on Transnational Stardom', in Meeuf, R. and Raphael, R. (eds), *Transnational Stardom. International Celebrity in Film and Popular Culture*, New York: Palgrave Macmillan.

Dennison, S. (2013) 'National, Transnational and Post-National Issues in Contemporary Filmmaking in the Hispanic World', in *Contemporary Hispanic Cinema. Interrogating the Transnational in Spanish and Latin American Film*, Woodbridge: Tamesis.

Deshpande, S. and Mazaj, M. (2018) *World Cinema: A Critical Introduction*, London and New York: Routledge.

Diestro-Dópido, M. (2015) 'London 2014 Roundup: "esperpento" Iberian grotesque', available at: https://www.bfi.org.uk/news-opinion/sight-sound-magazine/comment/festivals/london-2014-roundup-esperpento-iberian-grotesque (accessed 9 April 2020).

Durovicová, N. (2010) 'Preface', in Durovicová, N. and Newman, K. (eds), *World Cinemas: Transnational Perspectives*, London: Routledge.

Durovicová, N. and Newman, K. (eds) (2010) *World Cinemas, Transnational Perspectives*, New York: Routledge.

Dyer, R. (1997) *White*, London and New York: Routledge.

Dyer, R. (2011) *Stars*, new edition, London: BFI/Palgrave Macmillan.

Ezra, E. and Rowden, T. (eds) (2006) *Transnational Cinema: The Film Reader*, London: Routledge.

Falicov, T. (2008) 'Latin America: How Mexico and Argentina Cope and Cooperate with the Behemoth of the North', in McDonald, P. and Wasko, J. (eds), *The Contemporary Hollywood Film Industry*, Oxford: Blackwell Publishing Ltd.

Fantino, A. (2013) *Animales Sueltos*, 18 September, Buenos Aires: America TV. https://www.youtube.com/watch?v=30SH75EtxcM (accessed 13 March 2020).

Felperin, L. (2016) 'Truman Review: Last Goodbye to a Doted-on Dog', in *The Guardian*, 5 May. https://www.theguardian.com/film/2016/may/05/truman-review-last-goodbye-to-a-doted-on-dog (accessed 9 April 2020).

Garavelli, C. (2013) 'A Shared Star Imagery: The Argentine Actor Ricardo Darín Through Spanish Film Posters', in *OI3Media*, 13. http://host.uniroma3.it/riviste/Ol3Media/Stardom.html (accessed 11 February 2020).

García Oliveri, R. (1986) '"Deadly" mortífero film de Aristarain', in *Tiempo Argentino*, 23 August.

Godin, M. (2018) 'Ricardo Darin, le George Clooney argentin', in *Le Point Pop*, 4 January. https://www.lepoint.fr/pop-culture/cinema/ricardo-darin-le-george-clooney-argentin-04-01-2018-2184046_2923.php (accessed 13 April 2020).

Góes, B. (2017) 'À espera do fator Darín', in *O Globo* blog, 12 June. https://blogs.oglobo.globo.com/lauro-jardim/post/espera-do-fator-darin.html (accessed 15 April 2020).

Gomez, C. (2014) 'Les amours françaises de Ricardo Darin', in *Gala*, 12 February. https://www.gala.fr/l_actu/news_de_stars/les_amours_francaises_de_ricardo_darin_308444 (accessed 13 April 2020).

González, L. (2018) 'Cruzando el Atlántico: cine argentino en España', available at: https://www.academia.edu/35102913/Cruzando_el_Atl%C3%A1ntico_cine_argentino_en_Espa%C3%B1a (accessed 20 August 2022).

González, L. (2021) *El (nuevo) devenir global del cine argentino. Políticas y mercados externos*, Buenos Aires: Teseo/Leandro González.

Hemardinquer, D. (2012). '"El Chino" en Argentine', in *L'Est Républicain*, 8 February. http://www.estrepublicain.fr/art-et-culture/2012/02/08/el-chino-en-argentine (accessed 16 March 2020).

Hershfield, J. (2000), *The Invention of Dolores del Río*, Minneapolis: University of Minnesota Press.

Higbee, W. and Lim, S. H. (2010) 'Concepts of Transnational Cinema: Towards a Critical Transnationalism in Film', in *Transnational Cinema*, 1.1, pp. 7–21.

Hjort, M. (2010) 'On the Plurality of Cinematic Transnationalism', in Durovicová, N. and Newman, K. (eds), *World Cinemas: Transnational Perspectives*, London: Routledge.

Hopewell, J. (2013) 'Ricardo Darin's B.O. Appeal Proves Inter-continental', in *Variety.com*, 14 April. https://variety.com/2013/film/global/ricardo-darins-b-o-appeal-proves-inter-continental-1200356177/ (accessed 24 February 2020).

Kemp, L. (2017) 'Stardom in Spanish America', in Delgado, M., Hart, S. and Johnson, R. (eds), *A Companion to Latin American Cinema*, UK: John Wiley and Sons.

Kilday, G. (2018) 'Academy Invites Record 928 New Members', in *The Hollywood Reporter*, 25 June, available at: https://www.hollywoodreporter.com/news/new-academy-members-2018-revelead (accessed 9 March 2020).

King, J. (2000) *Magical Reels: A History of Cinema in Latin America*, London: Verso.

King, J. (2004) 'Cinema in Latin America', in King, J. (ed.), *Cambridge Companion to Modern Latin American Culture*, Cambridge: Cambridge University Press.

Lodge, G. (2020) 'Streaming Art-house Latin America-Style', in *The Guardian*, 11 April. https://www.theguardian.com/film/2020/apr/11/streaming-arthouse-latin-america-style?fbclid=IwAR0ROMT7eqCVDpraLqrqJtDBWCzleM95EUyAvzTsD-j9u7WavA8Y8s2THtU (accessed 13 April 2020).

López, A. M. (1993) 'Are All Latins From Manhattan? Hollywood, Ethnography and Cultural Colonialism', in King, J., López, A. M. and Alvarado, M. (eds), *Mediating Two Worlds: Cinematic Encounters in the Americas*, London: BFI Publishing.

López, D. (1986) 'Eficaz puesta en escena para el retorno del hijo pródigo', in *La Razón*, 16 June.

McDonald, P. (2013) *Hollywood Stardom*, West Sussex: John Wiley and Sons Ltd.

McIlwaine, C., Cock, J. C. and Linneker, B. (2011) *No Longer Invisible: The Latin American Community in London*. https://www.trustforlondon.org.uk/publications/no-longer-invisible-latin-american-community-london/ (accessed 8 April 2020).

Medeiros, M. (2019) 'Ricardo Darín nao é apenas um grande ator, mas um grande ser humano', in *O Globo*, 10 November. https://oglobo.globo.com/ela/martha-medeiros-ricardo-darin-nao-apenas-um-grande-ator-mas-um-grande-ser-humano-24070468 (accessed 15 April).

Meeuf, R. and Raphael, R. (eds) (2013) 'Introduction' and 'Discussing Transnational Stardom', in *Transnational Stardom. International Celebrity in Film and Popular Culture*, New York: Palgrave Macmillan.

Milian, C. (2017) 'Extremely Latin, XOXO: Notes on LatinX', in *Cultural Dynamics*, 29.3, pp. 121–140.

Miller, T., Nitin G., Mc Murria, J. and Maxwell, R. (2001). *Global Hollywood*, London: British Film Institute Publishing.

Negra, D. (2001) *Off-White Hollywood: American Culture and Ethnic Female Stardom*, London and New York: Routledge.

O'Brien, D. (2017) 'Latin Lover or Latin(o) Loser? Rodrigo Santoro and the Hollywood Stereotype', in Bergfelder, T., Shaw, L. and Vieira, J. L. (eds), *Stars and Stardom in Brazilian Cinema*, New York and Oxford: Berghahn.

Page, J. (2009) *Crisis and Capitalism in Contemporary Argentine Cinema*, Durham, NC and London: Duke University Press.

Ramírez Berg, C. (2002) *Latino Images in Film: Stereotypes, Subversion, and Resistance*, Austin: University of Texas Press.

Ribke, N. and Bourdon, J. (2017) 'Peripheral Stardom, Ethnicity, and Nationality: The Rise of the Argentinian Ricardo Darin From Local Celebrity to Transnational Recognition', in *Communication, Culture & Critique*, 10, pp. 712–728.

Rodríguez, C. (ed.) (1997) *Latin Looks: Images of Latinas and Latinos in the U.S. Media*, Boulder, CO: Westview Press.

Rosa, J. and Flores, N. (2017) 'Unsettling Race and Language: Toward a Raciolinguistic Perspective', in *Language in Society*, 46, pp. 621–647.

Ross, M. (2010) *South American Cinematic Culture: Policy, Production, Distribution and Exhibition*, Newcastle upon Tyne: Cambridge Scholars Publishing.

R. P. (1986) 'Aristarain vuelve a filmar, ahora con producción norteamericana', in *Tiempo Argentino*, 21 June.

Sánchez, R. (1995) *Telling Identities: The Californio Testimonios*, Minneapolis: University of Minnesota Press.

Shaw, D. (2013) 'Deconstructing and Reconstructing "Transnational Cinema"', in Dennison, S. (ed.), *Contemporary Hispanic Cinema. Interrogating the Transnational in Spanish and Latin American Film*, Woodbridge and New York: Támesis.

Shaw, L. and Dennison, S. (2007) *Brazilian National Cinema*, Abingdon: Routledge.

Shohat, E. and Stam, R. (1994) *Unthinking Eurocentrism: Multiculturalism and The Media*, London: Routledge.

Smith, P. J. (2011) 'Transnational Cinemas: The Cases of Mexico, Argentina and Brasil', in Nagib, L., Dudrah, R. and Perriam, C. (eds), *Theorizing World Cinema*, London and New York: I. B. Tauris.

Tierney, D. (2019) *New Transnationalisms in Contemporary Latin American Cinemas*, Edinburgh: Edinburgh University Press.

Ugolini, C. (2016) 'Truman, quando è il padrone l'amico più fedele. Darín: "Un animale straordinario"', in *La Repubblica*, 19 April. https://www.repubblica.it/spettacoli/cinema/2016/04/19/news/truman-137909798/?ref=search (accessed 11 April 2020).

Vaucher, A. (2001) 'Coming to America: Foreign Talent Learns How to Make It in the U.S.', in *Variety*, 29 August. https://variety.com/2001/film/news/coming-to-america-1117852003/ (accessed 20 February 2020).

Villazana, L. (2013) 'Redefining Transnational Cinemas: A Transdisciplinary Perspective', in Dennison, S. (ed.), *Contemporary Hispanic Cinema. Interrogating the Transnational in Spanish and Latin American Film*, Woodbridge and New York: Támesis.

Chapter 11

# Discourses of scandal, politics, activism and legacies

The lead vocalist of the Irish rock band U2, Bono, who is well-known for participating in global charity efforts, has said that celebrity is a kind of currency that needs to be used wisely (quoted in Assayas 2005: 103). The same could be said about stardom. Embedded in that currency there is an inherent cosmopolitanism that goes beyond the aforementioned debates on the transnational, global and international dimensions of a performers' career. Even though cosmopolitanism 'has a history of being associated with imperialism and colonial thought' (Baban 2013: 135; Young 2001), in recent years there has been a growing body of literature that is rethinking the cosmopolitan ideal for a globalised world (Appiah 2006; Hiebert 2002), embracing 'some fundamental values and qualities that connect us together despite our visible differences' (Baban 2013: 136; Nussbaum 1996). It can be argued that part of those cosmopolitan tropes, when it comes to bringing together the stardom community, include scandals – with their power to unveil truths concealed behind the star image (deCordova 2001) – and the signifying power of the star to enact potential social, political and even economic change. These characteristics seem to be universal, beyond any specific industry, albeit normally being anchored in local particularities. As will be explored in the following pages, it is indeed the cosmopolitanism of the star/celebrity currency that reconfirms Darín as a star beyond his native nation.

Martin Shingler and Lindsay Steenberg have wondered about the place of the film star in what they called the 'age of (digital) celebrities' (2019: 446). The contemporary shift in cinema distribution, such as the rise of streaming platforms, and 'the theatres of stardom and celebrity (e.g., the rise of social media)' (2019: 446), generate new forms of interactions with the audience, further breaking down the boundaries between the private life and the public image of a star (Qiong Yu 2018; King 2015). Under these circumstances, whether scandals are still playing a role in the rise and fall of stars, and whether stars have enough power within global and national politics to really instigate social change, are key aspects we need to delve into to grasp the current effectiveness of the star currency. These are also some of the questions raised by Shingler and Steenberg in their review of the relevance of Star Studies today, which will be explored in connection to Darín and his son, 'el Chino' who brings a perspective of generational comparison to the debate.

Considering the conceptual explorations of stardom/celebrity and the national/transnational previously discussed, this chapter seeks to continue examining Ricardo Darín's stardom outside Argentina, but contemplating as well the proximity of his star image to celebrity activism and what has been called 'philanthrocapitalism' (Fridell and Konings 2013; Bishop and Green 2008). Accordingly, the following pages will look at Darín's paratextual performances as humanitarian, ecological activist and political dissident. Questions of whether he is a star symbolising change at home and/or abroad, the issue of to what extent the nature of his public, socially committed persona is fabricated, and whether that persona follows the pattern of Hollywood stars and/or of other 'Hispanic' stars, are all matters that inform the type of cosmopolitan stardom he embodies. Moreover, these considerations allow for the examination of commonalities among various star systems, and particularly of how Argentina, and Latin America more generally, stand vis-à-vis the production of stardom in Europe and in Hollywood's post-studio era (McDonald 2008).

## Political economy of celebrity activism

In the introduction to his edited volume entitled *The Political Economy of Celebrity Activism*, Nathan Farrell explains how the structures of the Western media landscape have facilitated the perception by some of celebrities as legitimate political spokespeople, and how the nature of contemporary celebrities 'has, in some ways, necessitated this' (2020: 2). As Darín's case demonstrates, these structures predate the existence of digital communication technologies, opening up this aspect of celebrity beyond the contemporary star.[1] His work in philanthropic causes started during the *galán* years in the early 1980s. Chapter 5 discussed how, back in those days, a group of actors were taking their work on TV to the theatres to extend the popular domain of their small-screen characters. Known as '*los galancitos*', they also toured the country playing football for different charity organisations, filling stadiums and gaining significant

**Figure 11.1** Darín enters the football pitch in one of the *galancitos* games in Almirante Brown, courtesy of Fernando Fuentes

media attention.[2] In their golden years, not only many renowned actors participated in those games – including Darío Grandinetti, Carlos Calvo, Raúl Taibo, Pablo Codevilla, Miguel Ángel Solá, Hugo Arana and Jorge Mayorano – but famous sports personalities, such as Maradona, and prominent musicians like Sandro, also joined them.[3] Considering how the media success of those games fed into the audience turnout successes at the theatre – and vice versa – it can be argued that these charitable events evinced how celebrity humanitarianism is tarnished (Kapoor 2013: 30).

Stars, and even more so celebrities, embody the potential and promise of capitalism, with its commodification of human relations and cult of the individual based on unequal social connections and vertical aspirations. A major contribution to celebrity studies, Fridell and Konings remind us, has been to make explicit 'the powerful linkage between celebrity and the politics of consumption' (2013: 13). They further explain that 'celebrities are at the forefront of encouraging acts of consumption without genuine self-reflection on their social and ecological impacts' (2013: 13). In fact, they stated, the political power of stars and celebrities depends on the suppression of awareness of the roots of injustice and inequality (2013: 7). These structural characteristics of our globalised world have led in recent years to shift part of the celebrity's associative value to humanitarian causes and ideals.[4] Despite the implicit selflessness of the altruistic philanthropic acts, many scholars have argued that these acts might be the latest manifestation of celebrity branding (Kapoor 2013; Tsaliki, Frangonikolopoulos and Huliaras 2011; Marshall 2010; Littler 2008; Long 2006). Stars may not be fully aware of the extent to which they are part of the problem they are claiming to want to eradicate through their charity work, but they are certainly conscious of the power they have – their 'currency', in Bono's words. Darín is no exception.

When analysing *Elefante blanco*, Beatriz Urraca related the success of the film to the actor's celebrity value, exploring the interconnections of humanitarianism with entertainment. She highlighted that in the interviews to promote the film, Darín was self-consciously using his stardom to draw attention to the social problems addressed in the plot (2014: 356) – namely, the challenging socio-political circumstances of the slums and the role of drugs and the Catholic priests and Church in them. Urraca's analysis also comes to ratify Kapoor's statement that celebrity humanitarianism is bound up with a nationalist/occidentalist discourse (2013: 35). In this respect, she has said that Darín's involvement in awareness-raising activities has always been connected to Argentina:

> for example, he has participated in several Greenpeace campaigns to save native lands in the provinces of Salta and Chaco, lent his voice and image to announcements designed to fight gender violence and discrimination against people with disabilities in Argentina, and made phone calls for Red Solidaria, an Argentine network that connects people in urgent need with those who can help. For these and other activities, he was awarded the Save the Children prize in 2012. (2014: 358)[5]

Darín himself has highlighted/acknowledged the need to focus on local realities. During the campaign to protect the Wichí nature reserve in 2005 he stated that 'we know more about what is happening in New Orleans than what is happening with the Mapuches in the south of our own country, whose lands are been devastated. This has been happening for decades. There are a lot of people that have been fighting against these issues for years but they have never garnered the necessary media attention' ['sabemos más de lo que pasa en Nueva Orleans, que sobre los mapuches del sur cuyas tierras son devastadas. Esto pasa desde hace décadas. Hay gente que hace años lucha por este tema y no consigue acceso a los medios'] (quoted in Ochoa 2005). Even when he briefly relocated to Madrid (Spain) in 2003 to perform *Art* at the theatre, he continued his support for national NGOs. Both he and Germán Palacios attended the ceremony to mark the agreement between The Real Madrid Football Club and Father Mario Pantaleo's Foundation, declaring that 'of course we needed to come! It is a lovely gesture from a Spanish organization towards our country' (quoted in Pisano 2003).[6] This focus on national problems is similar to that of the actions taken by other Latin American stars, such as Gael García Bernal and Diego Luna. Through their production company Canana Films, they are bringing attention to human rights abuses in Mexico (Aho 2010), whilst also supporting various local campaigns, such as the relief fund to help the victims of the earthquake in 2017 (Miller 2017).[7]

Nations as imaginary communities (Anderson 1991) build their identities through common history, myths and the related concepts that include 'heroic figures' such as the humanitarian celebrity (Kapoor 2013: 35). As Rojek (2001), Dyer (1998) and others have explained, 'celebrities – through their imaginaries – unify, explain and shape everyday life by providing sites of belonging, recognition, and meaning' (Yrjölä 2011: 179). When celebrities embark on beneficent causes, investing precious time and resources, it is said that their actions reflect on the nation, producing what Kapoor described as 'a generous and benevolent national community or Western identity' (2013: 35). Questions remain as to whether these assumptions can be applied to the global south. Most of the analyses that centre on this connection between nation, capital and the 'potent psycho-symbolic return' embedded in giving, focus on how the so-called 'First World' singles itself out from its Others (Kapoor 2013: 35). Nevertheless, it can be claimed that there are micro levels of 'aid dependency' within each country, regardless of their geopolitical position in the world order. Argentina, as a nation formed from Western ideals and cultures, responds to the model of neoliberal capitalism that celebrates individualism and encourages commodification. Thus, celebrity humanitarianism can indeed be read in terms of promoting cohesion and a sense of national pride, whilst arguably increasing star visibility and careerism. In fact, for some scholars, social action in the neoliberal era is characterised by the increasing presence of celebrities 'who have stepped in where the state used to be, proliferating privatized forms of welfare and redistribution' (Banet-Weiser and Mukherjee 2012: 93).

Even though the causes Darín has focused his attention on are mostly connected with his homeland, they still stand for cosmopolitan and humanitarian values. A good example is his support of campaigns and organisations fighting Chagas disease. Although it is a common problem in the north of Argentina, he continually emphasises that this is an epidemic that tends to be neglected because it affects the poor, but that it does have a global significance.[8] In this vein, in 2006 he participated in a special TV programme called *Hoy me desperté* [*Today I Woke Up*], broadcast on World AIDS Day,[9] to raise awareness of the spread of HIV infection and commemorate those who have died from AIDS-related illnesses. Full of local characters and tropes, the final sequence mixed voices from various famous personalities and unknown everyday people, including Darín towards the end pronouncing a hopeful universal message: 'I know that one day, not far off, together we will be able to overcome prejudice.'[10] Another case where the local becomes global/cosmopolitan is the short film dedicated to those who died in the AMIA terrorist attack called *Libro de la memoria: Homenaje a las víctimas del atentado* [*The Book of Memory: Homage to the Victims of the Terrorist Attack*] (Bertilotti 2017).[11] Made on the twenty-third anniversary of the suicide bombing that destroyed the Jewish community centre in Buenos Aires, the video gathers more than sixty performers and interweaves statements from Argentine writers on the topic of the nation and the importance of memory.[12] When campaigning for the International Red Cross, Darín stated that 'action should not be reaction, but creation' ['La acción no debe ser reacción, sino creación] (Darín quoted in CICR 2009) in an attempt to sensitise new generations to global humanitarian problems – a campaign that attracted the support of international celebrity philanthropists such as Barbara Hendricks, Lionel Messi, Marc Forster and Ana Ivanovic.[13] In all these public interventions there is always the emphasis that, despite their local particularities, these cases touch upon universal issues.

In this sense, Darín's actions follow the characteristics of what Sydney Tarrow (2005) identified as those of the 'transnational activist'. These encompass the ability to mobilise domestic and international resources – either financial or symbolic – 'in favour of goals [s/he] hold[s] in common with transnational allies' (2005: 29). Tarrow further explained that these activists emerge from domestic political or social events, and that they are better connected than most of their compatriots, having the ability to move between the country of origin and the international level to mobilise change (2005: 43; Huliaras and Tzifakis 2011: 32). Their constant relationship with the domestic sphere, Tarrow argued, allow these transnational activists to be conceived of, in Mitchell Cohen's terms, as 'rooted cosmopolitans' (1992), who work within a nation-state framework, but respond to the dynamics of a world governed by overarching principles of rights and justice. In this sense, the recognition of Darín's humanitarian work in Argentina by an international non-governmental organisation such as *Save the Children*, which has its headquarters in the UK and related branches in various countries around the world, demonstrates this rooted transnational impact.[14]

Although Darín feels at ease with this sort of social activism, and he has been using his star currency over the past five decades to draw attention to specific causes, his political activism has been more problematic.[15] As we will explore in the following section, his public statements overtly challenging specific party politics have led to more criticism and scandals than substantial change. In their analysis on celebrity and politics, Drake and Higgins declare that 'celebrities perform a public service in bringing politics to an audience that traditionally feels excluded from political discourse' (2006: 99). Yet, the tendency of recent years is that celebrities no longer pose a radical or anti-establishment discourse as they used to in the 1960s (Huliaras and Tzifakis 2011: 38). In relation to this, in her explorations of different modes of celebrity political activism today, Kathryn Gregg Larkin (2009) identifies three types: the entertainer, the spokesperson, and the advocate models, which range from minimal to maximum involvement. The first involves contributing a performance for a cause, rather than acting on behalf of the cause. The second one is an endorsement of policy changes, lending a voice of support to judicial processes. The third, also called 'the Bono model', follows through with greater commitment – the star becomes the face of the cause. Even though Gregg Larkin explores these models specifically in connection to celebrities in the US, these strands are also perceived in other latitudes. As the above-mentioned examples show, Darín falls mostly within the 'entertainer' mode. When he managed to visit the Casa Rosada – Argentina's main government building – in 2005, and spoke with president Néstor Kirchner about the Wichí, he was embodying the role of the spokesperson. The advocate model, however, has proven a step too far for him, thus far.

When he played the role of president of Argentina in the film *La cordillera* in 2017, he declared in several interviews that he lacks the necessary coldness to work as a politician (AFP 2017). He has always tried to remain outside party politics, defining himself as 'politically incorrect and socialist by nature' (Fantoni 2012). This positioning has not come without confrontation with some political parties. During the ongoing COVID-19 crisis, he participated in different media programmes, encouraging people to stay at home to avoid the spread of the virus, and talking about the socio-economic, psychological and cultural impact of lockdowns.[16] In an interview with a Spanish TV show called *Lo de Évole*, Darín controversially declared that it was shocking how many people were profiting from the coronavirus.[17] Right-wing supporters soon exclaimed that these comments were the actor's way of 'sell[ing] the socialist control of production', a move they considered hypocritical for someone of his professional stature and economic cache – 'a communist manifestation that backfires' (Puglisi 2020).

The debate over celebrity humanitarianism seems to be divided between those 'optimistic' scholars, who see the actions of stars and celebrities as an enhancement of democracy, and those 'pessimistic' scholars, 'who link it to capitalist imperialism or a throwback to older colonial tropes' (Biccum 2016). Darín is conscious of the potential cynicism embedded in philanthropic acts.[18] During the course of this research, his actions have gradually inclined this author's prose to the so-called 'optimistic' strand. For even though his support for humanitarian causes has been in the media in one way or another, this has been too low profile to be considered of significance for his career prospects. His international reach in this respect is even more scant, with no mentions, for instance, in the *Look to the Stars* database.[19] When an impostor stole his identity in an attempt to scam charity organisations in Argentina, his representatives made it very clear that he would never profit from social support (Emol 2011). There is, of course, the symbolic profit to consider: Kapoor explains that charity works tend to aid in 'humanizing the celebrity', softening the image of 'crassly mainstream and commercial entertainers' (2013: 31). But Darín already had the friendly image of 'the-guy-next-door' when he started collaborating with humanitarian causes and did not need to do any charity work to sustain it. Moreover, as the next section demonstrates, his scandals have tended to far surpass the positive media attention given to his philanthropism.

## Scandals and political polemics

In his seminal work *Picture Personalities* (2001, originally published in 1990), Richard deCordova explored how scandals can be considered the ultimate point of evolution for performers to become stars. Scandals expose the discourses at play in the divide between public and private life, and thereby also reveal the mechanisms of the star system (Watts 2008: 244). While scandals used to be devastating for a performer's career, the expanded affective connection with the audience generated by the internet – i.e. our greater access to stars' private lives and thoughts – has shifted the power of scandals, to becoming, to a certain extent, a potent promotional tool. During the *galancitos* years, when Darín was gaining media visibility, in addition to the above-mentioned charity work he also saw various scandals that, undoubtedly, further contributed to his public exposure and construction of his stardom. In 1981, for instance, he started dating the TV star Susana Giménez. The fact that she was thirteen years older than him – an unusual age difference especially where the woman is the older partner – and her great popularity constantly caught the tabloids' attention.[20] Sexual affairs in the public eye are almost a universal characteristic of film stars. When relationships are non-normative, or when there is a perceived shift in power as an outcome of the affiliation with a more popular star, the press dedicates more time and space to those news, which can help the career progression of a performer. Arguably, this was the case with Darín and Giménez, and it can be compared with other contemporary Hispanic stars who made headlines in recent years for similar reasons, such as Penélope Cruz's relationships with Matthew McConaughey and Tom Cruise, and Gael García Bernal's with Natalie Portman.

Additionally, some of the aforementioned charity football games got heated. In 1982, when participating in a match to support the Argentine Red Cross in Bahía Blanca, Darín lost his temper with the linesman and the situation got out of hand, ending with charges of assault and him having to attend court hearings throughout the next year.[21] One of the local newspapers reporting the incident emphasised the fact that most of the members of the team were at a point where their careers were on the rise (*La Nueva* 2012), suggesting the media attention caused by the scandal was therefore to their benefit. Hence, it is interesting that Darín's CD, *De a dos*, which was initially, and unsuccessfully, released in 1979, sold an unprecedented 7,000 copies precisely in Bahía Blanca – a fact that Darín himself does not know how to explain (*La Nación* 2000). Arguably, this may well be connected with the fascination with the star's veridical self, which is unveiled by scandals such as that of the football match.

The *autos truchos*'s affair illustrates how scandals tend to surpass celebrity philanthropism in media attention, greatly contributing to stardom and celebrity construction. '*Autos truchos*' was the name given by the press to a judicial process against Darín for the irregular acquisition of an imported car.[22] The actor bought the car in 1988 from one of the biggest car dealers in the country without realising that it had been brought into the country illegally. In 1991, he was briefly sent to jail on charges of 'smuggling' and his car was expropriated by the government – which then sold it at a highly-publicised public auction later that year.[23] In 1998, he declared that he felt privileged, because 'for far less some people have disappeared from the public eye (...) They have been trying for seven years, without success, to find out if I'm a smuggler or an actor' ['Por muchísimo menos hay gente que ha desaparecido de la faz de la tierra (...) hace siete años que están tratando de averiguar si soy contrabandista o actor. No lo han logrado dilucidar'] (*La Nación* 1998). In an interview in the year 2000 he explained further:

> No one was interested in finding out the truth. I spent many years playing football for different charity organizations and suddenly I appeared in the newspapers. They said 'the rich and famous use a customs exception for disabled people to buy imported cars', and they accused me as if I were one of those assholes who actually benefited from this clause (...) I was on the cover of *Crónica* for ten consecutive days (...).
>
> [a nadie le interesó averiguar la verdad. Me pasé varios años jugando a beneficio de diferentes entidades, y de pronto aparecí en los diarios. Dijeron: 'Ricos y famosos se valen de una excepción aduanera para discapacitados, para comprar autos importados', y me acusaron igual que a otro pelotudo que sí lo hizo para ahorrarse diez lucas (...) estuve diez días seguidos en la tapa de Crónica (...).]
> (*La Nación* 2000)

The *autos truchos* affair was brought to public attention again in 2013, amidst heated public discussions that Darín had with President Cristina Fernández de Kirchner (CFK) and which made headlines. In an interview for *Brando* magazine, he talked about the increasing social divide and wondered how the Kirchners – both the president and her late husband, former President Néstor Kirchner – managed to increase their patrimony (*La Nación* 2013a). This questioning enraged the dignitary, who published a lengthy response to Darín on her Facebook and Twitter accounts which, among other details, reminded him of the case of the car and how he got away with it thanks to bureaucratic technicalities.[24] He replied, also through the media, that he was the one who was tricked in that case, and whilst claiming the money for his car back from the government, invited the president to have a private conversation with him. What these exchanges demonstrate is that 'when Darín speaks, people listen', even the President (Urraca 2014: 359), and that his neutrality when it comes to party politics is gradually changing with both age and, we may argue, with a higher international stardom status.

As Urraca (2014) explains, Darín's authoritative public discourse is based on the authenticity of the public persona that he has constructed over the years. By mentioning the *autos truchos* affair in CFK's response to Darín's remarks, the intention was to tarnish that image – and, therefore, to lessen the effect of his enquiry. At a time when the majority of the artistic community in Argentina was adhering to Kirchnerism (Rebossio 2013), Darín's words sparked what we can term 'K-gate'.[25] Fellow actors, such as Federico Luppi, called him 'un pelotudo' [an asshole] for making those public statements and, while defending CFK's position, reminded Darín that he 'also had a fiscal setback' in the 1990s – referring to the *autos truchos* affair (*Página/12* 2013). Darín's sister, actress and president of the Argentine Association of Performers, Alejandra Darín, toned the discussion down. She stressed the importance of having actors express their political opinions, to demonstrate that they are real people and not fictional characters, whilst also supporting CFK's administration, as 'the government chosen by the people' (*La Nación* 2013b). In later interviews on TV, Darín softened his criticism, explaining that he did not want to hurt Cristina, that his observations were not intended to target her specifically, but rather to reflect on the origin of the patrimony of all public officials, and that he felt his words were taken out of context (*Cadena 3* 2013).

P. David Marshall explains that scandals are a form of transgression of the structured and industrial branded persona in entertainment. According to him, a scandal 'can allow the individual to transcend that identity, or it can lead to the disappearance of the celebrity from public consciousness' (2014: xxiv). When it comes to 'K-gate', the fact that Darín managed to surpass the scrutiny of many of his peers, without any damage to his reputation, nor any major enemy in the political front, speaks of the power he holds in the local public domain. The divisions in Argentine society are now even more profound than in 2013. The so-called 'grieta' [the fracture] defines two clear sides in the political milieu, making statements like Darín's in *Brando* magazine less provocative. Whether he was a pioneer in voicing the discontent of part of the population, or he was an 'opportunist' – as Luppi hinted in his radio interview (*Página/12* 2013) – 'K-gate' shows, to paraphrase Marshall, that his stardom has the power 'to represent the active construction of identity' in Argentine society (2014: xlix). It remains to be explored whether, as Trope has discussed in relation to Angelina Jolie's case, 'such an alignment neatly satisfies the star's necessary negotiation of public and private personae [whilst] potentially and problematically blur[ing] the line between altruism, self-promotion, and self-preservation' (2012: 155–156).[26]

Even though Tsaliki, Frangonikolopoulos and Huliaras inform us that 'changes in the organization of publicity and in technology have had a profound impact on the operation of celebrity' (2011: 10), allowing audiences to gain greater access to a star's private life and, therefore, softening the power of scandals to impact on performers' careers, celebrity still depends on the hype of scandal. Harvey Weinstein's case and the #MeToo movement (2017) have shown that there *is* a line that cannot be crossed. In Argentina, the *Ni una menos* manifestations against gender violence started in 2015, experiencing their peak in 2017–2018, as an outcome of the media response to #MeToo and demonstrations in support of the legalisation of abortion.[27] In the midst of this dynamic wave of feminist activism, Darín found himself at the centre of a new polemic, probably the most challenging of his career. Valeria Bertuccelli, his co-star in the play *Escenas de la vida conyugal* until 2014, declared on a TV programme in June 2018 that Darín 'mistreated' her.[28] At the time the press said that Bertuccelli left the play because she fell in love with Darín and had to preserve her marriage (*Redacción LA* 2015; Monfort 2018). When Novaresio, who invited the actress on his show to talk about the abortion law and her new film, asked her whether those rumours four years ago were true, she declared that she could not hide the truth any longer and that she felt now was the right time to talk about male dominance and power abuse (Monfort 2018; Infoshow 2018). Erica Rivas, who replaced Bertuccelli as Darín's co-star in *Escenas* – and left the play at the beginning of 2018 without a clear explanation – supported her testimony, declaring on her Twitter account that she was 'very brave' (*La Nación* 2018a).

When actress Laura Novoa supported Bertuccelli's and Rivas's allegations through social media, she declared that this was a particularly historical moment for feminism, suggesting, as Bertuccelli also did (Monfort 2018), that there should not be any 'sacred cows' and women should not be afraid of talking about their feelings in public. These comments manifested that the real issue was not Darín himself, but a more ingrained problem in society – i.e. the patriarchal domination for which the media is greatly responsible.[29] It was precisely the relationship of performers with the media that Bertuccelli tackled in a later interview, stating that nobody accused him – as they did her – of taking advantage of the scandal, even though he promoted his film during these debates (Infoshow 2018). All this seems to indicate that this shift from a specific person to a global problem allowed Darín to emerge fairly successfully from this maelstrom – even when, in January 2019, model Romina Seferián accused the actor of touching her inappropriately in a bar back in 2011. The *Actrices argentinas* [Argentine Actresses] collective, formed in 2018 to campaign for the legalisation of abortion and to act as a safety net for women fighting against patriarchal abuse in the entertainment industry, did not stand by Bertuccelli's and Rivas's accusations – a decision that ended up fracturing the collective.[30] Its president, Verónica Llinás, declared that the case was democratically voted on and did not have the support of many of its members – including Dolores Fonzi, Andrea Pietra and Carla Peterson (*La Nación* 2018b).

It is too soon to know the long-term implications of the Bertuccelli-Rivas case. When asked about it at the launch of his latest film in September 2019, Darín declared that it is a 'baggage that weighs on him' and he feels he does not deserve to carry it (*La Nación* 2019). The fact that *La odisea de los giles* became the most successful Argentine film that year, with more than 1.8 million tickets sold in Argentina alone, shows that the power of Darín's stardom persists.[31] His experience of being in the spotlight for decades helps, and his sense of the dynamics of the public sphere seems sharper than ever. Since 2014, he has been more openly manifesting his respect for women. He wrote the prologue to Tini de Bucourt's book *Mujeres felices* [*Happy Women*] (2014), a self-help book to encourage women to find their true beauty. In 2017, he shot a spot to support Susana Giménez's campaign against gender violence, where he declared that: 'We, men, also have to get involved. Gender violence is everyone's business. Violence is not only physical, but also psychological' ['Los hombres también tenemos que involucrarnos. La violencia de género es un asunto de todos. La violencia no es sólo física, es psicológica también'] (Caras 2017).

## Ricardo 'Chino' Darín: legacy and new forms of stardom?

The latest scandals, gossip and philanthropic actions discussed attest to the important role of social media in the construction of stardom today.

Celebrities and stars are no longer just a product of representation but, as Marshall (2010) notes, the outcome of their own presentational skills. What platforms like Twitter, Facebook and Instagram have facilitated is a personal control over the presentation and circulation of stars' public personae (Turner 2014: 71). The differences between the way Ricardo Alberto Darín has been building his career compared to that of his son, Ricardo Mario 'Chino' Darín, are not so much different in generational terms but as a result of technological competency and fluency. Although Darín comes from a family of performers and has been dealing with the press from a very early age, the widespread reach of networked social media gives 'Chino' the possibility of self-branding and of pursuing a more de-territorialised career trajectory than his father.

Chino's first steps in celebrity construction were, like his father, in a *telenovela* – an Argentine TV melodramatic serial called *Alguien que me quiera* [*Someone Who Loves Me*] (Channel 13, 2010) – but he soon moved away from the types of roles that were iconic for Darín senior in the 1980s and 1990s.[32] In 2011 he continued, briefly, in another TV programme, *Los únicos* [*The Only Ones*] (Channel 13), while performing at *Los Kaplan* in a Buenos Aires theatre – so far the only play he has worked on, unlike his father, who is more pulled towards the stage. The following year, he started working in cinema, in Spanish director David Marqués's *En fuera de juego*, where his father had a small uncredited role. From that moment, a series of important roles, both on TV and cinema, have been shifting his celebrity status to stardom – including *Historia de un clan* [*The History of a Clan*] (Telefé, Argentina, 2015), *La embajada* [*The Embassy*] (Antena 3, Spain, 2016), *La Reina de España* [*The Queen of Spain*] (Trueba 2016)[33] and *El Ángel* [*The Angel*] (Ortega 2017). Before the advent of COVID-19 lockdowns around the world, Chino was constantly moving between Argentina and Spain, to a certain extent de-anchoring his work from a specific national context.

The growth of consumers' choice in the new media landscape is challenging for traditional film stars like Darín. As a millennial who came of age in the information age, Chino seems more at ease in the construction of his image in the uncontrollable realm of the worldwide web. A perfect example is how he has taken control of the media narrative surrounding his relationship with Spanish actress Úrsula Corberó – star of the Netflix series *La casa de papel* [*Money Heist*] (Piña, Atresmedia, 2017–2020). The constant use of selfies to share their love with the world via social media demonstrates a redefinition of star construction in the twenty-first century. This degree of control over their image reveals a symptom not only of cultural but also of industrial change. Intermediaries – or 'gatekeepers' – between the star and the general public seem to be becoming increasingly obsolete. Additionally, Chino's creation, with his father, of the production company Kenya is also a sign of this new era, when film stars are not just performers, but hyphenated professionals – producers, directors, scriptwriters, etc.

In several interviews Chino has declared his blissful ignorance of stardom and how he despises its sacralisation (Plotkin 2019). This approach comes as a result of a long process; partly because of his upbringing among celebrities and his overexposure to the media – he has mentioned how, when he was born, he appeared in the cover of *Gente* magazine (Plotkin 2019), which normalised the visibility of his private life – and partly due to his coming to terms with the way discourses are now constructed in the on-demand culture.[34] While his disregard is genuine, he still abides by the commercial rules of the acting profession, in a culture that continues to be fascinated with image. Whether he likes it or not, he has become today, in Turner's terms, a discursive category, a commercial commodity, and the object of consumption (2014: 4). In this respect, he

**Figure 11.2**  *Revista Gente*'s cover, January 1989

continues the legacy of his father. Nonetheless, our community bonds are rapidly changing – and even more so in a world suffering the effects of a pandemic – which means that a conceptual shift is coming in the way we conceive stardom and how we relate to these extraordinary beings that keep feeding our expectations of human greatness.

## Final remarks

Argentina, Brazil and Mexico continue to be the largest producers in Latin America (Falicov 2019: 1), but their star systems present some important differences. They all feed on and have a close connection with their national television programming, including most significantly *telenovelas* and sitcoms. But, in contrast to the other two countries, the lack of state support in Mexico and its proximity to the US has led some critics to talk about its industry – and, we could argue, its star system – as Hollywood's backlot (Falicov 2008: 270). It is undeniable, however, that all three possess a culture-specific star phenomenon, and Darín is a good example of that. As Bandhauer and Royer rightly state in their introduction to *Stars in World Cinemas*, 'stars are firmly situated in the local' and, as shown in this section and in their book, they are 'constructed by local politics and ideologies, film industries, linguistic contexts, and by specific films and directors' (2015: 3). Nonetheless, as both Bandhauer and Royer also point out, 'the local is also composed of specific transnational connections' (2015: 3). The extent and level of impact of those connections – what Kemp (2017) calls 'the cinematic kingship' – in the general public beyond the country of origin determines the level of international dimension of a star. In Darín's case, sharing the screen and red carpet with Javier Bardem and Penélope Cruz – two A-list Hollywood stars and Spain's most beloved contemporary actors – and receiving the Donostia Award for Lifetime achievement in San Sebastián in 2017, marked his true transnational stardom.

Whether Darín signals new forms of film stardom that are emerging from Latin America, or he is an exceptional case, remains to be confirmed. When Martin Shingler and Lindsay Steenberg encouraged scholars to move beyond Hollywood and Western studies of Stardom they urged us to open our 'field of vision to the ways that global and local star systems are adapting and feeding into the Hollywood model of stardom and Western modes of celebrity' (2019: 451). Darín's case shows that, despite

Latin America being dominated by Hollywood productions at the point of distribution and reception (Falicov 2008: 265), when it comes to their own films there is a vibrant star system that is not adapting or feeding into the Hollywood model, but rather finding its own way to survive. The new globalised patterns of reception and the support in Argentina from governmental policies and the national film institute provide hope for the expansion and consolidation of an industry with a solid star system in place. One that is heavily cross-pollinated by TV but where significant media distinctions seem to remain – at least at the time of this writing. We need to consider, in a world that is increasing its 'parasocial' interactions – i.e. those that occur across significant social distance with people we do not know – how we are using celebrity and stardom 'as a means of constructing a new dimension of community through the media' (Turner 2014: 6). Undoubtedly, during the worst moments of the coronavirus lockdowns in the UK, Darín has made me feel connected to my Argentinian self.

## Notes

1. It was not until 1995 that the internet was commercially distributed in Argentina (CABASE 2019).
2. Newspapers stated that they used to play in support of children's hospitals. Darín says that they did not have a visible person driving a specific agenda. They found out, for instance, that the Red Cross was in need in a specific region and they went there to help. They had an administrator who was in charge of dealing with the logistics (personal communication, interview with the author, May 2020).
3. In various interviews it was stated that the football team was originally formed by Adrián 'Facha' Martel – an actor known for his works with the famous comedian Alberto Olmedo – but that it only gained visibility and was rebranded under the label of '*los galancitos*' mainly when Carlos Calvo and Ricardo Darín joined the squad. They used to play against various reporters and press people. In 1991, however, in what was recognised as their last game together, they played against members of the football player's union to support the Hernández Hospital and also in honour of the actor Adrián Ghio, who was killed that year by police negligence in a car accident (*Escribiendocine* 2020).
4. For further information on the causes of celebrity activism please see Huliaras and Tzifakis (2011).
5. These Greenpeace campaigns have been vital in the preservation of native lands in Argentina, which were being sold to private companies for the harvest of soy. As many reporters have stated, it was not until Darín brought up the issue of the Wichí communities and the Pizarro reserve on Diego Maradona's TV show *La noche del*

*diez* – on 26 September 2005 – that the issue caught the media's attention and, as a consequence, saw government action, after months of unsuccessful attempts (Ochoa 2005). In an interview in 2013, it was mentioned that graffiti could be seen at the front of Darín's house saying, 'Thank you Ricardo Darín for helping the Wichís' (Perantuono 2013). Darín has been a close friend of the president of Red Solidaria, Juan Carr, for many years, being involved in many campaigns launched by the organisation (personal communication).
6. The agreement, signed in 2003, continues to this day. It supports sports activities with the aim of keeping vulnerable children in a safe environment after school. Father José Mario Pantaleo was known for being a healing priest who established, in conjunction with 'Perla' Gallardo-Garavelli, two foundations that transformed González Catán, a deprived area at the outskirts of Buenos Aires. For further information, see: https://padremario.org/
7. Another local cause Darín has participated in since the 1980s that bears mention here is the 'Tenis por la vida' [Tenis For Life] games, which in 1988 saw him joined by Alberto Olmedo, Carlos Calvo, Emilio Disi and Paz Martínez, among others, in support of the Asociación Pro Ayuda a la Niñez Desamparada, APAND (Zeballos 2014).
8. In 2014 he shot an advertising spot for Iniciar For Global Action where he stated that ten million people were affected by this tropical disease – for further information see: https://vimeo.com/79719781 (accessed 12 May 2020). In December 2019 he joined the campaign #NingúnBebéConChagas, which highlighted that even though the disease originated in Latin America, it is now a global problem – for further reference see: https://ningunbebeconchagas.com/#compromiso (accessed 12 May 2020).
9. On 1 December.
10. The one-off episode was written and directed by Darío Lanis and Bruno Stagnaro and was produced by Fundación Huésped, in conjunction with Pol-ka Producciones, Cecilia Felgueras, Flehner Films and Boga Bogagna. Cast members included Eleonora Cassano, Adrián Suar, Cecilia Roth, Gustavo Garzón, Leonora Balcarce, Boy Olmi, Jorge Lanata, Iván Pineda and Víctor Heredia. The programme received a special award at the New York TV Broadcasting Festival Awards in 2008 and was praised for its originality – not only for covering the topic for the first time on TV, but also for doing it in an unconventional format that combined fiction, documentary and videoclip fragments (*La Nación* 2008b).
11. AMIA: 'Asociación Mutual Israelita Argentina'.
12. The video started with Darín and Dolores Fonzi reciting words by canonical Argentine writer Jorge Luis Borges: 'la patria amigos, es un acto perpetuo, como el perpetuo mundo' ['homeland, my friends, is a perpetual act, like the perpetual world'] – followed by performances by a myriad of stars, including Facundo Arana, Cristina Banegas, Valentina Bassi, Leonor Benedetto, Max Berliner, Antonio Birabent, Nicolás Cabré, Gloria Carrá, Gabriel Corrado, Lito Cruz, Alejandra Darín, Federico D'Elía, Emilio Disi, Nancy Dupláa, María Fiorentino, Guillermo Francella, María José Gabin, Gustavo Garzón, Esther Goris, Antonio Grimau, Martina Guzmán, Silvia Kutica, Osvaldo Laport, Juan Leyrado, Luis Luque, Luis Machín, Leonor Manso, Jorge Marrale, Mercédes Morán, Laura Novoa, Florencia Peña, Carla Peterson,

Diego Peretti, Andrea Pietra, Enrique Pinti, Carlos Portaluppi, Arturo Puig, Gerardo Romano, Cecilia Roth, Soledad Silveyra, Adrián Suar, Eugenia Tobal and Eleonora Wexler.
13. Those words pronounced by Darín come from Mao Zedong.
14. The awards ceremony took place in Spain in September 2012. Among those receiving a distinction that day were the Nobel Prize winner Tawakul Karman, Kim Phuc Phan Thi, Gervasio Sánchez and Vicente del Bosque. Save the Children works with many celebrities, including Ben Affleck, Gwyneth Paltrow and Julianne Moore (Huliaras and Tzifakis 2011: 35).
15. The distinction between social and political activism is purely functional here. We cannot deny the fact that all actions at a social level are political.
16. He participated, in, among others, a campaign to support the audio-visual industry during what has been identified as a paradoxical moment: film theatres closed and productions were cancelled, and yet consumption of audio-visual culture is higher than ever (*Escribiendocine* 2020).
17. The interview took place on 12 April 2020 via videoconference.
18. In a personal communication, Darín stated that he always felt the need to give back to the people a little bit of the love that he has been lucky to receive. He acknowledged the complexities of combining fame with philanthropy, which is why he said he does not judge colleagues who decide not to participate in humanitarian causes. He also mentioned that he is careful not to participate in any campaign at times when his image is being used for commercial purposes, such as beer adds, in an attempt to 'keep some sort of balance' (interview via videoconference, May 2020).
19. The *Look to the Stars* database, known as 'the world of celebrity giving', includes information of charity work carried out by film stars. Among those referenced there are several Hispanic stars, such as Diego Luna, Penélope Cruz, Gael García Bernal, Javier Bardem and Salma Hayek.
20. The relationship lasted seven years.
21. The case was found in favour of Darín thanks to a video recording which demonstrated how the linesman knocked him down, leaving him unconscious for a few seconds, and how this sparked Darín's violent reaction that ended with the linesman's nose being broken (personal communication, interview May 2020).
22. In fact, the case affected many famous people, including Darín's girlfriend at the time, Susana Giménez, but Darín was its principal face – as clearly evidenced by the file name logged with the judicial system being 'Darín et al.'.
23. Darín went indignantly to witness the auction, and when asked by the press if he was there to buy it, he said: 'I'm not going to buy again a car I bought in good faith and through the effort of my work.' Interview by Channel 13 news programme: https://www.youtube.com/watch?v=n3RZJKLkWQ4 (accessed 30 April 2020).
24. The case of *autos truchos* was closed in 2002 due to the statute of limitations having run out post its dismissal.
25. Néstor Kirchner's administration (2003–2007) and CFK's subsequent two terms in office (2007–2015) have generated a political movement known as 'Kirchnerism', which is popularly associated with the letter 'K' in the media – i.e. the K government, the K supporters. At the time of writing, CFK has been Vice President of Argentina since 2019.

26. Other controversial remarks made by Darín that year involved the national film institute (INCAA). As Urraca explains: 'in a radio interview with the outspoken anti-Kirchner journalist Jorge Lanata, Darín questioned the INCAA's method of granting subsidies. This prompted its president, government appointee Liliana Mazure, to detail how the Institute functions in her lengthy remarks addressed to him and published in the online journal *Haciendo Cine*' (2014: 369).
27. On 3 June 2020 the movement celebrated its fifth anniversary (Chaina 2020).
28. Instead of 'mistreatment', in subsequent interviews the actress talked about 'destrato' – disregard.
29. The fact that the media disseminated the rumour of Bertuccelli being in love with the actor as a reason for leaving the play demonstrates how patriarchal discourses are ingrained in Argentine society.
30. For instance, the collective backed Thelma Fardin's legal process against actor Juan Darthés for rape. In December 2018 it initiated the media campaign #Mirácómonosponemos, which became a viral phrase used to denounce acts of sexual abuse in Argentina. In a recent edited volume on #MeToo, it was suggested that because Darín did not 'conform to the image of the expected perpetrator, many were not ready to put their relationships with him and his wife on the line' (Garibotti and Hopp 2019: 195). Although the chapter signals the crucial need to develop theoretical aspects of anti-rape politics, and should be praised for that, Darín's example challenges the core of its argumentation – not only there are facts that are incorrect, such as the mention of Darín's wife leading the Actresses Association, there is also the important factor that he was not accused of sexual abuse or harassment by Rivas nor Bertuccelli and, thus, cannot be compared to the other cases mentioned in the chapter.
31. For further information on box-office figures in 2019 in Argentina, see: https://premiososcarlatinos.wordpress.com/taquilla-argentina/2019-2/ (accessed 4 June 2020).
32. The programme was created by Adrián Suar.
33. In this film, his character has a romance with the character played by Penélope Cruz.
34. He explained how, when he was a teenager, he submerged himself in a multiplayer first-person shooter game. The anonymity of his avatar, Hankamonic, gave him the pleasure of being an unknown for a while (Plotkin 2019).

# References

AFP (2017) 'El actor argentino Ricardo Darín dice carecer de "frialdad" para ser un político', in *France24*, 26 September. https://www.france24.com/es/20170926-el-actor-argentino-ricardo-darin-dice-carecer-de-frialdad-para-ser-un-politico (accessed 24 May 2020).

Aho, M. (2010) 'AQ Talks to Diego Luna on Documenting Mexico's Human Rights Abuses', in *Americas Quarterly*, 12 February. https://www.americasquarterly.org/fulltextarticle/iaq-i-talks-to-diego-luna-on-documenting-mexicos-human-rights-abuses/ (accessed 13 May 2020).

Anderson, B. (1991) *Imagined Communities: Reflections on the Origin and Spread of Nationalism*, London: Verso.
Appiah, K. A. (2006) *Cosmopolitanism: Ethics in a World of Strangers*, New York: W. W. Norton.
Assayas, M. (2005) *Bono on Bono: Conversations with Michka Assayas*, UK: Hodder and Stoughton.
Baban, F. (2013) 'Cosmopolitanism Reinvented: Neoliberal Globalization and Thomas Friedman', in Fridell, G. and Konings, M. (eds), *Age of Icons: Exploring Philanthrocapitalism in the Contemporary World*, Canada: University of Toronto Press.
Bandhauer, A. and Royer, M. (eds) (2015) *Stars in World Cinema*, London and New York: I. B. Tauris & Co.
Banet-Weiser, S. and Mukherjee, R. (2012) *Commodity Activism: Cultural Resistance in Neoliberal Times*, New York and London: New York University Press.
Biccum, A. R. (2016) 'What *Might* Celebrity Humanitarianism Have to do With Empire?', in *Third World Quarterly*, 37.6, pp. 998–1015.
Bishop, M. and Green, M. (2008) *Philanthrocapitalism: How Giving Can Change the World*, London: A&C Black Publishers Ltd.
CABASE (2019) 'Historia Argentina de Internet', online video report available at: https://www.cabase.org.ar/documental-historia-argentina-de-internet/ (accessed 30 April 2020).
*Cadena 3* (2013) 'Darín, sobre la polémica con Cristina: "La herí sin querer"', in *Cadena 3*, 15 January. https://www.cadena3.com/noticia.asp?categoria=noticias&titulo=darin-sobre-la-polemica-con-cristina-la-heri-sin-querer&id=108433 (accessed 1 June 2020).
Caras (2017) 'Susana, Lali y Darín, contra la violencia de género', in *Caras*, 8 March. https://caras.perfil.com/noticias/actualidad/2017-03-08-109697-susana-gimenez-lali-y-darin-se-sumaron-a-la-campana-contra-la-violencia-de-genero.phtml (accessed 4 June 2020).
Chaina, P. (2020) 'Cinco años de Ni Una Menos: "La deuda permanente es con nosotras y nosotres"', in *Página/12*, 3 June. https://www.pagina12.com.ar/269932-cinco-anos-de-ni-una-menos-la-deuda-permanente-es-con-nosotr (accessed 4 June 2020).
CICR (2009) '"La acción debe ser creación" – El actor argentino Ricardo Darín apoya la campaña "Nuestro mundo. Tu acción"', press release, in *Comité Internacional de la Cruz Roja*, 22 December. https://www.icrc.org/es/doc/resources/documents/news-release/2009-and-earlier/owym-news-141209.htm (accessed 11 May 2020).
Cohen, M. (1992) 'Rooted Cosmopolitanism', in *Dissent*, 39.4, pp. 478–483.
deCordova, R. (2001) *Picture Personalities. The Emergence of the Star System in America*, Urbana: University of Illinois Press.
Drake, P. and Higgins, M. (2006) 'I'm a Celebrity, Get Me into Politics', in Holmes, S. and Redmond, S. (eds), *Framing Celebrity. New Directions in Celebrity Culture*, London: Routledge.
Dyer, R. (1998), *Stars*, London: British Film Institute.
Emol (2011) 'Ricardo Darín es víctima de estafador que suplantó su identidad', in *emol. espectáculos*, 14 November. https://www.emol.com/noticias/magazine/2011/11/14/512596/ricardo-darin-es-victima-de-estafador-en-argentina.html (accessed 10 May 2020).

*Escribiendocine* (2020) 'Coronavirus: Darín, Oreiro y Cecilia Roth en una campaña iberoamericana en apoyo al cine y la TV', in *Escribiendocine* online journal. http://www.escribiendocine.com/noticia/0017035-coronavirus-darin-oreiro-y-cecilia-roth-en-una-campana-iberomericana-en-apoyo-al-cine-y-la-tv/?fbclid=IwAR3F8-puOgzJkWE5SlR-sOxaPYOuH9NyJ0_nnYkOsdyu941yIs4lTG_2J1g (accessed 28 April 2020).

Falicov, T. (2008) 'Latin America: How Mexico and Argentina Cope and Cooperate with the Behemoth of the North', in McDonald, P. and Wasko, J. (eds), *The Contemporary Hollywood Film Industry*, Malden and Oxford: Blackwell Publishing Ltd.

Falicov, T. (2019) *Latin American Film Industries*, London and New York: BFI & Bloomsbury Publishing Plc.

Fantoni, E. (2012) 'Darín es un encanto, Darín es un hipócrita', in *Etiqueta negra/Programa Ibermedia*, 1 November. https://www.programaibermedia.com/darin-es-un-encanto-darin-es-un-hipocrita/ (accessed 25 May 2020).

Farrell, N. (2020) 'Introduction: "Getting Busy with the Fizzy" – Johansson, SodaStream, and Oxfam: Exploring the Political Economics of Celebrity Activism', in Farrell, N. (ed.), *The Political Economy of Celebrity Activism*, Oxon and New York: Routledge.

Fridell, G. and Konings, M. (eds) (2013) *Age of Icons: Exploring Philanthrocapitalism in the Contemporary World*, Canada: University of Toronto Press.

Garibotti, M. C. and Hopp, C. M. (2019) 'Substitution Activism: The Impact of #MeToo in Argentina', in Fileborn, B. and Loney-Howes, R. (eds), *#MeToo and the Politics of Social Change*, Switzerland: Palgrave Macmillan.

Hiebert, D. (2002) 'Cosmopolitanism at the Local Level: The Development of Transnational Neighbourhoods', in Vertovec, S. and Cohen, R. (eds), *Conceiving Cosmopolitanism*, Oxford: Oxford University Press, pp. 209–223.

Huliaras, A. and Tzifakis, N. (2011) 'Bringing the Individuals Back In? Celebrities as Transnational Activists', in Tsaliki, L., Frangonikolopoulos, C. A. and Huliaras, A. (eds), *Transnational Celebrity Activism in Global Politics: Changing the World?*, Bristol and Chicago: Intellect Ltd.

Infoshow (2018) 'Valeria Bertuccelli reveló detalles de su denuncia contra Ricardo Darín: gritos, insultos y "un empujón de más"', in *Teleshow*, 28 September. https://www.infobae.com/teleshow/infoshow/2018/09/28/valeria-bertuccelli-revelo-detalles-de-los-maltratos-que-sufrio-por-parte-de-ricardo-darin-gritos-insultos-y-un-empujon-de-mas/ (accessed 2 June 2020).

Kapoor, I. (2013) 'Humanitarian Heroes?', in Fridell, G. and Konings, M. (eds), *Age of Icons: Exploring Philanthrocapitalism in the Contemporary World*, Canada: University of Toronto Press.

Kemp, L. (2017) 'Stardom in Spanish America', in Delgado, M., Hart, S. and Johnson, R. (eds), *A Companion to Latin American Cinema*, UK: John Wiley and Sons.

King, B. (2015) *Taking Fame to Market: On the Pre-History and Post-History of Hollywood Stardom*, London: Palgrave Macmillan.

*La Nación* (1998) 'El hombre orquesta', in *La Nación espectáculos*, 10 August. https://www.lanacion.com.ar/espectaculos/el-hombre-orquesta-nid106448 (accessed 7 May 2020).

*La Nación* (2000) 'Ricardo Darín', in *La Nación espectáculos*, 1 October. https://www.lanacion.com.ar/espectaculos/ricardo-darin-nid585078 (accessed 6 May 2020).

*La Nación* (2008) 'Premiaron al programa Hoy me desperté', in *La Nación Espectáculos*. https://www.lanacion.com.ar/espectaculos/television/premiaron-al-programa-hoy-me-desperte-nid984063 (accessed 6 May 2020).

*La Nación* (2013a) 'Ricardo Darín: "Quisiera que alguien me explicara el crecimiento patrimonial de los Kirchner"', in *La Nación Política*, 4 January. https://www.lanacion.com.ar/politica/ricardo-darin-quisiera-que-alguien-me-explicara-el-crecimiento-patrimonial-de-los-kirchner-nid1542756 (accessed 31 May 2020).

*La Nación* (2013b) 'Alejandra Darín, sobre la reacción de Cristina: "no lo siento como un ataque"', in *La Nación*, 9 January. https://www.lanacion.com.ar/politica/alejandra-darin-no-soy-kirchnerista-no-soy-cristinista-soy-argentina-nid1544149 (accessed 1 June 2020).

*La Nación* (2018a) 'Erica Rivas apoyó a Valeria Bertuccelli: "Sos valiente. Tus palabras reparan"', in *La Nación*, 13 June. https://www.lanacion.com.ar/espectaculos/erica-rivas-apoyo-a-valeria-bertuccelli-sos-valiente-tus-palabras-reparan-nid2143545 (accessed 2 June 2020).

*La Nación* (2018b) 'Verónica Llinás explicó por qué Actrices Argentinas no respaldó la denuncia de Valeria Bertuccelli contra Ricardo Darín', in *La Nación*, 17 December. https://www.lanacion.com.ar/espectaculos/personajes/veronica-llinas-explico-que-actrices-argentinas-no-nid2203264 (accessed 3 June 2020).

*La Nación* (2019) 'Darín volvió a hablar de Bertuccelli: "Todos los días me pregunto por qué lo hizo"', in *La Nación*, 14 August. https://www.lanacion.com.ar/espectaculos/personajes/darin-volvio-hablar-bertuccelli-todos-dias-me-nid2277465 (accessed 4 June 2020).

*La Nueva* (2012) 'Los galancitos por Bahía', in *La Nueva Sociedad*. https://www.lanueva.com/nota/2012-3-10-9-0-0-los-galancitos-por-bahia (accessed 3 May 2020).

Larkin, K. (2009) 'Star Power: Models for Celebrity Political Activism', in *Virginia Sports and Entertainment Law Journal*, 9.1, pp. 155–180.

Littler, J. (2008) '"I Feel Your Pain": Cosmopolitan Charity and the Public Fashioning of the Celebrity Soul', in *Social Semiotics*, 18.2, pp. 237–251.

Long, R. (2006) 'Using Your Star Power', in *Foreign Policy*, May–June, pp. 74–78.

McDonald, P. (2008) 'The Star System: The Production of Hollywood Stardom in the Post-Studio Era', in McDonald, P. and Wasko, J. (eds), *The Contemporary Hollywood Film Industry*, Malden and Oxford: Blackwell Publishing Ltd.

Marshall, P. D. (2010) 'The Promotion and Presentation of the Self: Celebrity as Marker of Presentational Media', in *Celebrity Studies*, 1.1, pp. 35–48.

Marshall, P. D. (2014) *Celebrity and Power: Fame in Contemporary Culture*, Minneapolis and London: University of Minnesota Press.

Miller, M. (2017) 'Gael García Bernal, Diego Luna Start Charity to Help Mexico Earthquake Victims', in *Entertainment Weekly*, 22 September. https://ew.com/news/2017/09/22/diego-luna-gael-garcia-bernal-charity-mexico-earthquake-victims/ (accessed 13 May 2020).

Monfort, F. (2018) 'Escenas de la vida patriarcal', in *Página/12*, 28 September. https://www.pagina12.com.ar/144887-escenas-de-la-vida-patriarcal (accessed 2 June 2020).

Nussbaum, M. (1996) 'Patriotism and Cosmopolitanism', in Cohen, J. (ed.), *For Love of Country*, Boston, MA: Beacon Press, pp. 3–20.

Ochoa, S. (2005) 'El reclamo wichí llegó a la Rosada', in *Página12*, 30 September. https://www.pagina12.com.ar/diario/sociedad/3-57220-2005-09-30.html (accessed 12 May 2020).

*Página/12* (2013) 'Una discusión de "teléfono descompuesto"', in *Página/12*, 8 January. https://www.pagina12.com.ar/diario/elpais/1-211401-2013-01-08.html (accessed 1 June 2020).

Perantuono, P. (2013) 'Ricardo Darín: "somos un país niño"', in *#LaÉxito*, 6 January. https://radioexito.com.ar/nota/1053/ricardo-darin-somos-un-pais-nino (accessed 11 May 2020).

Pisano, S. (2003) 'Convenio con la obra del Padre Mario Pantaleo. El Real Madrid ayudará a unos 1000 chicos bonaerenses', in *La Nación*, 1 March. https://www.lanacion.com.ar/sociedad/el-real-madrid-ayudara-a-unos-1000-chicos-bonaerenses-nid477427/ (accessed 14 May 2020).

Plotkin, P. (2019) 'La odisea interior del Chino Darín, la estrella más encantadora del cine de hoy', in *Rolling Stone*, 31 July. https://www.lanacion.com.ar/espectaculos/cine/chino-darin-estrella-cine-encantadora-nid2271458 (accessed 8 July 2020).

Puglisi, J. A. (2020) 'Ricardo Darín "se dispara al pie" ante Évole: una recomendación "comunista" que se le vuelve en su contra', in *Periodista digital*, 13 April. https://www.periodistadigital.com/periodismo/tv/20200413/ricardo-darin-dispara-pie-evole-recomendacion-comunista-le-vuelve-noticia-689404290779/ (accessed 25 May 2020).

Qiong Yu, S. (2018) 'Introduction; Performing Stardom: Star Studies in Transformation and Expansion', in Qiong Yu, S. and Austin, G. (eds), *Revisiting Star Studies: Cultures, Themes and Methods*, Edinburgh: Edinburgh University Press.

Rebossio, A. (2013) 'Darín se enzarza con Cristina Fernández por el patrimonio de los Kirchner', in *El País*, 7 January. https://elpais.com/elpais/2013/01/07/gente/1357570036_004381.html (accessed 1 June 2020).

*Redacción LA* (2015) 'Valeria Bertuccelli ¿Se flechó con Darín y dejó todo?', in *Los Andes*, 16 May. https://www.losandes.com.ar/article/valeria-bertuccelli-se-flecho-con-darin-y-dejo-todo (accessed 2 June 2020).

Rojek, C. (2001) *Celebrity*, London: Reaktion Books.

Shingler, M. and Steenberg, L. (2019) 'Star Studies in Mid-life Crisis', in *Celebrity Studies*, 10.4, pp. 445–452.

Tarrow, S. (2005) *The New Transnational Activism*, Cambridge: Cambridge University Press.

Trope, A. (2012) 'Mother Angelina: Hollywood Philanthropy Personified', in Mukherjee, R. and Banet-Weiser, S. (eds), *Commodity Activism. Cultural Resistance in Neoliberal Times*, New York: New York University Press, pp. 154–173.

Tsaliki, L., Frangonikolopoulos, C. A. and Huliaras, A. (eds) (2011) *Transnational Celebrity Activism in Global Politics: Changing the World?*, Bristol and Chicago: Intellect Ltd.

Turner, G. (2014) *Understanding Celebrity*, London: SAGE Publications Ltd.

Urraca, B. (2014) 'Rituals of Performance: Ricardo Darín as Father Julián in *Elefante blanco*', in *Revista de Estudios Hispánicos*, Tomo XLVIII, 2, June, pp. 353–372.

Watts, A. (2008) '"You Can Blame the Editing but you're Still a Bitch": The Search for the Authentic Self in Reality-TV Celebrity', in Hart, K. (ed.), *Film and Television Stardom*, Newcastle: Cambridge Scholars Publishing.

Young, R. J. C. (2001) *Postcolonialism: An Historical Introduction*, Oxford: Blackwell Publishers.

Yrjölä, R. (2011) 'The Global Politics of Celebrity Humanitarianism', in Tsaliki, L., Frangonikolopoulos, C. A. and Huliaras, A. (eds), *Transnational Celebrity Activism in Global Politics: Changing the World?*, Bristol and Chicago: Intellect Ltd.

Zeballos, H. (2014) 'Torneo de actores y tenistas de 1988', in *La Capital Mar del Plata*, 16 January. http://www.lacapitalmdp.com/noticias/Deportes/2014/01/17/254297.htm (accessed 20 May 2020).

# Appendix 1

## Filmography

*He nacido en la ribera* (Catrano Catrani 1972)
*Así es la vida* (Enrique Carreras 1977)
*Juventud sin barreras* (Ricardo Montes 1979)
*La fiesta de todos* (Sergio Renán 1979)
*La carpa del amor* (Julio Porter 1979)
*La rabona* (Mario David 1979)
*Los éxitos del amor* (Fernando Siro 1979)
*La canción de Buenos Aires* (Fernando Siro 1980)
*La discoteca del amor* (Adolfo Aristarain 1980)
*La playa del amor* (Adolfo Aristarain 1980)
*Abierto día y noche* (Fernando Ayala 1981)
*El desquite* (Juan Carlos Desanzo 1983)
*La Rosales* (David Lipszyc 1984)
*Expreso a la emboscada* (Gilles Béhat 1986)
*Te amo* (Eduardo Calcagno 1986)
*Revancha de un amigo* (Santiago Carlos Oves 1987)
*The Stranger* (Adolfo Aristarain 1987)
*Perdido por perdido* (Alberto Lecchi 1993)
*El faro* (Eduardo Mignogna 1998)
*El mismo amor, la misma lluvia* (Juan José Campanella 1999)
*Nueve reinas* (Fabián Bielinsky 2000)
*El hijo de la novia* (Juan José Campanella 2001)
*La fuga* (Eduardo Mignogna 2001)
*Kamchatka* (Marcelo Piñeyro 2002)

*Samy y yo* (Eduardo Milewicz 2002)
*Luna de Avellaneda* (Juan José Campanella 2004)
*El aura* (Fabián Bielinsky 2005)
*La educación de las hadas* (José Luis Cuerda 2007)
*La señal* (Ricardo Darín and Martín Hodara 2007)
*XXY* (Lucía Puenzo 2007)
*Amorosa soledad* (Victoria Galardi and Martín Carranza 2009)
*El baile de la Victoria* (Fernando Trueba 2009)
*El secreto de sus ojos* (Juan José Campanella 2009)
*Carancho* (Pablo Trapero 2010)
*El destino del Lukong* (Gonzalo Roldán 2011)
*Un cuento chino* (Sebastián Borensztein 2011)
*Elefante blanco* (Pablo Trapero 2012)
*En fuera de juego* (David Marqués 2012)
*Una pistola en cada mano* (Cesc Gay 2012)
*Séptimo* (Patxi Amezcua 2013)
*Tesis sobre un homicidio* (Hernán Goldfrid 2013)
*Violet* (Luiso Berdejo 2013)
*Delirium* (Carlos Kaimakamian Carrau 2014)
*La chica más rara del mundo* (Mariano Cattaneo 2014) – short film
*Relatos salvajes* (Damián Szifrón 2014)
*Torrente 5: Operación Eurovegas* (Santiago Segura 2015)
*Truman* (Cesc Gay 2015)
*Kóblic* (Sebastián Borensztein 2016)
*La cordillera* (Santiago Mitre 2017)
*Libro de la memoria: Homenaje a las víctimas del atentado* (Matías Bertilotti 2017) – short film
*Nieve negra* (Martín Hodara 2017)
*El amor menos pensado* (Juan Verá 2018)
*Todos lo saben* (Asghar Farhadi 2018)
*Héroes de la conservación* (Marcelo Viñas and Juan María Raggio 2019)
*La odisea de los giles* (Sebastián Borensztein 2019)
*Argentina, 1985* (Santiago Mitre 2022)

## Theatrical plays and musicals

*El tema es el amor* (1978)
*La vida fácil* (1980)
*Hasta mañana, si Dios quiere* (1982)

*La extraña pareja* (1984)
*Taxi* (1985)
*Sugar* (1986–1987)
*Pájaros in the nait* (1990–1991; as director)
*Rumores* (1990)
*Necesito un tenor* (1991–1992)
*Pizzaman* (1994–1995)
*Algo en común* (1995–1996)
*El submarino* (1998; as producer)
*Art* (1998–2004 and 2008–2010; in Spain, 2003 and then 2005–2006)
*La madre de . . .* (2003 – voiceover)
*Escenas de la vida conyugal* (2013–2022)

## TV shows

*La mesa redonda de los niños prodigio* (1967/1969)
*La pandilla del tranvía* (Channel 9 – 1968)
*Las grandes novelas* (Channel 7 – 1970)
*Estación Retiro* (Channel 9 – 1971/1972)
*Alta comedia* (Channel 9 – 1974)
*Ayer fue mentira* (Cascallar, Channel 9 – 1975)
*La familia Super Star* (Channel 9 – 1975/1978)
*Los que estamos solos* (Migré, Channel 13 – 1976)
*El tema es el amor* (Migré, Channel 13 – 1977)
*Pablo en nuestra piel* (Migré, Channel 13 – 1977)
*Vos y yo, toda la vida* (Migré, Channel 13 – 1978)
*Una escalera al cielo* (Galván, Channel 9 – 1979)
*Casa de muñecas* (Álvarez, Channel 13 – 1980 – TV mini-series)
*Un día 32 en San Telmo* (González Márquez, Channel 9 – 1980)
*Vivir con todo* (De Cecco, Channel 9 – 1980)
*Me caso con vos* (González Márquez, Channel 13 – 1981)
*Juan sin nombre* (Álvarez, Channel 9 – 1982)
*Nosotros y los miedos* (Álvarez, Channel 9 – 1982–1983)
*Compromiso* (Channel 13 – 1983)
*Mi chanta favorito* (Channel 13 – 1983)
*Cuentos para ver* (Channel 7, ATC – 1984)
*Estrellita mía* (Channel 11 – 1987)
*Rebelde* (Channel 9 – 1989)
*Buenos Aires, háblame de amor* (Channel ATC – 1991)

*Mi otro yo* (Channel 13 – 1992)
*Mi cuñado* (Channel Telefé – 1993–1996, in 1998 new final episodes were shown)
*Chiquititas* (Channel Telefé – 1998 – Eduardo)
*La mujer del presidente* (Channel Telefé – 1999 – Agustín Moyano)
*Por ese palpitar* (Channel América TV – 2000)
*Tiempo final* (Channel Telefé – 2000 – Juan, electrician)
*Hoy me desperté* (Channel 13 – 2006 – one episode)
*Para vestir santos* (Channel 13 – 2010)
*El Host* (2018)

# Appendix 2

**Table 9.1** Films starring Darín released in Spain. Further information is available online at the Institute of Cinematography and Audiovisual Arts (ICCA) – Spain (available at: https://infoicaa.mecd.es/CatalogoICAA/ [accessed 22 May 2022]).

| Release dates in Argentina/in Spain | Production | Title of film | Director | Distributor | Box-office results: income/spectators |
|---|---|---|---|---|---|
| 1993/20 May 1994 | Argentina | *Perdido por perdido* | Alberto Lecchi | VHERO FILMS S.A. | 50,416.74 €/ 18,073 |
| 1998/22 May 1998 | Argentina, Spain | *El faro* (in Spain: *El faro del sur*) | Eduardo Mignogna | PRIME FILMS S.L. | 464,740.55 €/ 123,591 |
| 1999/19 July 2002 | Argentina | *El mismo amor, la misma lluvia* | Juan José Campanella | ALTA CLASSICS S.L. UNIPERSONAL | 2,804,629.26 €/ 609,566 |
| 2000/23 August 2001 | Argentina | *Nueve reinas* | Fabián Bielinsky | ALTA CLASSICS S.L. UNIPERSONAL | 2,257,369.85 €/ 475,058 |
| 2001/11 October 2001 | Argentina, Spain | *La fuga* | Eduardo Mignogna | WANDA VISION, S.A. | 50,103.09 €/ 12,432 |
| 2001/23 November 2001 | Argentina, Spain | *El hijo de la novia* | Juan José Campanella | ALTA CLASSICS S.L. UNIPERSONAL. | 7,231,323.19 €/ 1,575,039 |
| 2002/11 October 2002 | Argentina | *Samy y yo* (in Spain: *Un tipo corriente*) | Eduardo Milewicz | FLINS Y PINICULAS, S.L. | 748,950.15 €/ 160,975 |
| 2002/29 November 2002 | Argentina, Spain | *Kamchatka* | Marcelo Piñeyro | HISPANO FOX FILM S.A. | 2,983,604.50 €/ 628,099 |
| 2004/4 November 2004 | Argentina, Spain | *Luna de Avellaneda* | Juan José Campanella | ALTA CLASSICS S.L. UNIPERSONAL | 1,738,036.39 €/ 346,654 |
| 2005/21 October 2005 | Argentina, Spain | *El aura* | Fabián Bielinsky | ALTA CLASSICS S.L. UNIPERSONAL | 397,883.37 €/ 79,125 |

| Release dates in Argentina/in Spain | Production | Title of film | Director | Distributor | Box-office results: income/spectators |
|---|---|---|---|---|---|
| 2007/21 June 2006 | Argentina, Spain, Portugal, France | *La educación de las hadas* | José Luis Cuerda | ALTA CLASSICS S.L. UNIPERSONAL | 1,865,842.40 €/ 353,923 |
| 2007/21 December 2007 | Argentina, Spain | *XXY* | Lucía Puenzo | WANDA VISION, S.A. | 237,209.70 €/ 43,840 |
| 2007/5 October 2007 | Argentina, Spain | *La señal* | Ricardo Darín and Martín Hodara | WANDA VISION, S.A. | 214,696.59 €/ 38,214 |
| 2009/25 September 2009 | Argentina, Spain | *El secreto de sus ojos* | Juan José Campanella | ALTA CLASSICS S.L. UNIPERSONAL | 6,306,339.97 €/ 1,033,740 |
| 2009/24 September 2009 | Spain | *El baile de la Victoria* | Fernando Trueba | VERTICE CINE, S.L. | 1,415,112.12 €/ 234,708 |
| 2010/22 September 2010 | Argentina | *Carancho* | Pablo Trapero | GOLEM DISTRIBUCION S.L. | 660,119.18 €/ 105,211 |
| 2011/17 June 2011 | Argentina, Spain | *Un cuento chino* | Sebastián Borensztein | ALTA CLASSICS S.L. UNIPERSONAL | 2,284,050.23 €/ 353,511 |
| 2011/1 June 2012 | Argentina, Spain | *En fuera de juego* | David Marqués | A CONTRA-CORRIENTE FILMS S.L. | 179,643.65 €/ 33,270 |
| 2012/13 July 2012 | Argentina, Spain, France | *Elefante blanco* | Pablo Trapero | ALTA CLASSICS S.L. UNIPERSONAL | 1,002,614.81 €/ 156,999 |
| 2012/5 December 2012 | Spain | *Una pistola en cada mano* | Cesc Gay | CASTELAO PICTURES, S.L. | 1,911,285.51 €/ 265,558 |

| Release dates in Argentina/in Spain | Production | Title of film | Director | Distributor | Box-office results: income/spectators |
|---|---|---|---|---|---|
| January 2013/5 March 2013 | Argentina, Spain | Tesis sobre un homicidio | Hernán Golfrid | TORNASOL FILMS S.A. | 1,528,759.43 €/ 217,104 |
| 2013/8 November 2013 | Spain, Argentina | Séptimo | Patxi Amezcua | HISPANO FOXFILM, S.A.E. and FILM FACTORY ENTERTAINMENT | 3,002,608.93€/ 484,845 |
| 2013/18 February 2014 | Spain, USA | Violet | Luiso Berdejo | KOWALSKI FILMS, S.L. and NEW MORNING FILMS | 316.70 €/ 94 |
| 2014/17 October 2014 | Argentina, Spain | Relatos salvajes | Damián Szifrón | WARNER BROS ENTERTAINMENT ESPAÑA S.L. and FILM FACTORY ENTERTAINMENT | 4,810,764.55 €/ 807,971 |
| 2015/30 October 2015 | Spain, Argentina | Truman | Cesc Gay | CASTELAO PICTURES, S.L. FILMAX | 3,589,119.96 €/ 634,665 |
| 2 October 2014 | Spain | Torrente 5 | Santiago Segura | BUENA VISTA INTERNACIONAL SPAIN and FILMSHARKS INTERNATIONAL | 10,634,693.53€/ 1,811,276 |

| Release dates in Argentina/in Spain | Production | Title of film | Director | Distributor | Box-office results: income/spectators |
|---|---|---|---|---|---|
| 2016/17 June 2016 | Spain, Argentina | *Kóblic* | Sebastián Borensztein | DEA PLANETA, S.L. | 412,171.20 € / 67,648 |
| 2017/29 September 2017 | Spain, France, Argentina | *La cordillera* | Santiago Mitre | WARNER BROS ENTERTAINMENT ESPAÑA S.L. and FILM FACTORY ENTERTAINMENT, S.L. | 885,650.89 € / 143,890 |
| 2017/29 December 2016 | Spain, Argentina | *Nieve negra* | Martín Hodara | A CONTRACORRIENTE FILMS, S.L. | 562,332.49 € / 90,933 |
| 2018/14 September 2018 | Spain, France, Italy | *Todos lo saben* | Asghar Farhadi | UNIVERSAL PICTURES INTERNATIONAL SPAIN S.L. | 3,157,087.92 € / 580,427 |
| 2018/30 November 2018 | Argentina | *El amor menos pensado* | Juan Verá | CASTELAO PICTURES, S.L. | 815,755.49 € / 132,614 |
| 2019/29 November 2019 | Argentina, Spain | *La odisea de los giles* | Sebastián Borensztein | ALFA PICTURES, S.L.U. and FILM FACTORY ENTERTAINMENT, S.L. | 954,044.74 € / 155,680 |

# Index

*Adiós Argentina*, 28–9
Adjemián, M., 71–2, 93n
ageing star, 13, 68, 172–86
Alarcón, A., 25
Alarcón, M., 147n, 187n
Alarcón, P., 91n, 108, 111n, 123, 167n
Alfaro, E., 58–9, 142
Alippi, E., 24–5, 29, 37n
*Alta comedia*, 12, 108, 113n
Alcón, A., 11, 38n, 51, 59, 60, 62n, 64n, 92n, 105, 111n, 113n, 145
Alcón, M., 39n
Aleandro, N., 3, 11, 25, 50, 58, 71–3, 79, 80, 87, 91n, 103, 105, 119, 145, 162, 174, 176, 193
Alemán, S., 104, 123
Altavista, J. C., 57, 64n, 110
Alterio, H., 3, 11, 25, 48–9, 58–9, 71, 73–4, 79–80, 91n, 92n, 102, 107, 112n, 167n, 176, 187, 197–9
Amadori, L. C., 32, 33, 38n, 51, 61n, 111n
André, A., 111n, 119–20, 130
*Antena*, 31, 43, 103

Antín, M., 11, 47, 53, 62n, 78, 85
Arata, L., 38n, 101–2, 110, 111n
Argentina, 3–6, 9–12, 22–38, 44–5, 47–9, 53–6, 64n, 68, 70, 72, 76–8, 80–3, 88, 92n, 100–1, 104, 109–10, 111n, 113n, 116, 123, 126–7, 138, 140–1, 143–4, 159–60, 163–4, 177, 180, 182–3, 193–8, 200–6, 214, 220, 222–3, 232, 234–8, 241–4, 246–7
*Argentina, 1985*, 1, 70, 89, 90, 226n
Argentina, I., 37n
Argentina Sono Film, 10, 28–9, 32, 38, 58–9, 61n, 62n, 75
Argentine Actors Association, 25, 73–4, 100, 103
Arias, I., 194, 206n
Arias, P., 29, 30, 38n, 39n
Aries Cinematográfica, 59, 75, 78, 127, 157, 167n
Aristarain, A., 83, 92n, 126–7, 160, 179, 193, 217–18
Armendáriz, P., 5, 38n
*Art*, 13, 135, 143–5, 173, 180, 198, 235
*Así es la vida*, 13, 30, 75, 110

audience, 4, 5, 8, 12, 13–14, 22, 24, 26–7, 33–4, 36, 44, 53, 55–7, 62n, 63n, 71, 77–9, 88, 90–1, 99, 107, 128–9, 134, 138, 145, 154, 163, 165, 166n, 174, 176, 178, 183–4, 193, 197–200, 202–3, 207n, 211, 215–8, 220–1, 224, 231, 233, 237, 239, 242
Ayala, F., 47, 53, 59, 62n, 111n, 127, 157

Balá, C., 57, 64n, 92n
Banderas, A., 81, 83, 202, 215, 217
Bardem, J., 14, 15, 201, 219, 246, 249n
Bardem, P., 72
Bardot, B., 44–5
Battaglia, G., 62n, 64n, 79–80
Bebán, R., 59, 112n, 119, 130, 136, 157, 167
Beltrán, N., 63n, 167n
Bengoechea, F., 25
Bertuccelli, V., 11, 88, 105, 144–5, 187n, 242–3, 250n
*Betrayed by Rita Hayworth*, 5
Blanco, E., 176–7, 186n
Bo, A., 39n, 45, 62–3n
Bores, T., 57, 63n
Borges, G., viii, 11, 50, 60, 62n, 64n, 86, 93n, 140, 178
Borges, J. L., 248n
Boyano, A., 23
Bozán, O., 31, 38n, 59, 61n, 63n
Brandoni, L., 48, 71, 73–4, 82, 108, 144, 153–4, 178, 185, 186n
Brazil, 92, 162, 167n, 213–14, 220, 222, 225, 226n, 246
Bredeston, G., 57, 62n, 110, 136, 167n
Brédice, L., 61n, 80, 112n, 165, 167n, 187n

Briski, N., 71, 73–4, 112n, 167n, 188n
Bushman, F., 26

Calvo, C., 76, 111n, 124–5, 131n, 132n, 137–41, 147n, 233, 247n
Calabró, J. C., 64n, 76, 102, 157
Campanella, J. J., 1, 80, 87, 89, 120, 165–6, 175–8, 180, 194, 198, 204, 219, 226n
Cantinflas, 5, 38n
Cárpena, N., 57, 92n, 104, 119–21
Carreras, E., 13, 30, 62n, 75, 112n
Casaux, R., 25, 36n
Castaña, C., 76, 126, 132n, 157
Castro, A., 82, 187n, 224n
celebrity, 6, 8, 12–13, 15n, 56, 90, 99, 104, 116–19, 121, 123, 129–30, 137, 153, 185, 222, 224, 226n, 231–47, 249n
Cervantes theatre, 9, 102, 111n
Institute, 15, 195, 204, 221
Chaplin, G., 71, 82,
child actor, 3, 99, 106
childhood, 12, 99, 100, 176, 180
performer, 12
star, 99, 100, 110, 113n, 124
Chiqui Fornari, 13, 143, 153, 161–2, 166n, 173
Codevilla, P., 104, 106, 108, 112–13n, 121–2, 124, 137, 140, 233
Colmenares, G., 12, 130, 167n
comedy, 13, 46, 57, 75–6, 103, 109, 136, 138, 140–3, 152–7, 166, 179, 201
Corrado, G., 130, 156, 167n, 188n, 248n
Cosimi, N., 27, 37n
Cruz, P., 14, 15, 71, 81, 201, 203, 207n, 215–16, 219, 240, 246, 249n, 250n

Daniel, E., 50–1, 56, 62n
Darín, A., 25, 74, 100, 112n, 166n, 187n, 241, 248
   R. 'Chino', 25, 81, 89, 90, 104, 110n, 148n, 201, 203–4, 207, 232, 243–5
*De a dos*, 128, 239
De Ajuria, J., 26, 36n
De Grazia, J., 62n, 78, 82, 160, 167n, 218
De la Serna, R., 81, 89, 186n
Del Boca, A., 12, 108, 113n, 124, 129–30, 161, 167n, 222
Del Carril, H., 10, 35, 37–9n, 43, 50
Del Río, D., 5, 6, 34, 38n, 39n
*Delirium*, 1, 213
Demare, L, 38n, 62n
democracy, 47, 70, 78, 80, 158, 238
Deneuve, C., 4
dictatorship, 6, 11, 44, 46, 53, 58, 69–82, 89, 91n, 121, 123, 126–7, 158–60, 178–9, 195–6, 200, 202
Disi, E., 92n, 148n, 248n
*Divine Lady, The*, 28
Dumont, U., 76, 82, 92n, 102, 112n, 158, 160, 186n

Echarri, P., 3, 81, 88–90, 130, 145, 167n
*El amor menos pensado*, 14, 185
*El aura*, 3, 178–9, 226n
*El conventillo de la Paloma*, 29
*Elefante blanco*, 2, 3, 226n, 234
*El hijo de la novia*, 1, 3, 14, 80, 87, 144, 165, 175–6, 194, 198, 200, 219
Ellis, P., 26
*El secreto de sus ojos*, 1, 2, 3, 14, 89, 93n, 105, 120, 176–7, 194, 219, 221, 223

*Escenas de la vida conyugal*, 13, 143, 242
*Estación retiro*, 12, 107, 121, 131n
*Estrellita mía*, 12, 113n, 129–30, 161, 222
*Expreso a la emboscada*, 159

Fairbanks, D., 26
Favio, L., 11, 47, 51, 53, 63n, 64n, 126
Félix, M., 5, 7, 38n
Ferreyra, J. A., 27–8, 37n
Figueroa, D., 24
*Flor de durazno*, 24
Fonzi, D., 80, 104, 181, 187n, 243, 248n
Foras, C., 27
Francella, G., 3, 11, 81, 88–91, 167n, 177–8, 187n, 248n

galán, 48, 51–2, 119–20, 142
galancito, 125, 129–30, 136–39, 141, 143, 146, 147n
Gallo, M. R., 62n, 101
García Bernal, G., 130n, 197, 211, 221, 224n, 235, 239, 249n
García Buhr, A., 30, 39n, 167n
García Satur, C., 57, 119, 130, 136
Gardel, C., 3, 5, 10, 24, 29, 30, 35, 37n, 148n
Giménez, S., 46, 63n, 73, 102, 106, 108, 110, 112n, 124–5, 129, 131n, 135, 139–40, 142, 147n, 161, 163, 173, 239, 243, 249n
Glücksmann, M., 28
Golden Age, 5, 23, 25, 28–9, 31, 35, 38n, 50, 55, 59, 68, 178
Gómez, A., 23–4, 29
Good Neighbour Policy, 33, 215
Grandinetti, D., 1, 3, 82, 147n, 159, 167n, 197, 233

*Hasta después de muerta*, 23
*He nacido en la ribera*, 12, 105, 108–10, 112n
Hill Mailes, C., 26, 36n
Hispanic academia, 1, 2
  identity, 207n
  imaginary, 195
  star, 2, 3, 14, 15, 191, 214–17, 225n, 232, 239, 249n
  stereotype, 217–18, 223
Hollywood, 1–3, 5, 195, 202, 204, 211–20, 223–4, 225n, 232, 246–7

Italian Neorealism, 48–9, 85
INCAA, 84, 214, 250n

*Juventud sin barreras*, 13, 127

Kirchner/Kirchnerism, 12, 69, 70, 88–9, 237, 240–1, 249n, 250n
Kohon, D. J., 11, 47, 51
Kraus, G., 78, 112n, 124, 148n
Kuhn, R., 11, 47, 51–2
Kuliok, L., 111n, 123, 160, 167n

*La cordillera*, 14, 182, 237
Ladrón de Guevara, F., 23
*La fuga*, 56, 174–5, 194, 222, 226n
Lago, C., 81, 178
*La historia oficial*, 11, 72, 79, 80, 111n, 158
Lamarque, L., 3, 10, 28, 29, 33, 35, 37n, 39n, 102, 111n
Landriscina, L., 110
Lanzani, P., 81, 89, 90
*La pandilla del tranvía*, 12, 107, 113n
Laplace, V., 51, 82, 102, 107, 167n
*La rabona*, 30, 127
*La Rosales*, 31, 102, 110, 158, 226n
*La señal*, 2, 175, 181, 226n

Latin America, 5–10, 195–7, 199, 205, 206n, 214–15, 220, 222, 225n, 232, 246–7, 248n
  cinema, 6, 154, 165, 220
  films, 6, 202, 221, 223, 224n, 225n
  stardom, 4, 9, 13, 116
  stars, 2–4, 187n, 214, 221, 223, 235
Latino, 1, 8, 37–8n, 116, 195, 216, 220
Leblanc, L., 46, 102
Ledesma, A., 33, 37n
Legrand, M., 31, 33, 39n, 43, 51, 59, 60, 62n, 73, 91n, 105, 111n, 167n
Liss, L., 27, 37
Llinás, V., 89, 143, 185, 243
Logan, J., 26
López Rey, M., 46, 59, 62n
*Los tres berretines*, 29, 30
*Luces de Buenos Aires*, 30, 37n
Lumiton, 10, 30, 32, 38n
Luna, D., 130n, 165, 215, 235, 249n
Luppi, F., 3, 11, 48, 58, 63n, 71, 73, 82, 91–2n, 119, 159, 161, 168n, 182, 197–8, 218, 241

Mafalda, 78
Maipo theatre, viii, 29, 82
mainstream, 1, 3, 79, 87–9, 152, 164, 184, 216, 238
Maizani, A., 29
Maradona, D. A., 226n, 233, 247n
Marconi theatre, 25, 101, 111n
Marinelli, A., 57, 59, 119, 167n
Mario, A., 23
Marshall, N., 30, 32, 39n, 61n, 111n, 140
Martel, L., 86, 223
Martínez, O., 1, 81, 102, 112n, 144, 167n, 178, 206n
Martínez De la Pera, M., 23

Mazza, J. L., 75, 141, 143–4, 166n, 188n
Menem, C./Menemism, 11, 83, 88, 180
Mentasti, A., 29, 62n
Merello, T., 10, 29, 30, 35, 38n, 43, 51, 62n, 111–12n
Mexico, 116, 126, 131n, 196–7, 214, 235, 246
*Mi cuñado*, 13, 142, 153–7, 161, 166n, 173, 186n
migration, 21, 31, 91n, 195
Migré, A., 61n, 103, 105, 112n, 118–24, 130–1n, 136
Miranda, C., 34, 39n, 217
Mirás, F., 80, 145, 167n
Mitre, S., 1, 14, 70, 89, 90, 104, 182
modernity/modern life, 6, 21, 46, 48, 55
Moglia Barth, L. J., 28–9, 37–8n
Monroe, M., 43–4, 140
Monsiváis, C., 5, 9
Morán, M., 11, 86, 91, 177, 185, 248n
Moreno, Z., 35, 39n, 43, 51, 109
*Mosaico criollo*, 37n
Múgica, B., 50, 58
Múgica, R., 38n, 47, 51, 56
Muiño, E., 24, 29
Murúa, L., 11, 11, 25, 29, 47, 50, 52–3, 56, 62–3n, 71–2, 74, 92n
musical, 13, 25, 28, 34, 37n, 58, 102, 112n, 128, 139–40, 142

nation, 22, 34, 117, 206, 211–14, 222, 224, 231, 234–7, 246
Navarro, F., 43, 61n
Negrete, J., 5, 37n
New Argentine Cinema, 11, 13, 46, 54, 56, 62–3n, 69, 70, 81, 83–9, 93n, 164, 168n, 175

New Latin American Cinema, 6, 11, 52–3, 63n, 85
*Nieve negra*, 14, 81, 181–2, 224
*Nobleza gaucha*, 23–4, 36n
*Noches de Buenos Aires*, 30
non-professional actors, 11, 49, 54, 85, 174
*Nueve reinas*, 1, 3, 88, 144, 155–6, 163–6, 173–5, 178–9, 181, 194, 198, 219, 221–2

Ochoa, F., 30
O'Connor, E., 31
Olivera, H., viii, 59, 61n, 80, 127, 141
Olmedo, A., 52, 57, 63n, 78, 92n, 152, 157, 167n, 147n, 247–8n
Oreiro, N., 3, 88–90
Ortega, P., 52, 57–8, 74–5, 126
Ortiz, H., 5, 52
Ortiz, M., 4, 5, 43
Oyarzábal, F., 30

Padín, M., 23
Pagano, A., 24, 39n
Palacios, G., 104, 112n, 144, 167n, 206n, 235
Parodi, S., 23–4
Parravicini, F., 23–4, 36n
Patria Film, 24
Pauls, G., 11, 164–5, 167n, 226n
Paz, O., 7, 9
Pecoraro, S., 76, 80, 82, 206n
Pellegrini, H., 51–2
Perciavalle, C., 139
Peretti, D., 3, 81, 88–9, 143, 201, 249n
Perón/Peronism, 12, 32, 35–6, 45–6, 54, 61n, 116, 196
Perugorría, J., 197, 221
Petray, C., 23–4, 36n
Petrone, F., 31, 101

Picchio, A. M., 49, 82, 102, 104, 119, 129, 142, 162
Pietra, A., 104, 145, 167n, 188n, 243, 249n
Pinky, 55–7, 140
Pirovano, I., 24
Podestá, 24–5, 36n, 92n, 103
  Blanca, 24–5, 101, 141, 148n
Politti, L., 71–2, 74, 92n
Porcel, J., 57, 63n, 78, 92n, 152, 157
Power, T., 9
Puig, A., 105, 108, 110, 112n, 121–2, 129, 136, 139, 142, 188n, 249n
Puig, M., 4–6
Py, E., 23, 28, 36n

Quartucci, P., 23, 92n

Radal, A., 23
radio, 2, 26–7, 29, 31, 37n, 55, 101, 104–6, 110, 111–12n, 118, 124, 128, 152, 241
  Belgrano, 27, 39n
  El Mundo, 51, 102–3, 105, 113n, 119
  La Nación, 28
  LRA, 37n
*Radiolandia*, 31
Rago, P., 148n, 177, 187n
Ranni, R., 52, 82, 112n, 119, 129, 138, 157, 168n
Ratti, C., 25
Razzano, J., 24
*Rebelde*, 12, 130, 193
*Relatos salvajes*, 1, 3, 14, 81, 93n, 145–6, 183–4, 202, 220–1, 223
Renán, S., 62n, 76–7, 82, 107, 127
Rico, O., 23–4
Rivas, E., 145–6, 187n, 242–3, 250n
Romano, G., 90, 104, 174, 187n, 249n

Romero, M., 30, 38n, 61n
Ross, M., 58–9, 71, 73–4, 157, 167n
Roth, C., 71–2, 80, 82, 92n
Roth, S., 39n
Rueda, B., 183, 201

Sábato, M., 92n, 180
Sandrini, L., 10, 29, 30, 37–8n, 59, 61–2n, 75–6, 102, 105, 110, 167n
Sandro, 57–9, 110, 126, 233
San Martín theatre, 9
Santoro, R., 225n
Sarli, I., 44–6, 62n, 112n
Saslavsky, L., 30, 111n
Save the Children, 234, 237, 249n
Sbaraglia, L., 1, 3, 11, 80–1, 88–90, 92n, 140–1, 164, 181, 197, 207n
Scarcella, J., 23, 36n
Segré, M., 23
Serrano, E., 24, 31, 39n, 62n
silent cinema, 22–3, 26, 28, 37n
Silveyra, S., 11, 57, 90, 102, 112n, 119, 167n, 249n
*Sintonía*, 31
Soffici, M., 30, 35, 62n
Solanas, F., 53, 63n, 74, 80, 167n
Solá, M. A., 81, 92n, 129, 131n, 174, 197, 233
Soriano, P., 52, 59, 62n, 92n, 111n, 167n
sound, 5, 23, 27–8, 30, 37n, 80, 106, 110, 113n, 140, 218
Spain, 14, 23, 33, 37n, 63n, 70–2, 80–2, 91–2n, 112n, 144, 165, 180, 187n, 193–9, 201–7, 214, 217, 219, 226n, 235, 244, 246, 249n
Spanish, 4, 6, 14, 15, 26, 31–2, 71–2, 76, 81, 91–2n, 144–5, 162–3, 177, 193–207
stage acting, 21, 134

stardom, 2, 4–6, 9–11, 13–14, 27, 31–5, 38n, 45–6, 53, 55, 68, 77, 81, 83, 89, 116–17, 133, 135, 146n, 152, 155–6, 172, 176, 180, 185, 193, 202–4, 231, 232, 234, 239–40, 242, 244–6
  Argentine, 4, 9–10, 68
  collective, 53–4
  international, 7, 211, 224n, 241
  local, 23, 37n, 69
  peripheral, 6, 211
  transnational, 15, 195, 213, 214, 216, 224
star image, 11, 21, 30, 32, 44–5, 50, 58, 180, 182, 184–5, 199, 204, 224, 231–2
Star Studies, 3, 6, 10, 54, 68, 146n, 211, 232
star system, 2, 3, 6, 10–12, 21, 27, 29, 31–6, 36n, 37n, 43–4, 46, 48, 50–1, 53, 55–6, 59, 60, 63n, 64n, 68, 70, 81, 87, 89–91, 100, 117, 146n, 166, 173–4, 194, 197, 204, 219–21, 224, 232, 239, 246–7
stereotype, 2, 14, 48, 153, 155, 161, 166n, 195, 199, 203, 205, 207n, 212, 214–15, 217, 223, 225n
Stivel, D., 58–9, 64n
Suar, A., 3, 11, 81, 87–9, 140, 187n, 248n, 250n
*Sugar*, 13, 106, 129, 139, 140, 142, 147n, 148n, 173
Susini, E. T., 30, 38n

Taibo, R., 112n, 131n, 136–8, 233
tango, 24, 29, 35, 37n, 47, 61n, 80, 108, 112n, 148n
*¡Tango!*, 28–30, 37n
*telenovelas*, 13, 58, 63n, 83, 89–90, 111n, 116–30, 165, 217, 222, 246

television, 7, 10–13, 15, 43, 52, 54–9, 61n, 63–4n, 69, 77, 80–3, 89–90, 101–8, 110, 111–12n, 116–19, 123–4, 127, 129, 134–5, 138, 142, 147n, 152–6, 160, 164–6, 173, 175, 179–80, 246
theatre, 2, 12–13, 21, 23–6, 29, 31 n, 36–7n, 47, 49, 51, 55, 57–9, 63n, 72, 74, 79, 81–2, 89, 91n, 101–2, 104–6, 110, 111–12n, 121, 125, 134–42, 144–5, 146–8n, 153, 155, 161–2, 173, 194, 197–8, 224, 233, 235, 244
*The Divine Lady*, 28
Third Cinema, 53–4
Tinayre, D., 30, 61n, 73, 91n, 102, 105, 112n, 167n
*Todos lo saben*, 14, 201, 220, 226n
Torre Nilsson, L., 11, 47, 51, 53, 56, 62–3n, 111n
Torres, D., 60, 140
Torres, L., 43, 61n, 102
Torres Ríos, L., 37n, 38n, 51
transition, 6, 11, 23, 57, 71–2, 78, 80–3, 88, 99, 106, 126, 157–8, 172, 196, 213, 224n
Trapero, P., 84–6, 89, 183
Trento, G., 26, 36n
*Truman*, 14, 194, 199, 201, 205, 226n
Turgenova, M., 27, 37n

*Una escalera al cielo*, 122
*Una nueva y gloriosa nación*, 26

Valenzuela, D., 85, 93n, 188n
Valenzuela, M. C., 108, 112n, 121–2, 136, 141, 153, 166n
Valle, F., 23–4, 28, 37n

Vaner, M., 50–1, 62–3n, 71–2, 92n
Vehil, L., 38n, 82, 103, 110
Velez, L., 34
Viale, J., 60
Viale, O., 52
Vidarte, W., 48, 62n, 71–2
Vignoli, A., 29
Villamil, S., 88, 130n, 175n, 177, 179

*XXY*, 3, 222, 226n

Yankelevich, J., 27, 116

Zanca, A., 122–3, 131n, 137, 157, 167n, 186n
Zubarry, O., 59, 64n, 92n, 110, 129, 167n
Zuviría, M., 24

EU representative:
Easy Access System Europe
Mustamäe tee 50, 10621 Tallinn, Estonia
Gpsr.requests@easproject.com

www.ingramcontent.com/pod-product-compliance
Lightning Source LLC
Chambersburg PA
CBHW071700160426
43195CB00012B/1526